THE EUREKA MYTH

THE EUREKA MYTH

CREATORS, INNOVATORS, AND EVERYDAY INTELLECTUAL PROPERTY

Jessica Silbey

STANFORD LAW BOOKS
An Imprint of Stanford University Press
Stanford, California

Stanford University Press
Stanford, California

Printed in the United States of America

Library of Congress Cataloging-in-Publication Data

Silbey, Jessica, author.
The eureka myth : creators, innovators, and everyday intellectual
property / Jessica Silbey.
pages cm
Includes bibliographical references and index.
ISBN 978-0-8047-8337-8 (cloth : alk. paper) —
ISBN 978-0-8047-8338-5 (pbk.   )
1. Intellectual property—United States.   2. Creation (Literary, artistic, etc.)
3. Technological innovations—United States.   I. Title.
KF2979.S59 2015
346.7304'8—dc23
2014028756

ISBN 978-0-8047-9353-7 (electronic)

Designed by Bruce Lundquist
Typeset by Newgen in 10/15 Sabon

To Robert and Susan Silbey

Contents

Acknowledgments

WRITING THIS BOOK was challenging and fun. Yet I am glad to be done. By contrast, conducting the interviews and speaking with the people whose stories fill the pages that follow was not only fun; I had a hard time stopping. Long after my fiftieth interview, I continued to seek out people with whom to speak. The interviews were pure pleasure. I could have spent many more years sitting with artists and scientists and lawyers and businesspeople talking about the creative and innovative work in which they engage. I still struggle to resist the temptation to add to my interview list. I still carry my digital recorder with me. But the book needed to be written, especially when the patterns within the interviews became sufficiently clear, convincing me that despite the diversity of interview subjects, I had enough data to investigate and analyze their common themes. And so first, I thank the people who sat with me and shared details about their work and their professional biographies and aspirations. I am grateful to you. And I am sure the stories you shared with me are the reasons most people will read this book.

I had many voices in my head as I wrote this book, voices encouraging and challenging me to be more precise, more analytical, more ambitious. Some of those voices are from a long time ago when I began my career as a writer and teacher. They are stuck in my head for good, and I am grateful for them: James Boyd White, Joseph Vining, Tom Green, three teachers who long ago helped me think hard about law as a system of language and meaning that is deeply human and worth spending a life writing about. Other voices are from the intellectual property community, a community of which I am so glad to be a part, a community that is open, embracing, constantly evolving and looking to the future with excitement but without losing track of its human values and historical roots. Voices from this community for which I am particularly grateful and who lent their invaluable support include Barton Beebe, Julie Cohen,

Peter Decherney, Stacey Dogan, Brett Frischmann, Wendy Gordon, Laura Heymann, Mark McKenna, Bill Patry, Rebecca Tushnet, and Martha Woodmansee. I also thank these very special friends who supported me in ways that only dear friends can, by listening to me obsessively talk and talk and talk about this project. I am blessed they care so much about me and push me to do this work better. Thank you to Elizabeth McGeveran, Bill McGeveran, Mary-Rose Papandrea, and Elizabeth Trujillo.

Suffolk University Law School, the administration, my faculty colleagues, and the law librarians, especially Rick Buckingham, provided me with substantial support over the years. Also, I was particularly lucky to have stellar research assistance from Todd Thurheimer, whose experience as a computer engineer, a musician, and a budding lawyer were invaluable to this project. I could not have made the progress I did without Todd to work the data with me. Todd's perspectives and insights were often different than mine and therefore he added significant dimensionality to the project. I owe him a huge debt of gratitude.

There is a hidden gem (or perhaps no longer so hidden!) in Nausicaa Renner. At the tail end of this project, she became part of this book and a partner. Sharp and wise with language, she improved this book immensely. I also must thank the editors at Stanford University Press, especially Michelle Lipinski and Kate Wahl, and the anonymous peer reviewers, all who dedicated time to improving this book.

I have been lucky to share this work as it evolved with colleagues and students around the United States and abroad, at Boston University Law School, Harvard University Law School, Harvard School of Education (and Project Zero), New York University, Yale Law School, University of Pennsylvania, Cardozo Law School, University of Maine Law School, American University Washington College of Law, Northeastern University Law School, University of Washington School of Law, Case Western Reserve School of Law, Chicago-Kent College of Law, Loyola University of Chicago School of Law, Loyola Law School of Los Angeles, Osgoode Hall at York University, the London School of Economics, and the International Society for the History and Theory of Intellectual Property in London and Paris. Questions asked during these visits enriched my engagement with the material. And the enthusiasm of colleagues at these institutions helped propel me when the project felt overwhelming and unwieldy.

My husband, Keith Dresser, and our daughters, Charlotte and Harper, deserve a prize for patience and resilience in the face of my obsessive work habits. They are my prizes. I do not take them for granted, but knowing they would be there each day, supportive and with hugs, made the long nights easier. I would be remiss if I did not also thank Ruth Walsh, whose unfailing presence in our family life since its beginning has made everything better.

My mother read every word of this book. She remains my first and most influential teacher, and, I believe, my best champion. I am proud to be her daughter, and I hope this book reflects how extraordinary a teacher she is, even of stubborn students. This book is dedicated to her and to my father, both who earned deserved reputations as gifted and generous teachers and scholars in their fields. My father died while I was writing this book. He was particularly passionate about art, music, and literature and was himself a superb scientist. This book made perfect sense to him. When I learned that, I knew I was onto something.

Introduction

> I wanted to make paintings. I wanted to publish them. But
> I didn't want to own them. . . . It's like having a litter of
> puppies and you [find] a good home for each one of them.
>
> *Joan, an internationally known public artist*

WHAT COULD IT MEAN for this artist, Joan, to compare her paintings to cuddly canines? In what plausible way is an artist's creative process like the daily labor and intensive care that is required to nurture a pregnant bitch and whelp her puppies? Is the professional satisfaction in building an appreciative audience and receiving feedback from the art world like the satisfaction received from children's joy when they take a puppy home? What does it mean to own a painting (or a puppy) when the purpose of making it is to give it away? Does one author puppies the way one authors a painting, hoping to retain some subsequent control over attribution and integrity?

The epigraph to this chapter is from an interview I conducted with an internationally renowned sculptor about her creative process, professional development, and studio business. She took and loved studio art classes in college, but she loved English, history, political science, and psychology as well. She graduated college unsure of her career path. As a graduation gift, her mother gave her a set of beautiful and expensive paints, with which she began her career as a painter. From there, this artist made her way around the world to find space, people, and creative inspiration. She has worked full-time as an artist her entire professional life, producing giant sculptures and wall-size watercolors. Twenty years later, she lives on the East Coast of the United States with her husband and two school-age children. She could support the family with her public art commissions, but her husband works as well (and as hard) as she does.

When I asked Joan about some of the difficulties she experienced being a painter, I was surprised that she responded by talking about the burden of storing all her finished work. My questions were driving at the relationships among making a living as an artist, intellectual property, copying, the digital age, and creative influences. But she seemed puzzled by my persistent questions regarding her business strategies, her tolerance for unauthorized copying and misattribution, and her desire for widespread distribution. Instead, she told me that she didn't think or care that much about others copying her work. Nor was she very concerned about the contours of ownership and control she had over her paintings. Indeed, the very fact that she had to maintain the paintings or sculpture—archive them, store them, protect them—was a burden. This turned out to be a common concern among the many artists I subsequently interviewed. Being worried about space and storage was not how she wanted to spend her time as an artist. She just wanted to "make paintings." She wanted to "publish" them by sharing them with the world. But she didn't want to "own" them. And then she compared her magnificent, colorful, slightly erotic, feminine paintings to puppies. What in the world did this have to do with intellectual property, the legal regime that ostensibly regulates, facilitates, and progresses creative art?

* * *

> Steve Jobs and Wozniak created the personal computer, all right? . . . Cohen and Boyer created biotechnology, the concept of moving genes around through man's intervention. OK? But most of the rest of us mere mortals just—you know, you learn from other people, and then . . . you know, the frontiers of science are pushed back . . . gradually through similar antlike persistence by scientists.
>
> *Dennis, in-house patent lawyer for a pharmaceutical company*

The myth of the inventor hero is deep and strong. It is common to hear that a world-class scientist was a child math prodigy, to explain how his mind sees the physical world in unique and distinct ways. His aha moment transforms our understanding of outer space or molecular biology.

And yet this quote from a patent lawyer with more than twenty-five years working alongside groundbreaking scientists in the pharmaceutical industry compares most of the important work in medical science to antlike drudgery. This IP lawyer suggests that the inventor heroes he names (Jobs and Wozniak) are hardly human. Instead, he says we should recognize and revere the labor of everyday scientists; they work in droves and teams to transform the frontiers of our physical experience bit by bit, like colonies of ants building and supporting a hill of dirt.

Is it degrading to compare scientists to ants? Is the exalted work of the medical technology that has drastically improved human life over the course of the twentieth century anything like the transport of dirt grains and leaf scraps over insignificant distances in a suburban backyard?[1] In what way does hard work and "persistence" correspond to rights in inventions and competitive advantages that might attach thereto? Why is this patent lawyer talking about trivial everyday work and manual labor when inventions (and patents in particular) are made by novel and nonobvious ideas that spring from the mind? In calling antlike persistence heroic, even as he downgrades himself and his collaborators as "mere mortals," he seems to suggest that hard work and targeted investment will and should reap well-deserved rewards.

I interviewed this patent lawyer over nearly two hours. His office, cluttered with piles of papers, was at the center of a building complex that housed many similar pharmaceutical companies. He has been an intellectual property lawyer for many leading pharmaceutical companies since the mid-1980s, which marked the beginning of the modern biotechnology movement, the rise of the pharmaceutical giants, and the centralization of patent law in the US Court of Appeals for the Federal Circuit. He spoke quickly and passionately about the importance of patents to his industry and the missteps of so many of his former employers in undervaluing even the "smallest" of inventions. But in the next breath, he lamented the development of patent law to include broad subject matter that championed trivial and undemanding developments in financial services and electronics manufacturing, echoing the sentiments of many other lawyers and businesspeople. He seemed to be saying that these patent-rich fields were truly the anthills of invention: ubiquitous and unoriginal. And yet, hadn't the ants been venerated as frontier explorers a moment before?

Given the complexity of his experiences, what is the relationship between patent law and lawyers, pharmaceutical breakthroughs, and anonymous daily drudgery? When does it make sense to assert patents against other pharmaceutical companies, and when are affordability, access, and collaboration more important? Skilled in technical legal doctrine and passionate about patent policy from years working alongside bench scientists in highly profitable companies, this lawyer had a lot to say about when the intellectual property system resonated well with its underlying principles and when it required retrofitting to the industry's practices and public need.

*　　*　　*

This book is full of quotes such as the two that have been presented so far, excerpted from fifty face-to-face interviews that I conducted with a wide range of scientists, engineers, musicians and artists, their business associates, and intellectual property lawyers over the course of four years. The interviews were part of an effort to learn more about the intersection of intellectual property law on the one hand, and creative and innovative work on the other. At the most fundamental level, this book is devoted to understanding statements like those from the artist and lawyer on their own terms. I sought to learn how creative and innovative work occurs from the ground up, from individuals to loose organizations of people to large and small institutions. My goal was to discern whether and how intellectual property laws that purport to "promote the progress of science and the useful arts" play a role in the making, claiming, and disseminating of art and science. What effect, if any, do our intellectual property laws have in facilitating innovation and creativity in the United States?

The US Constitution speaks of "promot[ing] the progress of science and useful arts, by securing for limited times to authors and inventors the exclusive right to their respective writings and discoveries." To this end, incentivizing the creation and dissemination of art and science by granting rights that resemble property rights to creators and inventors has been the stated goal of intellectual property law since the United States' founding. But more than two hundred years later, we remain unsure—indeed, we are deeply conflicted—about whether the laws that protect intellectual property work as intended. Does preventing anyone but the patent owner from making, using, or selling an invention without payment or permission promote progress? Does granting a copyright that endures for the life of the author plus seventy years promote more learning and more creativity? How can we gauge the success of laws designed to promote science and art for the public good?

Innovation and creativity are buzzwords of the twenty-first century. The United States asserts its dominance at the cutting edge of both technology and culture, whether in medicine, computer design, film, or music production. Today, copying and disseminating art and science are easier than they ever were, but earning and profiting from exclusive rights appear to be harder. In a world in which global wealth is determined in part by who benefits from innovation and creative output, discerning how art and science are made, by whom and why, and how they benefit the communities in which they circulate are enormously important questions. This book does not aim to address all of these questions. But it begins with the question of how intellectual property law in the United States promotes science and art, assuming as I do that the United States remains one of the global leaders in IP policy and in the production and dissemination of creative and innovative work.

This book describes how intellectual property intervenes, if at all, in the professional lives of artists and scientists and the companies for which they work. Interpreting the descriptive accounts these artists and scientists provide, the book traces the professional development of chemical engineers, classical composers, Internet architects, sculptors, filmmakers, and genetic biologists, to name just a few, in a wide range of formal and informal organizations. In doing so, and in conversation also with IP lawyers, business managers, and employers, the book delineates the presence and absence of intellectual property, as well as the shapes and roles it takes. As a qualitative study of intellectual property that investigates the mechanisms and motives of a range of creators and innovators and their professional managers and organizations, the books aims to chart new terrain for our understanding of and future in scientific and artistic innovation and the intellectual property that purports to sustain them. Although the focus of the book is on the interviews, and their common themes and critical distinctions, the empirical and theoretical analyses framing the discussion of the interviews may inform present innovative and creative communities and companies as well as law reform efforts aimed to support them.

Psychologists and social scientists have long studied innovative and creative communities to discern their contours and their contexts. Those scholarly projects tend to study creative personalities and the evaluative standards for creativity or innovation.[2] This book focuses less on the kinds of people who produce creative and innovative work and the values society ascribes to them. Instead, it focuses on the motives and behaviors of the creators and innovators and their professional organizations. How and why do they do what they do? What are the mechanisms that help or hinder their continual engagement in creative or innovative endeavors? How does intellectual property play a role in their aspirations and well-being as professionals in IP-rich fields? In other words, this book makes sense of the intersections between creative and innovative activity and intellectual property law using the experiences and explanations of those engaging with both.

THE ARTISTS, SCIENTISTS, AND ENGINEERS

Contrary to the dominant stories of monetary incentives and wealth maximization, the interviews in this book elaborate intellectual property's *diverse* functions and *sporadic* manifestations in the lives and work of artists, scientists, and their business partners and managers. Filled with stories from, for example, sculptors, bioengineers, filmmakers, chemists, novelists, software engineers, business attorneys, publishing executives, venture capitalists, and music agents, this book reveals assorted (instead of singular) ways of achieving a flourishing livelihood in science and art.

Interviews followed a standard protocol, asking the same questions of each interviewee despite the diversity of their careers and situations. (Appendix A describes the data collection and analysis in more detail; Appendix B describes the interviewees in more detail.) When warranted, however, conversations wandered in order to follow and pursue whatever was important to each interviewee and to clarify or connect earlier statements. Statements like that of the artist Joan, comparing paintings to puppies, invariably provoked a more in-depth conversation.

And Joan was far from unique; I was constantly challenged by statements packed with deeper assumptions about the boundaries of ownership claims, the nature and characteristics of personal investment in creative and innovative work, and the diverse desires for how a professional life in such fields optimally proceeds. During an earlier interview, a photographic journalist described his relationship to his photographs: "At the time, I understood that they, the organizations I worked for, owned the photographs, and I think I fully thought of them as mine." One of my goals in writing this book is to understand contradictions such as this one. How can art belong to its maker and to a company at once? In what way is the art one makes like a beloved pet (or, more commonly throughout the interviews, like a child)? What are the implications for the analogy of work to family relationships or animate beings? How do these feelings and explanations about the relationship among art, scientific discovery, employment, and ownership affect the manner and circumstances of innovating alone or within an organization and controlling work through intellectual property law?

Interviewees demonstrate diverse ways in which IP law helps and hinders artistic and scientific productivity. In this way, the book begins to dismantle the stunningly persistent and monolithic explanation for intellectual property protection in the United States: that IP is necessary to facilitate robust production and dissemination of art and science. For example, some musicians lament the copyright royalty system, wishing instead for a consistent salary to make music on a regular basis. They need to earn money to live, but they are ambivalent about whether they earn money from royalties or from a salary paid by a standing organization. Many want regularity in their revenue stream so they can compose and play without worry. Some of these same musicians, however, wish for control that would prevent other people from misusing their work. In copyright parlance, these musicians value the derivative work right (protected through copyright law) and also moral rights (which are largely unprotected under US copyright law). Copyright law thus does not ably protect musicians' interests or incentivize their work, as IP law claims; musicians write and play music because it is what they do and will do, with or without US copyright. The stories these musicians tell about how and why they became musicians; their interactions with agents and music publishing companies; the challenges and joys of being a musician; and what, if anything, they would change about their lives professionally, provide a window into the intersection of creative work and copyright law in the music business.

I was surprised to learn that engineers and scientists often sound like artists, musicians, writers, and filmmakers in their ambivalence toward the full panoply of rights intellectual property law provides. They too value hard work, professional autonomy, intellectual challenge, and professional and personal relationships. Indeed, entrepreneurs in the high-technology space directly resemble some of the artists and scientists in their drive to create something: an object, a network, or a marketplace that benefits a larger community. As Andrew, a successful entrepreneur with a computer software background, said, he came from a "culture of entrepreneurs," and most of his life he "just wanted to build something." When asked about how patents, trademarks, and copyrights might function in his successful companies (and in his failed ones), he talked about how his large patent portfolio was just "detail and documentation":

I would . . . make time for the engineers to meet with the lawyer and patent different things. Like, I . . . would talk to people and say, "What do you have that you think we can patent?" And then they would tell me, and then we would go in and patent those things. But you know, for any one of these companies, there is typically one or two ideas that are really valuable, and that are the patent. And then the company ends up getting a dozen or two dozen patents. The rest of them are just the blocking stuff that—or not even that: . . . I think they're just something you build to look very attractive to a potential buyer. But they're not real—they're like detail and documentation.

Andrew's fairly dismissive attitude toward patents contrasts with the intensity and pride with which he describes the excellence of his team of engineers. The engineers, not intellectual property, are what drove him to negotiate a multimillion-dollar offer for his company because he wanted the price to reflect the benefits he and his team bring to the digital marketplace:

We were like a military—you know, my engineering group was unbelievably predictable. . . . And we had done work for [a large public company] that was really highly regarded as a very high-quality job on a [similar product] that worked. So the [giant media corporation looking to buy us] knew they were getting a very good technical group.

This entrepreneur confirms that the value of the company was as much in the people as it was in its inventions.

Parsing the stories of these musicians, visual artists, biologists, and engineers, and comparing them with the stories from their managers and lawyers, provides a layered account of the multidimensionality of US intellectual property law in action. The interviews demonstrate in the aggregate how motives and mechanisms of creativity and innovation are multifaceted and interconnected. And yet intellectual property law, as we have come to implement it in the United States, is a one-size-fits-all model. Statutory regimes governing trademark, copyright, and patent law were drafted and continue to be interpreted to protect particular economic interests based on incomplete and sometimes inaccurate assumptions about cultural and scientific production and the people engaging in it. The accounts in this book provide empirical evidence that these legal frameworks and policy-driven foundations are mistaken. In doing so, the book describes the profound mismatch between motives and mechanisms of art and science and the structure of US intellectual property law.[3]

THE BUSINESS PROFESSIONALS

I expected to hear a different perspective from business and intellectual property attorneys. I thought they would rehearse the unbending position that intellectual property is necessary for making and commercializing art and science, but the lawyers in this study had a lot to say about the ways intellectual property fails and succeeds for their clients. They did not uniformly—or even consistently—support the incentive theory of intellectual property. Instead, because of the perceived mismatch between IP and clients' professional goals, attorneys develop a range of strategies for encouraging their clients to participate in an intellectual property system of which even the lawyers seemed somewhat skeptical:

[T]he way I try to describe it to [the company's engineers and scientists] is that it's the way . . . we represent value. I mean, to be perfectly callous about it, I've used this approach a number of times: "Look: we're a start-up company. All these venture capitalists who are going to be investing in us, they are going to look for IP. They don't know what it is any more than you or I know what it is, right? But they are going to look for something that says 'it's IP,' so it's the way to show them what the really amorphous stuff you're doing in the research lab, how that translates into something that they can put their hands on." . . . And the more of it we have—and it's fuzzy what the "it" is, but the more of "it" we have, then the more successful we're going to be.

Admitting that intellectual property may largely be for show but that it is critical to funding ventures, lawyers turn intellectual property and the regime that regulates it into a kind of shell accounting game. Attorneys do not intend to mislead or misinform (although many talk about their strategies as "tricks"), and they do not describe their behavior as an ethical challenge to or against the public interest. Instead, they say they adhere to the "rules of the game" in counseling their clients. Throughout my conversations with intellectual property and business attorneys and with company representatives in IP-rich industries, respondents describe IP as just another legal regime or organizational maze through which they guide their clients in order for them to reach professional or personal goals. To lawyers and firm agents (such as CEOs and vice presidents), IP is a pliable legal fiction—as is the notion of the corporation itself—that can be molded and exploited for particular purposes.

Whether through intellectual property law, employee relations, real estate, or securities law, lawyers keep their clients' interests in mind, and the interests of creative and innovative clients are rarely to maximize wealth or a financial return on investment. Instead, lawyers shape and reify the perceived importance of intellectual property law by molding it to correspond with other values about which their artistic and scientific clients care deeply: their professional reputation, their community's enhancement, and consistency and control over their everyday labor. In this way, even for the IP lawyers and the business folks, intellectual property law does not function as an investment vehicle that incentivizes the production of art and science. Instead, when able, it gives a name to the ephemeral nature of what scientists and engineers do, and it concretizes the value they create. An in-house attorney describes this process of correspondence in terms of coaxing software engineers in her company to participate in the patenting process:

It was just hard for them because there was a struggle philosophically around all of this, and a real skepticism—the concept of law, legal, and compliance was 180 degrees away from this very fluid, creative, libertarian open environment. . . . The concept of people wearing jeans and Hawaiian shirts, the concept of people having these open cubes and working until two o'clock in the morning, and having a corporate ethos that basically embraced flexibility and dialogue and consensus building, and to a certain extent rebellion and questioning authority—that was anathema to the corporate cultures that had preceded them. So just getting a law department in a company like that where they would even trust what "the lawyers" would say required an awful lot of effort on our part, and a completely different perspective on how we approached our internal clients. You could not come top-down as authoritarians. You basically had to come bottom-up, as having gained their respect through your relationship, your appreciation for what they did, and their true belief that you just have to instill that you really believed in the company and its proposition. . . . In terms of software [patents], that became actually something developers really understood. They personally benefited from it, but there was a long, long history of invention in this country. Patent invention goes [way] back. . . . So you become part of a storied legacy of the great inventors. So patents were, in a way, a much easier sell. And you have to get the developer involved. I mean, they write the invention statement, and they work all the way through, and their name is on that in the Patent Office. So there's real ownership and pride and [a] coolness factor to being an inventor, and being part of the company, an IBM or an HP and Microsoft, and some of these others companies that own thousands of patents.

This attorney emphasizes a mutuality of interests between the individual employees and the company when she encourages participation by firm employees in a patent system of which they originally were skeptical.

Reputation, ego, and being part of something much bigger than oneself are all personal and professional interests of the employee-innovator. When lawyers describe intellectual property as affecting these outcomes instead of others, the justification for intellectual property and its mechanisms shift and diversify beyond the function of financial incentives.

I also expected to hear a different perspective on behalf of corporate interests. Corporations are not really people, after all.[4] Whereas individuals might prioritize autonomy, optimal work conditions, reputation, and relationships over maximizing wealth, companies are said to exist to make money.[5] Thus, I thought that when I asked CEOs, vice presidents, and other corporate agents to describe their firm's business strategies and goals, they would provide accounts of behaviors and experiences in which the right of exclusion in intellectual property does incentivize more production.[6] And indeed, the corporate agents' understandings of intellectual property's benefits and limitations more faithfully aligned with the traditional IP incentive story than lawyers' or artists' accounts.

Swapping the corporation for the individual in the IP story of creative and innovative progress jettisons a long-standing IP myth: that copyright and patent rights exist to benefit "authors" and "inventors."[7] And yet connecting strong IP rights with financial incentives may confirm the percolating fear among those witnessing the growing dominance of corporate interests in both national and international politics that threaten distributive justice, political accountability, governmental transparency, and democratic engagement. Because, celebrating the alignment of IP's financial investment function at the corporate level minimizes, if not largely abandons, the reigning and original importance of the public interest in intellectual property law. An alignment between firm incentives and IP policy is therefore worthy of critique and concern. Moreover, there is evidence in the interviews that alignment is partial, missing important features about which key employees and corporate principles in creative and innovative fields care.

Corporate agents agree that IP facilitates some development and distribution of creative or innovative work *but rarely the initiation of that work*. Initiation—beginnings and persistent effort to achieve innovative or creative breakthroughs—is almost always intrinsically motivated. In other words, even for the companies that may exist to make money (although as I will discuss, even that characterization is debatable), the progress of science and art requires passion for the work, which does not appear to be incentivized by IP's investment function. Thus, it may be more accurate to say that IP functions subsequently as a form of postindustrial corporate capital, to borrow Julie Cohen's insight.[8] Like bank loans, real estate agreements, and employment relations, IP law intervenes later in the corporate "life" of creative or innovative work. Only haphazardly does it serve as a mechanism to recuperate sunk investment costs, and oftentimes it serves goals relating instead to relationship building and business flexibility.

Intellectual property law in the United States has been shaped and reformed to address interests of *both* individuals and businesses, assuming that they are one and the same in terms of behavior, motives, and aggregate benefit to community welfare. We may believe that they are not the same, and yet it is difficult to identify or isolate a corporate motive or business interest to study when companies cannot and do not speak the way individuals can and do. To be sure, many of the individuals I interviewed worked for or were members of firms. And their interests often aligned with those of the firm. The company's "interests," therefore, may be discerned by looking to the interests of the individuals who direct or shape the company's actions. Indeed, companies can speak only through their representatives. But truer to the point, corporations cannot hold attitudes or beliefs of their own: "If [the company] possesses anything, it is because of the legal theory that endows it with fictive personality. . . . Just because it is legally constituted, a group cannot be said to 'behave'—still less to think or feel."[9] This mistake of ascribing "motives" or "desires" to corporations specifically or institutions more generally—be those motives pecuniary or otherwise—is widespread in scholarly literature and contemporary politics.[10] The data grounding this study, as well as data from other studies, alongside prominent theoretical literature about institutions, demonstrate how the "thinking" and "desiring" that are said to occur in and through institutions are mutually constitutive of the individuals who form the collective.[11] Not only do institutional acts depend on individual choices; those choices are rendered meaningful and available because of the institutions themselves.[12] It is therefore not worth distinguishing between organizational and individual motives in terms of whether or how each may harness and harvest intellectual property. The question—and its underlying assumption—is based on false premises. And so this book proceeds to identify a range of motives and mechanisms for making and disseminating creative and innovative work both independent of and through corporate structures in the hopes that further research can evaluate how such motivations cluster. Throughout the book, I highlight instances when industry-specific differences arise in the interviews. Given the sample size, it is not possible to generalize from these observations and instances.[13] But when my observations and analyses correlate with existing quantitative data studies, I note the relevance of peculiar institutional structures and organizational prerogatives.[14]

WHAT THE INTERVIEWS SHOW

Given that corporate behavior channels individual motivations, and that corporations are said to chase financial gain, it is perhaps surprising that both individuals and corporate agents identify motives other than money for pursuing creative and innovative work and for protecting it through intellectual property. The empirical data in this book show how the classic justification for property rights of "reaping what you sow" is grossly overstated. Interviewees in this study, through their accounts of their involvement in creative and innovative professions, illustrate a diversity and balance of values to achieve professional well-being, including professional autonomy, control over time and space, relationships with others (community building and sustaining personal ties), challenging oneself and others, and earning a living. Their descriptions of corporate culture and management choices reject the monolithic identity of the corporation whose only goal is to make money, denying that the company "is a kind of shark that lives off the community rather than . . . a member of a community with important agency in the construction, maintenance, and transformation of our shared lives."[15] Privileging monetary objects invites the claim that nonmonetary objects are subordinate to pecuniary interests.[16] The data do not support this claim. To be sure, pecuniary interests and an appreciation of market dynamics are not irrelevant to professional well-being, but the interviews indicate that the market "requires for its operation the existence of conditions that cannot be accounted for, or maintained, on its [own] terms."[17]

Taking the data from these fifty interviews as a starting point, we begin to understand that the long-standing and resilient incentive story of IP—that strong property rights are necessary to promote science and the arts—is false. There is a range of interests and values that motivate and sustain creative and innovative work. What good, then, does the incentive story achieve? What explains its durability and believability? I have two tentative answers, which justify this book's qualitative and interpretive approach to analyzing and relating accounts of lived experiences to intellectual property law. First, the incentive story is a shorthand for something much more complex. When we let the shorthand take over, it slowly reifies the more multifaceted experience into a singular account about monetary gain. *Incentive* originally meant much more than "incentivized by money" but its variations have been lost in the drive toward an uncomplicated and presumably objectively measurable standard. Although such simplification is a common mechanism both socially and organizationally (it is, after all, how myths are made and ideological discourses sustained), the simple story has negative consequences. When the story of monetary gain becomes a refrain, it has a tendency to be self-fulfilling. Law is habitually made and remade by courts and legislatures that rely on the common stories being told.[18]

Second, no one really believes the incentive story in its pure form. We forgive the shortcomings of shorthand because it is a useful heuristic for those who must explain their professional choices despite their nuanced experiences. "Working for money" (and protecting work through durable property interests to recoup one's investment of money and time) is perceived to be a common denominator. But it is not remotely the whole story. While justifying work with the need for money is reasonable, money is also a means to achieve ends that we all have in common but that are often left unarticulated because the incentive story is so trenchant, and because these other ends are felt to be idiosyncratic, private, or subjective. This second answer has some traction in the interview data, especially among respondents who work in industries that rely heavily on intellectual property, such as pharmaceutical and medical device companies, novelists, photographers, and some text publishing companies. People in these industries first explain how IP is required to start a company, collect investments, and jump-start research and development. After further conversation, they explain how starting in the business or continuing in the business also satisfies their individual interests and the collective interests of their institutions. Diverse goals—such as maintaining professional and personal autonomy, developing and sustaining relationships with others, and advancing social welfare—demonstrate the multiple bases and explanations for pursuing creative and innovative work, as well as the need to excavate alternative stories from beneath a dominant narrative of wealth maximization.

The interviewees' accounts are narrative in form: temporal, emergent, multiple, and moral.[19] The diverse narrative explanations undermine the one-dimensional IP incentive story and belie the categorical principles of a legal approach that masks more complex realities. For example, the rule that rights of exclusion will apply to certain creative and innovative work is often explained by the principle that these rights incentivize investment in creative and innovative work because people worry about the risk of underpriced copies. This uncomplicated explanation obscures ill-fitting and unsatisfying applications of the law, which misfit reflects textured and differentiated experiences, situations, and desires that produce creativity and innovation. Creators' and innovators' own reasons for when to make claims over their work, when and how to distribute their work, and when to relinquish control emerge in the interviews as stories with strong and consistent morals that emphasize hard work, adequate ownership and remuneration, self-direction, intellectual challenge, and sustainable but evolving professions and communities.

THE INVESTIGATIVE METHOD

The stories collected here comprise informal and cultural arrangements within creative and innovative fields of production, some of which diverge from IP's formal legal rules, revealing that intellectual property law is less relevant than previously assumed. Through a narrative approach to law, I attempt to unearth the personal dimensions of progress and the contours of the IP law and to connect both to larger frames of reference, such as creative communities, professional associations, and legal regulations. Indeed, the stories told are themselves the frameworks through which individuals situate themselves within larger social structures.[20] Because situational accounts both interpret and constitute one's relationship with the law, they are not to be dismissed as anecdotes or caricatures. The qualitative analysis of these accounts that forms the basis of this book is strongly rooted in rigorous social science methods and duplicates well-regarded studies in psychology, sociology, and anthropology.[21]

Instead of conducting and analyzing interviews, I could study outcomes. Do pharmaceutical companies with more patents make more socially beneficial medicines? Do filmmakers and production companies who exploit the full range of their copyrights remain viable for longer? Measuring outcomes would be easier—there is a tangible dependent variable to count. But such quantifiable outcomes can use ambiguous metrics.[22] Which things or events should we measure or compare? Which patented medicines fulfill the constitutional "progress" rationale—those that save the most lives or those that generate the most revenue? And, importantly, how do we know whether intellectual property law that protects the patented invention is the mechanism that is causally responsible for its development? Instead of focusing on outcomes, this book focuses on processes and investigates the initial and ongoing dynamics of originating, producing, and distributing creative and innovative work. It asks those who are creating and innovating (or their business associates) how intellectual property law has enabled or constrained their output. Qualitative research collects and analyzes lived experience from the ground up and on the terms set by the people and organizations being studied, thereby providing an inroad into the understanding of lived experience and situational complexities that other kinds of analysis (theoretical and quantitative) cannot. Quantitative research is not truly meaningful without a qualitative component. And yet despite a growing body of quantitative research on IP law and policy, we rarely see qualitative research to complement, enrich, and challenge the conclusions of that research.

Language—words and stories—makes sense of the world. Close attention to language can tell us things that surveys and quantitative research do not. Whether called narrative, rhetoric, or interpretation, stories explain and justify the situation in which we find ourselves and that frames, enables, and constrains creativity and innovation. At the same time, stories are inherently political. They can justify the status quo or affect change. The repeated use of words and phrases reifies categories and expectations, and in turn structures relationships in our communities. This has certainly been the case with the incentive story, but this books discerns other narratives that dispute it. They should be added to the anthology of stories that lawyers and lawmakers use to apply and reform intellectual property law in the future. The factual accounts of creative and innovative production in this book provide the groundwork for intellectual property retrofitting. In the ongoing legislative reform debate, we should pay attention.

The fifty interviews at the foundation of this book create a database of language—cultural tropes and meanings—that are the accounts of people's engagement with creative and inventive processes and intellectual property regimes. This book's contribution will be to supply a thick description of the varieties of intellectual property's interventions in the lives of artists, writers, scientists, and engineers. When the data in this book confirm the traditional IP incentive story, I highlight this consistency. But the accounts often diverge from IP law's long-standing and unbending rationales. With substantial narrative detail in the interviewees' own words, I hope the book will be both enjoyable and informative. It will also add much-needed diversity to the stubbornly one-dimensional explanation for intellectual property protection in the United States.

The book's chapters trace the development and dissemination of creative and innovative work, weaving into it the various roles of legal protection in the professional goals of the creators or innovators and their businesses. Chapter 1 details the beginnings of creative and innovative work—how people got started and why. Chapter 2 explores everyday work, how beyond the inspired beginning people continue working (and working hard!) at a professional endeavor that may never pay off. Chapter 3 describes the various ways interviewees misconceive or even fail to consider intellectual property. It then describes how, despite those misconceptions, omissions, or an otherwise ill-fitting IP regime, creative and innovative endeavors may form sustainable businesses. Chapter 4 focuses on the importance of reputation to the professional well-being of creators, innovators, and their businesses. This chapter also discusses how intellectual property doesn't protect reputation, except narrowly through trademark law, and the implications of this particular misfit. Chapter 5 explores the roles of lawyers in the creative and innovative process, describing how intellectual property usually emerges from legal counsel. Lawyers are described (and describe themselves) as coaches or instructors and are not always welcome interveners in creative and innovative processes. The friction between lawyers and their clients has implications for the experience of and attitudes toward intellectual property as a legal regime that is intended to promote progress. The last chapter, Chapter 6, describes the myriad ways creative and innovative work is distributed, given that dissemination to the public is the ultimate goal of intellectual property law. This chapter builds directly on Chapters 3 and 4 by highlighting an ill-fitting intellectual property regime whose creation of exclusivity often frustrates the interests of pursuing intellectual challenge, the presentation of work to audiences, and the public good of sustaining and development communities.

The book concludes with several thoughts on the theoretical and practical implications of the IP mismatch with hopes for ongoing law reform and client counseling. The diversity of motives and mechanisms by which creative and innovative work proceeds, and the absence or only partial presence of IP as a critical mechanism, suggests that our IP system is misaligned with the requirements and desires of creators and innovators. My conclusions, though less specific than the compelling accounts in the interviews, hopefully provide sufficient detail to prompt robust conversation and further investigation into the needs of individual industries as regards intellectual property. Critically, my conclusions do not advocate for a more comprehensive and better-fitting IP regime. Some misalignment is a good thing.[23] But better attention to why and how creative and innovative work is produced by people who are willing to devote their life to its laborious endeavor will lead to evidence-based lawmaking and effective law enforcement. Hopefully, such attention will also have the salutary effect of enhancing distributive justice regarding the benefits and pleasures of science and art.

*   *   *

Although this book is about intellectual property law, the following chapters focus on the practice of creativity and invention and not on the language of the federal statutes that aim to promote both. Nonetheless, I provide here a brief explanation of copyright, patent, and trademark law to help orient the discussion that follows.

The Copyright Act and the Patent Act, both federal statutes, are nearly as old as the US Constitution. Both were passed in 1790. The Copyright Act protects original expression for the benefit of authors. In 1790, the stated purpose of the Copyright Act was the "encouragement of learning," and yet its scope was quite narrow, protecting only "maps, charts and books" for a term of fourteen years. Over time, the Copyright Act's exclusivity has broadened in scope and duration, so that it now protects, for example, architectural works, pantomimes, sound recordings, photography, and film for the life of the author plus an additional seventy years. (If the work was a work for hire, then copyright persists for 120 years after creation or 95 years after publication, whichever is shorter.) The enumerated list of subject-matter categories covered by the Copyright Act is nonexhaustive and deliberately meant to be flexible and inclusive. The touchstone of copyright protection is originality, and starting in 1976, the work also has to be fixed in a tangible medium of expression to be covered by the act. Prior to 1976, original works had to be published to be protected. Although copyright does not extend to facts or ideas, the originality standard is otherwise broad and generally understood to be a very low bar. And copyright registration is not necessary for ownership, although it is a prerequisite for a lawsuit. The combination of a low originality standard and the lack of "copyright formalities" (e.g., copyright registration, the requirement of the copyright notice © for protection) creates a culture in which almost anything that is fixed on paper or screen or is otherwise tangible is protected by copyright law.

Copyright law grants to authors six exclusive rights: the rights of reproduction (the "copy" right), distribution, public performance, public display, preparation of derivative works, and public performance of sound recordings by a digital transmission. Notably, copyright law does not require attribution, nor does liability attach for misattribution. Copyright law contains important limitations and exemptions to liability for infringement. The three most deeply entrenched limitations are the right to make "fair use" of the copyrighted work; the exemption of facts and ideas from copyright protection; and the first-sale doctrine, which exhausts the right of distribution and public display upon the first sale of the copy of the work. For example, the fair-use doctrine is what allows users to transform preexisting works into new expressive works; to write book reviews and quote the underlying work; to parody a novel and transpose character, setting, and dialogue into the parody. The exemption of facts from protection allows writers to rewrite history and repeatedly report on current events without infringing one another's writing. And the first-sale doctrine authorizes the used-book market and the secondary art market. It also (though not without controversy) allows owners of books and paintings to alter their tangible property—to write in the margins of books and paint a mustache on their purchased portrait. By common-law extension, secondary liability exists in copyright law, usually described as "contributory" or "vicarious" liability. Internet web hosts, digital intermediaries and content distributors of all kinds may also be subject to secondary liability if they materially contribute or otherwise facilitate the violation of copyright owner's exclusive rights.

The Patent Act protects novel, nonobvious, and useful inventions, but only once the Patent and Trademark Office (the PTO) examines the patent application and determines that the invention fulfills these three requirements. Patents are therefore harder than copyrights to acquire, although the amount of patents issued every year continues to grow. Patentable subject matter is limited by the Patent Act and by federal law to "anything under the sun that is made by man."[24] Courts and practitioners have interpreted this quote from the 1980 case of *Diamond v. Chakrabarty* to mean that both "laws of nature" and naturally occurring things are not patentable.[25] Abstract ideas and mental processes are also not patentable, but the transformation of an object into a different state or thing using abstract ideas or processes may be patentable. Since 1980, the scope of patentable subject matter has expanded to include business methods, laboratory-isolated genomes, and software.

The inventor discloses the invention to the public through the patent application, describing with specificity the invention so that an "ordinary person skilled in the art" could understand, replicate, and improve upon the invention if desired. This disclosure is intended to foster learning and progress. In exchange, patent law grants to the inventor the right to exclude others from making, using, selling, or offering to sell the invention for a period of twenty years without permission from the patent holder. There are very few exceptions to patent exclusivity. One, which has been limited over time and subject to ongoing debate and controversy, is the experimental-use exception. This exception is based in common law (i.e., it is not in the Patent Act explicitly) and permits the use of another's patented invention when such use is for research, philosophical inquiry, or curiosity. It is a very narrow exception and has been further limited over time, even denying immunity to research universities when its researchers engage in research or conduct experiments using patented inventions. Indeed, the experimental-use exception is considered so narrow as to be unavailable in most practical circumstances. The accumulation of patents since the 1980s and the consolidation of patents in firms (in "patent portfolios") has led to reasonable complaints about "patent thickets" and hold-up problems that some say significantly reduce the value of patents to foster further invention and commercialization.

The Lanham Act, which governs federal trademark law, describes a trademark as "any symbol or device that is capable of identifying the source of goods."[26] Trademarks function in two ways: to identify the origin of a good or service in the marketplace and to distinguish a good or service from others. Trademark law is not an anti-copying regime in the way patent and copyright law are. Trademark law primarily protects against use that confuses consumers as to the source of the good or service. There can be multiple owners of the mark "Delta," for example (e.g., Delta Dental, Delta Airlines, Delta Faucets), as long as each other's use of the word or symbol that includes the mark "Delta" does not confuse market participants as to the source of the good or service branded with it. Preventing source confusion helps consumers: we can shop efficiently and with precision. Preventing marketplace confusion also assists manufacturers and service providers in developing their company's goodwill as embodied in their trademark, which associates them with their commercial product.

There are few limitations on trademark subject matter. Words that are generic for the good or service are barred from trademark protection. And trade dress (product packaging or design that indicates source) that also serves a useful function cannot be protected as a trademark. These limitations promote the principles of fair competition. Trademark law is supposed to facilitate markets, not hinder them. Because trademark law is a restraint on both speech and marketplace behavior (e.g., it limits the use of symbols, words, or designs by market actors), it excludes from trademark protection uses that hinder descriptive marketplace speech and functional product design. It protects only against trademark uses that confuse consumers and threaten the goodwill of the mark holders. Trademarks endure in perpetuity insofar as they remain distinctive of the source of the product or service. And trademarks need not be registered with the PTO to be federally protected, although registration has significant benefits. Trademark rights arise out of use, not registration.

Trademark dilution and cybersquatting (i.e., contests over domain names) are also part of the Lanham Act. Dilution concerns only the most famous of trademarks, but it is a very broad cause of action because source confusion is not a prerequisite harm. Dilution occurs when another's use of a famous mark impairs the mark's distinctiveness. It can also arise from the similarity between a mark or trade name and a famous mark that harms the reputation of the famous mark. This latter harm is dilution "by tarnishment." Dilution would be a substantial restriction on speech without the existence of strong defenses in the statute: of fair use, noncommercial use, comparative advertising, parody, criticism, and commentary. Cybersquatting prevents the bad faith intent to profit from another's trademark in a domain name. Enacted in the 1990s, both of these claims are indicative of the broadening of trademark rights over the past several decades.

The strength of these federal intellectual property rights is indifferent both to the amount of time spent to create or invent and to the difficulty of the creative or inventive task. Labor does not matter to the strength or scope of the intellectual property right. Only the patent regime applies a novelty standard. Originality under copyright law and distinctiveness under trademark law are quite low hurdles. And although the three regimes are supposed to be distinct, evolving practice and case law has led to troubling overlaps between copyright and trademark, copyright and patent, and design patents and trade dress.[27] Overlapping regimes allow IP owners to elect the regime that is most protective (e.g., stronger, broader, longer) despite long-standing policy to the contrary. Overlapping protection interferes with carefully crafted IP doctrines that balance private rights in intellectual creations against public access to such creations and future progress.[28] And yet, overlap seems inevitable given the interview data's illumination of persistent misalignment between creative and innovative work and statutory IP regimes.

Inspired Beginnings

THE "EUREKA" MOMENT experienced by artists and scientists is a well-known cliché, depicted in cartoons as a lightbulb appearing over one's head. Indeed, artists and scientists do experience these moments of transcendent discovery as they work. Throughout the interviews I conducted for this book, I heard some version of the eureka moment in response to questions such as, "How did you become an artist?" or "What influenced your path toward scientific research?" This chapter unpacks the mythology of these moments to examine how they arise.

Despite the frequency of these moments of discovery, the language and story types that accompany them are more complex and varied than simply "I woke up one day and the idea came to me." To be sure, whether in the arts or the sciences, many of the interviewees describe ideas coming to them as if unconsciously, or as one writer says, as "a voice passing through" her. But these individuals also, *at the same time*, describe various activities and complex social structures that nourish their work, particular reasons for being in certain places at certain times, and diverse circumstances that led to the production of work that may eventually become intellectual property. The eureka moment is only one facet of the creation stories that interviewees tell. And yet the law that purports to govern the origination, production, and promotion of art and science does not reflect this situational complexity; instead, it appears to be structured around or explained by the stereotyped eureka moment.[1] The law appears to rely on individual will and luck and eschews the connected and communal creativity and innovation that is the everyday work of creators and innovators.

When asked about their beginnings in the creative or innovative fields, many interviewees described some sort of origin story—a personal beginning pregnant with meaning beyond simply its causal role in producing a career or identity. Origin stories permeate our culture, from the creation of humanity in Genesis to the special meaning that the story of our children's birth takes in our own family ("the day you were born"). Genesis is the preeminent origin story, establishing the beginning of human civilization with God's creation of man in God's image and the subordination of Eve through her birth (origin) from Adam's rib. The myth of the United States' constitutional founding, the manner and motive for signing of the Declaration of Independence, and the deliberative engagement of the founding fathers continue to justify political and socioeconomic relationships among citizens and the government. Origin stories, like all narratives, make sense of the present in terms of a past moment, seeming to speak to "the essential nature of self and society."[2] They are uniquely persuasive as explanations for an individual's life or a society's contours by conflating the inquiry "Where did we come from?" with the question "Who are we?"

I therefore analyze the origin stories in these interviews closely. When people answer questions about how they began their career or why they pursued a certain direction and not another, they do not provide just one explanation. To be sure, they often answer the question with a single starting point, to which they ascribe special importance. For example, a theoretical chemist (whom I'll call Robert)[3] explains his start in molecular modeling this way:

My girlfriend [in graduate school] . . . happened to be an applied mathematician, . . . and I just learned all the applied math stuff . . . [which] turned out [to be] . . . useful in doing theoretical chemistry . . . but a lot of people in chemistry didn't know that stuff because they hadn't had this experience.

A visual artist, Sadie, recounts her beginning in art as a consequence of her mother dying at a young age and thereafter searching to be more like her mother and close to her even in her death.

We tell stories to make sense of our lives, as individuals and a society. (Perhaps there is no other kind of sense than that which we make through narratives.) Often, these stories take recognizable forms; on their face, these inspired beginnings seem to be generically straightforward origin myths. But no story has a singular meaning or significance. Within these stories of inspired beginnings are descriptions of diverse influences and resources that shaped their paths. When studied in light of the entire extended conversation we shared and the many additional details about the interviewees' career, the "once upon a time" quality of these origin stories recedes as the complexity of life's circumstances manifests more broadly. In this chapter, I examine both the commonalities and the variations among inspired beginnings in order to move us from a clichéd beginning to a fuller comprehension of how creativity and innovation happen. This will subsequently enable a fuller critique of the law's regulation of creative and innovative production.

Law and policy discussions of creativity and innovation do not dwell on the moment of creation or discovery, although "first in time" and "originators" of work are glorified and specially protected by US law.[4] Instead, most legal policy conversations today revolve around incentives, either conflating extrinsic motivations (e.g., financial reward) with intrinsic motivations (e.g., emotional pleasure) or presuming a hierarchical relation between them, thus subordinating intrinsic motivation to financial reward.[5] As the Supreme Court famously wrote about copyright, quoting Samuel Johnson, "No man but a blockhead ever wrote, except for money."[6] In other words, as the dominant legal story goes, we work (at art or science) primarily to earn a living.

Despite driving intellectual property law and policy discussions, the pecuniary gains to which an intellectual property owner is entitled are at best obliquely mentioned among the artists' and scientists' accounts of inspired beginnings, if at all. The absence of an economic incentive *in the beginning* correlates with recent studies that highlight the role of intellectual challenge and personal interest as intrinsic motivations.[7] Empirical studies also track the positive role that attribution and contribution have on collective social goods in motivating artistic and scientific production.[8] In asking interviewees questions about how they got started writing a draft novel or conducting a scientific experiment, such as "How did you get into this line of work?" or "What prompted you to embark on that project?" I expected to hear a variety of answers, including "To earn a living" or "I was looking for remunerative work." But these were rarely the responses. In fact, when pushed, many interviewees expressed surprise that they could earn a modest living from the artistic or scientific work about which they were passionate.

The dynamics of these origin stories do not completely displace the economic incentive used to justify intellectual property protection. But the diversity among the interviewees' accounts of how and why they embarked on a life of innovation in the creative and scientific fields stands in stark contrast to the romantic ideal of eureka moments and the monolithic language of monetary incentives. Additionally, and importantly, the diversity illuminates how the roots and offshoots of creativity and innovation are integrated into social organizations and legal relations.

*   *   *

Throughout the fifty interviews, stories of unconscious or serendipitous breakthrough are surrounded by other, specific conditions that also account for the beginning of creative or innovative endeavors. One of these conditions is playfulness; the individual's pursuit of pleasure manifests in the interviews as deeply individual preferences, united only by the common desire to explore as freely as possible. While the language of luck and serendipity populates these stories, respondents say that happy accidents occur when they are open to experiencing them and when they allow themselves (or are allowed by others) to follow meandering paths, whether or not a path is ultimately fruitful.

Another common condition that situates the origin story of creative or innovative work is *a problem in need of solving.* The problem might be personal, institutional, or social. The solution might be individual specific and then unpredictably expand, or it might initially be intended for a large audience. The interviewees vary in their expectations for dissemination, a point I more fully explore in the last chapter. But felt need and urgency around identified problems often drive creative or innovative beginnings.

If there is a consistent moral across the stories of inspired beginnings, it is in the interviewees' refusal to resolve tensions between individual gains and community welfare. It is clear from the interviews that an artist's or innovator's capacity to engage the work and extend the work's value comes from a combination of supportive relationships with others and historical or intellectual debts to past artists or scientists. Autonomy and freedom feature prominently in the stories of inspired beginnings, but so do the recognition of social connections and the necessity of (if not also the desire for) formally organized societal relations. The simultaneous emphasis in these origin stories on individual autonomy and ties to the social collective offers lessons for intellectual property policy that has conventionally favored the individual's contribution over that of the community.

UNCONSCIOUS ORIGINS

Several interviewees compared the moment they knew they created something worthwhile to an alarm going off. Here is a journalist and novelist, Jennifer, describing the beginning of a writing project. We were sitting at her dining room table, which was strewn with papers and children's toys, on a weekday morning: "It feels like you are almost like a filter, with a little alarm, and the alarm is, 'Oh, that's a story. You know, that's a story that people would be . . . interested in reading about.'" Jennifer experiences her alarm as an external signal that prompts an internal moment of clarity and purpose indicating that it's time to dig in and work on the project. Andrew, a software engineer, describes a similar moment when he discovered his next entrepreneurial project. When describing it to me, he is highly animated, gesticulating with his hands and leaning forward with his tall frame from the couch on which he sits: "It was so obvious . . . [I]t was so clear to us that the presence was going to have to move out to the network . . . that is the moment of invention, it's not like, sitting around drawing a drawing, it's actually like a little when you see the concepts coming together." Both Jennifer, the writer, and Andrew, the software engineer, took leaps of faith to pursue their respective work despite lacking validation or encouragement from others. They would invest significant time, labor, and money in their projects, and risk failure, to make something they believed worth their effort.

As it turns out, both Jennifer and Andrew earned enough money to live off their projects. Jennifer was a salaried journalist for more than a decade and then later sold her book to a publisher (transferring the copyright) and lived off the royalties for a while before returning to journalism.

Andrew accumulated venture capital on the basis of his innovative software and his patent portfolio, and he later sold his nascent company to a large publicly traded company. But these intellectual property jackpots were by no means preordained. Nor was money the original motivation for pursuing a life in art and science.

Jennifer became a writer because of her interest in both the Soviet Union and journalism. High school teachers strongly influenced her decision to pursue a job as a Moscow correspondent after college, and she had a strong desire to "do something useful":

So in tenth grade . . . I started these two interests, and I decided for some reason, at that point, that I wanted to be a Moscow correspondent. And then I just—in a very linear way, I pursued that goal, and . . . so basically, that's what got me into journalism. . . . [I]n the old days, you know, the world was on the brink of nuclear catastrophe, and it seemed like we really needed to understand the Soviet Union, and they needed to understand us.

Andrew, the software engineer, has a similar origin story, linking his work in the software industry to early teenage influences and activities:

[M]y background is in engineering and physics, and it's specifically in computer science doing both engineering and physics. So I was doing programming in school for ten years, and I was doing programming before that since I was thirteen years old. And I think that that's been very important to everything I've done since I left graduate school for physics. You know, straight out of physics, the fact that you have so many years to kind of learn your trade while you don't even think that that's what you're doing, learning the trade.

Both of these people describe their origin in very different fields as a product of serendipitous factors born of their unique biographies. And both also ascribe the moment of invention to something beyond their conscious choice. The metaphorical alarm bell—a symbol of time and readiness—was a sign to them that they could move forward with confidence, as if someone were waving a flag to say to them, "The time is now, this is it—ready, set, go."

In lieu of an alarm, the interviews also contain metaphors for creative moments or invention related to nature or magic. Jennifer mentioned "an element of alchemy" in writing her first book, implying a magical and unexplained process. Andrew, the software engineer and entrepreneur, compared the process to a mirage: something before his eyes that made itself perceptible to him in an unexplained and thrilling way. The beginning of the project was not like sketching or brainstorming—"not like . . . drawing a drawing"—but like an idea appearing before him of its own force: "you see concepts [come] together."

A web designer echoed this sentiment in terms of a portal he was asked to create: "We did the research on how their business was organized, and it was almost—it was one of those things where it was almost obvious what needed to happen, and all I needed to do was kind of not mess it up, you know?" Karen, a sculptor and installation artist who lives and works in New York City, describes how the idea for an award-winning work "just struck" her. She was brainstorming an installation project that would be outside and on view for months. She had to consider the durability of materials against the elements and throngs of passersby:

I was walking over where the [street hits the wide pedestrian path] . . . so you don't have any buildings, it's just more open. And so you've got the big sky, and I realized, oh, yeah—the street trees are here. So you don't have the buildings, you don't have the people, but the trees. And then I realized, well, they'd been here all the time, from day one. . . . So that's why it was—when it struck me, I think I sent [my partner] a text or I called him and I said, 'What about the street trees?' Because . . . while I was walking and it just kind of hit me, I was like, 'Oh, yeah.' It would be immediately an easy way—I could see how I could connect and work with the entire length of the street.

As with the alarm, the magical appearance of an idea compels these artists and engineers forward. It is understandable that a moment of clarity or a sign from nature (or God, or whatever your mystical preference) would encourage the commitment of time and labor that intense productive work entails. The personal and business risks involved in doing art and science are serious considerations. But the feeling of lucidity eases those risks, at least as far as committing to hard work and experiencing personal satisfaction in its outcome.

A patent attorney, Carol understands the invention of one of her clients, a biologist, in a similar way. We are sitting in a conference room in her law firm and she is telling me about the initial interview with her client when they discussed the process of drafting a patent:

[He said,] "Look, I am just a scientist, you know? I go into my lab, and I come up with theories." And he said, "This was a complete sea change"—and that was his word: a complete sea change. No one—and no one—believed him. And we wrote a patent, and we got him an application, and we got him patents . . . and he's in Europe, and he's all over—worldwide jurisdiction. And now, people are . . . employing this particular method to help a population of people for which there was very little hope, and it's working. And he's just . . . very touched by that, that he did something that . . . was just sort of like this [snaps fingers] flash of genius. He looked at the data with one of his students, and he was like, "You know what? I don't think it's that—I think it's *this*. And so let's test it." Well, no one believed him.

It is common that "creation stories" render the moment of inspiration into myth.[9] Serendipitous and natural forces conspire to characterize creation stories as beyond the control of those who will be credited with the creation or invention, whether amateurs and professionals. In these interviews, the mythic form does not discriminate between those who are commercially successful and those who are not. The interviewees relish the lack of responsibility attributable to their own conscious behavior. For instance, the inspiration for one of singer-songwriter Mary's most popular songs was, as she describes it, an accidental confluence of natural beauty and canine companionship. As with the journalist, the biologist, the software engineer, and the web designer, the valuable creative work appeared almost fully formed to Mary:

I was walking [my dog] . . . it was the most beautiful night. I wasn't trying to write a song; I was just walking with her. And the song, it was one of those weird songs that just came to me in my head. . . . I heard the music. The whole thing came to me on the course of a two-and-a-half-mile walk. Got back to the car, wrote it down on a map of New England. I didn't have anything else in the car. And it was like, *there*. It was complete.

Mary was also careful to specify that "this almost never happens," but that she is grateful it did because the popularity of that song ended up paying for unexpected medical care her dog would need later:

And so then almost a year later—April of this year—literally the morning I was taking [her] to the vet, [I] opened the front door—I mean literally with her and the suitcase . . . to go to our vet—the mailman is standing there, hands me this big envelope from satellite radio. I open it up, and it's $1,600. And I just squealed. . . . I was like, "You have got to be kidding!" Because . . . I knew we were going in for a big surgery, and I didn't know what it would cost, but . . . you never think about that. . . . [T]hat's what credit cards are for. But . . . it was primarily for that song. . . . And so it was just . . . really amazing.

To Mary, who was speaking with me in her living room strewn with guitars, amplifiers, and papers, the mysteriousness surrounding the song's quick conception, and its rarity, was explained a year later when the money was necessary for her dog's life-saving surgery. The musician's own work and the benefit it brought her was an unexpected gift.

Both Jennifer, the journalist, and Andrew, the software engineer, tie their professional successes to early childhood circumstances and to many years of hard work in the field. Mary, the musician, and scientists experience eureka moments after years of musical or scientific training. Their language of accidents, randomness, and happenstance implies a lack of control and a fortuity. But another important facet defines them: their discoveries and creations are products of their particular material conditions, especially the people they've known and the places they've been. This may seem a banal observation. But the excavation of the inspired beginnings of art and science is central to recognizing how origin stories may hide or suppress other explanations. This book aims to appreciate how multifaceted narrative explanations can be. It is important to remember that the "point" of the story determines its significance for future application across similar circumstances. The dominant point of origin stories is often the unconsciousness, magic, and fortuity that stimulate creativity and innovation. But to discern their undercurrent of material circumstances and biographical specificity is to comprehend another message. When we perceive the circumstantial and biographical complexity of creative and innovative beginnings, we can begin to ask whether the intellectual property regimes aimed at stimulating creativity and innovation align with the actual practices of creativity and innovation.

Here is a prolific and successful children's book author, Barbara, talking about her authorial beginnings. Barbara invited me to her home in the country. It is a cozy, cabinlike house on a small body of water with an open floor plan that looks onto a lush garden. She began her professional career as an editor, not a writer, while raising two children as a single mother:

While I was [an editor at a children's trade publisher], my son at that time was about six years old, and I was reading books to him, and I went to bed one Saturday night remembering the book that I had read to him over and over and *over* again. And during the night, I had an idea for a book, and when I woke up in the morning, it was about half written. And I got it on paper, showed it to a friend at [at work] who said—and I will never forget these words . . . "You're a writer!" And then I became a writer.

Barbara combines all these characteristics of origin stories—natural alarms, unconscious discovery, fortuitous relationships, and biographical specificity. She describes the moment of recognition—"You're a writer!"—as if it sprung, uncontrolled, from within her. But she also explains how being an editor at a children's trade publisher and a mother combined to make her into a writer. The children's book writer anchors her eureka moment to the fact of her being a parent and an editor. Similarly, Mary ties her song's origin to the night sky and her dog's companionship. Robert, the theoretical chemist we met at the beginning of this chapter, situates his own breakthrough in terms of his voracious reading habits and his girlfriend. Robert also attributes scientific genius (a quality of those he calls "superstars") to essential characteristics of a person's mind rather than to learned behavior or habit.

The interviewees describe creation as both serendipitous (a function of situations or experiences that are unplanned and beyond one's conscious control) and organic (being driven by natural or unknown forces). But it is also important to remember that while the interviewees describe the experience of inspiration as passive, they are active participants, responding to and taking advantage of the opportunities presented to them.[10] They are moved to make something of the eureka moment, as if *called* to write the song, the book, or the algorithm. The respondents recognize value in what becomes "their" innovation from external signals and are moved to harvest it in some way. Mihaly Csikszentmihalyi describes similar elements of luck and serendipity in his book *Creativity: Flow and the Psychology of Discovery and Invention*, suggesting that luck is not the only or most important element. He says luck is "easy to overstate. . . . Being in the right place at the right time is clearly important. But many people never realize that they are standing in a propitious space/time convergence, and even fewer know what to do when the realization hits them."[11] Before exploring how these origin stories unfold as tales of work and labor, I want to elaborate on the variations of serendipity and circumstance embedded in the origin stories themselves.

PROBLEM SOLVING AND PLAY

Generally, beyond the experience of "Eureka!" interviewees describe two primary contexts in which creativity and invention happen: problem solving and play. Individuals play by experimenting with freedoms they take or are granted. They can also be motivated by the need or desire to understand and resolve problems. Both of these states of being bring pleasure to the artist or scientist. They describe both the play and the problem solving as enjoyable activities in and of themselves. This may be different from everyday life, in which problem solving is necessary but not always fun. In these interviews, by contrast, play and problem solving are intertwined, and both are deeply enjoyable, ludic experiences.

Problem Solving: A Need and Desire

In unpacking how innovators and artists work, creativity theorists have written about "problem finding" and "problem solving."[12] Csikszentmihalyi defines the problem as a "stimulus" that triggers the creative process, with three possible sources: personal lives, domain (within a person's field), and social pressures.[13] He says, "The creative process starts with a sense that there is a puzzle somewhere, or a task to be accomplished."[14]

Csikszentmihalyi applies his concept of problem to a larger intellectual or historical scale, as in exploring the problem of colonialism or disease.[15] But even on a smaller scale, my interviewees confirm his conclusion, citing acute problems in their personal or material lives, and sometimes in the larger community. Problems ranging from quotidian habits to global issues can serve as the original motivation for creative or innovative output.

Dan became a librettist and musical composer after spending his earlier life as a successful chemical engineer. He attributes his career change to parenting troubles. His son, who has perfect pitch, is also autistic and as a young boy had trouble joining group activities:

We couldn't get him involved in a conventional activity of any nature, and we didn't really know why. It turns [out] he's a high-functioning autistic. . . . But we didn't know that. All we knew is that there was no way to get him to really explore his voice. . . . We went and we saw [the children's opera] *Dracula*, and [my son] . . . couldn't sit still for it . . . but the kids who were in it just thought this was the greatest thing. And I decided that we'd go home and we'd write our own opera, because, you know, [my son] saw that his friends were in this opera. He could never do it, but if I were to write some music for him to sing on a subject that interested him . . . he would sing it, and we could sing together. So we talked about what kinds of stories he liked, and what caught his attention. . . . [And] I started writing some [operatic] music [for him].

Dan studied music theory in college and describes becoming a composer of operas to involve his child in music under circumstances that are conducive to his son's particular disability. Our children and their needs are inextricably bound with the structure of our professional lives and are often catalysts for creative or inventive output. Indeed, children feature frequently in origin stories, as in the case of Barbara, the children's book author mentioned earlier.

Other problems to be solved may have roots in everyday material life, beginning a new and innovative project through urgency or need. Joan is a contemporary artist known around the world for her gigantic installations. She describes how, as a young artist, the necessity of making do with very few art supplies shaped her future career as a sculptor. Now in her forties, she lives with her two children and her husband in New

England. She speaks with me from her studio, which is attached to her house. Her studio assistants pop in and out of her office as we talk for many hours. She tells me how, when she was a young painter in India on a Fulbright fellowship, she was preparing for an exhibition and her paints got lost in the mail:

I had arranged for this big exhibition that the embassy was going to sponsor, and I had no paint. [She laughs.] And I was very lonely, and very nervous about—you know, here I was; what was I going to do? . . . I met a . . . senior Fulbright artist . . . and she was a sculptor. And . . . she told me that she had been a painter, and that all the women sculptors had been painters. . . . I think it gave me permission. . . . I was like, "Oh, if she can do it." . . . And so I started making sculpture there. And in India, I could afford to work with materials and have people help me. . . . [But] I didn't have enough money to make big bronze sculpture to fill this exhibition, and I was going for a walk every evening, and a swim on the beach. And that was when the fisherman were bringing in their nets. And I started looking at those forms on the beach, and I thought, "Well, there's another approach to volumetric form, without weight." And I could ship them around; they'd fold up, and they could be extended. And I'm still working with those ideas.

Joan's explanation strongly resonated with themes throughout the interviews. She needed a reason or external sign to push her to try something new, and she found it in those who came before her ("if she can do it . . ."). Like Mary, the singer-songwriter describing her evening walk with her dog around the reservoir, Joan adapted natural and material forms around her. But also motivating Joan's shift from painting to sculpting was the urgency of time constraints and her lack of material resources. She needed to fill the gallery halls, but her paints were lost, and she lacked the funds to cast large bronze sculptures. Moreover, she had to get her sculptures home, so they had to be movable. The malleability of the found material (nets and wire) with which she began working has been one of the hallmarks of her work as a sculptor ever since.

Scientists and engineers describe their creative impulse as a direct response to urgent problems. Biologists need to solve certain medical problems and find that challenge pleasurable.[16] Carol, the intellectual property attorney we met earlier, began her professional life as a biologist. She describes her early work as a scientist this way:

Just being in a lab was fun to me, you know? And then [in college] I became a lab dishwasher, and . . . I was making the media and solutions, and helping the grad students, and . . . I thought it was fun. And so I went to grad school. And that was fun. . . . [Y]ou have a hypothesis, I mean, that's what science is all about. . . . [Y]ou look what's out there, and you formulate a hypothesis . . . and then you design experiments to test that hypothesis. And then you sort of move on, and you build into other things. Just to me, it . . . was great, because it was fun, it was like solving a mystery with . . . not really knowing what's at the end of it.

Carol left science when the laboratory work and faculty politics ruined the fun of the problem solving and interfered with the autonomy and freedom to pursue her own research. The playfulness was muted by destructive relationships at the university. Now, Carol is a lawyer and a partner at her firm, content to work with scientists to further their research and its dissemination. She therefore speaks from a particularly knowledgeable vantage point when she characterizes one of her clients as a "proud" and happy scientist, deriving pleasure from his lab's collaborative work to address the medical problems of a needy population.

Similarly, Paul, an IP lawyer representing a small device manufacturer, relayed the reasoning behind one of his client's inventions: a device for a gutter that prevents ice dams, which are particularly thorny problems in his New England community:

[H]e had a problem, and he thought, well, it would be neat to do this, especially in New Hampshire, because people's gutters . . . almost every year, they have problems with their gutters where they splinter . . . because the ice expands. . . . And he had this device . . . where the gutter . . . folds. . . . It's a simple device. Everybody can understand it, but nobody thought of it. . . . [T]he technology is so basic, it's something where the second I saw it, I wanted it on my house.

The picture Paul paints about his client setting out to fulfill a particular need is typical—stereotypical even—of small-time inventors. Another lawyer in the financial services industry describes a similar client situation:

It was a business consulting firm, and I think that what happened was they developed their own software to do financial analysis, and then they began to think, "Wait a minute: other people might like to use this software. You know, if they don't—they might not need our services; why not . . . make money selling the software." So, you know, they had developed these things for other reasons, for other business purposes, and then it became valuable.

Needs can be material ("I lost my paint and so I am working with the materials I have" or "How do we make our business work better"), socio-emotional ("I needed to help my child" or "This is a medical problem I want to solve"), or consumer oriented ("We need a better way to keep our gutters ice-free").

Sometimes need is directed at a particular audience—those suffering with a particular disease, home owners in the Northeast with clogged gutters—but just as often the need is personal. An unpublished novelist, Elizabeth, exemplifies many of the interviews in emphasizing how her work is driven by personal need:

I also think of writing . . . having some similarities to exercise, it being something that I need to do every day, and that it's not really explicable—there are plenty of people who *don't* have to exercise every day. But when I do it, I feel better. And this is what I notice: that this is the year that I first . . . quit and moved up to Vermont [to write full-time]; I noticed that I felt less crazy as a person if I got my work got done. . . . I was like, "Oh my God! This really makes me feel calm!"

Many other respondents—both artists and scientists—confirm this sentiment. Frequently, when I asked why creators and innovators kept doing their work, they would answer, "Because it keeps me balanced and happy." For instance, Mary, the singer-songwriter, said:

I mean, I know that if someone told me right now, "You will never be able to make a record or perform again," I would not stop writing. Like, that's my filter on the world. That's how I recycle an experience and turn it into something [that] feels beautiful to me. And there is just so much chaos, and that's the way I've always made order out of all of this stuff that's so hard to navigate.

Whether working for start-ups or public companies, scientists and engineers tend to express the same sort of pleasure in pursuing solutions and challenging themselves. Thomas, a co-owner of a privately held software company, demonstrates his value to the company when he explains his sustained interest in the company's business, which has lasted seventeen years:

I want to understand what . . . the problem is, and I want to work with people to help solve their problem. And that has been more successful as a strategy, because people see that and they want to work with you because you helped them solve their problem. . . . I just think it's interesting. I mean, . . . complex problems are interesting to solve. I don't [feel], "I am going to create this big business, and do this and that." But I was always like, "Hey, this is kind of interesting. I'd really like to do this." Or if somebody has a problem, I'd really like to try and figure out how to help fix it.

Although Thomas directly profits from the company's success, how and why he works at his company is based in the feeling he derives from helping clients solve problems. He attributes the success of his company to his client-centered problem-solving focus. This focus is the origin of his interest in software and it has become the company's signature:

This is actually a big thing in the way the company evolved . . . [T]he software itself is very good, it's very clean; it does things very well. . . . But there are other programs that could do that. So that's not what makes it unique. It's the people that we've already done this for that can tell other [potential clients] that they should come to us because we could solve their problems. So it's the software is a third of the overall solution. It's like you need the software tool, you need the people to provide service, and you need to basically understand the business's need. You need to understand the business need in order to be able to solve the real problem. And that's where most programs fall down.

Matthew is another software engineer and works as an information architect for web-based business portals. He is currently not a direct stakeholder but an employee in a growing company. Matthew expressed nearly the same feeling as did Thomas about his work, how he got into it, and why he sticks to it:

It's very personal to me. I mean, it may be common in some ways, but . . . the way I think about it, it's the whole problem-solving aspects of it. It's the gathering of the different data, which includes things like understanding who the users are . . . what the users want to do, or are likely to want to do if you are making some assumptions, and also gathering whatever capabilities you are going to be able to put into this thing. So . . . what's feasible, what's possible, and then what you are trying to accomplish, and then . . . coming up with the thing. . . . [For the insurance company] it was both designing certain interactions, but then also . . . cracking the nut of "All right, here's the big thing, and if we don't solve this, it's all done," and finally figuring out how we needed to do it.

Need and desire entwine in how creators and innovators think about a day's work. It is important to note that the pleasure respondents describe is not in solving the problem and finishing the product; rather, *engaging* in their craft makes them happy (be it designing computer programs or writing and playing music).[17] I mentioned earlier that origin stories tend to conflate the question of who we are with where we came from. Similarly, we need to be careful about confusing the *need* to engage in their craft with the *pleasure* the craft brings to its maker. The origins of particular companies, works, inventions, and careers happen in the context of personal habits, traits, and conditions that are fundamental and enduring. But whereas particular needs might be momentary and circumstantial, desire characterizes an ongoing passion, satisfied only in part by the completion of a project. Interviewees describe the need to work as a craving; it is not a material desire but an existential and emotional one.[18] The pleasure and momentum of everyday work is the subject of Chapter 2. For now, I turn to the connection between pleasure and *initiating* work.

Freedom to Play

The common defining feature of pleasure among interviewees is the *freedom* they feel while engaging in their work—a kind of free play that is, simply, fun. Sometimes this feeling arises in the context of work autonomy, and other times through the exhilaration of adventure and exploration. Throughout many of the interviews, autonomous play seemed to foment even more creativity and innovative output in a generative cycle.[19] Similarly, the lack of freedom is often why people leave jobs, like Carol, the academic biologist who resigned her tenured post to become a patent attorney. Freedom to explore is both a state of being that these artists and scientists profoundly enjoy and the fertile beginning for creative and innovative work.

Leo, a lawyer in Manhattan for most of his life, is, in his sixties, becoming a well-known visual artist. We spoke at his summer house on Cape Cod, sitting in the living room overlooking a salt marsh. He told me how he began painting by "messing around" in his kitchen:

I didn't set out to be a painter. . . . I wanted to be a writer, and that was much more daunting, because I had spent a lot of time thinking about what great writing was. . . . It became sort of a big hurdle to overcome. But painting, I just started doing it because . . . I enjoyed it; it was meditative for me. A lot of the painting started out as what I would call getting into a mental space, where I would work for two to four hours a night in my kitchen. . . . One of the things that happened to me was that I discovered my own way of painting. . . . I work on the floor; I drip. . . . If I hadn't had the freedom to experiment—which is . . . the way I develop my painting [and] is very much . . . like . . . experimentation, because it was just an evolutionary process of working and what I call messing around which is just trying things and seeing what happened.

Leo's origin story was accidental and serendipitous, drawn out by the freedom to let his thoughts play and actions roam. For Leo, experimenting with all sorts of paint materials was essential to stumbling upon a winning combination of acrylic for his characteristic drip paintings.[20]

This combination of accident, need, and playfulness was common in the interviews, and true not only for the artists: scientists and their business managers likewise emphasize the benefit that intellectual autonomy and workplace playfulness bring to their fields.[21] Ted, an in-house counsel for a bioengineering company, jokingly calls the most prolific inventors at the company "juvenile delinquents" because they are always figuring out ways to break or circumvent rules to make something new and different. Ted and I sit at a conference table at his company in a low-rise building in the Boston-Cambridge area. His enthusiasm for law and his company's business is contagious. He smiles broadly and swivels constantly in his chair. He says:

I think the most successful inventors here are the people who are constantly looking for an edge, and looking at how to buck the system. They see it as a challenge. . . . Always looking to game the system or something like that. . . . Shortcuts, or just trying to get around things. They were probably horrible juvenile delinquents in their youth. [Laughs]

Patentable inventions, says Ted, come from the willingness and ability to play with the rules and adventure beyond established scientific and institutional boundaries.

Ted describes invention happening in the lab "by accident," suggesting the important roles of serendipity in triggering innovation and of fortunate accidents, which can happen only when scientists have the freedom to explore paths not previously taken. Ted intentionally fosters a playful and experimental culture in his company to encourage scientists to think outside of the box and break certain rules. In fact, his company incentivizes what he calls "playing hard" with monthly competitions for the "coolest idea," contests that are peer evaluated and celebrated in game-show style. Winners are awarded $10 gift certificates.[22] But the modesty of the awards indicates that the reward is less about money than the fun of the game, and the emotional and reputational kudos for having the "coolest idea." Other interviewees confirm this sense that free and flexible workplaces are more important than the money they earned at work and could be just as (or more) productive. Thomas, the software engineer with his own company, describes the early days of his business, when he was earning less money and was considering the business risk of his venture:

I had a tremendous amount of flexibility. The one thing that my job has always given me is a lot of flexibility and a lot of room. And I appreciated that a lot, because I could do pretty much anything I wanted, and I could pursue any projects that I wanted. So that, at that time, meant more to me than additional money.

Literature analyzing employee-management relations and company success, as well as a growing body of empirical work, asserts a causal relationship between employee satisfaction, employees' relative autonomy at work, and company performance.[23] The accounts in the interviews of work motivation and satisfaction lend support to this literature.

For some artists and innovators, freedom and play are not possible within the workday. In those cases, interviewees actively chose to take particular jobs that maximized their time and freedom to experiment outside their day job. For even the most established artists I interviewed, it was common that at times during their career they had to piece various paying jobs together to make ends meet while setting aside time to work on their unremunerated art. For example, David decided to teach part-time (as a computer instructor) to finance his studio photography. He had a very successful commercial studio for decades before the digital revolution. But since the mid-1990s, David has relied on other income to support his photography. Like so many artists and scientists, the individuals I interviewed could have taken higher-paying jobs unrelated to their creative passions, but they considered the freedom to pursue their art or science more valuable. And so they took jobs that maximized their time rather than their income.

The freedom to experiment with full creative license and autonomy is a vital starting point for creative or innovative output. For many of the interviewees, freedom is crucial to engaging in and enjoying the creative activity, and to its production of innovative technologies or creative works. Intellectual property scholarship is rich with critiques of how certain forms of intellectual property protection restrict development of creative or innovative work and can thereby stifle the very creativity and innovation the intellectual property laws are meant to incentivize.[24] Interviewees corroborate these critiques; ironically, for them, amassing a patent portfolio is important because patents can be "chits to trade" when another company's blocking patents threaten their research projects. That is, lawyers and scientists use patents not necessarily to collect rent but to leverage rights and clear the field so they can continue research and development potentially unrelated to the patents themselves. In this vein, Dennis, an in-house intellectual property lawyer, recounts his discussions with company scientists who resisted his request for invention disclosures by appealing to the freedom the scientists crave to continue their research.[25] Dennis explains to the scientists:

"I agree that this subject matter likely shouldn't be patentable. But . . . right now, it *is* being patented by other people, and we're having to analyze their patents, spend tens of thousands of dollars analyzing them, rendering opinions, telling business people they have to make business risks based upon infringement issues. And . . . we're taking licenses." So I said [to them], "What I want is something that I can trade with somebody." I said, "I'm not interested in necessarily asserting these against anybody. I'm looking for something that either (a) gives me a quid to trade with somebody, or (b) we patent it first so that some other company can't patent it and then come to us for $100,000-a-year royalty."

Other attorneys and scientists shared similar explanations, treating patents as tools for making room and reserving space so that more experimentation and innovation could take place.

The attorneys I spoke with did not discuss the role of copyright and trademarks in the same way. Perhaps this is because the boundaries of copyright and trademark are fuzzier and not sufficiently "tradable" as properties the way patents are (copyrights and trademarks notoriously have more limitations and exceptions to their exclusive rights than do patents). This, among other difficulties, may explain the more frequent and tolerated infringement of copyright (and perhaps even trademark) among artists and businesspeople.[26] Yet tolerated infringement can also be understood as a method of making room, by entering the space without permission. Whatever the legal rules, making room for play and experimentation was regularly described as a precursor to the act of creation or discovery. Having both the time and the intellectual space to play is essential to initiating and sustaining creative projects. Thus, when IP rules and practices get in the way of work, interviewees take risks to ignore the rules or work around them in order to continue with their art or science. (This need for time and space, discussed in more detail in Chapter 2, has implications for whether the misalignment of the US IP system needs retooling.)

Across the interviews, inventors and creators discuss the immense pleasure they feel when work leads to a discovery or creative experimentation generates a work. One general counsel told me he entered the e-commerce business because it built on his expertise, which had itself developed in part because he simply enjoyed working through the problems in the field. And really, this isn't surprising. Social scientists who study work and creativity have said the same thing about drive and motivation: they happen not because of the financial rewards from particular products but, at least initially, because doing the work itself is a fun challenge.[27] (Chapter 6 discusses skill development as a primary reason for distributing the work as well: to challenge competencies and build upon them.) What is surprising for our understanding of intellectual property, however, is that these creators and innovators do not describe the benefits of ownership (e.g., control, revenue) as a reason to embark on their life or project in art, science, or business. Their origin stories give other reasons for doing what they do *at first*, infusing their everyday life as writers, musicians, software engineers, entrepreneurs, or chemists with the gloss of inevitability, luck, free play, and material or existential need.

ORIGINS OF ORIGINS: BORROWING TO MAKE ANEW

What was special about that newly patented battery? What made this painting (as opposed to others) so highly acclaimed? When I asked artists and scientists about their sources of inspiration, I was hoping to elicit thoughts on what made creative or innovative work valuable: How did the originators of the work explain the successes or failures of their creations or inventions? Would those explanations resonate with the basis of protection in intellectual property law (or the comparable "creative spark" in copyright law; distinctiveness in trademark law; or novelty, nonobviousness, and usefulness in patent law)? Instead, in answer to my questions about "inspired beginnings," I heard the language of serendipity, of play and problem solving, which celebrates a combination of luck, individual context, and autonomy rather than a work's uniqueness and utility.

When I continued to ask about their sources of inspiration, the interviewees' descriptions were even more complex. Interviewees struggled to draw a line between their own contribution to the final work and works from which they borrowed in their field. This was the case with Dan, the composer and former chemical engineer described earlier. While working as a senior engineer, Dan was the named inventor on several patents that were owned by the companies for which he worked. For Dan, the label "inventor" was uncomfortable, despite being descriptively accurate. Dan told me:

I am a very creative person. I wouldn't think of myself as an inventor, but what I am good at is bringing ideas from different areas together that—and seeing something that, over here, "Wait a minute—that applies to *that*." And so that's where my strength is. . . . And you know, I came up with lots of ideas in all my jobs, and a lot of them didn't pan out, and some of them did.

Dan developed groundbreaking uses for plastic materials in the 1980s and patented software in the 1990s, which, to his knowledge, remains a critical tool in several environmental consulting companies. Nonetheless, he attributes his success to his ability to combine and build on other people's ideas and innovations from diverse fields. Bob, a general counsel, describes the value of his publishing company's profitable line of K–12 textbooks in a similar way:

[T]his is a fairly established product. . . . it goes through iterations, and the states want to try different things in terms of elaborating more standards and more of this or that, and the books get bigger and bigger. But the core approach in the major subjects doesn't change. Math and science [don't] change. The sequence of instruction doesn't change radically. They want to drive more and more instruction into it . . . but still . . . it's not highly inventive in the sense that . . . this is the 2000 [edition]. You look at the 2008 [edition], it's not going to look vastly different. . . . [T]he 2008 edition is going to be very much a derivative work . . . and that's what I was getting at, is that the process is to start with a very fulsome product, and then tweak, move it around, adapt it, look to the external curriculum requirements, and then add in whatever's considered best practices in pedagogy.

Both Dan, a chemical engineer, and Bob, a general counsel in the publishing business, describe the inventive contributions of their profit-making products as "bringing ideas together" from other people and as "iterative adaptations." Authors, painters, scientists, and software engineers I interviewed likewise say that works that earned them fame or fortune were inspired by earlier work of other artists and scientists. Some borrowed plot structure, some borrowed stylistic elements, and many drew directly from research protocols or the hypotheses of mentors and colleagues to evolve scientific investigations. This is not to say their work is not or should not be protected as intellectual property because it lacks requisite creativity or novelty (in a legal sense), but instead the people and companies developing useful and creative work accept, and even embrace, the fact that the creation and value of the new product relies on works that came before.

Although it is fairly commonsense, the understanding that creativity and innovation are inevitably iterative processes remains largely unacknowledged in the legal doctrine. And perceptible disagreements and distinctions arise among the interviewees, reflecting the policy debates in the legal literature about where the line should be drawn between unregulated borrowing and borrowing for which one must ask permission. Irene, a solo-practice copyright lawyer who primarily represents individual writers and small companies, reflects on the development of copyright law and evolving standards for creativity and ownership. She has been a lawyer for more than thirty years, and in that time she has seen copyright law struggle to adapt to changes in cultural production. As a young lawyer, Irene was one of the first women in the emerging IP group of a New York law firm in the early 1980s. Her career has grown alongside the development of the 1976 Copyright Act, the origins of which she witnessed firsthand. She eventually left "big law" to work in-house for several publishing companies, and then later she started her successful solo practice from a home office. In a café near her home, she tells me about her evolving experiences with clients and their work:

[Common conflicts about ownership] have to do with the changing nature of creativity. Because when I first started doing this, the creators truly were doing things much more from scratch. . . . [W]hat's happening now is that you see much more creative work that is, in fact, an accumulation, a compilation, a conglomeration of different elements, some of which were taken from other places. And that's because the technology makes it possible to strip—makes it so trivially easy. . . . You can strip the content out from however it was delivered to you and plug it in somewhere else, so people do it. . . . I think it's probably more typical now for people to not quite understand why . . . someone else is claiming a piece of what . . . they've done.

Irene bemoans the effects of the digital "mash-up" culture because she thinks it means the authors of the original works, from which pieces are snipped, or "stripped," as Irene says, are not getting paid: "I think that [original] vision deserves to be protected and respected. And if that guy has to do things like eat and pay health insurance, he needs to get paid. But that seems to be disappearing."

Elizabeth, a novelist with whom I spoke, develops this theme, making what seems to be a moral assertion about the value of novelty and an author's duty to develop new forms of expression. At the same time, she admits that she unconsciously based her main character on Jane Austen's character Emma:

I based [my character] on somebody I met. And then as I was thinking it through . . . I thought . . . this is kind of like *Emma*! That gives me confidence! . . . I think it gives writers . . . confidence when you can say . . . , "This book is just like this other famous book that . . . has lived in the public mind since . . . 1797.' . . . And it's not like I don't fall prey to this—to feel like human nature has been pretty stable for a long time, and we have probably said everything there is to say about it. But conditions, the conditions of human nature, of humanity, do change, have changed. You know, we produce new food stuffs, . . . and there are always these specific details that are new. So come up with a new story to tell me about those things.

Whereas Irene, the copyright lawyer, was concerned for the financial well-being of her authors, Elizabeth objects to copying less in terms of financial debts than as a personal trespass. Elizabeth speaks from her living room, where she sits on the couch her feet tucked beneath her:

Well, I just think, like, get your own idea. . . . That's how I feel about it. It just annoys me when people rip off other people's ideas. I mean, it just makes you think that those people are weak. Why would I want to read a book by somebody who has to take somebody else's idea to have a foundation for a story? . . . I think there's a line between imitating the masters until you find your feet, and just taking somebody's scaffolding for your own . . . [if the] book's not in the public domain. It's like, hands off.

These disparate descriptions of origins are united by an understanding that inspired beginnings to truly creative or novel works worthy of protection are quite rare. Dennis, the longtime pharmaceutical industry patent attorney, complained of a lost opportunity to patent an invention at his previous job: it could have been a breakthrough, he explained, but his colleagues failed to recognize the remarkable occasion of true invention. Dennis says, "In the past, I have gotten very upset with our business development colleagues who trivialize intellectual property and trivialize invention. . . . Invention is rare, OK!" But Dennis also recognizes the tension between the inevitability of borrowing and the appreciation for something new:

And this actually gets to the trouble of what you patent and what you don't patent, because it's . . . really rare to have true innovation. . . . Steve Jobs and Wozniak created the personal computer. . . . Cohen and Boyer created biotechnology, the concept of moving genes around through man's intervention. . . . But most of the rest of us mere mortals . . . learn from other people, and then . . . the frontiers of science are pushed back generally gradually through similar antlike persistence by scientists.

Innovation and creativity are therefore both produced by influence and valued for novelty. A consequence of this is the common phenomenon of simultaneous invention.[28] Within defined communities, it is no surprise that multiple, similar inspired beginnings take place. Indeed, inventions often slip through the hands of their creators, as in the case of Andrew, the software engineer and entrepreneur:

It never got executed by *us*. . . . [I]t was in the air, you see. It was just a matter of time. . . . [T]here are always many smart people that are exposed to the same conditions, and they will come up—I actually believe they are very few ideas that are such breakthroughs that you won't have, over a period of two years, many people come up with the idea.

An in-house lawyer explained it this way, when describing the scope of his company's patent portfolio:

They're not on the total core product. I don't think we invented [the whole process]. We were involved in it kind of a year or year and a half later, and we've protected some of the important functionality. But we certainly can't claim a monopoly on the whole . . . process. . . . And [our competitors] didn't get an application in either. And I think really, what happens is this stuff gets invented, and the first user just doesn't get an application in.

Interviewees in both high-tech and biotechnology discussed the fact of simultaneous invention and iterative, overlapping discoveries, much of which is not (or they think shouldn't be) patentable. Kevin is a high-tech entrepreneur currently focusing on the telecom industry. He is also a former software and hardware engineer who spent his early career working with some of the computer giants that today dominate the industry. We're sitting on his front porch in the early summer. His phone rings every thirty minutes, but he ignores it and continues our conversation:

For a lot of entrepreneurship, it's about finding a business model. You know: "exactly what should I put together, and exactly to whom should I sell it, and when do I catch them, and how much do I try to charge them for it?" Very little of entrepreneurship, in fact, is about developing really fundamentally new things. . . . You don't fund a start-up to do new, . . . solid-state device physics. It's too risky; it's too expensive; it takes too long. Usually, it's people taking an existing thing, reconfiguring it, maybe being clever. . . . Take Twitter as an example: there is no new computer science behind Twitter. . . . Google, . . . the [existing] scientific citation ranking algorithm . . . and they solved tons of problems in terms of figuring out how to . . . scale. . . . [But] it's a lot of optimization. There is . . . not much new science [that] came out of that.

Ted, the in-house biotechnology lawyer who described his colleagues as juvenile delinquents, did so precisely because his colleagues took experimental risks working around and building off other people's published work:

They see it as a challenge, like, "OK, those guys are doing *that*. Well, what if we do *this*? Will that get us around that? And what if we do *this*? Or hey, I read this article where they said they were going to do *this*. What about if we do *this*? Or what if we cut them off, and we file on this? Because we're doing something similar."

The conversation about the relationship between being new and borrowing from the past is an age-old one in intellectual property law. Typically, the legal argument concerns whether permission is needed to build on previous work and where the property line is drawn to distinguish one person's work from another work. But that is not how the interviewees describe it. Indeed, whether permission is required or new IP results from borrowing is not their focus. They care about doing the work, and they emphasize the inevitability of their work's relationship to its predecessors and how inspiration is a combination of both new and old. Sometimes the stories appear illogical: critiquing a borrowing as a form of stealing and then admitting that borrowing is inescapable, or praising the uniqueness of an invention while explaining that all inventions owe their origin to those that came before. These stories are not incoherent, however, so much as a challenge to the myth of individual genius and inspired moments.

But do they really challenge these fabled origins? The origin stories in this chapter highlight (in the words of the interviewees) the importance of autonomy and freedom in the pursuit of creative and scientific work, values around which our intellectual property system are organized. Although the origin stories commingle influence and novelty, none of the interviewees actually denigrates the central importance of the individual's role, be it moral or intellectual, in the creative or inventive breakthrough. To the contrary, even those interviewees who appear the most communitarian with respect to the influence and credit of a work strongly value the role of the individual's freedom and autonomy in its creation, even as they describe the communities and relationships that make their work possible—teams of scientists, communities of writers, influential teachers and friends.

The dual emphasis on the individual and the collective is no more irrational or irreconcilable than understanding creative work as both new and borrowed. As the beginnings dissolve into daily work and ongoing productivity, the individual easily melds into, and is sustained by the relationships in, his or her community. Just as the fact that the interviewees accept the simultaneity of borrowing and novelty has implications for intellectual property policy, the simultaneous emphasis on individual autonomy and ties to the collective in these origin stories has lessons for intellectual property law, which continues to valorize the individual over the collective for the purposes of ascribing property ownership.[29] As Chapter 4 describes in more detail, individual autonomy and reputation are strong drivers of the work these interviewees pursue. Yet the interview data strongly suggests that the creators' and innovators' reasons for valuing (and protecting) autonomy may be separate from the reasons for assigning property rights that encourage investment: they cared much less about intellectual property as a form of financial investment than as a feature of their identity and personality.[30] The language of serendipity and luck, of play and problem solving, which reportedly motivated much of the work, focuses on their lives and self-definition, and it relates only tangentially (or only later) to making a living.

Intellectual property law's role as an investment mechanism, meant to stimulate creative or innovative work through incentives, appears absent in these inspired beginnings. To put it differently, intellectual property law is largely unfelt and unseen by these interviewees either as a guide or as a constraint in the early development of works of art and science. The field is open (or made open when hurdles exist) to play within their respective professions or in their free time: where accidents and serendipity are allowed to happen, where pleasure is encouraged, where instinct can be explored or followed. We might say with confidence that, of course, law is present here, as it is everywhere—in the employment contracts, book contracts, or loan agreements, in the private law that facilitates business relationships and personal well-being. But if these interviews measure the popular consciousness of intellectual property as an *incentive*, intellectual property law does not productively structure the beginnings of creative or inventive experience. Instead, the creative or innovative impulses described by the interviewees arise from diverse and serendipitous personal experiences, from doing what pleases them, from pursuing what appears necessary and important, from the pursuit of personal and professional freedom, and from within communities of influence.

I am not suggesting that intellectual property as a legal construct or a cultural object is unimportant in the creative or innovation industries. But these accounts from scientists, artists, intellectual property lawyers, and businesspeople offer accounts of the *beginning* of professions and projects in the creative and innovative fields that run counter to the understanding of intellectual property ownership as an investment vehicle. Intellectual property appears not to be the initial trigger for creative or innovative work. If it exists in the beginning at all, it is a hurdle to clear or a rule to ignore and often because a lawyer has brought it to the attention of the artists or scientist. (Chapter 5 discusses this role of lawyers in more detail.) But IP does emerge more prominently in the respondents' later professional trajectories, especially in the context of business negotiations, growth, and conflict. In particular, as Chapters 3 and 6 describe, intellectual property serves some of the interests that arise later in the life of creative or innovative work—facilitating focused and controlled distribution, and, in some contexts, commercialization.[31] If these interviewees are to be a guide, intellectual property intervenes later and yet in more limited ways than the law, and the myth of origin story, claims.

CHAPTER 2

Daily Craft
Work Makes Work

WHAT MOTIVATES WORK on a day-to-day basis? After all, the beginnings of inspired creations or innovations are insignificant without a finished product, whether to sell or share, and this requires work. Are the features of inspired beginnings I identify in Chapter 1—serendipity, playfulness, and problem solving—present in the daily work of creators and innovators? This chapter explores the everyday work that leads to creative and innovative output, most of which is eventually commercialized and distributed to make a living, be it for an individual (artist or inventor) or a company (as part the company's business).

The interviewees' stories resonate strongly with literature on the psychology of work and sociology of organizational behavior. Those familiar with the work of Mihaly Csikszentmihalyi and the optimization of intrinsic motivation will recognize the accounts of "flow" that populate the interviews.[1] So on the one hand, the data from the interviews confirm well-established research on and analysis of creativity and innovation. On the other hand, the interviews shed new light on the individual relationships between motivation to work and property claims, some of which do not align with traditional views on intellectual property rights. This chapter is organized around two commonly mentioned features of ongoing creative or innovative work: (1) hard work and labor, and (2) autonomous time and personal space. I found that, while discussing their everyday work in these two ways, interviewees frequently invoke nature metaphors, combining the inevitability and regularity of natural processes with the dignity of human handicraft and exertion.[2] They describe laborious, painstaking, and time-consuming efforts that are also rhythmic, organic, and comforting. The result is good work—both the activity of work and its output. And the present analysis asks how relevant this result is to the motivations and mechanisms for its being done in the first place.

As this chapter will show, interviewees focus only implicitly or tangentially, if at all, on the product of the workday, like a painting or a software program. While these products may become assets for reproduction, distribution, or commercialization, interviewees infrequently cite these typical intellectual property values. Instead, whether explicitly or metaphorically, their language reflects alternative values in how and why the work gets done, which highlights the importance of habitual routines, integrity of both the individual and his or her labor, and community building. The emotional and personal rewards derived from these commitments eclipse the financial payoffs from the work, be they uncertain or robust. And where the financial and material necessities of daily life are present in these interviews, they do not align with intellectual property entitlements. This chapter concludes with a spotlight on the mismatch between work values and intellectual property values, which is the focus of Chapter 3.

ON HAVING SPACE AND TIME

Many respondents describe their workday spatially. The laboratory, office, or studio often enables work by providing a designated space to focus on the details of a project and define its purpose. That space is a crucial and pleasurable component of work is unsurprising and also has a mythic history—think about Virginia Woolf's "A Room of One's Own" and the romance of the artist's garret. Barbara, a prolific author of children's books, describes how she enjoys sitting at her writing desk; being surrounded by pictures of her fans, juvenile readers, creates a safe and encouraging workspace. Another writer, of both fiction and nonfiction, describes an office she rents as an "unimpressive room"—importantly, it has no distractions. "Creativity comes out of solitude," one musician noted, lamenting that her blossoming career means less time and space to herself. A filmmaker told me that "it takes an office" to get a film made, putting both the human teamwork and organization into spatial terms.

The interviewees who work in laboratories and technological spaces express similar sentiments in terms of the productive freedom their spaces provide. Carol, who began her career as a biologist, describes her initial dedication to science in terms of her love of working in the laboratory and the community it created:

So the labs that I worked at . . . were smaller labs; they weren't huge labs. But there's always people there. And sort of, academic scientists are a loose group, you know? It's kind of . . . "anything goes.". . . You could just be whoever you were, and you were accepted in that community.

A high-tech entrepreneur recalls with fondness the "basement apartment" where he met other venture capitalists and technology entrepreneurs several times a week for many months, and where he developed several of his key ideas. A general counsel at a software company explains that the "culture of open space" at his company, which is intended to promote a sharing community through an open floor plan, is as much about sharing among his colleagues the view of the city through the windows as it is about optimal development conditions for the software products. Another general counsel at a publicly traded high-tech firm similarly describes his open office culture, where even the vice presidents and senior officers have cubicles instead of offices. Although in both cases confidentiality and privacy were at risk with this layout and culture, both lawyers emphasized that conference rooms were well placed around the building to facilitate private conversations when needed.

Both isolated and open spaces can be productive, from the perspective of the interviewees, when they facilitate certain aspects of creative freedom: isolated spaces can focus attention through solitude, and open spaces allow collaboration. Either can foster identity development through independence and lack of restrictions. In other words, the importance of space does not have to be about the fact of a room or desk of one's own. It can also be about being physically close to coworkers (open cubicles or populated offices) or whether the space is adequately stocked (e.g., sufficient tools, light, sounds). In this way, the physical space of creativity and innovation is not confining but defining: it not only sets the stage for work to be done but also sometimes shapes the work itself, determining its contours. This is often literally true, as when sculptors or architects work within predefined spaces, writers respond to particular environments, and scientists are restricted (or liberated) by laboratories and equipment. Leo, the painter, describes his transition from working at home to working in a studio as a way to focus his attention:

I started to go to the studio every day. . . . I adopted an attitude: "I'm going to make something every day." Even if I don't like what I'm making, I'm going to make something. And you know, I treated it like a job. And a lot of things came out of that. I mean, first of all, I started taking it seriously.

The physical space of the studio, a room of his own devoted only to his art, enhanced this artist's sense of purpose, driving him to produce more. Workspaces characterized by independence (a studio) and collaboration (a lab) fuel the progress of science and the useful arts.

Time is as much a force for productivity as space. Consistently and across fields, interviewees describe how their work takes a lot of time. A musician says that success is "definitely . . . about sheer hours that you put into it." An in-house intellectual property counsel describes the time scientists devoted to exploring a particular alternative energy technology as "years and years and years and years and years." A consultant in the pharmaceutical industry laments the "five or six years" he worked on a cancer drug, only to learn that the project would be discontinued because profits were not projected to be more than $40 million. Software engineers and book editors describe the months (and sometimes years) devoted to particular projects without the certainty of a payoff. Many remark that the amount of time sometimes "doesn't make sense," but they spend that time regardless because "putting that much time into the book . . . [is] what it needed," as one book publisher explained. Matthew, a website architect who once ran his own company and now is a manager at a marketing firm, expressed frustration with being prevented as an employee from spending the time necessary to get a project "right":

My assumption was working for a privately held company . . . that . . . if it took a year or a year-and-a-half to do right, we could take that time because we didn't have to show the return on investment right away. But I was naive, because the stakeholders themselves internally were incentivized on an annual basis. So it didn't matter that we were privately held: . . . you would be amazed how many deadlines were right before Christmas.

The tension between time and money runs throughout the interviews, no matter the interviewee's field. Generally, there are three kinds of tension. First, the interviewees commonly complain about a lack of time, and second, they lament that the amount of time one spends is never fully compensated with earnings. As one architect and public artist said about the work he performs with his partner, "We don't keep track of our time, because that would depress the hell out of us." Third, many interviewees find that they do not have enough time to focus on the creative or experimental aspects of work because of the demanding administrative or organizational tasks their projects require. Building on the notion of an ideal space that fosters collaboration and teamwork, most interviewees described the desire for assistants and partners to take on the auxiliary work. Dan, a composer, says he would benefit from more staff in his organization "to free me up to go pursue these other things. . . . I haven't been able to find the person to do the other things so that I can just do the music." Sadie, a sculptor since college who also sometimes works as a curator, wishes she had a studio assistant. In her late forties, she is very well regarded in her field. But she struggles to earn a consistently comfortable living from her art. She wishes she had a studio assistant to facilitate communication with galleries, to manage correspondence, and to pack and unpack her shows so that she could focus on making the art to sell and display: "I've been trying to figure out as the show comes up in April, [how] . . . to find someone to do the public relations, find someone to be my assistant, and work in the studio to just keep me on schedule." Elizabeth, a novelist who writes every day but remains unpublished, cannot be bothered to send her writing to editors and relies on her partner to do it: "He is going to send it out for me. We've realized that that's not my strength. . . . I don't like to be rejected. I think it's incredibly boring to send stuff out. It is. It's so boring. . . . And . . . they come back six months later, if they ever come back at all. It's just . . . not fast enough."

Tension over time also manifests between partners and associates. In-house counsel, firm counsel, and licensing officers for biotechnology, high-tech, and mechanical engineering companies uniformly describe the difficulty they have in directing the attention of the scientists and engineers away from the laboratories and workspaces so that discussions of invention disclosures and trade secret protection can take place. Their colleagues, they say, actively resist taking time away from their work, and work does not include legal paperwork. Throughout the interviews, I heard accounts of how disruptive and time consuming legal consultations could be for creators and innovators. For example, Donald, a senior in-house counsel at a software firm that has been building its patent portfolio to great success reported:

[My chief technology officer] jokes to me that it takes me an hour to read a patent application, but it takes him a whole day. Because they are fifty pages long, and he goes, "You're just skimming it. You're not paying attention to the claims," . . . And he has to read those claims with a ruler, sentence by sentence. . . . And he's right. It's a lot of work for him. . . . And so it is: it's an undertaking for him.

Lawyers and agents combat this resistance from artists and scientists by streamlining approaches to intellectual property development. Susan, a senior manager in a technology licensing office, describes it this way:

We educate [the scientists and engineers] that we're not going to let [the patenting process] take a lot of their time; that the invention disclosure form is one page long, and it's all you have to do. Clip your first manuscript to it or anything else you want to clip to it, and we'll send it to the patent attorneys, and they'll do the work.

Ted, the in-house counsel in a start-up energy company, developed a similar strategy, incentivizing disclosures with a low-stakes monthly contest:

We just encourage the scientists to submit cool ideas. This is separate and apart from . . . your standard invention disclosure form, which . . . [is] seven pages long and asks them to fill out all this information. Not that it's onerous, but it's still a . . . little bit of a hurdle for them to get them that far. So this way, it just really tries to capture stuff. . . . [T]hey're sitting around, and they have this little idea, this brainstorm where they see some interesting result or something like that. And it's like a one-page form: what's your idea; how is it cool; what's its value; have you done any research; have you seen any results in this, blah, blah, blah. . . . It's really grown amazingly. I think the first time we did it, we have seven, eight cool ideas submitted for the month, and last month we had twenty-five. It's just continued to grow and grow and grow.

In these cases, there is tension between the time taken to develop an artwork or invention and to establish intellectual property, which may or may not turn into a revenue stream for the individual or company. Both individuals and the company representatives try to minimize the time away from creative or innovative work for the administration of the business, which includes assessing the value of developing and protecting intellectual property from the work produced. Chapter 5 will say more about the relationship with lawyers and business agents to harvest intellectual property. For now, I want to note how intellectual property development and its value are separate from creative and innovative work. In fact, when it arises, the legal dimension is largely considered a nuisance by scientists and artists. Chapter 5 considers this dynamic in more detail and what it might mean for intellectual property law, which is explained and justified through its incentive mechanisms, and for the lawyers and business agents who encourage IP protection.

As I detail in Chapter 3, most of the people I interviewed make a living from their creative or innovative work. Fundamentally, the tensions regarding time do not convey an unpredictability or unfairness in financial payoff for work so much as they do the endlessness and indeterminacy of the work itself. Creative and innovative work takes so much time that appropriate compensation is hard to assess and, frankly, a fool's errand. And so, when asked how this problem of scarce time might be fixed, many interviewees state that having *free* time—a flexible and autonomous schedule—is optimal for their productivity and happiness, and avoids the red herring of assessing the time value of money.

Having freedom over one's work schedule does not mean, however, that individuals work erratic hours. To the contrary, many describe workdays that are highly regimented but that fit their personal and professional needs. All the writers I interviewed describe some variation of a steady schedule consisting of fixed hours during the day that they devote to writing. Lisa, an acclaimed writer, describes her work habits this way: "I just go [to my office] as soon as I can get there every morning after breakfast; I just go there, and I work 'til about four o'clock, and then I go home. You know, I never work at night or do any fancy stuff like that." Elizabeth, another writer, describes having "complete control over her environment" as optimal for writing: "I would get up at the exact same time every day, go to bed at the exact same time every day; . . . I mean, it was . . . a little crazy. But I could do it because I had complete control over my environment . . . be sitting in front of my computer at 9 o'clock, down. And that was it."

In a similar spirit but a different field, software engineers and entrepreneurs benefit from freedom and flexibility of their work life as central to their persistence. We already heard from Thomas in Chapter 1, a software engineer with his own company, who describes his work as providing him with "a tremendous amount of flexibility. . . . I could pursue any projects that I wanted. So that . . . meant more to me than additional money." For engineers and inventors like Thomas, who work long hours but often on their own schedule, time itself is a form of compensation. Being free to pursue their own hours is essential to their productivity.

Autonomy over one's time relates to the generative play that characterizes inspired beginnings, as discussed in Chapter 1. Indeed, the freedom to pursue projects and to dedicate as many hours in the day to work as needed to be productive defines the daily lives and personal identities of many I interviewed. When one forms an identity through the habitual time spent on work, the work is unlikely to end lest one loses the carefully crafted identity of artist or scientist. Indeed, the line between work and play (or the work-life balance ubiquitous in contemporary discussions of employment in firms and organizations) was elusive to many I interviewed. Often, interviewees simply did not register a distinction. Some interviewees were trying to figure out how to minimize travel or other business needs in order to spend more time at home, so that they could work while remaining close to family. "I have been working really hard at making it more the way I want already," says Joan, an acclaimed sculptor. "About my family time, I would say the thing I'd like to change: I'd like to travel less. I like travel, but I don't like to travel for work. And I'm doing more videoconferences, and . . . I've minimized travel for work more than any other artist I know." For many interviewees, marathon work—at home or away—is a point of pride. They seek not to work less, but to work on their own terms. Andrew, a high-technology entrepreneur, describes the initial stages of his company in terms of a grueling nine-month period of coding and cold calling every day:

And we coded for about—I don't know—eight months straight for a demonstration. And you know, this is coding. . . . [A]t that time, we were coding probably seventy to eighty hours a week. And it's *just* coding. And then . . . after six months, I started cold calling. So I would spend enormous amounts of my day just cold calling cable companies, all day long.

In-house lawyers, who closely identify with the creative and innovative company culture, also think about time spent at work in similar terms. One lawyer in a pharmaceutical company aligns himself with his scientist colleagues in working late nights because the work demands it, the culture of the place appreciates it, and—importantly—he feels good when he gets the work done and wants to be recognized as a hard worker. Irene, a longtime lawyer who primarily advises clients on copyright matters, loves all the traveling she does for and as work, but she also appreciates how, when she is not traveling, she can work from home in jeans and a T-shirt. She attributes the freedom of her daily work schedule to her success cultivating a clientele who also understand the value of autonomy for the purposes of maximizing creative production. She and her clients are members of the same moral universe.

How much control they can exercise over their time is, for these people, a measure of professional success in their fields. Working long hours—taking time as a matter of choice—is essential to the interviewees' identity, to the value of what they produce, and to their professional satisfaction and personal well-being. Both space and time are, of course, essential dimensions of life, and no social action can take place outside of them.[3] We all work to control our time and space in some manner. These interviews demonstrate that, when people engage in (or facilitate) creative and innovative work, shaping one's space and having autonomy over one's time are critical to being successful. The dominance of space and time in discussions of optimal work situations may imply that other dimensions, such as material resources and legal constraints, are less prominent in the minds of artists and inventors. Chapters 3 and 4 develop this implication when discussing the halfhearted role that intellectual property plays in creative and innovative professions.

ON WORKING HARD
(ECHOES OF LABOR AND CRAFT)

Given the time that interviewees commit to working, and the freedom they have in structuring their days, how do they manage to start such time-consuming work and keep at it? These creators do not live isolated lives; indeed, they celebrate their relationships and rely extensively on their interactions with others. This is, again, a question about motivation: when you are free to work however you want and whenever you want, what makes you strive to work hard and continuously so? Jennifer, a writer who began her career in journalism, described the relationship between drive and freedom this way:

Even though we do have a deadline, . . . it's not about just doing the best you can do by this deadline. It's about making it as good as it can possibly be, and that's different. . . . [T]he bar is higher. And in fact, I was just talking to [my coauthor] today about how we . . . could edit [the book] forever. You know, we could keep going back and forth with suggestions forever.

The language in the interviews that describes daily routines makes explicit the existential condition of creative work: it is never done and it is hard. If the interviewees recognize the perpetual nature of their work, how do they generate the momentum for projects and complete them?

These are especially important questions in light of the difficulty, and oftentimes boredom, that the writers, engineers, musicians, and artists express about their daily work. They echo one another in speaking of the dogged "pursuit" of their work, how the writing can be "painfully mechanical," and how producing software is like a "military" operation, predictable and exact. Kevin, the telecom consultant and former software engineer whom I interviewed on his front porch, recounts an interchange with a former boss about a major development project, "I don't think we realized that it was the hardest thing we were going to do. . . . Well, we have got [new functionality]. It works great. We are shipping it for three years."

A copyright lawyer who specialized in licensing talked about the work of writing and building a business around it as bricklaying and that the time and labor required was like that of becoming a "master bricklayer." Very similarly, a novelist describes how writing a novel is like "cobbling together [a] building." Another lawyer, an in-house IP counsel at a biotechnology company, describes how his colleagues, all scientists, "have got a research plan, and they are marching along that research plan, and they are trying to make the specific organism that does *this*." The words in these quotes—*pursuit, military, bricklaying, cobbling, marching*—all suggest physical labor, hard work, and persistence.

Karen, a New York City sculptor who primarily makes a living through a combination of commissions, fellowships, exhibitions, and sales, with financial support from her partner, says that momentum keeps her artistic work going. She contrasts the inspired beginning with daily exertion:

Work makes work. That's one thing. So that whole lightbulb theory. . . . I still remember . . . my first solo show, and I was in bed, and [she snaps her fingers] "Oh! Here we go!" I was able to come up with the title of the show. And that was . . . a big moment, because a lot of things fell into place. But in general, it's like work makes work, so you just work, and then you realize this is what it is, or what it should be, or what you should be doing.

Although Karen must produce objects to continue profitably as an artist, she rarely talks about the need to work for money (except to say that she is terrible with the business side of her work). Instead, in a matter-of-fact way, she says that more works comes by working every day. One project leads to another idea, and she is compelled to continue:

Because it has to be done. . . . [It's like] you're telling a story. And so I'm only at the beginning, so you have to keep going to finish it. . . . And there is . . . a puzzle, so I'm trying to figure out the puzzle. And one thing leads to the next, so that's what I just did, now I kind of have to do this one to finish it, and then there's the next one.

Karen's description of her work rhythms resonates with the notion of flow, documented and explained by Mihaly Csikszentmihalyi.[4] Certainly there are aspects of the obsessive and addictive elements of creative work that Csikszentmihalyi described in these interviews. Losing oneself in the challenge of the project—in a meditative or very focused way—is a common feature of the work habits described by interviewees. David, a photographer, said, "It's an adrenaline rush," so much so that he loses track of time completely:

My wife asked me to . . . put an alarm on my computer every hour on the hour [and I did] because here when I start focusing on one of the things [I'm working on], you look for an hour at that picture and you are going to start seeing things that you didn't see before, and . . . that is what I'm looking for in my work. It's one hour, hello, one, two, three, four [hours go by].

As described in Chapter 1, problem solving is a common reason to begin scientific or artistic projects in the first place.[5] But beyond the original impetus, fixation on their craft also keeps the interviewees at work. Andrew, the high-technology entrepreneur, talks about the momentum of his work this way: "So there was an aesthetic side. I remember going back to my house and thinking for three days how the system would be architected. So that's a very good sign. You . . . already know you're in the right area if you can't stop thinking about the problem." Having the idea may be momentary, but elaborating the idea and testing it and then implementing it demands a continuous engagement. Barbara, the well-known children's author, similarly finds a rhythm in her work: "I know that sometimes, I get in the zone. . . . [N]othing else is there. There is me and the screen, and I am standing right there with the characters, and I am sweating with them, I am laughing with them, I am simply a part of it." In addition to the inertia of the day's rhythm, interviewees report a willful determination to continue. "Keep doing it," says one writer. "Do it every day," says another. Leo, the lawyer turned painter, explains how once he treated painting "like a job" and decided he was "going to make something every day," his new career developed and became more rewarding.

The enjoyment and focus derived from the momentum of work is as prevalent in the copyright industries as in the patent industries. Contrasting the momentary flashes of genius to the quotidian work of laboratory scientists, recall Dennis's statement about the pharmaceutical industry: "most of us [are] mere mortals . . . learn[ing] from other people, and then . . . the frontiers of science are pushed back . . . gradually through similar antlike persistence by scientists." Dennis finds solidarity with the bench scientists at his company in feeling that everyday toil is not drudgery but part of the character of scientific progress. The language of "antlike persistence" was originally used to describe patent lawyers and their own resolute pursuit of valid claims in a court opinion from the 1920s authored by the famous judge Learned Hand.[6] Indeed, that working hard, working everyday, and depending on others is the foundation and mechanism of creative and innovative output is neither new nor surprising. The description of everyday laboratory work also resonates with the analysis of communalism, a binding norm and methodological goal among scientists, described in Robert Merton's work, *The Sociology of Science*.[7] It also recalls Isaac Newton's famous epistolary statement: "If I have seen further it is by standing on the shoulders of giants." Despite its ubiquity among artists and inventors, however, hard work and long-term investment do not justify intellectual property protection. "Sweat of the brow" is no basis for copyright or patent protection, as the Supreme Court reminded us more than twenty years ago in *Feist Publications v. Rural Telephone Service Co.*[8] Intellectual property law glorifies the individual over the collective and genius over hard work. Collective creativity is uncomfortable both statutorily and in the common law.[9]

Although these fields are populated with intellectual property, the way that the interviewees spoke about their occupations is oriented less toward objects, discoveries, or products than toward the practice, routine, and minute-by-minute detail that constitute their professional lives. In these accounts, the identity, satisfaction, and honor rooted in doing work are not necessarily manifest in its outcome. Karen's contrast between the lightbulb and the fact that "work makes work," or Dennis's juxtaposition of the rare genius-inventor to the "antlike persistence" of scientists, suggests that the value of the work is its everyday structure not the rare moment of inspiration. This has implications for the labor theory of property (and the anti-labor theory of intellectual property), which I have more to say about at the end of this chapter.

As Alasdair MacIntyre explains in his groundbreaking *After Virtue*, the value—indeed, the virtue—of practice is that its embodiment in everyday activity binds people within particular communities around shared standards.[10] MacIntyre means *practice* quite literally, the way musicians practice, athletes train, and artists and scientists study (or anyone else who works repetitively everyday within a community with common goals). My interviews illustrate this focus on daily detail. Writers talk about developing the pacing of stories and working on consistency of characters. They talk about the number of pages they write every day and the details of character and plot development as physical milestones. Painters, filmmakers, and photographers talk about refining color and lines and losing track of time as they manipulate their equipment. Scientists and engineers emphasize how long it takes to become proficient in their field—years of schooling and working alongside mentors in laboratories with equipment and machines—and eventually to be on the cutting edge to develop the science and technology. Here, Mary, the singer-songwriter already mentioned, differentiates her love of performing and her passion for recording music, which is detail-oriented and painstaking:

I love performing, but my favorite part is that secret place where you are all alone and you are writing, and . . . you are really living in a world as an artist. And I love the recording process. I love just tinkering away in the workshop doing—crafting it, and having that time to polish it and sculpt it, and perfect it in a way.

Mary combines the spatial aspect discussed earlier ("all alone" in the studio) with the time commitment ("having that time to . . . polish") and problem-solving nature of hard, detail-oriented work ("tinkering"). She does not highlight the finished product—its aesthetic qualities or its end value—but instead expresses her enjoyment of the process, of engaging with the music and writing words. This is the language of craft: the development and exercise of technical skill within a particular field, which often elides physical purpose and function with aesthetic value.[11] And although the end result of craftsmanship is a purposeful object—a wooden bowl, a patchwork quilt, a cuckoo clock—that object carries with it the story of a life or a community.[12] Ironically, although the law grants creators and innovators the rights to *intangibles* (i.e., intellectual property), in the context of my interviews, the overwhelming focus of pleasure and drive concerns *tangible* work output, physical skills, and personal connection to the work (and to appreciative audiences). That is, in most of the interviews, the process, not the result, of creation or discovery defines the interviewees' professional and personal lives and keeps them engaged. We might consider the language of tangibility and everyday engagement as evidence of "virtue" described by MacIntyre, an ethic that defends against the corrosive effects of capitalism. Or we could interpret it as evidence of the primacy of the material dimensions of life. Either way, the interviewees define themselves by what they do and how they do it and less (if at all) by the output as a commodity, whether or not it is protectable as intellectual property.

Even lawyers or businesspeople (both in copyright and patent fields) value similarly arduous, routine work. This is counterintuitive. After all, generally lawyers and business managers are not the creators or innovators themselves, but organizers of the bigger picture, connecting the parts to facilitate a successful whole, connections and parts that individual artists and scientists might take for granted. And yet a businessman working with "entertainment properties" praises how his team "take[s] *every* aspect of whatever that driving platform is . . . and we examine *every* single one ad nauseam, to the point where you can go in any direction and take one of those characters and go off and create something." A pharmaceutical consultant recalls how his company helped produce a drug-delivery system for a prostate cancer treatment "that [was] pretty unique. [And a] very hard thing to do. . . . I worked a long time on it, and . . . it's probably one of the biggest technical challenges I ever faced. It was a very, very difficult thing to do." A publishing agent appreciates how his company's unique efforts in translating books—efforts in which most publishing houses do not engage—earned it best sellers:

And the reason [others] didn't do it . . . is because it took *way* too much work to translate this giant tome from . . . Italian to English. . . . [But] we are constantly translating books from English . . . into French, German, all of these languages. [P]utting that much time into the book, what it needed, . . . we were willing to do all that work, [so] we reaped the benefits of having [a] best-selling [book] of the season.

Each of these businesspeople bears the burden of daily work admirably, driven by a commitment to quality of the work and pride of the craft. To be sure, especially in these latter examples, the long, hard work eventually becomes an explicit justification for strong intellectual property rights on behalf of firms. But the value of the work is unmistakably derived from physical and intellectual efforts coordinated, combined with pride, and propelled forward by everyday momentum and routine.

In all these examples, there are distinct echoes of Marxist theories of wage labor and capital. Marx says that when the employer owns the end product and any capital surplus, wage labor alienates the employee from the work, from its product, and from him- or herself. By describing work in physical and burdensome terms, interviewees (employees or independent contractors) seek a union between their physical labor and its outcome. Preserving and validating the worth of both is to recognize themselves in their work. However arduous, they describe daily labor in virtuous terms and that shape their identity, which is embodied in work and invested in its output. Likewise, interviewees on the business side connect everyday work with their firm's or company's output, attributing its successes to the coordinated efforts of its committed employees. They seek a union between the company's employees, their output, and the company mission—also a kind of identity formation, based on collaboration and unity of purpose. In their descriptions of daily good work, interviewees resist the alienation that capital accumulation and its system of economic exchange might cause.

HARVESTING IP AND OTHER METAPHORS

The interviews' emphasis on everyday labor should not obscure the claims of control and ownership that the interviewees assert over their work. The time devoted to work, the space it occupies, and the challenge and skill it requires can translate into strong claims of entitlement. These claims resound in moral rights or theories of labor. But they do not correspond well to the justifications for intellectual property law. Even when interviewees occasionally describe a claim of ownership in terms of recouping investment of time and incentivizing risk taking, the governing metaphors used to explain why ownership and rights should apply to the work refer to physical or natural things or processes—"things to put your hands on."

Elizabeth, a novelist, describes her work using this analogy: "Writing, for me, it's like fishing. . . . [S]ome days you catch something interesting, and other days you catch a bunch of carp, and some days you catch really pretty much nothing." The interviewees often use naturalistic metaphors like fishing when speaking about their daily work, as if to say that the physical labor of the job dignifies the output because it is made with the body and time of a person. A remarkably similar metaphor to Elizabeth's arose in my interview with Ted, the in-house lawyer at an alternative energy biotech company. Although Ted is in a strikingly different field from that of Elizabeth, he also refers to nature and physical processes to describe the company's intellectual property. He characterizes a difference between in-licensed work and "home-grown" technology by describing his role, which "is to basically try to harvest innovation across the entire process chain," and that of the vice president for research, who "seeds" ideas to his scientists to generate invention. In yet another context, a university licensing officer describes how his colleagues shepherd the invention from its "birth to its death."

Child rearing and caretaking are two other analogies that arise frequently in the interviews to express the physical care that successful creative output requires (these analogies come up again in the detailed analysis of reputational interests and ego harms in Chapter 4). One agent complains that nowadays, music labels refuse to foster the artist. Before, she says, labels used to "teach [music artists] how to . . . do a show. . . . [T]hey might send them opening for some people just to . . . learn how to do what they do. . . . [P]eople just think people come out of the womb a touring artist." Another business developer, who works mostly in the film industry, pitches to companies this way: "You have a decision to make. Are you going to nurture your property, or are you going to *milk* your property? The decision is yours. You can milk it 'til it's dry, and then put it to bed for how many years, or you can nurture your property." A copyright lawyer at an aggregating and licensing company said something nearly identical: "if we try to maximize money, we'll milk the cow and then kill it. The idea is to optimize it so that over time we do the right thing."

Harvesting, fishing, child rearing, nurturing, and other natural processes evoke both the mystery and the challenge of natural bounty, rooting the processes of creation, and justifying the assertions of ownership in timeless features of human existence. These metaphors reinforce the enduring quality of innovative and creative output, likening the scientific and artistic fields to the natural world, where claims and fights over rights are all tied together. A copyright lawyer believes that being paid for intellectual work is necessary and in large part inevitable in our modern society because "intellectual property is in the genes of every human being." Several lawyers discuss the "landscape" of intellectual property, commonly using the metaphor of "fencing in" to describe what intellectual property rights do. Another lawyer describes how technological changes produce shifts in the capacity and tolerance for trespassing on intellectual properties; digital music, he says, is on the "bleeding edge of infringement," and digital rights management systems were merely "speed bumps" along the way. Individual inventors describe themselves "catching" concepts; writers say that they are "cracking open a kind of carapace"; and their lawyers, when charged with commercializing the creative expressions or innovations that result, acquire a "license to hunt." These phrases are vivid and evocative of physical existence, a far cry from the conception of intellectual property as intangible, or as located in the mind.

When explaining IP rights to assert quality, ownership and right to compensation, the interviewees use another set of metaphors that shift allusions from the natural world to the world of craft, things handmade and owned. They claim intellectual property rights in terms that emphasize the physicality and material concreteness of the most conventional conceptions of goods and chattel. Kevin, a telecom consultant and software engineer, asks me rhetorically: "[W]ould you call a cell phone a software product? [I]t's a nugget. You sell someone a nugget. But it's loaded with software." Kevin also laments the perceived monopoly on encoding and decoding video (MPEG technology) because a single entity owns a "giant pile of patents on . . . the core technology." In similar fashion, an in-house lawyer for a biotechnology company describes the "equal *chunk* of stuff that we've in-licensed." Another in-house lawyer for an e-commerce company says of first joining his company, "We were . . . being over-friendly to our customers. We were letting them overuse our software. . . . And so I've really tightened up the screws."

Lawyers and business folks are not alone in identifying the desirability of having something to touch or hold in creative and innovative work. Artists and scientists embrace their work this way too, shifting back and forth between the language of nature and the world of things. For instance, Sadie, the sculptor and curator, talks about why, after writing a poem, she did not feel finished. She told me she had to do something with it. She had to "find a place to put this poem, and I had more interest in trying to convert it into being art. . . . I like the mechanics of it, internally. And I like that that's an object. I mean, I like looking at things, I like putting stuff in my pocket, taking 'em home." Of all the interviewees, sculptors most directly work with their hands, but this sentiment is in no way limited to them. Musicians also "polish" and "sculpt" their songs. A writer defines plagiarism as resting on someone else's "scaffolding." Patented inventions are "chits" for trading and patent clusters have an "architecture" and a "landscape" that can be full of "land mines." Looking for patentable inventions is compared to a "treasure hunt." Taking someone's idea for an invention is akin to "stealing someone's homework." Breaking through digital rights management to access copyrighted work is like "shoplifting" by evading metal detectors. Legal claims for misappropriation or infringement demand that wrongdoers keep their "hands off" stuff. Here, Ted, the in-house lawyer at the alternative-energy company, articulates just this transformation of intangible to tangible for the purposes of describing value. He is excited about this description, leaning in and tapping on the table when he talks. He acts as if he is sharing with me a secret about how he successfully communicates with investors and does well for his company:

It's the way that we represent value. . . . [W]e're a start-up company. All these venture capitalists who are going to be investing in us, they are going to look for IP. They don't know what it is anymore than you or I know what it is, right? But they are going to look for something that says it's IP, so it's the way to show them . . . the really amorphous stuff you're doing in the research lab, how that translates into something that they can put their hands on.

Both the time-space dialectic described earlier and the metaphors that relate intellectual work to natural processes and tangible goods resonate with Lockean notions of property.[13] Locke's notion is that when we mix our labor with the natural world we have a right to own the fruits of that labor. But although this philosophy is considered one basis of property law, it has been rejected in the United States as a basis for intellectual property protection and is therefore tangential to IP. As the Supreme Court said in 1991, presumably restating a long-standing principle in the United States, "The primary objective of copyright is not to reward the labor of authors."[14] And although it may seem unfair to denigrate the sweat-of-the-brow doctrine for copyright protection, the Supreme Court noted that its demotion in the law was not "some unforeseen byproduct of a statutory scheme."[15] The same is true of patents and patent law. Effort is not the touchstone of patent protection, only novelty, nonobviousness, and utility.[16]

Many interviewees—including lawyers and businesspeople—lament that time and work spent on a particular project is irrelevant to its legal protection and value in the marketplace: months to draft the code, weeks in the recording studio, months to finalize the public installation of a sculpture, years to bring a drug to market. By elaborating on natural processes and tangible goods, how long the project took and how hard they worked, they invoke a Lockean theory of property, which, as opposed to a state of nature, preserves their rights on the basis of their physical labor by protecting their output from appropriation by others through law. Indeed, artists, scientists, lawyers, and businesspeople describe finding the marketplace and the IP rules that ignore the value of hard work quixotic and mystifying. In fact, some respondents when creating or innovating do not consider the law or regulation at all. Instead, they may be concerned with their (or their clients') personal interests in relation to others, moral claims that may resonate as much with the view of "property as personhood" as with Locke. This latter notion, which has roots in Hegel, has been developed most prominently in the twentieth century by Margaret Radin. She argues that there are some kinds of things in which we invest so much time and energy and to which we become so attached that we see ourselves in them.[17] As such, claims about "things" are akin to claims of personhood; choices regarding things include those concerning self-definition and relations with and expressions toward others. Interestingly, among the diversity of descriptions of work and justifications for protecting it, interviewees do not resort to descriptions of their work as products of the mind—although that is what it certainly is—but as real or personal property, tangible and closely held things, with justifications for traits of legal property, like excludability and exploitability, that are more deeply rooted in traditions of classical liberalism and its Hegelian critique than the more prominent economic and utilitarian theories of IP.

MISFIT BETWEEN WORK AND IP VALUE

The language evoking tangible goods in the intellectual property context may be unsurprising given the ubiquity of real property rhetoric in intellectual property policy debates.[18] But it is nonetheless puzzling. So many of these artists and scientists, and their business partners, collaborate and share their work. Few respondents speak about their creations or inventions in possessive terms in the way that real property language encourages. Words such as *mine* or *ours* (or corollaries, such as *copying* or *taking*) are used infrequently, if at all, in most interviews. Even when property rights are clear and could be asserted, few respondents—including business managers representing firms—behave in an aggressive manner. That is, rarely do they express a desire or take actions to fully exercise their exclusive rights in their IP by sheltering it from the world or sharing it only for full-extraction value. Much more will be said about the underenforcement (and overenforcement) of intellectual property rights in the next chapter. For now, suffice it to say that most interviewees dismiss minor incidents of copying or illegal borrowing as inevitable and rarely worth doing anything about, a finding that is reflected in other scholarly literature.[19] "What goes around comes around," people seem to suggest. Very few say they would bother filing a lawsuit even if faced with clear infringement as long as their personal or company welfare was not at stake.

Interviewees do, however, express outrage and use possessive language when infringement causes reputational harm or interferes with their long-held plans. In these cases, they are also more likely to contest uses of their (or their company's) work. Chapter 4 discusses these claims and conflict in more detail. For this chapter, it is important to note that the claims are asserted with language that suggests physical violation or trespassing, thus extending the connection between creative or innovative work and the value of tangible things to one's identity and sense of place and work. Leo, a painter whose success and reputation are growing, explained that while he would tolerate someone emulating or even copying his work, that tolerance would end if the copying would embarrass him:

Ultimately . . . I paint because I want to share . . . my sense of how I see the world, how I see color, with other people. I think I've got to . . . not be totally possessive about that. . . . [A]s long as someone was [copying me] in a way that I felt was up to the quality [it might be OK] . . . but if you think they are degrading your work, that's [another] thing.

In the scientific context, lawyers must explain the value of patents to libertarian-leaning colleagues who do not see scientific value in having patents as chits to trade with other companies, who can thwart research agendas with extortionist licensing practices. Recall, Dennis, an IP lawyer, explaining to the scientists in his pharmaceutical company: "What I want is something that I can trade with somebody. . . . I'm not interested in necessarily asserting these [patents] against anybody." Even firm employees (who have no ownership interest in patents at all) can be offended by minimal or nonactionable patent infringement, resorting to personal property language tinged with moral dimensions, using phrases such as "rip off" or "stealing homework" or "shoplifting."

More situations concerning the protection of reputation and the freedom to operate are discussed in Chapters 3 and 4. Crucially, however, IP law doesn't easily protect these kinds of reputational or personal harms in a way that artists, scientists, or business managers might hope. Copyright law does not compel attribution, prevent misattribution, or protect reputation.[20] Patent law does not compel attribution (beyond being named on an obscure patent document) or require collaboration. And patent law provides the opportunity for a newcomer to improve upon and thereafter block the use (and commercialization) of an earlier patented invention, despite the desire for collaboration and credit on the part of scientists and engineers in follow-on innovation and improvements. And so the misfit widens between the expressed value and desires for control over creative and innovative work and the manner in which the law (and the state) may value and protect it.

How does this language of nature, tangibility, and materiality function within the narratives of those engaging with creation and innovation in their everyday lives? The rhetoric of real and personal property appears to be a moral end in itself. Their goal resembles the protection of tangible property—the individuality and personality of goods—which displaces the incentive policy of intellectual property that purports to progress science and art. Yet assessing the value of people's work in material terms—as a function of their time, labor and identity—strengthens the creators' and innovators' possessive impulse. In turn, feeling possessive can manifest as assertions of control that are more robust than current intellectual property law provides, what one copyright lawyer described as the predictable "instinct of overreach."[21] In this way, the characterization of work predetermines the justification for its protection in a potentially dangerous circular logic.[22] Notably, the interviewees appear to desire protection through their IP rights for affronts that US intellectual property law cannot protect against (reputation, moral harms, and rights of integrity). And they underutilize the aspects of US intellectual property law (rent seeking) that intellectual property law is better suited to provide. Overreach in the context of moral outrage (the subject of Chapter 4) contrasts with the underprotection of IP in cases of everyday commercial infringement (see Chapter 3).

In short, the time and exertion of labor dominates the discussion of how to value creative or innovative work among the interviewees, as evidenced by linguistic patterns that invoke nature or personal property. Moreover, the time and burden of everyday effort is a source both of pride and worth, of personal identity and professional merit. Legal and moral language surfaces when respondents experience reputational affronts or challenges to their person or plans. And yet intellectual property law does not help much here. As with the stories of origins, intellectual property policy simply misaligns with this second stage of creative and innovative work. Policies that undergird the law of intentional torts and unjust enrichment more clearly resonate in this second stage of "work makes work."

Is anything new here, really? Combining the data and analysis in the previous chapter with the current discussion, we learn that beginnings are spontaneous or lucky and investing time and labor in one's work makes it personal. This sounds familiar, even clichéd, if one thinks about myths of the romantic author or the mad scientist. But what *is* new and surprising, at least to IP advocates, is that intellectual property doctrine and policies misrepresent creative or innovative activity. Intellectual property law is imagined to be a rational set of goals and a coherent structure by many lawyers and judges, essential to incentivizing art and science from its inception. But even the business agents and lawyers I interviewed, who are more self-reflective concerning legal rules and applications than their clients, assert that their clients' beginnings and the mechanisms of creative or innovative activity do not map onto the traditional justifications for and structure of intellectual property law and policy. (Chapter 5 is devoted entirely to the relationships among lawyers, business agents, and their clients.)

To be sure, there is variation among those interviewed. As Chapter 3 details, company spokespeople, as opposed to independent contractors or individuals, more consistently consider how and which research to pursue on the basis of the firm's ability to leverage intellectual property. In this sense, the people or entities that control the research and development are incentivized by intellectual property rights early in production, even when the individual creators are not. Why is intellectual property law justified by granting rights to incentivize creators (the myth of the romantic author or mad scientist) when it appeals more directly to firms? This is a serious question, because although individuals are at the foundation of our system of rights, it is at the firm level where intellectual property appears to do much of its work, when it works at all. There is some literature on this point (albeit largely only in the law and economics vein).[23] If it is true, and if the IP incentive structure is worth maintaining, then intellectual property law should address the organization of work within firms (its conditions, relations, and means of production). Doing so would enable the realignment of IP's incentive policy with the interests of the firms to whom it most directly applies. And it might also thereby develop optimal relationships with employees or independents, who, while they have strong feelings about and claims toward their work, do not necessarily have strong claims based in law.[24]

What might happen if we talk more about how intellectual property facilitates firm development and the distribution of intellectual goods than about how it incentivizes their initiation? The Supreme Court case *Eldred v. Ashcroft* upheld the Copyright Term Extension Act, the 1998 law famously passed to extend the copyright term on Disney's Mickey Mouse by an additional twenty years.[25] It argued that longer duration provides more incentives for artists and authors, which results in more copyrighted works and that is good for progress.[26] The Court explained how longer copyright terms may hypothetically incentivize distributors to maintain (and even repair and redistribute) older works no longer in circulation. But there was no congressional testimony supporting this assertion (as to films or books), only individual artists and the register of copyrights, who explained how longer copyright durations would hypothetically benefit authors and support them as they continue to work.[27] (Justice Breyer's dissent largely refutes the economic rational for preservation and redistribution as a basis for justifying longer copyright terms.[28]) Would *Eldred* have been decided differently if it were not taken for granted that creative work originates with the promise of a copyright, at least for individuals? Without the ability to fall back on romantic authorship as the sine qua non of copyright (or the genius inventor as the basis of patent law), legislators, lawyers, and business interests might be forced to focus on the distributional consequences of intellectual property entitlements, who benefits exactly and how from longer and stronger terms for protection.[29] My data make clear that individual artists and scientists are not initially incentivized by intellectual property rights, and only some firms are so incentivized. Reckoning with this evidence of emerging knowledge in IP-rich fields should force a frank conversation about how IP may only maximize firm capital and the firm's managers and shareholders without obvious benefits to their employees, other individuals, or the public, other than through a discredited and oversimplified "trickle-down" economic theory.

The fact that intellectual property entitlements more directly incentivize and benefit companies than individuals might also prompt a reconsideration of how we should evaluate the fair-use defense in copyright and the statutory defaults for patent ownership. With firms rather than individuals in mind, would fair use in copyright emphasize transformativeness less and commerciality and market harm more?[30] Would ownership and inventorship be allocated differently as a statutory matter (not to inventors but to firms who employ inventors)?[31] The ramifications for this kind of shift in focus would be significant. If we really want to benefit the distributors of intellectual property or those firms that are in fact incentivized by intellectual property rights, we would define and highlight the value these content distributors and product manufacturers bring to creative and innovative culture much more than is currently the case in our laws and society. Aligning IP doctrine with the empirical evidence about incentives and economic rewards would certainly shrink the focus on authors and inventors as the ultimate beneficiary of our intellectual property laws.[32]

In conclusion, let me emphasize that this discussion about beginnings and everyday work should not be misunderstood as an argument for intellectual property's absence or irrelevance in the lives of artists and scientists. This close reading of the interviews, and analysis of the accounts of how one begins and works daily in a life of art and science, shows that actors describe *multiple* motivations for initiating, engaging in, and building a life and a business around innovative and creative practices. Importantly, however, the various valuations of creative and innovative work among these actors coalesce in a heterodox account of intellectual property's role, challenging and perhaps weakening the orthodox account on which much case law and legislation is built.

CHAPTER 3

Making Do with a Mismatch

WHERE, WHEN, AND HOW is intellectual property claimed and asserted in the professional lives of artists and scientists? Chapter 1 demonstrates how assertion and interest in IP rights do not manifest in creativity's early impulses. In Chapter 2, the daily work of creativity and innovation is only sporadically or tangentially related to IP incentives, be it for exclusivity or rent. When law does emerge in the early professional lives of these creators, it manifests in joint ventures and employment relations, not as exclusive rights in the IP sense. Moreover, social relations develop and become legal or quasi-legal associations before IP rights are perfected or commercialized.

Recouping investment through IP arises infrequently in the discussions I had in the interviews about the early stages of artistic or scientific development. When they do come up, the IP rights are usually only one small part of a more complex business model. As this chapter shows, IP rights are misaligned with the goals and behavior of innovators and creators. IP rights do not fit well with the needs of individuals or the organization of businesses. This is not to say that the people I spoke with do not value IP protection—they do, especially in the context of particular businesses, which I highlight in this chapter (e.g., pharmaceutical and medical device companies, some novelists and photographers). But even professionals in industries in which IP features prominently—textbook publishers, software, musicians—assert IP rights in ways that challenge traditional justifications for IP protection. In many ways, IP takes a backseat to other creative and innovative practices and business strategies.[1]

The interviews demonstrate at least two ways in which IP entitlements are unsuccessful in providing the potential benefits of IP law and policy to businesses investing in creative and innovative production. First, IP's legal protections are frequently unknown, irrelevant, or misunderstood. Individuals and corporations alike overlook or misapprehend IP's potential role in protecting work and generating rent from exclusivity. Those who do not understand how IP can function in their professional careers do not use it as a tool to harness the property, or they misuse it in their business transactions. Those who do see IP as an available tool may misunderstand its contours, leading to a failure of IP to function as property in their daily work or business. Missed opportunities, misunderstandings, and misclaiming of IP rights can both undermine the law's effect and weaken its authority.

Second, IP does not meet the desires of those who seek to protect or benefit from their creative or innovative work. Some individuals actually wish they could demand *more* or *different* protection for their work than IP law provides, seeking attribution and control of downstream re-use of inventions or creative works. Corporate actors describe situations in which, on behalf of the company, they would overenforce or stretch IP rights to protect interests when IP doctrine and policy did not neatly align with their claims. Arguably, asserting an IP entitlement when it is not squarely covered by the particular legal or business problem harms the balance that IP law and policy is supposed to achieve. In recent years, overenforcement of IP rights has been a much-studied phenomena, maligned by scholars who popularly label the behavior, "trolling," "bullying," "copyfraud," or "copywrongs."[2] The interview data also contain examples of the opposite tendency: a deliberate underenforcement of a recognized right. Interviewees, speaking as individuals or agents for companies, recognize IP as an available tool but reject it as a suboptimal mechanism. This kind of misfit occurs when IP creates too many hurdles for ongoing transactions, thereby frustrating the goals of making, disseminating, and earning a living from work. In these cases, they tolerate infringing uses or affirmatively allow or encourage uses that would otherwise require permission. Forms of underenforcement vary, but the point is the same: IP rights are unnecessarily broad or strong for the purposes they seek to achieve.

As a regulatory system, IP aims to provide just enough incentives to encourage productivity while avoiding the excess burden of holdout behavior that frustrates IP's primary dissemination function. Too much IP and transacting around it becomes cumbersome, both for those who seek permission who may not need it and for those who control access and want to avoid arbitrary enforcement. Too little IP and overreaching or inefficient workarounds distort its production and dissemination mechanisms. If the over- and underenforcement of IP described in these interviews is as widespread as the data suggest, the IP system needs recalibration to avoid these hazards.

Instead of focusing on the diverse reasons that IP may fail to achieve its presumed goals of a monopoly return on investment, some interviewees conceive of IP pragmatically. In this articulation, IP is less a legal fiction to be applied or ignored than a flexible and adaptive construct for achieving one of three ends. First, IP can be strategically formed and deployed depending on changing business circumstances. Business models that seek agility in a changing market can benefit from the functional malleability of IP and its ability to enhance wealth. Second, IP functions as a right: it facilitates freedom, enhancing autonomy and self-definition. As a legal construct, it refers to an unalienable, enforceable claim tethered to personhood and social justice. Third, IP helps form and sustain essential social relations—like those with collaborators, the consumer base, or an audience. These three pragmatic concerns are frequently cited as diverse justifications for IP protection under the law.

In the context of these pragmatic approaches to IP's function, many interviewees (both makers and users of IP) indicate that they prefer IP entitlements to be leaky or pliable, more accessible and freer than the law otherwise provides, so that the benefits of the work spill into the public at minimal risk to owners while still preserving sufficient choices for making and distributing work.[3] This raises provocative questions. Is there a difference in the degree or nature of perceived or desired leakiness between the different IP regimes and industries? Do individuals, as opposed to those speaking on behalf of companies, experience one kind of misalignment—misunderstood or unnoticed IP—more frequently than another (e.g., over- or underenforced IP)? Surprisingly, my data suggest that the answer to both questions is no. Ill-fitting IP entitlements exist across industries and IP regimes, among both individuals and corporate actors. But a pattern does arise in the correlations between misaligned IP and pragmatic functions of IP. As Table 3.1 demonstrates, there are

TABLE 3.1   Alignment of IP uses with objectives

| | THE IP MISFIT | | |
Pragmatic uses of IP	Misunderstood or misformed	Overenforced	Underenforced
Making money	–	+	+
Establishing essential relations	+	–	+
Enhancing freedom	+	+	+

NOTE: A plus sign (+) indicates the existence of interview data; the minus sign (–) indicates the absence of interview data.

nine variations, two of which are largely absent from the data. Notably, underenforcement of IP achieves all three pragmatic ends, and interviewees attain freedom and autonomy with all three types of misalignment.

The first part of this chapter animates Table 3.1 with interview data. It describes the various ways IP law is misaligned with or tangential to the professional and personal expectations of those interviewed. Many respondents express frustration with the misfit between IP rules and the professional values that they cultivate in their daily work, like personal control over their time, fair earnings, and relationships. Too much or too little IP disturbs the flow of their work and its qualities they seek to develop. This is true for both individuals and companies working in IP-rich industries and across the statutory intellectual properties (copyright, trademark, and patent). While some do not understand how IP functions at all, leaving it largely irrelevant to their conscious endeavors, others describe misapplying IP (overreaching or leaving it underenforced) to maintain the level of autonomy they desire over their work, even at the expense of maximal wealth.

The second part of the chapter addresses the following question: if IP persists in its mistaken or misshapen form, underused or overused, what facilitates the making, distributing, and commercializing of creative and innovative work? I offer various accounts of how the individuals interviewed for this study make a living, or how the companies with which they are affiliated earn profits in industries populated with IP assets. Cataloging the varieties of ways in which revenue is generated—some *because* of IP, some *without* any thought to IP, and some *despite* IP—begins to diversify the conventional and one-dimensional explanation for IP protection in the United States. This explanation claims that IP is essential to the progress of science and the useful arts because through exclusivity it enables a monopoly return on high-risk investment. But as the data from these interviewees show, IP takes on multiple roles in creative and innovative businesses, and sometimes plays no part (or a limited part) in generating revenue from exclusivity. By documenting the diverse mechanisms that sustain IP-rich fields, I present emergent knowledge regarding the roles of IP in these industries, with the goal of revising and improving upon the utilitarian focus of IP theory.[4]

The chapter concludes with a discussion of the consequences of the misshapen and mistaken assertions of IP, especially because IP does play an important role in many of the professional lives and workplaces of those with whom I spoke. Should IP's misalignment and sometimes irrelevance lead us to conclude that the IP regime needs retrofitting to more easily apply and enforce the laws? Or, does the persistence of IP's misalignment suggest that the legal regime should stay leaky because an accidental or purposeful malleability that is subject to individual variation optimizes the progress of science and the useful arts? Whatever the answer, the data make clear that IP rights on which interviewees rely are less robust than the current legislative debates arguing for more and stronger rights would have us believe are necessary.[5] Whether we seek a better alignment with the actual ways in which IP is harnessed depends on our best guess for the social welfare outcomes of that alignment. For instance, if the hypothesized relationship between underenforced IP entitlements and the accomplishment of all three pragmatic dimensions of IP ownership (illustrated in the table) is persuasive, we might consider a system that provides for more opportunity for strategic underenforcement and where discretion to underenforce is less risky and less arbitrary. Indeed, we might want to maintain the imprecision—or even formalize a looser regime to allow for more gaps—to maximize certain underlying liberal values (freedom and autonomy) rather than recalibrate the legal rules for a more perfect fit that may end up frustrating core values.

The prevalence of misalignment in IP law, as demonstrated by the data, may resemble other areas of law (e.g., criminal law, tax law) in which imperfect enforcement is the norm.[6] A question, then, is whether IP law is different in the effects of its misalignment than other legal areas. Is there a flaw in an IP system that broadly defines numerous uses as infringement that nonetheless remain unenforced by a substantial number of rights holders? Do we have reason to worry about the arbitrary nature of enforcement and its potential chilling effects on further creativity and innovation? Is the fact that interviewees voluntarily opt out of enforcing their IP rights to continue their professional work in creative or innovative fields evidence of an IP system that is not calibrated at an optimal level of protection? Or, is leaving the discretion with the IP owner the nature of a rights regime? The conclusion to the chapter considers that IP is different from other legal fields and that the misalignment is problematic for rule-of-law concerns and because the rights regime of IP includes the public as much as it includes the IP owner. The chapter's conclusion also considers how the imprecision may be recalibrated—either in the informal suspension of law's application or with more formal legal declarations of breathing space.

MISFIT AND MISFORMED: TIME AND MONEY

The value of time, oft repeated in employment and business, echoes throughout the interviews. Whether earning a salary and benefits from an employer or making a living from individual contracts for goods and services (e.g., commissions, licenses), most interviewees describe the value they create in terms of their spent time. People want to be paid for the time they put into the work as a measure of the value they produce. They want the duration of their labor to be reflected in and recuperated through the exchange value of the objects they make. And they try to minimize the risk of losing time, money, and reputation by optimizing payment structures and distributional networks to align with the perceived value of time and energy spent. Often, this entails minimizing IP as an investment vehicle, because its payoff is highly uncertain and other opportunities for achieving goals exist.

Time and Value

In describing how creators and innovators hope to align time with value, Karen, a visual artist from New York City, says:

If you make a drawing, they don't [price] it by the amount of hours that you spend working on the drawing—it's the size of the drawing. That's how they calculate the cost. . . . They don't care [that] you might have spent one hundred hours working on a drawing; it doesn't matter. . . . [O]nce it reaches a point where things are getting resold, then there will be different valuations for them . . . [My agent] was the one who . . . explained it to me. . . . I was like, "Oh, well, these drawings are . . . on . . . small sheets of paper," because I usually work pretty small, just in notebooks . . . And [my business partner] was like, "Oh, well, you need to do bigger ones." And the gallery said, "You need to do bigger ones." [Laughs.] It was like, "Yeah, but you know, I could spend a long time working on the little ones, so you could charge for them." They were like, "No, it's that size, it has to be that price." . . . I don't understand it.

Karen correlates the quality and value of art with time and skill. Although she has been making art for more than a decade and, despite her business partner describing the market dynamics, the size-based valuation of the art market is foreign to her. She just doesn't "understand it."

Michael, a pharmaceutical consultant, illustrates this frustration as it arises in scientific fields. Michael began his career as a pharmacologist, putting himself through school so he could earn a living wage. He became more entrepreneurial in his early thirties and started his own business consulting with drug companies to help scale their products and bring them to market. When Michael described his clients from the past fifteen years, he named the A-list roster of pharmaceutical companies from around the world. Michael brought a perspective to the business that married science with the business aspects. He confirmed that it is common for pharmaceutical executives to explain that patent monopolies are essential to facilitate high drug prices, to recoup the significant investment in time and money required to develop and bring a drug to market. But he also described a related tension: companies engaged in drug research are insufficiently sensitive to the human labor (physical, intellectual, and emotional) that is invested in the early stages of development. The mismatch is especially acute when managers close lines of research as a result of insufficient profitability. Michael put it this way:

The lead investigator will be called into the VP of research's office [and] say, "We're shutting down the program. We decided, you know what? We spent too much, it's not economically viable for us; your program is dead." It's like being told your child is dead. Work on something full-time for six years? . . . [T]his is what drove me to consulting—I worked on [one project] for—my god!. . . . This is why I have no hair on my head.

Michael went on to describe what he perceived as the tension between emotional attachment to the time value of work and the unyielding profit expectations of large firms:

I worked on this drug for three years, [engaging in what were, at the time, dangerous development protocols], and I was on a plane flying home from one of these trips, and while I was on the plane, they canceled the program. And what made it worse is that I found out about a year later that a competitor company picked it up and finished it, and took it to market. So you put people in a situation like that, they think [claps hands], "All right—you want to cancel this program? Fine. I'm going out on my own. I'll find venture funding, and I'll finish developing it." Because, [big pharma] might not be interested. . . . Well, see, there are a lot of drugs at $20, $30, $40, $50 million. If you are in a position to take that drug and develop it, and make the $50 million yourself you think you could manage to be happy with $50 million? I think *I* could.

Whether Michael was describing a unique case or a common phenomena, the sentiment regarding the time value of human capital as persistently undervalued in some IP-rich markets saturated the interviews. Artists, scientists, and businesspeople want to balance the time invested with revenue that reflects their work, but they are not maximalist. As evident in Michael's quote, one solution is to settle for less ($50 million) to bring the drug to a needy population and to support and reward the human capital invested in its initial development. Karen, the artist, similarly resents having her pieces judged simply on the basis of size as opposed to effort or time.

The tension between time and value exists in part because the marketplace for IP-protected goods to the interviewees appears quixotic, counterproductive, and sometimes irrelevant. As Karen said earlier about the sizes of her work and the prices for which they may be sold, she just doesn't understand how or on what basis the market values art. Why size instead of detail and imagination? She determines artistic quality and value in terms of skill, emotional resonance, and high levels of originality. In her view, it appears that IP (with copyright's low threshold for originality) does not help to capture or transfer compensable value to her. Kevin, an IP-savvy high-tech entrepreneur, said the same thing with regard to patented technology in a field he knows well, the telecom industry:

The big problem in business with patents is that the implications are totally unquantifiable. What is it going to cost us—well, what are the odds we get sued? Impossible to figure out. What's the likely outcome? I mean, most other business activities, you can make a reasonable judgment. . . . "That might be a problem." "This might get us sued." . . . "It will cost us that." Patents? Completely unquantifiable.

Whether describing copyright- or patent-rich industries, the interviewees share a certain awe at how unpredictable or unintelligible the marketplace for IP-protected goods is. This unpredictability leads individuals and businesses to develop alternative strategies for achieving profitability while sustaining their artistic or scientific endeavors.

Minimizing Risk

Interviewees seek optimal payment structures that match their professional and personal goals, minimize risk of loss and work stoppage, and reflect hard work, high skill, and time spent. Most interviewees indicated that they would prefer consistently earning a moderate wage over sporadically or unreliably receiving a maximal sum. In many professions, profit can be inconsistent, especially in the early years. The interviewees, of course, assumed substantial risk in the very fact of their artistic, scientific, or entrepreneurial profession, so that, when possible, they seek financial stability in other ways, many of which are tangential to or in spite of IP entitlements. These more stable financial mechanisms (including contracts for goods or services and building a consumer base) are described more fully later in this chapter, but one tactic is pertinent to the discussion of misalignment. The interviewees often opt for salary- or hourly-based remuneration instead of revenue from licensing IP. For many interviewees, including highly successful artists and scientists, salary and hourly pay more often reflect the optimized relationship between time spent and work produced than holding out for IP royalties. As it turns out, quantitative studies are beginning to show that copyrights and patents make a significant amount of money only for blockbuster works or inventions, and in fact make the rest of the relevant industry professionals less wealthy.[7] The failure of IP to result in a substantial profit for the communities it is supposed to serve, on balance, undermines rather than promotes IP as an investment vehicle for creative and innovative endeavors.

Here, Lisa, a well-established writer describes an equitable balance between work and pay. This writer lives off her investments grown from copyright royalties, but early in her career, she taught part-time and wrote for a local newspaper to fund her novel writing:

I never sell a book until it's finished. I don't take an advance. . . . I don't take an advance because it's too nerve wracking to have a deadline. I have worked on deadline for years as a journalist, but that's a different matter. Because I'm always terrified with a book that I won't be able to finish it, or that some legal problem will arise that will stop me from doing it.

Lisa refused advances throughout her book-writing career, finding publishing deadlines restrictive, even though she is a seasoned writer and currently lives comfortably off publishing royalties. Lisa preferred having control over her time and for that reason refused advances that boxed her in. She relied instead on piecework and hourly wages while she worked on her books, which, now that she is in her sixties, number nearly a dozen. Another writer, Jennifer, also a former journalist and recently back from a national book tour, expresses a contrary perspective vis-à-vis her book advance. But she reiterates the observation that book royalties and advances are not dependable, and that all her decision-making and financial planning begin from that understanding:

I don't think that, in general, books can be a day job usually. You can't earn enough money with them to make it worth your time, usually. . . . It's possible. But . . . you wouldn't *do* a book unless you had a contract. But the contracts tend to be very modest. . . . [P]art of what I am thinking is I *would* happily do another book. I have this great agent now. But you need to be absolutely, passionately in love with your topic to commit a couple of years to it.

Both of these writers earn substantial money from selling their book to publishers, but neither could tell me the royalty percentages in their book contracts—they simply did not know. Were the royalties unimportant at the outset? Both writers sought dependable income early in their careers, and royalties are unreliable. Jennifer continues to draw a regular paycheck from a journalism-related job alongside writing books, which supplements the income she received from the book advance. In this interview, Jennifer talks about her book advance in terms of a salary even though its sum was not correlated with the time she spent and it is not part of an employer-employee relationship. Rather, it is a salary, in her eyes, because she distributes it evenly and predictably over several years, and because she worked to earn it. Her subsequent copyright royalties were unplanned and remain unpredictable.

In conversations about what interviewees want out of a relationship between time spent and value produced, the word *salary* appears often to describe a desirable model for compensation. It occurs frequently among artists and other independent contractors as well as among investors and entrepreneurs in start-up businesses. Joan, a well-established sculptor, deposits commission fees for her public art into the corporation she formed, and then distributes it as income to herself and her studio assistants, explicitly calling it a salary. Karen, the New York City artist, interchanges *salary* and *fee* when talking about how she would like to be compensated: instead of self-funding the costs of the commissioned project and her living expenses, she would earn a wage that covered both. For a recent job, she says:

I got the [money] that was to cover the flight and the studio, so the actual practical costs of what I was doing. But on top of that, then there should be a fee, which just is a fee; that technically, with every project, you should get a fee that's paying you for doing a job.

David, a photographer, expresses similar frustration. When asked what his ideal pay structure would be, he explained that the value he creates and for which he should be compensated derives from two sources: his time and his creativity. Most fees he received were for only one or the other. Clients, he said, often balk at the idea that time and creativity are independent values for a photographer, especially when they are faced with paying separately for the photographer's time *and* the copyrighted work (e.g., the digital file transferred without any restrictions on its reproduction or distribution). Investors in start-ups also describe the draw from their investment as a salary (or fee). In fact, the standard practice in structuring investment agreements for investors and entrepreneurs requires predictable and regular financial draws ("salaries") to minimize the risk of fluctuating revenue, despite the possibility that the young company might not earn a profit.

These financial arrangements work to offset the potential negative effects of IP's inherently risky payoff. Seeking salaried employment to balance the unpredictability of IP revenue and structuring commission income, patent, or copyright royalties to function as a "salary" are two ways in which the individuals I interviewed reconstituted the relationship between time spent and value created around inconsistent IP royalty streams. Salary seeking, for some people, is a buffer that allows them to take risks—risks that may eventually lead to large payoffs. Indeed, as compared to individuals and sole proprietors in IP-rich fields, several employees and corporate officers I interviewed find that the benefit of corporate structure is precisely that it spreads the risk of investing in creative and innovative projects; more research and development can occur in corporations because they distribute risk across their business model. In the same way, it appears that individual interviewees and corporate actors who participate in IP-rich industries similarly seek ways to spread risk and balance revenue-generating mechanisms to compensate for the inconsistency of IP revenue and its poor approximation of time invested and value created.

What Money Can't Buy

There is another side to the time-money balance that appears misaligned with IP's traditional incentive structure. People want to be paid for their time as a function of the value they add to the work. *But they also value their time independent of a financial bottom line.* At some point in their lives, many interviewees sought more control over how and when they work, and so they moved from working in a firm to a solo practice where the financial upside may be riskier but control over their days was greater. Either because of growing professional status or a life change, the risk of an inconsistent revenue stream shrinks or no longer outweighs the benefits of having freedom over one's time to complete work as desired.

The people who had left a creative or scientific job in a company to work for themselves describe how assuming the risk of inconsistent pay-off was necessary because autonomy over time became paramount. To many, the work they do, by its nature, is ongoing, and they need freedom to manage its flow. In particular, often they describe the change in terms of avoiding the constraints imposed by employers' demands for profit margins; instead, they want to work at their own pace and at a targeted quality, rather than for a designated price and profit level. Dan, the composer who left engineering to do music full-time, describes his decision. He sits at his dining room table in a modest house in an urban neighborhood. As a middle-age man with substantial freedom to spend his days working as he chooses, he appears both proud and humbled by his accomplishments. It is a Sunday, but it seems like a day as any other day of the week: both his wife and son are home, and the house is busy, with friends and colleagues dropping by throughout the interview:

Let's face it: this is a lot less lucrative than being a senior chemical engineer. And if I were in it for the money, I would have made a very poor choice of career. . . . [But] I get to see what I write realized the way I want it realized in my own company.

The downside of going it alone is the uncertainty of IP's payoff and the lack of commensurate pay for artistic production. For Dan, as for many others, freedom and control over time and workflow trump the fear of making a risky investment in creative or innovative work and is worth the risk of financial uncertainty. Although he worked a long time as a chemical engineer making a good living, Dan's shift to music was not without its risks. However, it appears for Dan that knowing the stability of a salaried job for many decades made the choice of leaving it behind to spend more time with his family, build a community around his music, and "realize the music the way he wants it realized in his own company" a straightforward choice.

This was as true for lawyers servicing IP clients as it was for the clients themselves. Irene, a solo IP lawyer, told me that she left a large firm so that she could spend more time on client tasks without having to charge for every bit of work (as the firm would have required). Working solo means she can specialize in particular kinds of IP and work for clients whose IP needs seem more vital to their businesses. Like many of her creative or innovative clients, Irene wants both the freedom to spend time in ways that make sense to her and compensation for that time in a way that reflects the quality of the work accomplished. Dennis, an in-house patent attorney, articulates the same sentiment when describing an exchange with a solo IP lawyer with whom he often works. Dennis reports that when he told the solo practitioner, "This is contrary to my interests, but . . . you really need to raise your prices," she responded:

No . . . [F]irst of all, I have so much work that if a client makes me mad, I can fire the client. . . . [S]econdly, I just don't . . . want to cut my time. I want to know that I'm charging what I think is a reasonable amount. So if I want to spend forty hours on something, I can do it.

Achieving Balance in Time and Value: Organizing Work and Business

In some cases, interviewees eventually achieved what they felt was an optimal balance between time worked, quality achieved, and amount of money earned. Other interviewees struggle to find an optimal work-earning balance, even when working independently. Especially interviewees still in a start-up phase of their business (be it art, science, or technology) explain how they had not yet achieved an optimal work-earning balance. Running a young business is time consuming, and the income is not automatically commensurate, especially when money is not the measure of success. Instead, whether the interviewees are seeking fame or some other professional goal, it was common to hear that "there isn't enough money in this business to compensate me or anybody who is involved in it for the effort expended." These folks add credence to the cliché that people work from passion rather than for wealth. (Chapters 1 and 2 presented data illustrating this orientation to work.) For these people, money is not the primary measure of their success, and they are satisfied with "having enough," rather than more than enough, especially when they have artistic control and a growing reputation. As a filmmaker said, "I just wasn't ever driven by monetary [gain]. . . . I am a working filmmaker, and that's the difference." Indeed, working in a creative field is sometimes defined as having a commitment to art over money. Another filmmaker, who is also in advertising, says about the creative arts generally:

You'd be crazy if you pick up a guitar, and go, "I'm playing guitar to be a millionaire." Anybody who knows the reality of the business would be out of their . . . mind. That's like saying, "The best way for me to be really wealthy is to play the lottery." . . . [Most often] the mentality [is,] . . . "If I work my butt off, and I am halfway right, [and] I have a decent idea, this can support a life."

These people find satisfaction in working regularly and making a living at it—indeed, they are quite proud that they earn enough to continue doing what they enjoy and doing it well.

In all cases, self-appreciation and pleasure derives from developing and practicing a skill. The pleasure is inherent to the everyday. And personal rewards, such as reputational benefits, worthwhile relationships, professional autonomy, wealth, more work, and daily challenges, are a function of this everyday work. Moreover, valuing the time spent in conceiving and shaping intellectual pursuits grounds the self-identity for the majority of the people I spoke with, and hence how they assess their working life. Because IP law does not value the owner's time, and because its payoff is risky (it often leads to no payment at all), individuals and organizations create diverse structures for their professional operations and compensation schemes, including, but not limited to, the use of IP.

Identifying the diverse payment and work structures within businesses infused with IP may seem like describing an obvious and common phenomenon in business. There are two points to be made here, however. First, legislative debate and case law identify businesses saturated with (or described as being organized around) IP as uniquely in need of stronger protection for their property assets. Yet if IP-rich businesses are in fact not different from other businesses in their diversified revenue streams, the debates and case law are misleading; they overemphasize a legal entitlement that many IP-rich individuals and businesses underenforce in pursuit of other ends (e.g., autonomy, reputational or relational benefits). Claims that stronger IP rights would encourage these businesses and individuals to rely more heavily on their IP rights, eliminating the need to diversify business and compensation processes, are not convincing given the evidence from the interviews. Second, stronger IP rights will not address underutilization because, as I explain here, many individuals and organizations purposefully underenforce their IP rights to maximize other healthy or predictable revenue streams or values. Still others do not understand how IP rights work, relying blindly on legal and business agents long after the production and distribution goals of their art or science are established. In these cases, IP plays an erratic or diminished role in the professional goals of the artists and scientists and their businesses.

MISFIT, MISINFORMED,

AND MISUNDERSTOOD

As described in Chapter 2, many interviewees use the language of real or personal property to articulate the value of their work and how they claim it. As creators and innovators understand them, IP rights do not align well with how they make a living nor how they create value in their professions. Likewise, metaphors for natural processes ("harvesting" and "fishing") are used to explain how intangible assets develop, thereby making sense of their intangible properties outside of the IP market context. Instead of invoking doctrinal meanings of IP, their interpretations more closely resonate with norms concerning the time value of labor and the consistency and stability of income than high-risk or high-payoff situations.[8]

Whether conscious attempts to reorient professional values around time and labor or misunderstandings of how IP rights create value, the metaphors are persistent. If IP is meant to incentivize the production of science and art, the wide circulation of these metaphors as expressions of value is significant.[9] The interviewees use language that contrasts with how IP actually works to describe how their output is valuable or produces value, exposing otherwise tacit commitments to and preferences for how IP might otherwise facilitate professional well-being. Metaphors for IP bring to light a popular consensus, and exploring those metaphors (and the misinformation and mistakes regarding IP) provides access to the lived experiences of artists and scientists and how their interpretation of IP claims is oftentimes distinct from how IP doctrine might actually apply.

In the interviews, people often misstate how the IP they are creating might benefit them or their company. This is true of both individuals and corporate actors, though not of the IP lawyers I interviewed. This misinformation comes in various forms. There are folks who simply pay little or no attention to how IP works in their IP-rich field. This is typical when the creators or innovators are employees. "Most of the scientists are . . . in the drug industry," says one in-house IP counsel, because "they can make a comfortable living. But I think . . . most of the ones I've met in my fifteen years of direct exposure . . . are very interested in finding drugs to help people. . . . They don't understand the pharmaco-economics." Similarly, Kevin, a high-tech investor and former software engineer who believes that IP slows instead of increases his rate of return, is nonetheless frustrated with newer business partners who have never thought concretely about the connection between revenue streams and product sales (whether protected by IP or not). He says of the innovators in one of his start-ups (who until now were employees, not owners):

That's been the challenge in all of the work with these guys, which is that they never had to answer any of these [profitability] questions, because the paycheck comes magically from the checkbook in the sky . . . every pay period, so they don't have to worry about the financial relationships. Everyone who uses the software works for the same employer so there is no negotiation about "Well, I'll give you the software if you give me $12." That never happens. . . . [T]his guy has a team; he doesn't really know what it fully costs to have a team. . . . [H]e doesn't pay for his office space, right? . . . So to swing out and think about what this looks like as a business has been a lot of work.

This is a recurring phenomenon: many innovators do not think at first about how their business makes money or, as a result, about how or whether IP is part of that process.

Most of the artists, writers, musicians, scientists, and engineers I spoke with understand ownership rights in the context of work-for-hire in an undefined, general way: the company or client owns the work. When pushed to describe what ownership entails beyond the right to broadly commercialize, their answers were myriad and inconsistent. Some understood that work-for-hire under copyright conferred authorship status; others knew that individuals were inventors and companies were owners. Many people nonetheless cared about the future use of their work in terms of reputation—whether they would get credit, and under which circumstances the work would be used—but mistakenly believed that, even if they did not own the work, having created it provided them with some control over the work's future use. Melanie, a filmmaker with her own production company, said that although it is her dream for a distributor to buy her first self-funded film, she did not know how distributors make money and whether she would have to convey her copyright to them. A different filmmaker described the frustrating process of licensing archival photographs and film footage—because institutions would charge too much or refuse to license—but did not know that many of the once-copyrighted works she sought to use were now in the public domain; she was purchasing access to the physical copy in the archive rather than a copyright license.

Even when asked to describe contracts or business arrangements directly relating to their livelihood—whether as bonuses or as independent contractors—interviewees often were uninformed about the relationship between their IP and their income. For example, at first I was surprised to learn that most creators and innovators paid little to no attention to the financial terms of their contracts that concern IP royalties. But after many interviews, it became common to hear that individuals who owned IP could not describe how their royalty payments were structured. Although they could provide detailed narration of negotiations they had over the advance sum or over artistic and editorial control, even if it occurred decades earlier, when asked about royalties and profit sharing, they almost uniformly said, "I don't remember. I can check for you." As if proud of the initial lump sums they received for work done in their early careers, artists and scientists alike could quote the bonus they got for an invention or the commission for their early art. Scientists and engineers could tell me their salary and explain their employment benefits, but few could describe with confidence if and how they got paid because of IP creation. Many said, "I'd have to look at the contract," or "I let my lawyer handle that." Some deferred questions about royalty stream and derivative rights to their agent or gallery. Mary said, "so much of this stuff I just . . . tuned out and let the lawyer and my manager deal with." Karen, the visual artist from New York, lamented that even though she needed to be more on top of the contractual and financial arrangements of her work, she is just "not very practical like that." This is true of business folks and creators or innovators. A marketing executive for a high-end press knows how much books costs to make, how much they could be sold for wholesale, and how to package them to maximize retail sales, but nothing about the authors' compensation or their cost to the firm: "royalty deals I really don't know," he said. There are some, of course, who do study the details of their contracts, but even they acknowledge this is unusual. Barbara, an author, distinguished herself and a discrete group of savvy editors-turned-writers from most other authors she knew in being particularly well informed about royalties and other contract details. Barbara went further to explain that her distinctive expertise, being more knowledgeable about IP rights, is a product of her extensive work in publishing before becoming a best-selling author. She says, "I bring an insider's notion to what [the contract] is, and to what a negotiation is, and to what . . . matters to the person you are negotiating [with]."

Beyond simply not knowing about IP, some creators describe how they purposively ignore or distance themselves from the legal aspects of their work, especially the distribution of economic rights. (This was never true for the corporate agents or lawyers I interviewed.) Sometimes they expressed disinterest or assumed that the legal-economic language would be too complex to parse. (One writer said, honestly, "It bores me.") Other times, the distancing was strategic. Even though she considers herself unusually knowledgeable about her legal arrangements, Barbara says:

Remember also that I use an agent. And one of the best reasons to use an agent is that you never have to let business come between you and the editor. It . . . can always be about creative matters. You can always pretend you don't know what's going on. I have been in the middle of tough negotiations, yet I never had to address them whatsoever.

Steve, a media developer, said the same thing; he does not participate in contract negotiations with film studios and merchandisers because doing so makes it harder to work with the client that will eventually be distributing the content he and his company create:

[I don't involve myself with the contract details] . . . because once you do that, it makes things ugly. Because now you are arguing over percentage points, and you are arguing over payment series, and you are arguing over . . . things in a document that you should not be arguing about . . . we learned this lesson: it leaves a bad taste in the mouth of the client if we are going back and forth about petty stuff on a contract.

The "petty stuff" is the fee for service. As long as the agreed-to fee between his company and the client is within a reasonable range, he and his partner leave the contractual details to their lawyer and agent. Of course, Steve says, "there are deal breakers. There are people who wanted to whittle us down. And we said, 'You know what? Tell them no. We are done.'" But his intervention in the legal matters in these extreme circumstances is only to end the negotiations, not to refine their terms.

In general, the innovators in the high technology and biotechnology sectors I interviewed are more knowledgeable than the artists, writers, and musicians about the possible roles for IP in their businesses. This may be because of the overt teaching about profit models and strategy that takes place in these businesses, which are, by and large, more complex organizations with legal departments and business development professionals (see Chapter 5). In-house lawyers told me that it is necessary to instruct the engineers and scientists in their company about the benefits of patents and copyrights not only to capture and protect commercially viable products or maintain competitiveness but also to disabuse the developers and innovators of their distrust of IP in the first place. As members of an organization, collaborating daily on firm business, in-house lawyers regularly consult with innovators. Jacqueline, a longtime in-house lawyer in the software industry, describes her experience with the innovators in her company this way:

It was just hard for them because there was a struggle philosophically around all of this, and a real skepticism—the concept of law, legal, and compliance was

180 degrees away from this very fluid, creative, libertarian . . . open environment that was required . . . . So just getting a law department in a company like that where they would even trust what "the lawyers" would say . . . required an awful lot of effort on our part.

For many of the lawyers and innovators I spoke with, the relationship eventually becomes symbiotic: the innovators come to rely, however reluctantly, on the lawyer to facilitate the business process, its risk management, and its profitability. Part of this relationship involves encouraging and instructing the innovators on how to capture, protect, and commercialize IP, since the innovators may not know much about it or misconceive the function of IP law in their business. Ted, an in-house lawyer, considers himself "very lucky" because at his company (a biotech alternative energy company), in contrast to others he knows, he says:

[That his] company's very tuned into IP, and very interested in IP. . . . [T]he company has been very keyed in on IP from the beginning. . . . They understand the value of IP . . . from top down, there is this interest in IP, and this appreciation for IP. So it makes my job easier in trying to work with the scientists.

Nonetheless, Ted finds the scientists at his company to be more forthcoming and open to patent development than the engineers. Indeed, he describes a range of familiarity with and willingness to engage legal counsel for the purposes of IP development among the innovators at his company. In his experience, the scientists more freely communicate with the in-house lawyers regarding invention disclosures, whereas the "engineers, I think, are more comfortable dealing with trade secrets. . . . [T]hey are more . . . pragmatic, . . . they don't see things as 'create innovations,' or anything like that. It's just, 'Yeah, well, you've got to tweak it in this way to make it work.'" In response to the lack of familiarity and comfort with patents, Ted runs regular seminars with both the scientists and engineers at his company, focusing on their particular misconceptions.

Michael, a biotech consultant, now in law school, told me a by-now-familiar story about the resistance of some companies to developing IP protocols as a consequence of basic misunderstandings about the value of IP protection. To his advice, "Guys, you know, you've got to get confidentiality agreements with all your employees," he hears, "Well, no—everybody [here], we're all family." Michael groans when he tells this story, and rolls his eyes. But in this widespread misunderstanding regarding IP protection in his specialized industry, he sees a niche opportunity for his business:

It's a great business opportunity; it's one of the reasons I'm [in law school]— some of them don't, in the sense that they don't understand the trade secrets they are working with, they don't understand the patents that they should have. And so they put themselves in very vulnerable positions, in the sense that they could do a ton of work and then lose it.

It is likely that this misunderstanding or lack of attention to IP regulation has parallel misconceptions in other areas of law. For example, insurance company employees (other than attorneys) may have unsophisticated understandings of tort law. Police officers might not have a nuanced understanding of constitutional law. Contractors and other small businesses might not be well versed in contract, agency, and partnership law. Generally, it is reasonable to assume that laypeople charged with adhering to or implementing legal rules do not understand the details of legal regulation in the ways professional legal experts do, and instead resort to normative understandings of legal doctrine and processes. The question is whether the misunderstanding or lack of attention in the IP context is distortive or reinforcing: should the IP regime be calibrated to more accurately reflect certain behaviors and practices in hopes of optimally effectuating the goals of creators and innovators? Or is the IP regime's misalignment of central professional values with IP rights nonetheless effective—providing flexibility and choice with only minimal inconvenience? If the IP regimes were to more closely reflect the norms of creative and innovative practices, we would loosen and alter the legal rules in substantial ways related to reproduction and distribution and attend to differences in particular industries. We might also invigorate moral rights as regards attribution and integrity. By contrast, leaving things as they are may provide flexibility and choice to rights holders, but only those who know their rights and can effectively harness them. Doing this favors savvy rights holders over inexpert ones and disfavors secondary users and consumers under circumstances that may be unnecessary and even counterproductive. What do these data tell us about how and whether mistaken, misinformed, or misaligned understandings about IP progress science and the useful arts?

This is not a new question. Scholars and policy makers in other legal fields ask similar questions about how strict or loose legal regimes should be to achieve optimal compliance.[10] Indeed, these are some of the most basic questions for law and its effective enforcement. For example, with criminal and constitutional law, we often choose between enforcing rules through state action (the police or other state actors with detention power) or through private rights of action (private civil rights suits). Often, state laws allow for exceptions to certain crimes (e.g., medical marijuana) to balance competing interests; states choose the leaky form of law over the more draconian one, even though it makes enforcement of illegal possession more difficult. In contrast, some states pass stricter rules (e.g., zero tolerance for school bullying) with the knowledge that enforcement will not be perfect but the hope that the rule will have a strong deterrent and normative force. In other sectors, leaky legal regimes are common. In light of the digital age and the centrality of innovation for the world economy and public good, is the leaky IP regime different in ways that matter for the consideration of its future contours?

Whether the digital age shapes criminal law or constitutional law to the same extent it has changed IP law, we must reckon with how the profusion of digital media inextricably entwines IP creation with its dissemination, enforcement and further production. Today, most IP infringement occurs because of the ease of access, reproduction, and dissemination of digital representations—both the anxiety and the advantage of our current era.[11] This is true of patented technologies, copyrighted expressions, and trademarked products. Widespread digital dissemination (whether or not for direct commercialization and whether or not in violation of IP rights) enhances relationships with potential and actual consumers, strengthens product identity and drives more production. The digital age (like the printing press centuries earlier) has made the right of exclusion that defines IP both more relevant and less necessary for building professional identity, revenue, and reputation. And it is precisely because of this digital dimension that IP law can be more perfectly enforced and more pervasively evaded. IP scholars, such as Julie Cohen, ask if, with the digital era, there should come a qualitatively new way of thinking about protection and enforcement and whether "imperfect control of individual behavior" is optimal. She suggests that we should be "designing [IP regimes] for imperfection."[12] Citing other scholars such as Yochai Benkler, James Boyle, Larry Lessig, and Jessica Litman, all of whom take on the question of whether to choose imperfection in IP or settle for it, Cohen believes that "constitutive freedom" should animate the discussion and inquiry around IP.[13] Inquiries, including the present study, should investigate the "practices, spaces, and contexts within and through which individuals experience the information environment, and the ways in which authorization and constraint alter those experiences."[14] As the descriptions of misfits and misalignments presented here demonstrate, and as the remainder of this chapter shows, businesses and individuals engaged in creative or innovative work achieve personal and professional goals—autonomy, productive relationships, and revenue—under misaligned and ill-fitting IP regimes. But they function by substantially underenforcing IP rights and diversifying business strategies. Given this, it is unlikely that more enforcement and more perfect enforcement (as compared to underenforcement) will better accomplish creators' and innovators' goals. Indeed, IP law reformers might consider formalizing the informal restraint IP rights holders demonstrate when they tolerate certain kinds of infringement, permit uses that would otherwise require authorization, and generally underenforce their IP rights. Formalizing these choices minimizes the friction that risk-averse users and consumers experience in terms of their everyday interactions with and expectations of expressive and inventive goods. And it curtails the harm of arbitrary underenforcement, such as chilled creativity and innovation or transaction costs. Given the many ways that IP owners already make do in their professions with less-than-exclusive control over their work, formalizing a lower level of exclusivity (or different forms of it) is unlikely to effect productivity. It may even promote it.

How is the misaligned and underenforced IP regime productive? What are the "practices, spaces, and contexts" that individuals and businesses develop to sustain production and distribution in our copy-centered culture populated by IP-rich industries that use less than their full quota of exclusivity? The next section addresses the various ways these individuals and entities "make do" with misaligned IP. These adaptations include contracts for services and goods, first-mover advantage, market share optimization, and complementary products. As the discussion demonstrates, some people hope and expect to recoup investment in their work through some kind of legal right, but IP is only one mechanism (and not necessary the primary mechanism) around which people and entities structure their business to make a living. Generally, IP rights function in more varied, less rigid ways than the law formally indicates. Often, they are used or strategically relinquished to accomplish a variety of goals, only some of which involve recuperating investment. Other goals include developing relationships and preserving autonomy.

WAYS OF MAKING DO: CHOICE AND CONTROL

Differences exist among the interviewees regarding how IP functions in their work, but mostly the differences are of degree. By design, all the interviewees own or contribute to making work that is or could be protected by IP; IP is either in the background of their work or is available as an option. As such, each could theoretically assert their IP right to exclude others from using their work (or their employer could do so). But each interviewee, as a member of a particular creative or innovative industry, has a different experience with how valuable IP is as a tool in facilitating their professional goals. For instance, business models that require volume manufacturing and distribution to recuperate the significant costs of development and production tend to emphasize the rent-seeking function of IP and the importance of controlling competition. In interviews with people involved with medical devices, biotechnology, and some (but not all) text publishing, the traditional economic rationale of IP law as a mechanism for maximally exploiting copies is more present than in other industries. But even while the financial incentive remains prevalent, these same people emphasize various other goals that are less directly achieved through IP: control over their reputation and work flow, and building or maintaining a community around sustainable relationships. That is, they seek a balance of economic, ethical, and personal interests. By contrast, other industries such as web design, software products, music, visual art (excluding photography), e-commerce business systems, and home-goods manufacturing do not emphasize IP's right of exclusion as much as other ways of succeeding in their business. And they often describe the benefit of underenforcing whatever IP rights they have to facilitate their various professional goals.

Everyone I interviewed finds earning a living to be imperative to professional happiness. But many reach for IP for reasons unrelated to money (e.g., to control reputation), and others reach for alternatives to IP (like contracts or loyal relationships) as central ways of earning a living. IP does play a role in the professional development and personal well-being of those I interviewed, but on the whole its role is not critical to the ongoing sustainability of their artistic or scientific work. As described, IP's varied roles are not as vital to developing creative and innovative industries as the legislative initiatives and court decisions of the past thirty years that steadily strengthen IP rights would have us believe. IP protection is only one of many tools that individuals and businesses harness to sustain and grow their interests to generate more creative and innovative output. The diverse ways of "making do" in this case study (many that are at the *expense* of IP rights themselves) demonstrate how overstated IP protection is in the economic health and continued productivity of most creative and innovative industries. In the end, professionals aim to balance productivity and economic well-being with personal and ethical goals through a combination of business strategies. Choices about how and with whom art and science is pursued and control over one's economic, ethical, and personal circumstances (even if that means undermaximizing profitability) are ubiquitous throughout the interviewees' discussions about optimizing creative and innovative production.

An alternative explanation for the limited role IP rights have in individual work is that IP mainly incentivizes firms to invest in the development of creative and innovative products and to support the individuals who do the work. The data provide some support for this hypothesis. Firm actors in specific industries, like pharmaceutical and medical device companies, and some text publishing and photography professionals describe a business model that they claim requires monopoly profits at least for a limited time to be sustainable. However, even these industries rely on various sources of revenue, such as a first-mover advantage, contracts for services, and sales of complementary products. Also, firms do not have uniform incentives any more than individuals do. Pharmaceutical companies and publishing houses, for example, are hierarchical organizations built around duty and loyalty, comprising multiple, complex social and professional roles based on economic motivations and other incentives. These motivations are represented and enacted by the diverse individuals who are charged with making company decisions. In other words, according to these data, the "self-interested corporation" whose sole goal is to maximize shareholder value is an oversimplification and borderline inaccurate. Indeed, "to define a company's only goal as making money would define it as a kind of shark that lives off the community rather than as a member of a community with important agency in the construction, maintenance and transformation of our shared lives."[15] Corporations are made and directed by people, who themselves have various motives that are diversely balanced and depend on particular circumstances; like people, corporations are "complex organization[s] with many purposes and effects."[16] At least, this is what the professionals in this study say, and it informs how they direct and behave within the organizations for which they work. For these reasons, the conclusions here— that IP is an ill-fitting investment vehicle and its underenforcement optimizes professional goals in the creative and innovative fields—apply to both individuals and companies.

What follows is a catalog of the ways individuals and companies in IP-rich industries make do with and without IP. The purpose of detailing the variations drawn from the interviews is threefold. First, it follows from the above discussion concerning the ways in which IP is both misunderstood and misshapen, leading to under- and overassertions of creative and innovative work through an IP regime that does not fit people's specific and varied goals. The diversity of ways in which the interviewees generate income in their professional lives provides further clarification of this misfit—its relevance and context. Second, the various ways of making do demonstrate how the many different ways of earning a living lead to similar pragmatic goals: autonomy over work and relationships that are both sustaining and dynamic between individuals and within a community. Rent seeking through IP, when an available option, is usually only one way to achieve these ends. Finally, the catalog places the traditional and hegemonic explanation for IP protection in the context of dense and dynamic motives and mechanisms for engaging in creative and innovative work. Identifying the classic incentive story of IP alongside all the other reasons and means for progress in the arts and sciences provides a thicker description of precisely those activities and interests we claim IP law is designed to foment and protect.

The discussion begins with examples supporting the traditional explanation for IP protection: rent seeking as a return on investment. It then also describes defensive uses of IP as a way to protect a work agenda, the "freedom to operate" that IP can provide by guarding business interests, work flow, control and choice, and reputation. Then, the discussion catalogs six other mechanisms orthogonal to IP through which creative and innovative professionals build and maintain their professional practice. The discussion begins with first-mover advantage, building market share, and selling complementary products, none of which requires IP. I then describe how contracts for services and goods provide substantial business opportunities that sustain creative and innovative work, some of which rely on aspects of IP and some which do not. The section ends with a discussion of how valuable loyal relationships and reputation are to professional success and well-being in the diverse creative and innovative fields represented. In all, the variety of business practices described, many of which do not rest on IP and some that do, depicts stratified and diverse strategies to sustain professional work in creative and innovative fields. Longer, broader, and stronger IP rights seem largely superfluous to creative and innovative professionals. Most make do in addition to or despite IP. This is especially true when professional autonomy and maintaining relationships are paramount.

IP-Centered Revenue Sources
Rent Seeking and Perceived Value

Beginning with the most traditional and orthodox view of IP's productive function, several interviewees describe both copyrights and patents as a "foundation" for a business. An in-house lawyer at an alternative energy biotechnology company characterizes the company's early patent portfolio as the "foundation on which we started." This includes both "home-grown technology" and "an almost equal chunk of stuff that we've in-licensed." In other words, without the IP, there would have been no financing, no creation of more innovative products, and therefore no company. A copyright lawyer who represents mostly small-businesses and individual creators describes copyright as a "baseline," the central benefit of which is an "amount of exclusivity . . . and I can keep other people from doing things with it unless they ask me." The next step, as she describes it, is "to figure out what to do with [the copyright]," because after the essential exclusive right, "the rest of [the business] moves into other field[s]—parts of law, and just basic business negotiation." For her clients, copyright is the kernel around which she structures their business arrangements. Copyright does not constitute the whole value of the company, but it is a crucial starting point. A venture capital fund manager working exclusively to raise capital and develop global health technology for a medical device and services corporation makes it clear that if "we had no IP going in, we would never have been able to start the company." This finance professional cannot foresee a successful business in his field without an initial portfolio of pending patents, whether or not the IP in fact drives profitability for the company emerging from the investment fund's work.

Many of the professionals who characterize IP as the foundation of their business strategy are nonetheless skeptical about whether patents and copyrights *in fact* drive profits or whether, in the place of actual profitability, the option of exclusivity creates the *perception* of future value. The sheer existence of IP assets is often enough to attract early investment, which in turn enables further business development and the subsequent growth of market share. One lawyer says:

All these venture capitalists who are going to be investing in us, they are going to look for IP. They don't know what it is anymore than you or I know what it is, right? But they are going to look for something that says it's IP . . . And the more of it we have—and it's fuzzy what the "it" is, but the more of "it" we have, then the more successful we're going to be.

As Chapter 5 discusses in more detail, many in-house business agents and lawyers confirm this lawyer's account of the signaling function of patents and copyrights.[17] The existence of patents can be a sign of new or in-demand innovation, competitive strength in a specific innovative market, or the drive and talent of the founding innovators. Donald, currently in-house counsel for an e-commerce company, was previously general counsel at a media company. He describes his previous job as very different from the current one. At the media company, he deliberately used IP as part of building value:

The vision I had when I was the general counsel [was] . . . we knew that we wanted to sell that company eventually, so I was trying to build value. So literally, we . . . had one thousand or two thousand registered trademarks, we had at least two thousand copyrights, we have fifteen or twenty patents.

Expanding the list of IP looks like a growing treasure chest: IP are assets against which a company may borrow money for further expansion or appear as raw wealth to attract interested investors. Donald later praised a competing firm, calling its strategy of amassing of IP a "trick"—not fraudulent, but clever:

[Company X] had a huge patent portfolio. And that's where they did this trick. They had an in-house patent lawyer, and he really created value. . . . People looked at that company, the potential buyers, and said, "Wow! This company has one hundred issued US patents. This company has sued its two main competitors, and won one" . . . and already has an offer to settle the other one.

Whether or not the patents and copyrights in fact generate revenue, for these business strategists and lawyers, the presence of IP assets signals a strong competitive position because of its ostensible ability to exclude others from the same or overlapping commercial spaces. Many interviewees describe the assertion of IP rights as "slowing down competition" rather than stopping it. This slowdown occurs by actually filing lawsuits, threatening to file lawsuits, or being perceived as willing to file lawsuits. Most of the time, IP is asserted against competitors, but it can also be used against users or intermediaries to prevent the diminution of sales. In the copyright context (e.g., university course packs, scholarly journal publishing), interviewees describe IP rights as an effective tool for enforcing contractual terms of service rather than as a way to extract rent for the exclusive right. In some manufacturing contexts, the interviewees explain that copyright can prevent parallel importation. In both of these sectors, an overreaching assertion of IP (which depends on the nature of the use, the interpretation of the statutory provision, and exceptions thereto) can be used to preserve a competitive edge, although it may harm relationships with consumers and partners.

To be sure, IP rights are the basis of a healthy revenue stream for many companies and individuals. For example, copyright and patent royalties sustain several of the novelists and branded pharmaceutical companies with whom I spoke. But by and large, IP is only a small part of how many companies initiate and continue in business.

Defensive Assertions of IP

More frequently, the interviewees offer accounts of IP as a mechanism that provides operational freedom within a specific creative or innovative space. Justifications for defensive assertions of IP (as opposed to offensive assertions) are very common. Several lawyers describe how a patent could work to shield competitors who sought to extort fees for operating in similar commercial spaces or, as one lawyer describes it, as a "chit to trade": "It's the value of protecting things similar to what we're doing, so that we have chits to trade when, inevitably, we'll have to take a license from somebody else." The freedom to operate is how Dennis, an in-house attorney at a pharmaceutical company, justifies seeking patent protection, even in questionable cases, to the scientists at his firm; they understand and respect this freedom more than rent-seeking goals:

There's an anti-patent streak [] regrettably, in most people. . . . My response to [these scientists] was "I agree that this subject matter likely shouldn't be patentable. But . . . right now, it *is* being patented by other people, and we're having to analyze their patents, spend tens of thousands of dollars analyzing them, rendering opinions, telling business people they have to make business risks based upon infringement issues." And I said, "And we're taking licenses . . . What I want is something that I can trade with somebody. . . . I'm not interested in necessarily asserting these against anybody.

Dennis's company makes money selling drugs at monopoly profits, so seeking patent protection is essential for protecting ongoing research and development from being stymied by patent holders in related fields. This interview gives an example of a company that uses IP both to earn revenue and to facilitate freedom and autonomy in research.

Another in-house IP attorney, Donald, who works at an e-commerce company, describes his conversation with engineers about patents in the same way, but he finds the value of patents in his industry to be more ambiguous. Even though the patents are likely worth more in rent value in the pharmaceutical context than the patents in the e-commerce space, both attorneys believe that the primary value that patents have for scientists and engineers developing the products for the companies is as a defensive mechanism. Patents provide the so-called room to run within the industry. Donald explains, "They [the engineers and business developers] truly believe that [patent filings are] only for defensive purposes. . . . And that's why I am primarily doing it. I am never going to have a patent that will shut down my competitors." Donald also draws on the IP work he performed at other companies to distinguish among the roles of IP within diverse industries, pointing to the various ways that IP can contribute to building a company:

Patent lawsuits among competitors [are] really what I think the Constitution envisioned when it gave these monopolies. . . . [F]or twenty years, you get a monopoly to your invention. . . . Now, when I got here and when I was starting to talk to people to help define our culture of what we were going to do with our IP . . . I told them I was [previously] at a company where we sued our competitors. I said, "I don't envision that really happening here. . . . [W]e don't have those types of patents." Even doing that is something I found a little kind of reprehensible. . . . But to build a company, sometimes you have to be willing to do that. You know, if you are trying to get a leg up on a competitor, sometimes you have to be willing to do that. . . . [T]he best way is you have the best product and the best sales force, and the best support services, and you just go up and you beat them. And that's what we've done here: we've just driven other people away.

He sees patents as central to the ongoing health of the successful e-commerce firm but indicates that it functions more as an insurance policy than as a rent-seeking mechanism. In his experience, the way to excel in the field is "to be the best." This concept of being the best—or using the best equipment or people—arose frequently in the interviews as a key to success and will be discussed later in the chapter in the context of building market share.

In the copyright industries, IP is also used defensively—but not to provide breathing room to continue work. Instead, the interviewees describe asserting copyright to prevent deformation (a disfavored reuse) and misattribution of the copyrighted work. For them, deformation and misattribution disincentivizes the continued creation and dissemination of their work. However, both preventing deformation and misattribution are controversial uses of copyright law. The extension of the derivative work right to critical uses is highly debated, and copyright does not protect against nonattribution or misattribution. In other words, not all plagiarism is copyright infringement, and critical reuse is usually a fair use.[18] In my data, few artists registered their copyrights—a formality that is required to file suit for infringement. But when they did register, it was to protect their work from being used in ways they found offensive to their artistic integrity, a claim infrequently cognizable under copyright law, if at all. Here, a public artist describes registering a copyright to prevent misattribution and mass exploitation both nationally and abroad:

We got a little scared because people were kind of liking [the scupltures], and wanting plans, and . . . so we actually got a copyright out on it. But I don't know what that actually does. . . . Some woman from some other nearby city was sort of, on some art committee or whatever, desperately wanted us to . . . make her a little [sculpture]. . . . [W]e have to explain to people that we're not in the mass production business. . . . I would usually say to people, "Look, we don't sell these, but we would be happy to do something [similar] for your mall, or your whatever it is that you've got," and none of them amounted to anything. Because most of these people weren't really wanting to spend, you know, fifty thousand or more dollars. . . . [But] it was more that the Chinese government, I mean, somehow China could [copy the sculptures] for money.

Attorneys and business agents in the copyright field confirm that clients typically use registration to protect against unlawful or interfering uses of the copyrighted work as an injunctive mechanism rather than for rent seeking. Admittedly, the purpose of an injunction blurs when it prevents uses until payment is rendered. In some cases, especially in photography and publishing, suits are filed to enforce copyright licenses for reproduction and distribution of the copyrighted work. In these cases in particular, copyright law is used to extract rent and to prevent undesired uses.

But in most other cases, copyright is asserted either to prevent uses (and not for payment) or to demand attribution. (Attribution is discussed in significant detail in Chapter 4). Attribution, however, is not enforceable through copyright, and, as I've said, critical reuses of the underlying work are often permitted as fair use. Nonetheless, the interviewees assert their copyright to prevent certain undesirable uses, defensively protecting the work rather than offensively reaping rewards from it. Consider this story about a publisher's "flagship franchise," a famous animal character in children's stories that is both trademarked and copyrighted. When a small-town bar owner used the character in an offensive manner on T-shirts, the company, which owns the trademark and copyright, had to decide whether to assert their IP rights against the bar owner:

[I]t had a picture of [the animal character] . . . And it had gotten people very upset, as you might imagine, . . . and the first thing [our customers are] doing is calling us, saying, "You've got to shut this guy down." And of course, the intersection of free speech and commercial rights and IP . . . provide a rather interesting situation.

The publishing executive explained that the publishing company resisted asserting copyright and trademark rights against the bar owner because of the murky application of the First Amendment in the context of political speech. Instead, the audience and local population put significant pressure on the bar owner, demanding help from the publishing company and the local community to prevent the continued sale of the T-shirts:

[T]o a certain extent, we were baited to step in. You know, our customers were upset, and their view of IP was, "This cannot be allowed." . . . [But] this is political speech, and so there's a certain protection there. It's not a slam dunk . . . we got a number of phone calls from irate people, and a number of messages. And then the media was working to churn the thing. . . . So we were really in quite a situation. . . . [I]t was sort of funny: they almost felt possessive about [the animal character], because they had invested in the property. The thing that really got people most ticked off, the people that were most upset were people whose kids were watching the [television] series, because they felt that something that they were invested in and that had a certain meaning to them was being perverted in a way that was extremely offensive, and that therefore that couldn't be permissible. And it was interesting, because we got the first call literally before the protests had started. Because what had happened is apparently, they decided to do the protests . . . they contacted the [local newspaper]. . . . And then they're calling us immediately saying, "You've got to come in and do something about this."

This skirmish ended when the company issued a press release denying authorization of the bar's use of the character. The media and the local community subsequently pressured the bar to stop making and advertising the T-shirts: "We gave our press release and said we were going to consider further action. That . . . combined with the community pressure, . . . that was it. [The] guy was out of business."

In this case, the *audience* was behind the assertion of copyright and trademark of the creative property, not the owner, in part because the merits of the legal claim were ambiguous. As the publishing executive says, "We're sitting there as the custodians of the IP going, 'Well, this is a very complicated case . . . [and yet] the community activists want the publisher to come in and really beat up on this guy [the bar owner].'" This is the purest of defensive claims, asserting the exclusivity of the IP to prevent its intolerable use by others and to protect reputation and authentic identity, not to preserve or recoup profits.[19] And yet in this instance, a trademark tarnishment claim would have been viable and the First Amendment defense weak. However, the central aim of the invested fans and the IP owners (whose claim was ultimately left underenforced) was to protect the IP from the T-shirt maker's use because it was offensive, not because it diverted or reduced revenue.

Despite IP: Diverse Revenue Sources
and Other Pragmatic Ends

Compared to the variety of revenue-generating mechanisms, assertions of IP for rent seeking are relatively rare among the interviews. Rather, individuals and firms tend to rely on an assortment of business mechanisms to realize sustainable profits and achieve other personal and professional ends. IP rights are sometimes present within these other mechanisms as one feature among many that help the tools function (e.g., as an element of a contract). I collated the various business mechanisms across the interviews, finding that the majority fall into these six categories of revenue-generating tools: being the first mover in a market; building market share; developing and selling complementary products; contracting for services and goods; nurturing key relationships with vendors, agents, and clients; and developing and protecting one's professional reputation. The following section details each of these.

First-Mover Advantage

Many interviewees, from diverse industries, associate being the first to market a product or service with commercial success. Even when copycats compete for a share of the market, being first provides a comfortable margin of profitability. Across the interviews, first-mover advantage is strong in both the copyright industries and in patent-rich fields. This is surprising with regard to the copyright industries, since in the digital age, unlawful copying is easy, ubiquitous, and difficult to prevent. (This is less surprising in many fields dominated by patents and has been discussed elsewhere in both theoretical and empirical literature.[20]) Respondents who work in the business end of textbook publishing, software companies, and trade publishing (notably not in music or visual art fields) emphasize that being the first mover in their field is particularly lucrative. A vice president at a publishing company that specializes in K–12 educational texts prioritizes being one of the first to enter a specific geographic market to "set the standard" and establish market dominance:

[I]f you get on the list in Florida, Texas[,] . . . or California, and you get 25 to 35 percent of the market, you'll make your money back on the product, and then you can start selling to the rest. . . . The thing is, we get approval . . . on the list [in the specific territory]. So we'll know by November if we're on the list for reading in [California]. And then if we are, great. Then our sales force goes out into the school districts and say[s], "We're on the list."

This publishing executive said, "Our markets work" several times during the interview. For him, being the first to market a product to establish a market presence and thereafter maintain it is crucial to business health and product development. IP was not.

From the production end of publishing, two authors attribute their continued success as writers to their early work, which garnered substantial praise for being unusual or the first of its kind. One of Lisa's first books was about a university scandal shirked by the popular press. This early acclaim for courageous journalism established a reputation that sustains her readership levels; being one of the first female authors to write about that particular scandal set the groundwork for future projects and launched her independent writing career. Barbara attributes her successive novelization projects and her voluminous children's book series—the focal point of her writing career—to her early success at novelizing films. Despite writing more than one hundred books in the series, Barbara told me, her first books continue to sell the best. Both authors describe how being the first to shape their respective writing fields—cutting-edge investigative nonfiction and "tween" books—was the key to a successful writing career.

However, being first to a market also has its downside: deliberate copycats seek to benefit from a trend without investing their own labor and capital. Generally, the interviewees respond to this kind of free-riding behavior in two ways. On the one hand, they are unfazed by what has been called in literary studies the "anxiety of influence."[21] It is expected that artists will influence subsequent work and will themselves self-consciously borrow content and ideas from others. Indeed, some find this kind of copying flattering. Barbara, the children's book author just mentioned, describes her feelings about other writers copying her series:

I remember running into one of the people who copied me, who is a packager and somebody I had known I ran into at a local stationery store. And I said hi, and I said, "I understand you have got a new series coming out." And he blushed. I actually am the first person in the world, I think, to make [him] blush. He said, "Well . . . yeah." I said, "[I]t's the sincerest form of flattery." . . . [I]t didn't bother me. Not at all. . . . [Y]ou know you have succeeded when somebody tries to copy you. . . . I'd be annoyed if theirs succeeded more than mine did. But mine went into a television series. Theirs was optioned . . . and then they never did anything with it.

Besides genuinely feeling honored, tolerance in this context may also be explained by the lack of significant diversion of sales. However, this contrasts with strong intolerance for plagiarism (unattributed near-identical copying of expressive content), which is reported with anger by several authors, artists, and first-order creators. Plagiarism is felt as a professional and personal affront. Although plagiarism rarely affects revenue, the interviewees described it as "yucky," "weird," and dishonorable. Most interviewees could not tell me the legal difference between copyright infringement and plagiarism. But the emotional difference was significant. Moreover, asking permission to borrow, rely on, or be influenced by a previous writer or artist was unheard of, and yet failing to attribute or taking wholesale someone's work without asking was profoundly unsettling. Here, Mary (the musician) captures the sentiment across many of the interviews:

A total copy rip-off, you know, not so great. But if someone's just taking parts, I mean, and being influenced by it, that's totally great—or inspired in some way by it. . . . [I]t's all this big pool, and we're throwing stuff into it. So if someone is being inspired to write something by it, or stealing an image . . . yeah, that's unavoidable.

In the software business, business managers and developers also see being the first to market and establish a client base as crucial to the development of the product lines and business, as well as to ongoing innovation. In these businesses, copycats are anticipated, so companies actually build into their business models the time it would take competitors to copy certain features of the program. They expected to underenforce their copyright and comfortably rely on first-mover advantage to build their revenue stream. Likewise, the inevitability of copying motivates developers to innovate. Thomas, a software engineer with his own privately held company, describes this business strategy:

There are other businesses that are very large that did [property] software [like us but] for other things, like ticketing and events. . . . [I]t's a whole industry unto itself. And so in that period, all of them came out with modules that do exactly what we do. So it's sort of like . . . we hit it, we picked up a number of [clients], but it's a race until the other people catch up, and then it locks up again. So [in one sector], we have got about a third [of the business]. There is another software program with about 20 percent maybe, and there is a bunch of little ones. But . . . you hit it, you move into something, you get a certain amount of market share quickly, and then it solidifies and you're stuck. And now we're in exactly the same place [as in previous business cycles], where there [are] people that switch here and there . . . But it's usually just little one-off sorts of things.

Thomas also admits that it is not a priority to protect whatever copyrightable expressions or patentable subject matter his business owns. Rather, he is very protective of his company's reputation (and its brand name). As I discuss later here and in more detail in Chapter 4, building and preserving reputation is a more worthwhile financial and emotional investments for the interviewees than preventing copying.

By contrast, in the branded pharmaceutical field, copycat drugs are *authorized* under the rules for generic drug development. Yet they are maligned for this role because they undercut the earned-benefit value of being a first mover in the market; one person I spoke to compared it to "stealing someone's homework." Dennis, an in-house lawyer for a pharmaceutical company, pointed out that this also means generics hurt innovation:

[This company develops] novel targets, novel drugs—just very novel. Looking for unmet medical needs, and stuff like that. . . . [T]he *easy* money [in our industry] is where you are the second or third comer to the market. . . . The first comer to the market generally doesn't make the most money. . . . The only way you as a generic are going to exactly produce [our protein therapeutic] is if I give you the cell line I used for it, if I give you the broth that I grow the cell line on, if I give you the manufacturing technique or the harvesting technique. . . . Unless

I give you everything that I do, you will not be producing [the equivalent of our drug]. . . . [W]e need more innovation. I don't believe necessarily that we need more generics.

Dennis, longtime IP counsel for several large companies, worked in pharmaceuticals for more than twenty years and has seen company layoffs because of precarious profits. He was personally and professionally close with the research scientists at his various companies. To his mind, being first to innovate and occupy a market should (and usually does) entitle a person or company to sustainable revenue. But because of increased competitive and crowded fields, Dennis complained, being first may be a liability; generics and the related (but different) "me too" drugs may do better in the market than first-to-market branded drugs.[22] They certainly drive down the prices of the first-to-market drugs.

Dennis accepts that follow-on innovation and competitive copies are inevitable, and he agrees—as do many other interviewees in medical research—that affordability for patients is a critical concern. While we might assume that the first drug on the market is expensive because it absorbs and must recuperate the costs of research and development, when I asked Dennis whether patents are necessary to establish first mover advantage to recuperate those costs, he dissociated patents, market share, and affordability. Dennis identifies the problem of consumer affordability as an issue of excessive marketing by drug companies to patients, not of patent protection:

Sometimes we charge too much. I don't know what the solution is. . . . And our industry is not clean. . . . I think the worst thing that happened to the drug industry . . . [was] when they allowed the direct consumer advertising for drugs. I think it is absolutely embarrassing. You know, if I see one more Cialis ad, or Viagra, or Detrol . . . [O]ur client isn't the patient. . . . I believe our client is the doctor. . . . Because the doctor is the one that's interfacing with the patient, and I think it's wrong for us to advertise drugs and then create illnesses.

This executive's approach is to balance the need for profitability to pursue novel medical treatments with the importance of ethical professional behavior in the medical industry (which can lead to moderation of profits).

Dennis's experience coincides with data from various fields regarding diverse motivations of individuals within corporations.[23] I could not confirm whether (as he puts it) the folks "upstairs" in his company thought differently. But it is notable that this chief IP counsel seeks moderation in the revenue-driven IP strategy to align ethical beliefs with business practices.

To be sure, there may be cultural differences between pharmaceutical companies and software companies that explain the varying tolerance for copying. Certainly, the patent system historically treats the two kinds of innovation differently, favoring patents that result from medical research (device and composition of matter patents) over those that dominate the e-commerce and financial fields (business method patents). This was true until the controversial 1998 decision in *State Street Bank v. Signature Financial Group*, which substantially broadened patentable subject matter to include new methods for doing business, including tax strategies, insurance, and banking products. Cultural and legal distinctions aside, however, both the tech and medical industries represented in these interviews recognize the value of being the first to market for business vitality.

Building Market Share

Though being first to market is closely related to building a profitable market share as an essential tool for business development, developing a substantial customer base requires different strategies. Being first may be relevant to establishing rights in trademarks and patents, but strict enforcement of IP rights can frustrate the development of a growing market share. For many interviewees, underenforcing IP rights is an effective strategy for establishing relationships with consumers and growing their businesses.

One way of doing this is to offer products and services for free to attract customers or clients. Musicians play for free in the subway ("busk") to build mailing lists and sell CDs. Publishing industry actors benefit from open-source academic repositories, such as the Social Science Research Network, which drive on-line traffic to fee-subscription repositories, such as Project MUSE and Lexis/Nexis, thereby increasing their brand recognition. The main goal of several venture capitalists I spoke to is "scalability"—they focus their revenue stream on how large the demand for their product (and its production) can grow. Here is one such entrepreneur describing a current investment model in high technology:

One of the weird things going on right now is that investors have said, "If you can bring me a business that has tons of eyeballs, tons of users, with some kind of network effect where people who are on Twitter like to be on Twitter because other people are on Twitter, so you get a network effect . . . and it doesn't cost, in the grand scheme of things, all that much money to run the service; we are talking about a few tens of millions of dollars to run Twitter. . . . Go for it. Let the thing get up bigger and bigger and bigger and bigger, and somewhere along the way, we'll figure out how to make money." . . . Because when you get a huge number of people all doing some activity, you ought to be able to find some way of [building the network—]Craigslist, right? . . . Everything on Craigslist is free, free, free, free, free, free—oh, except for job postings and real estate in five cities.

The underenforcement of exclusive IP rights—copyrighted music, copyrighted academic content, patented or copyrighted software, access to products and services—is a common mechanism for building demand in the beginning.

Critically, underenforcement is both deliberate on the part of the IP owner (giving copies away) and haphazard but widespread on the part of the public (copying and disseminating without asking). Were underenforcement to require an affirmative act by the IP owner, market share would not grow as successfully as it does. Productive underenforcement requires market actors (consumers and secondary users) to engage in infringement with the hope they will not be sued.

Here is an example from the music business of the "economics of free" and the symbiotic relationship between fans and musicians from Mary:[24]

[Ripping CDs is] free marketing. . . . [T]he people that actually buy CDs [are] still there. . . . [I]f you're not going to buy it, but you're going to give it to your friend, great. If you're going to give it to five friends, that's fine. Because I'd rather you have it if you're not going to buy it. I mean, I'm not saying I want everyone to do that, obviously, because like I said, I'm still depending on the sales. But . . . I discover a lot of good stuff by someone just bringing me a CD. . . .

I think in a few years, it'll be more important to me that people aren't burning [CDs]. Right now, they are just getting the word out. And the whole point for me is people showing up at shows. So if they are burning it for a friend and the friend comes to the show, that all feels great. I think . . . in a few years, my answer will be different about that, because I'll feel like, "OK, people know it now." . . . [T]here'll be a strong enough fan base that then I'll be like, "OK, you don't need to share it with your buddy." . . . Whereas often, people think, "Oh, she's more successful—now I can really burn it." My ideal scenario, I think, would be that the bulk of my income comes from sales or placements—in things I believe in, not just random commercial stuff. And that I . . . play seventy dates a year with a good guarantee. . . . So the work-life balance is a little [better than it is now].

For Mary, copyright infringement can build an appreciative audience and generate new music. She assumes that, eventually, fans will buy her music and she will recuperate the cost of her work through ticket sales to her concerts and music sales or downloads. The copyright will be important *eventually*, but for *now* she embraces the notion of sharing freely. She acquiesces to the infringement of IP rights now to encourage lawful transactions later, and build her reputation. Were fans not able or willing to "rip" CDs, Mary's career might not be as vibrant. But fans who rip music can face gigantic and disproportional statutory damage awards against them given the wide monetary range in the Copyright Act.[25]

Thomas, the software entrepreneur, builds his business in a similar fashion as Mary:

[I]t's a running joke between [my partner] and I: there have been three times in our history where I spent a year working with [our largest client] for free, just working with them for—not full-time, but I . . . gave them the software, worked with them on it, kept running back and forth to different buildings of theirs, and, you know, for basically a year, I had to listen to my business partner saying, "This is a waste of time. This is a waste of time. This is a waste of time. This is a waste of time." At the end of that year, we got a contract for 150 buildings and it changed our lives.

The "running joke" between Thomas and his partner is the subtle difference between wasting time and money and building a profitable client base. The endurance and generosity of working for free—what some interviewees describe as a "business spirit"—turned Thomas's small software company into one of the most competitive in his particular niche field. His persistence paid off when he was able to expand the business because he worked free of charge and gave away his software product to several large potential clients. After about a year, each signed lucrative multiyear contracts for service and software with the firm. (Thomas's business model is discussed later under the section "Loyalty and Personal Relationships"). The primary value these clients sought in Thomas's company is the loyalty of one of its principles and the customer service he provides.

Giving service or goods away for free to build a market is a ubiquitous business strategy: free samples, a free trial-month membership, initial discounted terms of service. IP-protected products, however, are so easily reproduced and distributed in our digital age that free giveaways may have exacerbated financial risks and consequences. Nonetheless, the risks are worth taking for many of the people with whom I spoke and the infringements worth tolerating, not only to build market share but also to keep clients happy. This is true not only for corporate entities that might be able to absorb more financial risk but also with individuals who might not, and as much with copyrighted works (music, art, and software) as with patented inventions (e.g., drugs, medical and electronic devices).

An in-house IP attorney for a profitable business press with whom I spoke recognized that using a digital rights management system to provide the content for which customers had already paid made bad business sense, even if it protects against potential infringing uses. Underenforcing the copyrighted content—to the point of leaving it open—was the better business model for maintaining and satisfying existing customers:

Of course the whole emphasis . . . is in the opposite direction: we want people to copy and post it. We took all of our [digital rights management] off all of our content because it was driving customers crazy. And I don't blame them! I mean, we had two customer service people doing nothing full-time but . . . holding the hands of customers who had paid for stuff and then couldn't use it. . . . I said, "This is nuts!" You know, so we lose—so people shoplift. . . . It happens.

To be sure, this business press survives off the purchase of products. Free doesn't apply to everything, but underenforcing IP is essential for maintaining and growing the customer base.

Steve, the cofounder of a successful media development company, advises clients on just this strategy to build brands and expand merchandizing efforts. His company broadens the reach of specific media products—films or books—by developing diverse platforms through which the particular story and its characters can live and grow. An obviously important platform is the Internet. While moving media products to the Web is not as immediately lucrative as selling products and access directly to paying customers, Steve is confident that it eventually builds stronger networked communities of customers:

Is online going to make you a gazillion dollars? No. Is online going to enhance your story so that more people buy more books, and . . . go the movies more often? Yes. . . . And you can monetize that experience. *Battlestar Galactica*, if you remember that show . . . had a whole series online, and no one really knew about it unless you were an überfan. . . . But if you [were], you got *all* this other information about *Battlestar Galactica*, and . . . what happened was, then all the torchbearers who loved *Battlestar Galactica* went to their own little blogging stations and then told everybody else. Which drove more people to the SciFi Network.

"Free" has its downsides, of course. What if the risk doesn't pay off? What if customers expect free and refuse to eventually pay? Most people feel the risk is worth taking. Their experience shows that pursuing customers rather than infringers results in healthier business relations. Were they pressured to perfectly enforce their IP rights—either to establish precedent or to preserve future rights—they would spend time away from the work they love. Less art and science would happen. Building market share by tolerating copying or giving things away free serves all three pragmatic aspects of IP: it builds relationships, the reason for the giveaway; it eventually leads to financial transactions for products or service; and it reflects a choice about how to spend one's finite time and energy.

However, not all interviewees feel that underenforcing IP rights to build market share is optimal. Some find the practice to be potentially anti-competitive because established companies, by giving away products and services to maintain market share, can squeeze out smaller companies and newcomers.[26] This practice is particularly lamentable, they feel, in the context of high-tech giants like Google, Apple, and Amazon:

Our biggest problem is what I think is endemic to the world of technology; is you have got these very large, vertically integrated companies who don't need to make money from all the different layers of the stack. Like Apple, right? They don't make money, for example, on the telephone service. . . . They make money on the hardware. They make a little bit of money when they sell applications to you. Whereas Google gives away its phone operating system, doesn't make any money on the hardware, doesn't make any money on the software, but they make a lot of money when people access Google from their mobile phones and get to Google ads. . . . It's very challenging in the software business because they keep throwing more things into their phone operating system, Android, and it's free. Free! Oh, yes. "We are giving it away!" Not only is it free—they give away the source code. So talk about something that makes it very, very hard to be . . . nearby [market-wise] trying to extract value. So I call it the "tall value-chain problem." And you have got a competitor like Google, who has a really tall value chain . . . and they are just like, "Well, we are going to take all the money out of right here, and everything else we are going to give away." And it's an old, old strategy in Silicon Valley, which is you try to commoditize the thing that the person just below you or just above you in the value chain makes.

The "tall value chain" strategy is also a problem in the book industry, as described by Joseph, a publishing executive. Joseph has worked in the book industry his entire professional life, in bookstores as a book buyer, and now for a thriving niche press. We sat in his living room, which, as might be expected, was piled with books:

I think independent bookstores are trying where they bring in sidelines with higher margins. [It] seems . . . a necessary thing they need to do with their business model, given . . . the aggressive kind of approach of Amazon, [which sells] books at a 2 percent margin and [doesn't] care, because they are selling a TV along with it, . . . and they would love for the independent bookstore to be out of business. They would love nothing more. And they . . . have kind of gone on record as such. I mean, they don't really hide the fact that they . . . don't really come from the approach of "a rising tide lifts all boats." I mean, they come more from a . . . "We want to be the only person selling books."

Joseph explains how when certain industries are decreasingly diversified, the risk of consolidation and negative effects of monopoly grow. And yet Joseph admits that providing goods and services for free is "standard practice" and necessary for sales. Furthermore, he doesn't much worry about copyright infringement in his small press, much like the IP lawyer at the larger business press. Interestingly, however, Joseph distinguishes giveaways and infringement (neither of which is not worrisome) from price gouging (which is):

[Infringement] doesn't bother me. . . . It's not about downloads or whatever. . . . [B]ooks aren't going the way of the music industry. [The book industry problem is] the consolidation of . . . who *can* do it and who can't. In publishing . . . it's becoming increasingly hard for small bookstores to be around. They are shutting down . . . even small publishers. . . . [P]eople want to pay only $2.99 to download [a book]. They don't want to pay $26 for the hardcover. *That's* the monetary leak.

To Joseph, the problem is scale and consumer expectations. The protectibility of the good through IP law is less relevant.

Whether building market share with giveaways is a sustainable practice for every industry or company, it is nonetheless common. It grows the audience for and augments the reputation of the good or service. Underenforcing IP (distributing freely, tolerating infringement, or permitting uses that would otherwise require authorization) to build market share is essential for most business strategies, although it does make it difficult for small or new businesses to compete.

Complementary Products

Many of the business agents discuss "commoditizing complements" and "monetizing the experience" as a means of extracting profit from creative or innovative work. Like building market share, commoditizing complements is often connected to underenforcing IP-protected goods. In the example earlier, Google leaves its software open, sells only a small part of its email service (corporate and vanity emails), and largely profits from its advertising. And in the earlier quote about *Battlestar Galactica*, Steve's company helps to drive audiences from the Web to cable networks, movie theaters, and stores that sell related merchandise and service as a way to "monetize" the entertainment experience.

Accounts of the ways that businesses commoditize complements abound in both scholarly and popular literature: companies earning profits on razor blades rather than razors, or on printer cartridges rather than printers.[27] This kind of bundling strategy was described by the interviewees particularly in industries in which profits appear under siege due to rapidly changing market structures and customer behavior, such as in the software, music, and publishing industries. For example, musicians say that while selling tickets to performances brings in money, selling merchandise at performances—including notebooks, T-shirts, decals, and CDs—is equally important as a complementary sales practice. Bundling contracts for support services with software and text-based products is also common. In some cases, software is underpriced (and its IP right against copying underenforced), but the investment is more than recuperated through service contracts. Software can also be customized for specific clients, so the comparatively high price for the product includes both the customized software and its ongoing maintenance. The purchase price relates as much to the customization (which is harder for competitors to copy) as to the aspects of the software protectable through IP laws. As explained by an in-house lawyer for an e-commerce company, "AT&T spent about $4 million just to buy [our] software. They probably spent another $2 million in just professionals—which we also offer. We offer professional services to help install it."

In textbook, scholarly, and trade publishing, business agents adapt to make money. Frank, a lawyer for a medical and social sciences journals company describes business innovations in his company that are linked to online advertising revenue rather than pay-for-access:

One of the newer projects that we have started, which is actually neither a journal nor a book, is an online website. . . . It includes a fair amount of third-party content which we have managed to get permissions for, and is an advertising supported site designed for oncologists, and which has a kind of variety of information sources. There is a kind of a news feed. There is more detailed reference material. There [are] abstracts of . . . current developments in the literature. . . . [W]e're looking at a lot of kind of service options now in this space, and we're looking at services that are delivering that kind of product online. . . . I think it's the first kind that's exclusively advertising supported. We do have other services which are subscription-based services in the nursing space and a few other disciplines. But this is the first that is a deliberate attempt to be non-subscription-based.

As the publisher struggles to maintain profit margins, Frank actively worries about the future of copyright protection for his company's content (aggregated scholarship) in light of the recent "anti-IP" open-access movement for academic research and writing. He is clearly aware that the company must add value to the content it publishes beyond the (now-automated) aggregation and distribution service. The news-feed program offers a new service to readers alongside advertisements, thereby monetizing the content authors create for free but that the publisher distributes at a profit.

Bob, the vice president of a major publishing house, describes the complementary products in its "fulsome" program:

We also deliver . . . things called "one-stop planners." . . . We do precanned PowerPoints. We do test banks. . . . They really want us to deliver a full suite of . . . probably twenty additional products . . . so when they buy the book, they get the additional products. There will be workbooks for the life of it, so that the kids can write in the workbooks and throw them away. There will be all sorts of ancillary materials. So this is the sort of centerpiece of a fulsome program.

This system discourages other school districts from copying ancillary materials instead of paying for their own customized program. And since the materials change from year to year, the rapid evolution of the materials negates what illicit copying does occur. When I asked directly about how illicit copying hurts sales, and whether these complementary products make up for that loss, Bob said:

There's no effective way to work around [resale of used books or illicit copying] except to create new editions, get the teachers to adopt the new edition. But then as price resistance will creep in, *they* wouldn't do it. So it's hard not to sell it once and have to sit around for four years. The Internet became a great tool for linking in supplemental content, but then you would have to buy the book to get the password to get to the Internet for a one-year college term subscription. So now, to the extent that you could supplement the resource, you're providing a much more fulsome resource, but you are also driving it as more of a transactional sale.

Bob also told me that his company is involved in education lobbying and reform because "states tend to drive our business . . . [as] they aggressively refresh the product in the schools." This large publishing house's business strategy is to create and shape its market by complementing products with desirable consumer services or legislative fiat.

Smaller companies compete for business in the same way. Joseph, the publishing executive at the niche press, told me that when his firm felt threatened by the change in the book market, it developed a new strategy of placing his high-end books in stores, such as Urban Outfitters and Crate and Barrel. It has been a highly successful "complementary products" strategy, because people pay full price when the books are marketed as lifestyle products:

A lot of what I have been doing has been moving my business from sort of the traditional book market, because fewer people are buying books in bookstores or museums. . . . And I have been moving my business from those to boutiques—Urban Outfitters, Anthropologie, West Elm, Crate and Barrel, Williams-Sonoma—and I have been shifting all of my business over to that. And it's put us in a place to where . . . all the sales have gone down in . . . bookstores and museums overall. . . . But I have managed to keep my sales—I have actually gone up. I have managed to just take that money that is missing from there and transfer it over, and find this new . . . space for it. . . . [W]as I a visionary in seeing that coming? I don't think so. . . . [I]n sales, you . . . follow the dollar, and I saw that there was business there, and . . . I had an early foot in. . . . [I call it] the . . . 'Anthropologie effect,' . . . where [we] merchandise this book with a whisk and an apron that . . . have a similar color . . . or maybe complementary colors. Or . . . it might be a book on Indian cooking, and they have . . . an apron with . . . an Indian kind of fabric, and stuff like that. And it's merchandised with this whole thing, and people will gladly pay full price for it right there. And they'll buy the whisk and the apron, too. And not even think about, "Oh, I bought this for full price." It's because they are buying part of a lifestyle.

These strategies are also present in the science and technology sectors, where patented technology is sold alongside complementary services; communication devices are discounted but the service contract is locked in for twenty-four months; drug prices are subsidized but testing and diagnostic services are costly; patented software is thinly protected but customers pay for service and specific applications. Both copyrighted and patented products are bundled with profitable arms of the business (service and non-IP-protected goods). In some of these cases, the business leverage derives from a loyal customer relationship rather than from the creative or innovative good, which could be protected by IP if necessary. In other cases, the business is structured around a contractual relationship, a cornerstone of business and the subject of the next section.

Contracts

It seems commonplace to note that contracts for goods and services dominate business practices.[28] But where IP rights play a limited role in originating or developing the creative and innovative work, contracts are an important supplemental part of developing business relations. Indeed, the two benefits interviewees seek from contracts are absent from IP rights: (1) the predictability of the enforceable bargain and (2) the personalization of the business relationship. IP's unpredictability as a revenue-generating business feature is the source of complaint among diverse industry actors (most notably among artists, writers, high-tech and e-commerce players). Similarly, interviewees wrestle with IP's one-size-fit-all application no matter the industry, actor, or behavior at issue. Contract law provides an antidote to both of these problems with IP.

Many interviewees describe contracts as the most efficient mechanism for conducting essential business and fostering relationships. One person asserts that the benefit of a contract is that its critical terms—licensing fees or fees for work or service—are perceived as immediately understandable and reliable. Sometimes, these parameters implicate IP rights in terms of the scope of editorial control and future use, but the interviewees rarely mention how IP might act as leverage in contract negotiation. The contract terms that they highlight are aspects of business relationships over which they seek more control than they perceive IP law provides. While interviewees admit that they are inattentive to certain contractual details relating to IP (e.g., royalty rates), they are able to describe other terms with significant detail, including fees for service and attribution rights. Often times, IP law has little (or no) effect on terms that are actually central to the future of the business relationship and their satisfaction with the deal. The important and supplemental role contracts play in developing business relations contrasts with the background (or invisible role) the statutory grant of IP rights play in originating or developing the creative and innovative work in the first instance.

However, focus on contracts means that interviewees may end up extracting less revenue than IP rents would allow. Some might say that the IP's full value is realized in the contract's reallocation of benefits (e.g., a transfer of some IP rights in exchange for promise of attribution or non-derogatory use). However, as will become clear in the following pages, maximizing profit is not the primary motive in many contract negotiations. Revenue is important, but generating *predictable* revenue is the purpose of the contract. Moreover, interviewees believe that asserting contractual rights and waiving, minimizing, or even ignoring IP rights improves ongoing business relationships, cultivates an ethical mutuality of promises, and nurtures additional professional and personal values, like attribution and autonomy.

For example, Dan, the music composer who also directs his own performance company, talks about how "there isn't enough money in this business to compensate me or anybody who is involved in it for the effort they put in it. And that's true everywhere in the field." So when he negotiates the license fees for musical work his company will be performing, he considers other factors in addition to price:

[Licensors] have these very complicated formulas based on whether you are a for-profit or nonprofit theater, how many performances, how many people in your pit orchestra, . . . the size of your theater . . . But $3,000 [for a license to perform someone else's music] is generous . . . given the amount of money that we are spending on the production. . . . [W]e want [the composers] to be happy and feel like they are appreciated. . . . So given the amount of effort that these composers have put into these works, and the likelihood that they will just gather dust after one performance, . . . I think it's worth recognizing the value of what they've done.

This performance license represents a balance between the user's capacity to pay, the financial payoff to both parties, respect for the musician's effort, and the nature of the business generally. Dan thinks about the terms of the license to perform another person's music as a statement about the need to accommodate and address mutually beneficial aspects of professional production. For him, each actor should personalize the financial transaction to account for specific performance and professional contexts, which will inevitably moderate and mediate the royalty. To be sure, copyright is a baseline for the transaction itself, but the final agreement memorializes values other than exclusivity and its financial benefits, including quality of music production and performance and breadth of distribution.[29]

The owner and CEO of a lucrative media development company characterizes his individualized and generous approach to work-for-hire provisions as a way to work around the copyright system to benefit not only his employees but also his company:

I remember working at a Fortune 500 company, [my partner also] remembers that, and we don't treat our employees that way. So [you bring] something to me and we love it, let's go together. You will own certain rights; [the company] will own certain rights. You will get a majority of the publishing. . . . [W]e work out a fair deal because we want everyone here to be successful, and we want us to be successful, too. That's why we are a small company.

His approach contrasts with traditional work-for-hire relationships (in both copyright and patent) in which employees have little control over the end product and no ownership in it, although both approaches advance the same purposes: to manage quality output, provide acceptable compensation, and exercise meaningful editorial control (whether by employer or employee). These working conditions are more important than the provision of IP rights; several employees told me they could not remember specific IP terms of their employment agreement, including the work-for-hire provisions, but they could remember balking at (or negotiating) noncompete clauses, salary, and seniority (as a factor in creative control). Their attention to certain contract terms reflects concerns over autonomy and the value of human capital as indicators of professional success and satisfaction in IP-rich fields, which concerns can be protected through contracts more than through the IP they are hired to generate. This is consistent with evolution in business over the twentieth century that increasingly disassociates IP ownership from individual authors and inventors and shifts it to companies, leaving attribution interests as an inalienable right that employees or independent contractors value and on which they depend for professional success.[30]

The consideration and celebration of the individualized contract as a supplement to business strategies is not so much an evaluation of the efficacy of contracts as further evidence of the misfit of IP protection as a vital tool to developing and sustaining creative and innovative businesses. Some interviewees went as far as to say that service contracts, not the right to prevent copies or unauthorized distribution of IP-protected goods, keep business thriving. In several software companies, the value of the company's IP appeared negligible. As one in-house IP attorney says, copyrighting software

doesn't really give you any value. Copyright law is a joke. . . . I mean, it really is. . . . Unfortunately, it only costs, like, $25 a copyright application, or I wouldn't even [bother to register the copyrights]. . . . [I]f it was [as much as] $1,000 an application, I wouldn't . . . do it.

Instead, the company makes money from customer relations—with updates, maintenance, and training services. Could these businesses strengthen the value of the exclusivity their IP rights provide, for example, by tightly controlling the amount of computer terminals on which their software is loaded or closely monitoring client adaptations to their software? Yes, and they do, but they focus on the clearly profitable and growth-oriented aspects of their business embodied in specific contractual terms for service.

In contrast, some interviewees overenforce IP with the same goal: to promote compliance with critical contractual terms. For example, some patent holders will use even weak patents to intimidate competitors, and thereby obtain or enforce favorable contract terms regarding joint ventures or noncompete agreements. As Kevin, the telecommunications venture capitalist, describes:

All the companies that I work for, we all file patents. And we are pretty cynical about it, and we say, "We don't think these patents are really necessarily going to ever be worth anything to us," except [that] in this whole morass [it] is people wagging sticks at each other and saying, "I am going to sue you over your patents."

Similarly, a media consultant hired to create or produce copyrighted content describes threatening to file for an injunction on the basis that his firm owned the content—even when it didn't—to enforce the firm's contractual fees for service.

Contract and IP law are sometimes in sync and other times at odds. Whether it entails underenforcing or overenforcing IP rights, the goal of asserting the contract is to fulfill its central terms, which more precisely than IP articulate the priorities of creative and innovative industry players. Despite the commonly stated function of property to facilitate investment and productivity, interviewees generally perceive contractual bargaining to be more customizable and efficient than IP rights to facilitate production and trade. This is because IP is both too broad and too weak; it is miscalibrated for the goals of the business and for the customers and other users who seek access. As such, interviewees describe contracting around IP default rules, ignoring infringing acts, and relying instead on promises, and other normative business practices to sustain their work and livelihood. And although implied or express contract terms are by no means the whole business relationship,[31] enforcing formal legal rules (of IP in particular) to effect compliance for its own sake is infrequently worth the cost and conflicts with normative professional values concerning the production, distribution, and use of creative and innovative work.

Loyalty and Personal Relationships

It may sound mundane to highlight loyalty relationships as central to making do in business, yet every interviewee expresses the importance of professional and personal relationships with partners, clients, and fans for the vitality of their businesses. The mutual trust in these relationships is frequently the focus of conversations around the maintenance of creative or innovative professions, the reasons they work in the particular business, and the stimulus for signing and complying with contracts. Relationships with collaborators or consumers are also credited with enhancing products and services.

For example, authors and artists consider their agents to be more important than their publishers or lawyers in procuring and facilitating remunerative work. Agents are valued because of the personal ways they develop their client's career. Barbara, a self-supporting writer, describes her agent's qualities this way:

> She was a good boss because she had been a teacher before. . . . She had a very, very, very strong moral center. If you told [her] something and asked her to keep it confidential, believe me, she took it to her grave. She cared deeply about her authors, and it was a personal care. . . . [O]ne of her authors was . . . hardworking, and feeling depressed and down, and had a real problem, because her kitchen was a disaster. And . . . that seemed to be the focus on it, and she needed $10,000 to do her kitchen. . . . Well, [the agent] was selling a book for her. And I don't know where the negotiations started out, but it wasn't anywhere near $10,000. But when they got done, it was $10,000, because that was the amount. So [the agent] called her and said, "You've got your kitchen." That was the way she worked. . . . [S]ome agents have viewed it as their job to sell, sell, sell. She viewed it as her job too, she could do that; that's not a hard thing to do. But [she also viewed it as her job] to make a career, to plan.

The agent would fail if she did not help her client sell the book, but the quote illustrates how professional success and satisfaction involves taking care of her client's personal life as well.

Meredith, a music agent, confirms that sometimes the best business practice is to cultivate the person and hope that the product will follow:

I tend to do my best work when I am interdisciplinary, [that's] what . . . moti-vates me, as opposed to focusing on "I have one hundred dates I want to book for the year," . . . for an artist. And I just don't get the best deals, to be frank. I'm a bit of one of those nicer managers, which is something I kind of struggle with internally. [T]here's sort of people who are known for being nice manag-ers, who may not get everyone the most money they can possibly get, but you might work with them for years. And there are managers who . . . everybody hates, but they make big deals. People deal with them because they make big deals. It's just a really messed up kind of community, I think . . . [people] are not always professional. Like most people working in music never had a job before music. . . . They didn't work in the corporate environment. Some people did, like me. I worked in a corporate environment.

The general consensus in the music and writing communities is that happy, almost intimate relationships with agents and managers are central to professional development and sustainable business.

But the personal connection extends beyond individual artists and their agents to more traditional corporate business structures. Several investors (ranging in industry from telecom to web services to medical devices) also characterize relationship building as essential to financing business development; people invest money because they trust you and what you believe about the project. Many of the interviewees chose busi-ness managers or signed clients on the basis of loose networks of friends and acquaintances. Whether the company was "highly recommended" because it was large and impressive is less important than whether the individual sales person seemed "trustworthy" or "saw things similarly" as the customer.

This isn't surprising. Indeed, it's obvious, and the body of literature on the role of trust in the development of a competitive business is vast and growing.[32] Especially now, in the age of online commercial transactions, the in-person exchange is becoming rare and loyalty and reliability more valuable.[33] But the point here is threefold. First, the interviewees speak as often about developing and maintaining personal relationships with clients, consumers, and partners as they did about originating, creating, and distributing their creative and innovative work. Second, the development and maintenance of loyalty relationships is often pursued at the expense of or in spite of the assertion of IP rights. Third, the interviewees explicitly conflate organizational and firm structure with individual behavior and motivation, saying that firms have "personal relationships" with clients and consumers, or calling a business organization "trustworthy."

When these emotive descriptions ("trustworthy") are uncomfortably attached to legal abstractions ("corporations"), the interviewees are in fact talking about "two sets of individuals each of which is trusting the organization of which the others are members."[34] This redirection of individual-corporation relationship to individual-individual relationship may explain the complex and sometimes diverging obligations inherent in the particular roles within an organization (e.g., an agent with a fiduciary obligation to a client and to the firm in which he or she is a partner). The affective role of personal relationships in building and maintaining creative or innovative businesses and the imputation of emotional relationships onto organizational and firm behavior are prime examples of how the rational actor model and economic analysis of incentives and maximizing wealth is eclipsed by other interests, behaviors, and intentions.

A book publisher explains how getting a book from concept to sale is "all about personal relationships" between editor, author, marketer, and buyers. I understand this to mean that the motivation to get work done and do it well has a lot to do with enjoying working with certain people and not having to work with others. As discussed earlier, Thomas, the software engineer had a conflict with his business partner over how to retain clients, especially because their software is not unique or robustly protected. His eventual advantage in the dispute was that "every major client relationship is my personal relationship." Thomas builds and maintains these relationships with reliability and honesty, as an individual and principle in his firm, whatever contingencies might arise. A web designer says his most successful projects were those when he and the client worked well as a team with full authority over the project without having to defer to upper management. Productive teamwork, built around a trustworthy relationship in which vulnerabilities are exposed but not exploited, ensures a valuable product and ongoing client relationship for him. Michael, a pharmaceutical consultant, believes his best business contracts are with companies without too much ego and with which he could work as a partner:

They were smart. . . . They didn't get into any of this, "You hurt my feelings. Why wasn't I included in the meeting?" They didn't get into that. It was very, "We got work to do. Let's just get it done. Oh, you can do that? Fine, get it done. That's not in your area, but you want to do it anyway? Great." Everybody worked together. It was a really small, closely knit team. . . . [T]he tone [the leader] set was, "We are all brothers and sisters here, we are all . . . just going to work together."

These businesspeople confirm the common understanding that without cultivating honest and reliable relationships with clients, the business—whatever its sellable good (music, book, website, medicine, software)—suffers. In many ways, the importance of personal relationships overlaps with a business's good will and reputation, which is the subject of Chapter 4.

Relationships not only create business but also increase business and enrich the experience of pursuing it. Melanie, a filmmaker, finds that establishing personal relationships in the course of developing and shooting a film is particularly rewarding and, at certain times, key to doing her job efficiently. She recounts:

[A television station] called me and hired me to make a film for them as part of a series they were doing. That was a very hard series. It was about Native American history, and they teamed me up with a Native American filmmaker. And I feel very proud of that project, both for what the project ended up being, but also for the experience, sort of what I think I did, which was to make the relationship with this filmmaker. . . . [W]e made it work with . . . no help from [the television station], and that's what made the project as rich and strong as it was.

On another occasion, she mentions how these relationships translate into favorable licensing terms and productive dealings more generally:

The first thing I did when the project was just being conceived was go down to the [national charity], meet with the head of the archive, make sure he knew I was a serious person, that this was an important project, that I was interested—

and it wasn't inauthentic, but I was interested in what they do as an organiza-tion. . . . And so that human relationship with him . . . meant that when it came time to then hammer out a deal, he was willing to make a deal.

As these accounts demonstrate, personal relationships may translate into bottom-line benefits. While referrals in exchange for a reduced fee are common, many of these relationships are also based on nonmonetary interests—personal synergies, autonomy and control, or enhancing the work product and the satisfaction of teamwork. In addition to being an-other tool the interviewees use to "make do" in IP-rich fields, personal relationships in professional spaces also improve their experience doing creative and innovative work. These relationships feature centrally in professional development, successes and satisfaction, more so than the IP asset they may claim and license.

Reputation

Chapter 4 is devoted to reputation in the professional lives of those cre-ators and innovators I interviewed, but here I briefly describe its contours to complete the typology of ways of making do in IP-rich fields. The in-terviewees nourish their reputation as a primary value in their lives for three reasons: reputation is their identity (the self that acts in the world), reputation drives business (as form of goodwill and brand value), and reputation is a form of expression or representation of the self and one's thoughts (speaking, performing, and sharing). As with many of these cat-egories, reputational interests can be both under- and overinclusive of IP law's scope. Interviewees reach for trademark, copyright, or patent law to protect reputational interests, but only trademark comes close to ad-equately protecting the full dimension of reputational interests the inter-viewees describe. And sometimes they relinquish rather than enforce IP rights to enhance their professional reputation, to make money, to ensure their professional and personal autonomy, and to establish meaningful relationships.

Many interviewees identify with their work on a very personal level— it authenticates them to themselves and to others. Projecting themselves through their work is an extension of themselves (and of their company, if they feel closely affiliated). Because of this, many folks eschew "the marketing machine" (as one interviewee called it), and many only self-consciously cultivate their reputation when it feels authentic rather than manufactured. Many writers and artists decry the work of "promoting," leaving that work "to my manager" or "agent" or "husband"—despite the fact that they clearly care about how they are viewed by others, especially by their audiences. Mary's explanation of her views on reputation and professional development is typical of the individual creators I interviewed:

[My agent] and I talk about "brand" all the time. . . . When I first heard that word years ago, I just balked. I was like, "Brand? I'm an artist! I don't want to think about brand!" . . . But now I've grown to love that, because instead of forcing me into a brand that [my agent] wants, she is saying, "Let's look . . . closely at the way you are and make that your brand."

Company representatives similarly say that being "true to the company's identity" is central to its overall business strategy. "It's an identity," a book publisher says, referring to the books they commission and how they edit and sell them:

A lot of people talk about "love" and cooking. . . . [T]hey have to love what they do, to have that love, and that's why people can feel it. And I think that publishing, especially these type of books . . . with [so few] books a year, everyone is so closely identified to them, and it becomes personal.

For these interviewees, the development and protection of professional identity for a business's momentum and bottom line is vital. And when that reputation is tarnished or diminished, the response can include aggressive legal claims resembling (but also distorting) IP rights.

As is discussed in Chapter 4, these reputational concerns map very loosely—if at all—onto US IP law. Trademark law is primarily concerned with consumer search costs, assuring consistency in product and source based on brand identifiers. Only dilution in trademark law, which includes a right against tarnishment for famous marks, comes close to protecting against the kind of reputational injury interviews care about, and there, the dilution cause of action is fraught with difficulties of proof and only applies to a limited selection of marks. Copyright law protects the substance of original expression, not attribution or misattribution. And patent law (like copyright law) facilitates the disaggregation of ownership from inventorship (or authorship)—inventors may be credited on the patent but lack control over the invention's use. Where developing one's reputation is both a motive and a mechanism for sustaining creative and innovative work, IP law remains a weak and ill-fitting tool to accomplish that end.[35]

AUTONOMY AND ILL-FITTING IP

According to these interviews, IP protection is a weaker incentive to produce and commercialize creative or innovative work than courts and legal doctrine would have us believe. A consistent theme throughout is that people seek control over their time and the manner in which they work. The misfit between IP rights and how interviewees make a living exposes just how important autonomy and personal relationships are. The lamentation that IP rights do not facilitate such control only emphasizes the interviewees' desire for autonomy as a form of self-rule.[36] As one sculptor said, quoting advice she received from a mentor years before, "When you're an artist, no one can fire you, and it's as challenging as you make it." What function, then, does IP play? To start, the utilitarian explanation of IP overstates the importance of money in IP protection and transactions.[37] And the taken-for-grantedness of autonomy and personal relationships as fundamental to creativity and innovation reveals itself in the breach of IP law's formal application.

It is worth nothing that some interviewees say they would rather work independently (as a solo), whereas others prefer being an employee in a company. Self-rule, therefore, does not mean being an owner or chief executive—it means that within the work environment the person can exercise creative or innovative control over the object of work.[38] Sometimes, working in a company provides precisely the right situation—the tools, space, and colleagues—to foster creative and innovative behavior. As one chemical engineer says about his position within a large company, "That's one of the nice things about being in a team . . . even if you are not the guy who gets the inspiration, you have a role." At some companies, it is not the managers or owners who restrict the freedom of their creative employees, but the clients. As a web designer says, "No matter what I happen to think about the[] end results, if the client's happy and *they* consider it successful, and depending on the terms that they define, then they'll come back for more. . . . [But] I have different standards." Indeed, many of the artists, musicians, and engineers complain that a major hurdle in their work is capturing the attention of a paying audience. They describe the ongoing challenge of shaping their output according to the desires of consumers. This challenge exists for people whether or not they are their own boss. With freedom, therefore, comes risk. Some interviewees choose to manage that risk by being part of a larger organization, which affords some freedom, while others prefer to go it alone, which maximizes autonomy but usually heightens financial uncertainty.

Would strengthening IP rights provide interviewees more autonomy, stronger relationships, and less financial risk? From an economic perspective, it is not apparent from the interviews that more exclusivity to demand more revenue for longer periods of time would help the individuals with whom I spoke. While hypothetically, stronger IP rights would allow software engineers or musicians to collect more and higher licensing fees on a regular basis and for a longer time—thereby "freeing" them from a salaried or hourly job—none of the interviewees described the need for stronger or longer IP rights. Of the dozens of interviews with successful writers, scientists, engineers, and companies filled with IP, the dominant priority was to achieve consistency in an adequate income stream (rather than its maximization) in order to work and produce regularly. A musician explains, "I feel like I've structured my life for a really long time around just the opportunity to do music. . . . [O]nce I did get a job, how few days can I work so that I am free to be doing that?" A filmmaker, who believes she has found the optimal balance, says:

Since I became a producer [at a company], I have made enough money. . . . And then now that I have my [own] company, I actually make a little bit more money, and it's kind of been nice . . . but I didn't expect it. . . . I just wasn't ever driven by monetary [gain]. . . . I am a working filmmaker, and that's the difference.

From the corporate side, stronger IP rights do not translate to more freedom or control within a business sector, except to the extent that strong patents can be asserted defensively to protect certain research programs and offensively to generate revenue. These examples come primarily in the pharmaceutical and medical device industries. But the downside of asserting these rights, as explained to me by both the corporate agents and the individual creators, is the administrative work of producing and protecting IP: the internal facilitation of harvesting IP and policing of the IP rights. This is not to say the IP generation and protection is not worthwhile, but neither is it the central form of profit-making and professional development for most businesses. Some industries rely more on IP than others (in my data, pharmaceuticals and medical devices, photography, and some text publishing). Others downplay or minimize the importance of IP as compared to other ways of achieving optimal business success (music, documentary film, software, visual art, e-commerce business systems, and home-goods manufacturing).

The freedom or autonomy that most interviewees seek is the ability to work: at painting, writing, lab science, designing, innovating networks, or facilitating someone else in this kind of work. What they want is to continue to create and innovate; as Camille, another of the sculptors I interviewed, says, "I didn't set out thinking this is a great livelihood. I just set out: this is what I want to do." In the discussions about access and opportunity to do their work, there are echoes of Immanuel Kant and the roots of property ownership in possession and will. As Robert Merges has written, "The essence of property for Kant is this: other people have a duty to respect claims over objects that are bound up with the exercise of an individual's will."[39] Indeed, the people I spoke with desire to make their mark with the things they do or make, whether or not a consuming public consistently purchases their work. But Merges extends Kant's definition to say that the "full realization of [one's] autonomy interest in [one's] output] includes the right to make a living from . . . selling it."[40] The interviews bear out this economic conclusion only in part. Camille continues:

I don't think I followed any model. I think I created my own model, which was direct sales. . . . There was no gallery. I think I had a kind of belief that people believed in my being an artist, and when I connected with people, they liked helping that happen.

Camille eschews the intermediaries, even if it would make her more money, because she sought to balance autonomy with a reasonable living. Making money is one of three pragmatic uses of IP, but it is sometimes traded to accomplish other equally important goals. Individuals seek to primarily be recognized for their work—to be "known" or "credited." Even companies do this through brand recognition, building a corporate identity with a particular reputation for goodwill and community involvement, sometimes at the expense of maximum profits. Indeed, the interviews cover many examples of corporate agents underenforcing IP rights to sustain professional and community relationships and their own freedom to maneuver. Like people, companies seek to be recognized and known for what good they do or make, and the interviews with individual corporate agents reflect that.

The description of intellectual property in tangible terms (despite IP's necessarily intangible nature) reinforces the desire to make one's mark on the world. The "thingness" of a work means it can substantively reflect the will of the maker.[41] If "will is that aspect of a person which decides to, and wants to, act on the world," then the created thing is a stamp or mark of that personal will.[42] Indeed, the desire to wield influence and affect one's community by putting things of emotional vibrancy or aesthetic or practical value into it was overwhelmingly common throughout the interviews. Recall Joan, the painter-turned-sculptor, who describes her works as puppies:

I wanted to make [paintings.] I wanted to publish them. But I didn't want to own them. I'd rather they be in a public collection. . . . [M]y painting exists, I got to make it, and it's being well cared for. It's like having a litter of puppies and you found a good home for each one of them.

She does not necessarily give her work away for free, but the kind of control she asserts over it does not encompass "owning," either; instead, she makes sure that wherever it is, it is "well cared for." Many interviewees describe their ideal professional life precisely this way: "to be free to write the best book I can"; or, "I wanted to be an academic scientist . . . because I didn't want someone telling me the project that I had to work on." Seeing oneself in the work, or enabling others to recognize you through the work, motivates work and defines fulfillment for many of the folks I interviewed. As Leo, the painter, said, "I paint because I want to share my visual sense of how I see the world, how I see color, with other people." Whether talking to chemical engineers, biologists, e-commerce innovators, or to painters, photographers, and writers, in the interviews people regularly conflate "doing work" with "the work" they make (although IP law largely resists this conflation). The freedom to work is as important (if not more so) than the work product and one's exercise of control over it.

IP law does not always speak to this form of autonomy. Some of the interviews recognize IP rights as beneficial because they provide "freedom to operate." For instance, scientists are convinced to facilitate multiple patent filings because, they are told, doing so enables them to continue doing research at reasonable costs. In the creative arts, it is possible that IP rights sometimes enable creative control, providing artists with a veto over where and how their work is displayed. But in many other circumstances, IP rights impede or are irrelevant to the artists' and innovators' interests. Overbroad patents or patents of questionable subject matter are "sticks" to shake at competitors that divert resources and may sometimes quash collaboration. Digital rights management for copyright frustrates users and customers and is therefore strategically withdrawn. As I have said earlier, in rejecting the "sweat of the brow" justification for IP protection,[43] IP is not a reward for "doing work" except insofar as it protects some aspects and some uses of the work. Many interviewees were stunned to learn that copyright law does not require attribution or prohibit misattribution, or that patents can be granted for minimal work if it meets certain standards. Similarly, many wish that critical uses of their work required licenses. These interests are largely left unserved by US copyright law (and by patent law, to the extent that it does not require inventors to be "credited" except on the patent itself). Nonetheless, interviewees (other than lawyers) reach for copyright (or trademark or patent) to try to enforce attribution norms and prevent reputational harms. Here, overenforcing IP derives from misunderstanding and a frustrating misalignment, which may lead to subsequent misshaping and exaggerated claims of IP rights. In these instances, IP law is vulnerable because it does not fulfill the interests of autonomy and relation-building sought by those creating and innovating.

To this, one might say: so what if IP rights are flexibly applied? Sometimes they are asserted and sometimes they are not. All the diverse ways of making do are not evidence of a problematic misalignment but instead of a malleability that gives IP owners choices. Underutilization of the full panoply of rights granted under our IP system is simply that. It is not waste; it is freedom. But freedom for whom? And how is the waste measured? This critique ignores the users and the consumers, many of whom are also the creators. It assumes a clean bifurcation of rights holders and their audience, a division that defies real experience. It further leaves the public—the primary beneficiary of the IP system—in the hands of the whimsical generosity or intolerance of IP owners. Relying on the collective sufferance of rights holders has social costs relative to stymied creativity, innovation, and collaboration. Leaving the choice to assert IP rights with rights holders and the burden of legal uncertainty with audiences and downstream creators misconstrues the IP system as about owner welfare instead of cultural and scientific progress that requires conversation and circulation.[44] This is a regrettable mistake, given that my interviewees overwhelmingly indicate that IP rights are unnecessarily broad and generally out of sync with their goals and needs.[45]

Considering the misalignment as instead a beneficial malleability further ignores a trenchant rule-of-law problem. When claims of control over creative or innovative work are irrelevant or lead to disappointing results in court or private settlement, the formal rules purporting to protect that work may diminish in the eyes of those involved. What good is the law when precisely that which the artist or scientist cares most about (e.g., attribution, time, reduction of risk) is left unprotected or underprotected by the IP system that claims to incentivize them? "When enforcement is perceived as unfair not by a small marginal group, but by a larger group . . . the resulting rift between the legal norm and the social norm not only makes the benefit of compliance non-existent, it also tends to reduce greatly the degree of internalization of the legal norm."[46] The principle of the rule of law depends on a more accurate alignment between practice norms and legal rules.[47] In other areas of law—criminal law, tort law, real property, or constitutional law—rules exist that adapt to normative changes. Adverse possession is a clear example in property law. And the evolving definition of fundamental rights in constitutional law is another. Intellectual property law appears less flexible on this score. Indeed, most IP law reform over the past fifty years reflects isolated interests of IP owners protecting particular stakeholders in select industries and has moved at a glacial pace.[48] It has been a lopsided and unrepresentative process.[49] Given how rapidly creative and innovative developments occur and disseminate in our digital era, intellectual property's failure to reflect practices and expectations on the ground may lead to significant instability if not also to hostility.[50]

IP-rich creative and innovative industries sustain themselves in diverse ways, only a small part of which is through IP. That IP is sometimes relevant but not often central to the economic health of most creative and innovative industries—that it takes a backseat to many other strategies for making work and making do—undermines the long-standing utilitarian explanation for IP. This explanation has substantiated a century's worth of IP expansion through statutory and case law. If the explanation for IP is wrong, this expansion has been misguided. Optimally, we should instead seek an alignment of IP rights with the motives and mechanisms for engaging in creative and innovative work. This might mean formalizing the gaps where exclusivity is unnecessary (as either compulsory licenses or outright exemptions) so that relationships and markets can form more freely. It might also include providing for inalienable attribution rights to avoid stretching IP claims to cover complaints of defamation and other ego-based interests. I take up this particular issue in the next chapter, devoted to reputation, which is a commonly discussed interest but one that IP unsatisfactorily protects.

Reputation

IN *IMMORTALITY AND THE LAW: The Rising Power of the American Dead*, Ray Madoff writes that "even more than one's body or property, one's reputation is often essential."[1] She then makes "the obligatory reference to Shakespeare's" *Othello*, in which reputation comes up several times—although it means different things to different characters.[2] In act 2, Cassio, Othello's faithful lieutenant, laments the ruin of his reputation as "the immortal part of myself"—losing it leaves him nothing but "bestial." In act 3, Iago, in the process of planting a trap for Cassio and ingratiating himself with Othello, distinguishes pickpocketing ("'tis something, nothing") with "filch[ing] from me my good name . . . [which] makes me poor indeed." Is reputation that which, as Laura Heymann writes, "can be owned, . . . stolen, and has calculable value"?[3] Or is it the immortal in all of us, the identity we cultivate and seek to control against all odds and largely "outside the realm of law"?[4]

With the growth of the Internet, blogs, and social networking sites, reputation has become both more powerful and more fragile, and thus writing about reputation has taken on new importance.[5] With more at stake, individuals and companies may reach more often for the law to assert control over their work and manage risk to their professional and personal reputation. Most scholars and commentators agree, however, that the legal regulation of reputation is challenging, inconsistent, controversial, and complex. Part of the reason for this is the sheer variation among the facets of reputation—evident even in Shakespeare's warring formulations—and its role in both private and public life.

The interview data reflect the complexity of reputational interests and assertions made to protect them, but also the importance of building and maintaining one's reputation for personal fulfillment and professional success. Reputation, in fact, appears to be the aspect of professional and personal life that the interviewees care most about.[6] There is no doubt that reputational interests function both at the private level, in terms of self-actualization and self-identity, and at the public level, in terms of status, information sharing, and the social glue of affection and belonging. Concerns over reputation affect financial wealth, but also the autonomy interests and valued relationships described in the previous chapter. This chapter aims to determine the role of reputation and its various contours in connection with these central concerns of artists and scientists.

The interviewees say again and again that the value of a good reputation cannot be underestimated and yet many describe it as uniquely fragile. Although IP law features in the interviews when reputation is discussed, existing law is rarely satisfactory to protect it. Of all the legal doctrines available to professionals in the creative and innovative fields, trademark law—the development and preservation of "trade identity" and "business goodwill"—is the most useful for addressing business reputation and attribution. And yet today trademark law is primarily directed at facilitating commercial transactions and avoiding consumer confusion.[7] Except in the relatively small set of cases in which truly famous marks are subject to trademark dilution (especially dilution by tarnishment), and broad sponsorship or affiliation claims are viable, trademark law is not intended to cover claims for recognition, credit, defamation, or libel. This is especially true for the everyday artist, inventor, and his or her small business. In some instances described in the interviews, trademark law became the appropriate vehicle for protecting certain business practices and building (or protecting) revenue. And in these cases, intellectual property law obligingly aligned with the interests of the creative and innovative professionals. But in most contexts, trademark law does not map well onto claims about the importance of nourishing and protecting reputation for both personal and professional benefit.

Copyright and patent laws are even less relevant to protecting reputation. Copyright law neither requires attribution nor prohibits misattribution except in the case of a limited selection of visual art.[8] Patent law does not regulate attribution and credit beyond requiring that the proper inventor be named on the patent itself.[9] As many scholars have noted, common law actions for defamation, protection of privacy, and right of publicity more closely align with claimed harms and benefits concerning reputation than does IP law, and yet common law claims are notoriously hard to prove and expensive to bring.[10]

Despite IP's misalignment with reputational interests, if we take the interviews as a guide, the primacy of reputation directly affects IP production and transactions. Without clear avenues for redress or protection of either the public or private dimensions of reputation, individuals describe how they overprotect by withholding their creative or innovative work because their reputation is directly attached to it. In economic terms, this would be considered irrational holdout behavior, since there is no price at which they would license or otherwise share their work. This demonstrates both how serious the interviewees perceive that the reputational harm from disseminating their work can be and how unsatisfactory the benefits without adequate protection. In contrast, the fragility of reputation also fuels the impulse to broadly and liberally distribute work in order to nourish one's reputation in the public eye. To cultivate reputation, interviewees describe widely and freely sharing their work despite IP protection that controls access to maximize rent. IP's blunt protections disserve the multifaceted and contextually specific nature of reputational interests. Here, the misfit between normative claims concerning one's reputation for creative or innovative work and the legal claims is profound.

An explanation for IP law's misalignment is its inability to account for the coupling of the personal significance of the work with its public value. This deficit is particularly acute in the context of reputational interests because reputation is inevitably a product of the mutual relationship between producer (a private entity) and consumer (the public). Reputation depends on the engagement of an audience; collective judgment originates with the public.[11] The audience (be they readers, viewers, users, consumers, partners, or bystanders) participates in nourishing reputation by forming relationships, akin to personal relationships, with pieces of work. This may seem obvious in the context of a creative work—like a painting or a novel—in which the artist or author intends to become known by his or her signature or style. But it is also true with corporate output. Brand loyalty and product attachment are ubiquitous in our advertising age and are metaphors for friendship and affiliation. Moreover, consumers want and need the benefits that derive from reputational signals: "Consumers . . .

use trademarks not just as a shorthand for the physical qualities of a product but as a way of signaling their own emotional participation and identity, which then feeds back into the meaning of the brand in a continuous loop."[12] Reputation is the quintessential communal object, controlled and made by an anonymous crowd. And yet it feels uniquely one's own, profoundly precious and deserving of tight control. To be convinced, one need only think of Apple and other lifestyle brands that cautiously guard their brand but simultaneously seek personal affiliations with millions of people. Although reputation feels deeply personal, its lifeblood requires public circulation and engagement. How, then, can it be owned or controlled as a form of property? The circularity of reputational development—behaving less as personal property and more like a relationship—render disputes seeking to stabilize or protect reputation messy and contentious. Critical and yet capricious, in part because of its shared nature, claims to control reputation barely (if at all) correspond to well-defined and comprehensible IP claims.

And yet if we return to trademark law, its dual goals most closely articulate the web of concerns the interviewees express concerning their professional reputations. Trademark's dual goals are much discussed in the literature in terms of the mixed public-private nature of trademark interests: consumer interests (message clarity to render purchasing decisions optimally efficient) and mark owner interests (protecting investment in the development of product quality as represented by the mark). Indeed, "there is a deep historical ambivalence as to whether . . . trademark law is better thought of as a species of property law (i.e., *IP* law) or rather as a species of tort law."[13] Tort law focuses on duties between people and within communities, whereas property law (although it establishes relationships between people) traditionally focuses on the definitions and mechanisms of exclusion and the duties owed to each other with regard to things. The interviews reflect this situational and doctrinal ambivalence between public and private interests, and property and tort claims.[14] And because trademark law remains unsettled on this score, interviewees appear to provide accounts of overprotecting their reputation and underclaiming their work through trademark-like claims as a way to recalibrate for themselves a legal regime that feels awry.[15]

How is IP law awry? Specifically, the individuals and company agents I interviewed see the value of reputation in nonmonetary terms—as intrinsic benefits regarding their autonomy and identity or regarding their relationships (between people, among audiences, and within a community)—whereas IP law (including trademark law) largely focuses on market success or protecting financial investments. The interviewees infrequently describe reputational interests in terms of protecting or facilitating economic transactions or as a way to accumulate or protect wealth. Instead, they use emotional and expressive terms to describe the role of reputation for personal identity or community—reflexively to provide an account of a person's life or relationally to build connections with users, consumers and the broader community in which the individual or company is situated. These two interests parallel the pragmatic dimensions of IP described in Chapter 3. The reflexive relationship of identity further explicates the desire for autonomy: independence, self-directedness, security, and intellectual freedom. The relationship with an audience and in a community is integral to building and sustaining affiliations and connections. To be sure, these interests can have financial implications, but as interviewees tell it, a person or a company's reputation is first and foremost about emotional and expressive consequences.

While these interests may seem specific to individuals, companies also nurture their reputations, self-consciously, if not aggressively. By its nature, a company attends to its relationship with its audience, customers, clients, and what, in trademark terms is often called "goodwill."[16] What may be surprising, however, is that while the company's attention to reputation relates to its financial health (and ongoing existence), the company agents explain reputational harms and benefits in emotional terms, as if the company has human interests. In other words, they sound like personal torts not trademark claims: defamation, intentional infliction of emotional distress, misrepresentation, misattribution, and invasion of privacy. Protecting reputation via trademarks resembles—even for corporations—protecting a person.[17] As expanded in 1995, and amended in 2006, trademark law includes dilution by blurring and tarnishment, which comes closer to protecting against the kinds of harms the interviewees fear. Today trademarks "are simply one part of the overall brand experience, which aims to transform the brand into a persona, engaging consumers at an emotional level."[18] But dilution is restricted to famous marks and has an ineffective history in the courts.[19] Whether strong trademark claims do or should exist (and many argue that trademark claims are properly limited to unfair competition or consumer confusion harms[20]), the interviewee's injuries resemble bruised egos or more personal attacks. Of course, corporations don't have egos or subjectivities to injure. The "misplaced fiction of corporate personality," especially in terms of trademark dilution law, as Professor Sandra Rierson writes, has detrimental consequences for marketplace competition and free speech.[21] And yet the "age of the brand persona" is certainly upon us.[22] Indeed, as I discuss here, a common metaphor throughout the interviews is that of the *brand as offspring*.

The similarity between individuals and companies is also notable in discussions about the reputational interests of autonomy, control over identity, and cultivating relationships. Firm motives and individual motives overlap and their accounts and explanations resemble each other. Both individuals and corporate agents seek to build with their reputation relationships that will foster professional satisfaction and personal well-being. This undermines the standard narrative that corporations exist only to make money and that their assertions of control over their creative and innovative output is directed only to that end. More than a label or informational filter, a person's or company's reputation becomes a dimension of the good or service in and of itself (or in the words of many interviewed, a "priceless asset"). The word *priceless* came up as a trope throughout the interviews to describe a company's goodwill, and I am reminded of other things we deem "priceless" and therefore ostensibly beyond market control: people, body parts, and intimate relationships, to name a few.[23] When corporate interests begin to resemble nonmarketable subjects, and companies start to sound like individuals, the application of legal rules that considers them distinct may disappoint or distort.

Individual professionals unattached to large organizations rarely know much about the legal regulation of reputation—through trademarks, torts, or otherwise. And so when a musician, sculptor, or academic chemist describes reputational interests, the nature of his or her claim requires close attention to its legal character. The complaint may be an allegation of trespass (e.g., "she took something that belonged to me"). Just as often, it may reflect a breached duty of care (e.g., "he hurt my feelings"). Like the corporate actors, these individuals are motivated to rectify offense and police moral boundaries. Rarely are the reputational injuries attributed to market inefficiencies or defects. Even discussions about plagiarism and name stealing are less concerned with pocketing unearned value than with ethical and normative insult. Confusing property claims (of ownership and exclusion) with tort claims (of relationships and duty) further complicates the messy and diffusive role of reputation in creative and innovative work. Moreover, the frequent conflation of the public aspect of reputation (relationships with others) with its private aspect (professional and personal autonomy and self-fulfillment) heightens the urgency with which reputation must be protected. To many, protecting reputation becomes a matter of self-defense.

Collectively, the interviewees provide an account of reputational interests in creative and innovative work that, aside from trademark dilution law, is largely misaligned with available IP claims. This chapter describes the variations in reputational claims from the most to the least aggressive, illustrating a spectrum of strategies that individuals and companies deploy to manage their most prized "possession." Along the spectrum, individuals describe reputation in one of three primary ways, depending on how they balance private and public interests and autonomy and relationship building: reputation is identity (reputation is the self or organizational entity that acts in the world), reputation is social glue (reputation attracts and sustains audiences and communities around common ideas and principles), and reputation is a form of expression or representation of the self and one's thoughts (maintaining and performing one's reputation is expressive behavior). Each of these categories is an overstatement—reputation cannot fulfill any of these roles on its own—but this indicates how strong the expressed feelings are. These three categories overlap and sometimes conflict within the same interview, providing further evidence for the elusiveness of reputation but not of its unimportance. Reputation is a slippery concept, but the metaphors provide firmer contours using the interviewees' own words to help assess how, if at all, IP law may be relevant.

Professional reputation contributes to professional success broadly construed. But whether over- and underprotecting creative or innovative work to safeguard reputational interests, the dominant motives in the interviews are less focused on the pecuniary. The respondents rank the importance of reputation for autonomy interests and building desirable relationships as ends in and of themselves above the importance of reputation for economic wellbeing. Interviews may overreach with IP claims to protect these interests related to reputation, but they may also underprotect the work for the same reasons. This distinguishes the experiences of artists and scientists from the justifications for IP to encourage creative and innovative risk taking by facilitating the recuperation of financial investment through control over the work. The choices made in professional contexts, when the reasons for protecting or controlling reputation are to foster a fulfilling life doing creative or innovative work, primarily reflect matters of dignity and respect, not property.

"THE BRAND IS MY BABY"
AND OTHER FAMILIAL METAPHORS

Throughout the interviews, people compare works of art, innovation, and even goods or bespoke services to their "baby." It was particularly common to hear such familiar or emotional metaphors in terms of copyrighted content, but people also apply them to trademarked goods and some patented inventions. Lawyers say their clients refuse to license copyrighted content or trademarks because they want to protect "something that is like their child"—no deal is good enough to relinquish control over their work product. "I don't care about money. I really don't care," a lawyer recounts a client saying. "Don't let them do that with my work." A more graphic example of this sentiment can be found in the Steve Jobs biography from 2011. When Jobs's Pixar stock shares were worth $1.2 billion, he told the *New York Times* that "money did not mean much to him." He said, "There's no yacht in my future. . . . I've never done this for money."[24] What *did* Jobs care about? He cared about control and perfection. The success of Pixar meant that he and his partner John Lasseter could keep the *Toy Story* characters out of Disney's hands and prevent them from making bad sequels and unseemly merchandise. "That would have been like molesting our children," Jobs later recalled.[25]

The notion that work is like offspring reverberates in the interviews: it arises again and again in terms of legacy and identity. Comparing the work to a child is a variation on feeling that the work is an extension of one's self into the future. With both come the righteous expectation of control and ownership, akin to that which we have over our bodies. One writer talks about her novels in terms of finding her "place in the world," and another artist talks about approving (or disapproving) uses of his name and work in terms of whether the secondary use "honor[s] it." A sculptor who makes large-scale public art describes the maintenance of her work, and hence her reputation, "like child support." The work is a person, or enough like a person, to be supported with provisions and treated with honor and respect.[26] This is more than anthropomorphizing; the metaphors go further. The interviewees talk about the conception, birth, and raising of creative and innovative works, and they exhibit attachment and the desire for control. As one marketing professional says about work created in-house:

If someone here comes to us and says, "I have a story about a boy and his dog," and we read it and we go, "Wow, it looks great," we partner with them. We don't take it over. We are different than other companies, where we don't say, "All right, now we own your property." We partner with them, and we take it out together. . . . [I]t's an ethical thing for us. . . . [I]t's their baby, it's their child, and we don't believe in taking it away from them. We believe in partnering with them.

The notion that creative or innovative output is like a child—it needs nourishment and protection and constant attention, and is perhaps inevitably spoiled—speaks directly to the tendency to overprotect the work with exaggerated legal claims including overbroad cease-and-desist letters.[27] Many parents would do anything to protect their children, including stretch or break the law. Although this metaphor is familiar for creative expression (resembling the myth of creation springing from the genius's head), it is altogether inappropriate for trademarked goods with or without high brand value because legal protection of trademarks derives from use and consumer recognition, not creation.

The metaphors used for reputational exchanges also resemble family or tribal structures. "There's an endorsement that comes when *you're in-side*," a software entrepreneur says, describing how easy it is to pitch an idea to investors when you have ties to successful companies. Indeed, "the brand is my baby" reflects a sense of identity and identification with the work but also a desire to be affiliated with certain people or endorsed by certain entities. Interviewees want close-knit structures to foster belonging and worth. In addition, relationships with publishing houses, music labels, certification organizations, and high-profile clients strengthen public reputation and grow the relationships themselves, making such affiliations worth protecting at high costs. An in-house IP lawyer tells me that certain business deals (in his case, building a facility in a major US city) earn the company "street cred" with important industry actors who can help propel the younger company's business. A musician, initially very wary of branding strategies and overcommercialization of the music industry, decided to sign with a label to be "associated" with its "brand." She says:

I have tremendous respect for [the label]. They are small, but they are one of the leading . . . labels. . . . They have a really solid mailing list, and they have a really solid relationship with a lot of radio and . . . people everywhere I've done radio interviews, people are like, "When we see a [label] CD, we listen to it." Like it gets to the top of the pile. Where there are a million artists right now that are independent, and it's so hard for anybody to sift through that. There's so much crap, you know? . . . The label thing just sets you apart . . . enough that people are going, "OK, . . . they like her enough to put her on the label." And it just allows you a little bit more attention then.

To this musician, the association with a reputable label brings credibility and clout, and much-needed distinction in a sea of indistinguishable new, young musical talent. She describes courting the label (and it courting her), being nervous about signing, and then wondering later what the big deal was. She thinks that her decision to sign with the label in some ways resembles a romantic commitment; it entails long-term, significant obligations to each other that will reflect on both parties and contribute to the community at large:

I'm going to build really slowly people that I feel I can stay with for a long time, and people who I feel are going to represent me in a way that completes that brand and make me feel really comfortable. . . . And you know, it's very easy—I see it all the time, where people jump on immediately with someone who talks the talk, and it just burns out so fast.

The reputational benefits this musician gleans through the affiliation and sponsorship sound less like a business association and more like a family.

Several other businesspeople, one in web design and another in film and television, believe that being "loyal to the brand" and to "the core values and essence of the brand" makes for happy clients and a successful business. In this context, loyalty resembles the familial and tribal demand that community norms be followed to claim membership in the group. Several in-house lawyers I spoke with try to engage employees in IP development by playing on their company loyalty and their desire to be known as part of a certain community. Where some employees resist disclosing innovations for fear that patenting will prevent the work's widespread distribution, in-house IP lawyers encourage invention disclosure and patenting by playing to employees' drive for status and esteem in their particular community. One lawyer says:

Patented . . . software . . . [became] something that developers really understood. They personally benefited from it, but there was a long, long history of invention in this country. . . . [Y]ou become part of a storied legacy of the great inventors. So patents were, in a way, a much easier sell. . . . So there's a real ownership and pride and coolness factor to being an inventor, and being part of the company . . . an IBM or an HP.

Another in-house lawyer recounts a company ceremony during which employee-inventors are awarded a silver dollar in exchange for the patent as part of a "historical" ritual that dates from the company's founding; here, patents are "badges of honor." This language describes less the isolated hero-inventor or romantic creator than the person who is driven to be part of a collective, desiring the prestige and worth of working together toward common ends. The company or label is a family or home, and the product or service is the offspring. The individual is a contributor or partner in the collective whose reputation originates and grows through intimate association and membership. It is easy to forget that interviewees are speaking about creative or innovative work and trademarked goods or services when the language used and stories told resemble parent-child or other intimate and close relationships.

"A PRICELESS ASSET"

The interviewees also tend to exaggerate the value of their work when talking about their company's reputation in the marketplace. Specifically, they aggrandize the value of the brand name, asserting that "the company's value is its brand" or that the trademark is a "priceless asset" or that "branding is everything . . . it's huge." The root of exaggeration is the perception that the company's commercial success is necessarily tied to the purity of its name and its identity in the marketplace. And such exaggerations about the company's reputation in relation to the quality of the company's product typically results in the overprotection of trademarks (e.g., sending overbroad cease-and-desist letters to those using similar marks on unrelated goods or services) in an effort to avoid marring reputation by association with similar names or logos. This occurs not only between ordinary market competitors, in which case the trademark claim might be strong, but also when an unrelated company or product enters a distant market and uses the same or similar word or device in their marketing. As an example, an IP attorney for a profitable academic publisher says:

Our brand is 90 percent of what we do here. . . . I once made a joke that didn't go over very well. I said, "You know, if we changed our name to the 'State River Publishing Company,' and published everything we do now, without changing a word, we'd lose 90 percent of our business." . . . Our brand is . . . by far our most valuable asset.

Similarly, an in-house technology licensing officer at a major research university describes one of her important roles as policing the university's trademark: "We have to be real careful even when it's used on books and things. Real control. [We] police it properly [because we must] . . . protect a priceless asset."

The interviewees also exaggerate the value of their reputation by attributing skyrocketing or plummeting sales solely to the way they use their brand name. One vice president and general counsel for a publishing company describes "sales [going] off a cliff" because of a rebranding campaign. In all these cases, there is, of course, truth to the assertion that the trade name is valuable and sells products apart from their actual quality. As such, the reason to police the mark is twofold: to prevent free riding or unauthorized use of the company name and to protect the integrity of the name from being spoiled. The first is a breach of commercial morality,[28] and the second constitutes reputational harm. Both are akin to Iago's "filch[ing] from me my good name."

Even when it is unlikely that there will be confusion over the use of similar names because the markets are disparate, the interviewees nonetheless describe forceful policing practices to protect the unique identity of their company or organization. Susan, a university licensing officer, describes her policing practices as so broad that they prevent even truthful or nonconfusing uses:

[It's] a priceless asset. . . . We get involved because we've been given the responsibility of the use of the name. That is, when Sony Pictures wanted to film [a bad movie here]. . . . [W]e didn't want to let them, even though . . . it was a true story, it did happen [here]. We didn't want to let them, because we didn't want to be associated with [that kind of] picture.

This same IP professional explained how she "had to" prevent a local pizza place from using her employer's name. She recounts saying to the owner of the pizza store:

Look: you're a little business guy. I don't want to cause you trouble. But you've got to stop. . . . [I]t's not my choice. I have to make you stop. And if it costs us money—even a lot of money—I have to make you stop.

In both instances, the IP professional protects the organization's reputation from unauthorized use of its name (or a similar name), arguably beyond the scope of trademark infringement because no confusion will occur. Dilution might be available as a cause of action, and it is certainly cited in any cease and desist letter, but dilution law is reserved for those rare instances when the offended party is truly famous. And although I interviewed some individuals affiliated with companies with well-known marks, true fame of the kind the dilution statute was meant to protect is infrequent, as it was in the interviews. These policing efforts therefore concern not only commercial reputation but also, as I discuss here, moral outrage. Using someone else's name, even absent consumer confusion, is perceived by the interviewees as an indelible harm that the law should prevent, even though it often does not.[29]

The irony behind these examples is twofold. First, both the publishing company and the university thrive on and support First Amendment values, yet the overprotection of their employer's trademark (prompted by the exaggeration of their brand reputation) impinges on those very same values in others. Second, both entities are sufficiently well known that the likelihood of confusion and any real economic harm to the reputation from the possibility of use by others is small. Moreover, in the latter example, the use of the trademark by the putative defendants is not likely to be actionable given the existence of strong defenses (e.g., nominative and descriptive fair uses) and the substantial burden of proving the likelihood of confusion or dilution.[30]

To be fair, it is reasonable to consider trademarks to be valuable assets in a company's IP portfolio. Moreover, brand value (the reputation of the company beyond the particular product to its overall identity in the marketplace) certainly drives business. Many lawyers I interviewed confirm the importance of trademarks (as compared to copyright and patents) as a form of IP worth protecting, even overprotecting, for the overall business health of their clients.[31] As one IP attorney working in a midsize firm tells me, "I do their entire IP portfolio and their trademark is probably the most important thing out there." Whether or not this is true, the specific role that trademarks play in distinguishing the company and its goods or services is akin to naming, a personal and intimate act, and engenders strong claims for this kind of IP.[32]

NAME STEALING

Name stealing appears to cause particularly acute reputational anxiety among personal and business relations. Professor Laura Heymann writes about the importance of names (and the affront of name stealing) in terms of its relation (and nonrelation) to IP law.[33] In her view, and my data bear this out, a name is a creative act with the attendant claims of property and ownership. Moreover, embedded in naming are perceived elements of uniqueness and the desire for recognition, such that having your name adopted by another (whether or not knowingly) may feel like one of the most severe and personal forms of trespass: "they've taken *my* name." As Judge Learned Hand wrote more than eighty years ago in the context of trademark infringement and reputational harm, "For a reputation, like a face, is the symbol of its possessor and creator and another can use it only as a mask."[34]

Perceived harm to identity is reported by a variety of interviewees: lawyers, corporate representatives, and individual creators and innovators. One lawyer describes some of his clients this way:

They can appreciate how important it is to own a name. . . . When they see some other company come out with a product with their name, they know like *that* [snaps fingers]. But if somebody comes out with a [similar] technology [they may not know.] But they know [about the name]. They . . . have enough pride in their name where they are going to come to you and say, "Hey, they can't do that, can they?" While if it's a technology and a patent, [they are not so aggressive].

Recall how Bob, the publishing executive and general counsel from the previous chapter, told of an offensive and unambiguous use of his company's trademark as getting "people very upset . . . and the first thing they're doing is calling us, saying, 'You've got to shut this guy down. . . . We were baited to step in [because] . . . our customers were upset.'" This is similar to the example of policing, described earlier, in which Susan, the university licensing officer, prevented a film company from shooting a scene on campus that depicted a truthful historical event because the university "didn't want to be associated with [that kind of] picture." In each of these cases, using the trademark without permission or in a manner deemed offensive is not only a business harm but a moral affront.

One interviewee, Steve, who worked in marketing and the film industry for years before starting his own business developing merchandizing opportunities for highly branded companies, regards the most challenging clients as those who perceive their name as unavailable for varied commercial opportunities. He calls these "closed properties":

Closed ones are difficult to break into . . . but we also understand that the closed ones have their own agenda. [A famous author] is going to control [her book title and characters. Her] thing is that, "Yes, I am the only one, and I am not letting these people deal with [my characters] because I am going to launch [my own subsidiary merchandizing effort]." . . . We have an easier time containing the people who are all over the place, because again, closed is based in fear that we are going to come in and mess with their property. And we don't want to mess—we are not here to tell you about your property. We are here to help you enhance your property.

Steve's dispute with these kinds of clients stems from their lack of trust in his handling of "the property"—the brand name. The client-author clearly believes the brand name is off limits to anyone but herself, even off limits to agents and business partners. She trusts no one with her name.

To manage the use of one's name, interviewees describe requiring the approval of all the things, people, or events with which their names are associated. Sadie, a full-time sculptor and part-time curator, tells me she has a low tolerance for using her work (synonymous with her name) in promotional material, even as inspiration for what would likely be considered a derivative work under copyright law. And yet when she sold a piece to a museum, she assumed it would (and could) use her work in their promotional material without asking:

Because that's about the art, and it's about the institution, and where the piece is. [But if] you just make . . . one of these [pointing to a postcard], and then on the back you're selling carpeting, I'm not sure that I really like that. Especially if I didn't condone it. You know, it's one thing if you come to me and [ask].

Sadie expects people to seek her permission when using her art and name to sell something unrelated to its display in an art museum, but she assumes the museum is free to promote her work using her name without permission. As a matter of IP law, both situations probably require permission, whether explicit or implied, to avoid infringement of the work. But Sadie is not concerned with the copying of her work. She is apprehensive about her *reputation* and how repackaging the work might change it and its associations and thus will reverberate to her reputation as an artist. Because of this, despite seeking out "places where the work can be shown, where it gets good visibility, where there's some . . . positive experiences," Sadie turns down many more opportunities than she accepts because she is concerned about how appropriate the venues are: "I'm not sure [the work is] gonna be cared for. I don't think they know what they're doing. . . . I don't even know why there were picking me." She experiences her work as an extension of herself and her identity, and how it is displayed and promoted will affect how her work, her vision and her professional identity are appreciated.

Individual writers, artists, and musicians commonly express major concerns regarding the effects of naming or misnaming on reputation. This is unsurprising in light of the literature on the importance of attribution and misattribution in the arts and sciences.[35] For example, Dan, the opera composer, said that, although he does not mind when people copy his music or "reinterpret a character in a nonoffensive way, . . . to make something which would be offensive and then put my name on it would be a problem." Likewise, Barbara, a famous author, sometimes employs a ghostwriter for her sequels and series but maintains "very close control over [the book series]. My name is on the books." A music agent describes how upset one of her clients was when the client's albums were placed, without approval, all over a kitschy candle-store chain as part of a marketing ploy. The interviews contain many other such examples in which the subjective misuse of a name is so disturbing to its namesake that it is almost a form of *name-calling*. Concerns about professional reputation collide with wounded egos, and because there is often weak (or no) trademark interest given the nature of the good or service, the claims resemble defamation rather than IP disputes in which identity rather than market harm is the primary driver. More than a physical harm, harm to one's "good name" is, as Cassio says in *Othello*, harm to "the immortal part of myself."

US intellectual property law does not facilitate accurate attribution or prevent misattribution in the way that most interviewees would want. Other than fairly thin protection in the Copyright Act for certain rights like integrity and attribution (so-called moral rights) and only for certain forms of visual art, the requirement that creative or innovative work be accurately attributed or maintained (and not changed or destroyed) does not exist in US IP law.[36] Before 2003, there was some possibility that trademark and copyright owners might succeed in claims about misattribution or mutilation of their work via section 43(a) of the Lanham Act, which prohibits false designation of origin. For example, in the early decades of film and television, filmmakers and actors frequently wrangled for control over their products to prevent changes like colorization, adaptation, and sponsored advertising in the name of reputational injury. They relied on an amalgam of copyright, trademark, unfair competition, and defamation law. But as Peter Decherney describes in his work on copyright and the film industry, court decisions were unpredictable because of warring policies among technological innovation, market growth, and authors' rights to control their reputation through control of their work.[37] Eventually, most court decisions reached a consensus that US IP law protects economic, not personal or moral, rights. And in 2003, the US Supreme Court decision in *Dastar Corp. v. Twentieth Century Fox Film Corp.*[38] closed the door on the possibility that IP law could require attribution or prevent misattribution.[39] And yet the interviews are replete with expressions of how attribution and integrity are crucial to the work's optimal promotion and dissemination, whether or not for profit, because they safeguard and manage the development of professional identity and audience.[40]

Concerns over attribution are also contextual. Some interviewees describe being very particular, or "anal," about who is permitted to use their name as a job reference and when they themselves will claim a work as "theirs." Two academic scientists, a biologist and a chemist, discuss the importance of inclusive attribution—recognizing a group of contributors rather than single authors without accounting for relative size of each individual contribution. But the scientists, both of whom are successful entrepreneurs later in life, also said that when hiring or evaluating colleagues in their field, they distinguish primary and secondary contributors to a work. From this I gather that inclusiveness helps build community and maintain ongoing relations, but when it comes to substantial rewards (e.g., a job, a promotion), knowing the details of attribution is also important. No matter the circumstances, however, attribution is about accurately conferring credit so that reputation accrues to the right person. And in both of these cases, the use of a particular name has both an intrinsic value (seeing my name on the work makes me feel important and worthy) and an extrinsic value (the work is good because so-and-so produced it). The naming function foments attachment and identification with the work and shapes relationships with colleagues or choice audiences. As such, intentionally misnaming is a violation of community norms that could harm communal and individual welfare.

But sometimes, the benefits of attribution are not used for accuracy or due credit but for ego or greed. Steve, the media entrepreneur and marketing professional, told me that he named a character in his promotional merchandise after his client, a CEO, because he knows this pleases the client ("sounding touched they say, 'Oh, you named that character after me?'"). He is playing to the client's sense of importance and connection with the product, even if the client had nothing to do with the new media product's development. Steve is a savvy marketing professional who does this purely to strengthen client relations: he knows that name, identity, and work are intricately bound together and that seeing one's name on or in creative work (even if your labor is far removed from the end product) builds attachment and self-fulfillment. Michael, the pharmacologist and pharmaceutical consultant, emphasizes how many times he has witnessed outright lying to receive credit and compensation: "People want to get their names put on articles, they want to get their names put on patents they had nothing to do with. You see that a lot. . . . [It's] blind-ass pride." People falsify attachment through misnaming in an attempt to establish the feeling of true attachment. Dennis, a lawyer in a pharmaceutical company, finds this among scientists rushing to publish their work, unaware of the effects of early publication on patentability. "Foolish scientists," he says, "they want to publish it all . . . It's all about ego." Susan, the licensing officer, confirms this observation, saying that "most of the time you're not setting out to create IP, you're setting out to do research, get your tenure or get a medal."

Lawyers also strategically harness the desire to be named when seeking cooperation from their clients. Ted, an in-house counsel in a high-technology company, incentivizes innovative disclosures by appealing to "bragging rights." Recall that Ted created a companywide monthly contest for employees to submit "cool ideas" they discover while working, and at the end of the month, the company votes on the "coolest idea" (whether it's protectable by IP or not):

They aren't fully baked enough to consider for IP purposes. . . . People basically just get bragging rights. We then rank them, and we announce the winners. We incent[ivize] people, it's like a $10 gift certificate or something. Anyone who submits a cool idea gets the $10 gift certificate. . . . And so [eventually, if we can protect it or commercialize it] that particular piece of IP [is] . . . held up as "This was Sarah's. She was cool idea number one, and here it is."

The desire to be known as someone who contributes good ideas is strong among the interviewees. While developing a reputation as a smart or able person is important for both emotional wellbeing and financial remuneration, according to the interviews, it also develops feelings of belonging to a certain community. Although some of the examples here describe negative feelings about perceived arrogance (or "ego") relating to reputation, the motivation behind claims of attribution is both self- and other-directed. That is, in a work community, belonging is not one sided—not only do artists and scientists work to secure their affiliation; they also believe that their community is better off for their presence. These examples of claiming attribution—naming and identifying oneself as belonging within a particular professional space and to a particular product—demonstrate the constitutive nature of reputation, its driving role in community building, its structural force among members of the community, and its simultaneously public and private character. This complexity makes reputational interests particularly unfit for blunt or narrowly focused IP regimes.

* * *

In each of these three examples, the interviewees attach their creative or innovative work to their name, identity, or persona in stark and strong terms: as offspring, as priceless, and as a comprehensive identity. The forceful and emotionally charged nature of these descriptions may explain the tendency of owners and originators of creative or innovative work to over-reach through IP enforcement, the legal regime that explicitly regulates creative and innovative production. Thus, seeking protection through IP makes sense in these contexts as a defensive reaction, but IP law's lack of comfortable fit undermines its relevance to artists and scientists hoping to protect these particular reputational concerns.

Given this lack of relevance, it makes sense that the interviewees find ways to manage or control their reputation without strong property-like claims. As described in the following section, they avoid self-conscious marketing techniques—which might otherwise be driven by strongly as-serted IP rights—and instead maintain or cull their reputation through restraint and trusting audiences. This restraint may frustrate IP's goals of widespread dissemination. Even so, the same goals and values arise: the importance of controlling identity in a crowded market, maintaining authenticity in identity and expression, and selectively building profes-sional relationships. Despite an uncertain legal backdrop, interviewees manage to protect and develop these interests.

REFUSING THE MARKETING MACHINE

The people I spoke with demonstrate a range of resistance to aggressive marketing for the purposes of reputation building. For example, many of the small company representatives and the individual artists, scientists, and engineers describe themselves as "choosy" in how they market their work. For them, building authentic relationships with audiences and other professionals is essential to their success, and that means being discern-ing as to who and how they put their name and work into circulation. If being choosy means opting out of certain engagements or publicity, even when reaching a wide audience, many interviewees restrain themselves and avoid expansive promotion.

Mary, the singer-songwriter, who concedes that a large audience is crucial to her financial well-being, nonetheless resists her agent's advice on developing an identifiable and sellable persona for those purposes: "[My agent] and I talk about 'brand' all the time. . . . When I first heard that word years ago, I just balked. I was like, 'Brand'? I'm an artist! I don't want to think about 'brand'!" Similarly, Leo, a painter, criticizes the New York art scene as overly commercial at the expense of authenticity:

I think that the art world is . . . a marketplace. And there are brands, in effect; artists who are . . . brands. . . . [A] firm like Gagosian . . . [is] like Proctor & Gamble. . . . [T]hey created a marketing machine and it works. . . . [But] the recognition . . . can actually get in your way, because if you start worrying about what other people think . . . people come in and . . . have different ideas about where to go with what. . . . [But] I think ultimately, what's interesting about the creativity to me is that the more personal it is, the more authentic. But I mean, every artist is expressing themselves.

Both Mary and Leo consider marketing as potentially detrimental to their work; although their professional well-being requires an audience, developing that audience should not be at the expense of creative identity. Indeed, Mary says that when she writes she is "not thinking, 'What do people want? What will they buy?' But [instead] . . . , 'This is what I am, and I would like to be able . . . to translate it.'" Many other interviewees express a related anxiety that branding efforts change the underlying good or service and may, by extension, change them as well. The idea that marketing efforts shape or distort an identity rather than reflect the one a person already has is well theorized in marketing literature.[41] Desires and identities are shaped and changed by popular culture, through explicit or implicit advertising that reflects a way of living, speaking, and looking. And so it is unlikely anyone can "stay true" to oneself or avoid the manipulative effects of a formative market—although this is an ideal for many, especially for those who believe their talent comes from within.

Selectivity in marketing is common for both large and small entities, both individuals and companies. Slowing (or withholding) market exposure is a surprisingly common strategy, and it is accomplished not only through restricting the use of a trade name (a protectionist move) but also simply by withdrawing from certain markets entirely. For example, for a book publishing company trying to distinguish itself in the industry with special-edition and arty, large hardcover books, selectively partnering with retailers who can help build a particular kind of business identity is more strategic than saturating the market with its books. One of the company's marketing executives, Joseph, says of his company's books:

[They] just don't exist anywhere else. . . . [If] some other presses came along trying to do it, it just wouldn't have the same "oomph" that [we] have with it. We seem to . . . [have] carved out a spot for ourselves as being . . . able to curate almost . . . our own museum for a lot of books.

The press succeeds at being unique—through its selectivity and skill in curating its collection—and as such develops an exclusive image for itself. Contrary to concerns over counterfeiting in fashion and other luxury good markets, for this niche publisher, copycat books and presses are unlikely competitors because of the publisher's selective marketing practices.

For those engaged in restrained marketing strategies, the intrinsic value of the product is the reason for its commercial success, as opposed to market inundation. They maintain that the qualities of the product or service and not advertising drive the business. As Mary says about branding: "I've grown to love that, because instead of forcing me into a brand that [my agent] wants, she is saying, 'Let's look . . . closely at the way you are and make that your brand.'" In other words, Mary, like many other individuals and companies I spoke with, embraces "the marketing machine" only for what she considers "the right" reasons. Similarly, Joseph, the publishing professional, seeks partnerships only when they augment the press's brand in specific ways:

I have always been in sales, and I have always had a hand in marketing for the most part, but [I approach my role now] . . . more now through . . . a perspective of brand and partnership. Rather than looking for someone just to buy the books, I am looking for someone to partner with who can give as much to our brand as we can to them.

He is not looking to "just" sell books. His job is to build relationships that bolster the company's identity and reputation in the field as the producer and purveyor of a certain kind of book. He perceives this as the essence of the company's product, and he believes its partnerships should reflect the core values or goals of the company.

Of course, placing the importance of authenticity in creative and innovative work above business, protecting reputation through targeted relationships rather than aggressive branding strategies, and avoiding the marketing machine means potentially sacrificing (or at least stagnating) revenue. That is, many interviewees describe branding (building a professional identity and maintaining it with a particular market) as simply a form of identification, not consumer persuasion. They suggest that one doesn't (or shouldn't) develop a brand to convince people to buy more music or books but to convey a message about the creator and the work. The hope is that the message will attract an audience, but that is not its primary purpose. This limited (and somewhat conservative) notion of brand identity reflects the historical roots of trademark law, which began as the regulation of symbols or signs to designate goods as originating from particular sources, distinctive from other goods or services in the marketplace. In other words, trademark law began as unfair competition law, regulating truth in advertising.[42] Its development into the protection of the "brand persona" against dilution and false sponsorship goes far beyond its narrow purpose of authenticating the source of a commercial product.[43] Many interviewees seem to embrace the historical definition of trademarks, seeking identification in the marketplace rather than market control.

RATIONAL ACTORS AND TRUSTING MARKETS

There are yet more examples of how interviewees restrain from asserting strong IP legal claims over their or their company's creative or innovative work. Some of the professionals with whom I spoke downplay the importance of branding for their particular business. This differs from the interviewees for whom, as described earlier, brand was "everything." For example, Donald, in-house counsel (also a vice president), says that generally trademarks play a minimal role at his e-commerce company:

At this company, I'm not emphasizing trademarks quite as much. [Our name] is registered; our technology group is registered, but our other product names are more generic. . . . So [when] we came up with one new product line; it was called [X]. Well, we had abandoned the name—we had come out with a new version by the time I . . . even *heard* from the [developers]. . . . And then I did a registration. Now I'm just going to abandon it. . . . Trademarks are just not so valuable. Except for really important[] company names, and *really* important products. . . . [Even our logo is] on our letterhead . . . [but our company], it's not IBM. I'm not sure that [our logo] really adds to identifying the source of our goods and services.

Bob, general counsel for a large publishing company, expressed a similar ambivalence toward trademarks as a mechanism for protecting or building reputation and market awareness. Whereas Donald, the vice president, explains it in terms of a cost-benefit analysis, Bob characterizes his ambivalence in terms of market differentiation:

Many of our customers may not even know that the [book] series is [the publishing company's] line. . . . We've looked at doing family marks, because we have [products with similar names]. [W]e've done some trademark protection. We don't have a particular problem, again, because given the highly structured nature of our business channels, three guys in Long Island doing a paperback [with the same name as ours], no one's going to be confused about the product. And it's not going to deprive us of the established goodwill. It's not really dilutive in that sense.

Becoming identifiable as someone or something with a valuable product to share is the goal of any business or audience-oriented endeavor. Whether trademark (one's commercial identity in the marketplace) is the best tool for accomplishing that goal is a complex question. For many interviewees, it is not clear whether building and protecting trade identity as robustly or broadly as trademark law allows, for example, through broad sponsorship and dilution claims, is worth the costs of development and enforcement. Moreover, the availability of broad claims, as they exist in the statute and are applied through case law, may cause more mischief than benefit given the business practices and accounts described here.[44]

The calm attitude reflected in the two previous examples contrasts with the reputational anxiety evident in earlier sections. For instance, Bob, the publishing executive, explicitly says that he does not think of duplication of his company's brand in a related industry as "dilutive," whereas the IP professional at the university worried about that precise issue for *unrelated* products. Why would a well-known university overpolice its trademark while a global publishing company underprotects some of its particular product lines, when both clearly care about their business reputation in their respective industries? One answer may be in Bob's statement about his particular publishing market: it is "highly structured," he says, which reduces any likelihood of confusion or intentional free riding. This is consistent with other professionals who rely on the existence of distinct markets. As one in-house IP lawyer said, there "is not much point in trying to steal a trademark. . . . You can infringe it, but a trademark seems to me a much . . . less contentious field."

For some, protecting reputation through trademark law and maintaining a healthy business do not overlap. The variations in the interviews, even in similar fields, suggests that despite the near-universal focus on developing a good reputation, trademark law is useful only for some. When it is useful, though, it is an agile and threatening tool used to slow or divert others in the market, whether or not they are engaged in unfair competition (typically defined as source confusion or false advertising).[45] In these instances, the breadth of trademark law in the dilution and false sponsorship contexts aligns well and functions best only for large institutions with famous marks, as with the university previously mentioned.

It is not my experience that trademark law's utility or scope is any less contentious than copyright or patent law to those who value trademarks. But Bob's comment suggests that there are some industries in which self-differentiation is the norm and where reputation and goodwill are ably maintained in a self-conscious and self-policing fashion without express reliance on IP regulation like the Lanham Act (the trademark statute). As Jacqueline, a general counsel for a domain-name aggregator, puts it, "[Our company] ha[s] the flip side of a trademark infringement problem that's really significant. We have to be careful about the names we buy, that they don't infringe existing trademarks." Trademarks, like any other type of property or asset, can create liability as well as generate revenue. For these individuals, speaking on behalf of their companies, it is more rational to follow basic business norms that avoid unfair competition and source confusion than to pursue and protect against generalized or exaggerated reputational anxieties (akin to defamation or trade libel). This is especially true of businesses that view trademark overlaps as inoffensive to their business identity. In the publishing, e-commerce, and web development markets in particular, trademarks—as the essential identity, value, and character of a company—appear to be more remote from business reputation.

Indeed, a filmmaker, Melanie, with her own production company tells me she doesn't have a trademark—or at least she doesn't think so. She is quick to point out, however, that she does have a domain name and website where people can find her company and her films (i.e., she cultivates a spatial identity). To publicize her work and generate business, Melanie says she uses a process of referrals—based on her reputation from doing other films and working with well-regarded senior filmmakers. This process has generated confidence as it encourages outside investment in her films and allows her to say reliably, "Listen: I am a director, and I am a writer, and I . . . have a vision, and I can do it." In contrast to Melanie, however, Barbara, the famous and self-supporting author, does have a trademark for her best-selling series. Yet Barbara shows a similar level of confidence in her work and her reputation as revenue generating on its own. Like Melanie, Barbara is nonchalant about ownership and control over her trademark, leaving most of its development and dissemination via merchandising to a television and film producer with licensed rights to her book series. In the minds of both of these professionals, professional reputation is sufficiently distant from any "brand" or a specific trademark that identifies their work that they do not think much (or at all) about trademark law or concern themselves with trademark development. Each connects her professional reputation most closely to her expressive content, which is more akin to the authorship and attribution issues discussed earlier.

Trademarks are more of a focus in the interviews when the mark is also the name of the person or company and functions as a locator—either to find a web address or a telephone number. A music agent discusses with me how she works with clients to optimize searches on the Internet to return results linked to the music or the musician. This is a common practice across most businesses that have a web presence. Owning a domain name that incorporates the business's name is fundamental to this practice. And owning a trademark that incorporates the business name helps prevent others from "cybersquatting" with a similar domain name. The music agent describes how optimizing search for her clients is a fairly "easy" process, despite some clients' resistance to branding, because for many of her clients their professional identities are their personal names. There was no need for the musicians to "remake" or "rename" themselves, only to protect their name in cyberspace. Likewise, dispute resolution around domain name hijacking is fairly straightforward. So even those professionals for whom trademarks are not a focus depend on the logic of the World Wide Web—its users and its structure—to protect and promote their business identity. The formal legal regulation—trademark infringement, false sponsorship, and dilution—is mostly noise in the background for these creative and innovative professionals. Anti-cybersquatting protection, and the use of a name online to locate goods and services, is more useful to them. That the normative and technological development of Internet use preceded its legal regulation may explain the unusual alignment in the interviews between the business practices of creative and innovative professionals with significant online presences and trademark law. The logic of their particular marketplace and audiences satisfies them; and only true source confusion between related goods concerns them. In this way, the interviewees often refrain or refuse to engage the other robust enforcement opportunities trademark law might otherwise afford.

EFFECTIVE PUBLIC RELATIONS
AND INVESTED CONSUMERS

Like the rational actors and markets described so far, some interviewees appear to rely on their audience rather than the law to protect their reputation. This occurs in at least two ways. First, creative and innovative professionals and their companies consider their audiences sufficiently savvy to distinguish among marketplace actors. For instance, Bob, the publishing executive, admits that were another much smaller publishing company ("three guys in Long Island") to use a confusingly similar mark, "no one's going to be confused about the product. And it's not going to deprive us of the established goodwill." Second, *audiences* (rather than owners) can (and do) affirmatively object to another's use of the company's name or logo on behalf of the company in their own, consumer-oriented capacity.

Recall Bob's story of this second type of audience participation. A small-business owner used one of his publishing company's most lucrative franchises offensively on a T-shirt, which

got[] people very upset . . . and the first thing they're [the customers] doing is calling us, saying, "You've got to shut this guy down." And of course, the intersection of free speech and commercial rights and IP . . . provide a rather interesting situation. . . . We were baited to step in. . . . [O]ur customers were upset. . . . [Eventually] we gave our press release and said we were going to consider further action. That . . . combined with the community pressure . . . was it. [The] guy was out of business.

The publishing company sees consumers as a partner in reputational maintenance and an ally in the policing of the "brand persona"—so much so that it refrains from initiating action and lets the audience do the work. But relying on consumers and audiences to maintain a company's reputation also inherently recognizes that the brand persona is as much a consumer good as it is a business asset. As such, a company or individual can relax its aggressive policing tactics in favor of letting its engaged audience handle some of the public relations. The brand is made for, and in part made by, the public. To be sure, this kind of restraint (and lack of policing) sometimes leads to surrogate uses that might alter or even lead to the abandonment of a brand name (e.g., how Coca-Cola became "Coke" because of that frequent public usage, and how the trademark Aspirin became a generic noun). Nonetheless, relinquishing some shared control to audiences is an especially effective tactic in the age of social media and digital communication when audiences are more visible and engaged than ever. Harnessing their attention to build brand awareness and identity makes good business sense.

Some interviewees refrain from overprotecting trademarks and other branding strategies in an effort to preserve a loyal and core audience. For example, Barbara, who owns trademarked characters from her book series, was reluctantly involved in a trademark dispute between two foreign companies, one who publishes a translation of her work and the other who licenses the trademarks for a television show and merchandise. The trademark dispute was inadvertent—the mistake of unintended consequences from a foreign publishing contract that did not contemplate multiple venues for the book. Critically, Barbara, the author, is ambivalent as to whether the text publisher or film producer should win the lawsuit. "If I go where my money is, it's with the publisher and not with the [film] producer. On the other hand, I had said to the publisher, 'You know, the total is larger than the sum of its parts.'" Ultimately, Barbara does not care who wins the licensing dispute or whether she profits from it; she just wants it to end. As she explained to me, she has "no dog in the fight." She just wants her affiliated business partners to refrain from turning her award-winning book series into a front-page feud between two very large media companies. As her advice to the publisher demonstrates, Barbara believes the conflict is rooted in corporate ego rather than rational competition. After all, the television show fuels sales of the book, and the book generates viewers for the television show. She says that if she were to resolve the conflict by herself retaining control over the trademark, she would "as part of goodwill, . . . pass [the merchandising rights] on to [the] producer. They have the . . . English-language [rights]—of course they should have the foreign-language rights. . . . I am not looking for any more money for that." In trying to mediate the dispute, Barbara demonstrates trust in both entities to shepherd her book series to a fan base, and only moderate expectations for financial returns beyond the book royalties, which the trademarked characters promote.

Neither the publishing company (a trademark holder) nor the writer (a creative originator) perceives the lack of vigilance toward trademarks to be at the expense of professional reputation. This accords with the interview data that so many industries are "star driven," as one IP lawyer working in a small business press calls it. By this, he meant that where reputation is already established (presumably because of a previous blockbuster product), conflicts over the use or misuse of the brand name are less troubling than if the brand has yet to take off. "It's a real eye-opening experience," he says. "I mean, everything is marketing. The focus on the customer, . . . the attention to . . . sales numbers." A licensing officer in a university acknowledges her institution has an "unfair advantage": "it's called the brand. . . . If it came out of a guy's garage, it's hard to get any-one's attention. If it comes out of [here], it's already [a best seller]." Simi-larly, the sculptor who felt uneasy when her sculpture was photographed in the background of a car commercial eventually realized that this was a problem for the successful, and it wasn't much of a problem all things considered. "I should have such problems!" she said; that is, confusion over the work's unapproved appearances is a better problem to have than obscurity. She doesn't want to allow *all* photographic renderings of her work, but her growing fame makes her less worried about their unauthor-ized use in terms of reputational harms and benefits.

In smaller companies, I also heard accounts of decisions to avoid dis-putes and instead trust that time and a richer context will resolve some of the reputational issues. Cary, an in-house counsel to an energy company, tells me that in his prior job at a successful biotech company, he worked on a trademark lawsuit that was filed as a retaliatory counterclaim, which was really a false advertising claim. This experience led him to avoid all litigation, even meritorious litigation, because of its expense:

Litigators have a way of wanting to file a motion for everything, and . . . making sure that we're not just filing things to spite the other side is important. . . . [I]f the judge is suggesting mediation, I'm gonna do it. And even though the litiga-tors may say it's pointless, I'm gonna use every opportunity I can . . . to get us out of this so that we can start making money and forget about the legal bills.

Were counterfeiting a problem for his company, this lawyer admits, trade-mark law would certainly help, but he prefers to avoid formal legal disputes, including trademark disputes (even when factually incorrect assertions about the company are at issue), because they distract the focus of the business, which is to develop and sell products. Cary, vice president and legal counsel, is confident that the products' qualities and the consumer experience are enough to sustain the business, beyond any counterfeiting issues. Fighting over false advertising is a waste of time, according to him.

To be clear, in these examples, the trademark owner—individual or firm—is not relinquishing control over the trade identity and reputation to a hostile or crowded marketplace. Control remains critical. Instead, in these cases, IP law might be useful were it mobilized, yet the preference is to resolve the dispute outside formal legal practices. Like letting flood waters recede on their own rather than relying on mechanical pumps, the owners of valuable trade identities trust their reputational goodwill to maintain its own optimal level without engaging in legal processes. To some, like the attorney Cary, avoiding legal mechanisms like IP enforcement is consistent with the company's identity of making things that people want or need. IP law is not the central enforcement mechanism for reputation. Rather, consumer memory and ongoing investment in positive consumer relations are common and powerful tools, especially in light of the rapid changes in marketing and public relation opportunities on the Internet. This speaks to the current debate over the relative utility of stronger versus weaker IP rights, in trademark law and elsewhere, and the need for clearer defenses and shortened legal procedures to resolve meritless legal conflicts quickly.[46]

*　　*　　*

In my interviews, concern over reputation is rarely focused on harm to business goodwill because of mistaken identity or unauthorized copies. Most people think about reputational benefits and harms in terms of their personal attachment to the work and control over its message. These concerns map very loosely onto US IP law. Only broad sponsorship claims and dilution by blurring and tarnishment are particularly apt in these contexts, but they have been the focus of significant scholarly criticism, not the least because "sponsorship" is overly vague and proving dilution flummoxes even the most experienced attorneys. Likewise, copyright law protects the substance of original expression, and does not touch attribution or misattribution. Patent law facilitates the disaggregation of ownership from inventorship (or authorship), so that inventors may be credited on the patent but lack control over the uses of the invention.

When analyzed in the aggregate, the examples the data provides of the importance and protection of professional reputation present wide variation, and sometimes contradict one another. This is simply evidence of the diversity of the ways creative professionals imagine or nourish reputation—through IP law or beside it. In this chapter, I grouped the variations into categories, but most of the interviewees' conceptions of reputational value occupy more than one category. Again, this simply confirms that even critical professional and personal values such as reputation are fluid.[47] The diversity of ways in which creative and innovative work take shape and are meaningful against a backdrop of varying reputational interests and protective mechanisms further undermines the economically driven and utilitarian foundations of IP regulation.[48]

Moreover, the mismatch between reputational values and IP production, protection, and dissemination (and the law regulating IP) may be inherent to reputation's shared nature. Reputation is hard to "own" in the way that property (or IP) might be owned and defined. The mechanisms of exclusion for property rights facilitate protection and investment in the property assets. When the interest, such as a reputational interest, is necessarily shared, co-built, and contingent on cooperative development, exclusion (a signature of ownership) is less tenable. Overall, the interviews demonstrate a desire for exclusion, but less because of free riding (though that certainly was mentioned) and more because they seek targeted relationship building. The varied and fluid nature of reputational interests, like personal relationships themselves, means that it is nearly impossible to make them rivalrous: bounded, evaluated, traded, or sold. As one interviewee says, trademarks and the goodwill they embody are the "closest to moral rights" in US law. And moral rights are notoriously inalienable, in part because they form essential parts of a person.

Property ownership derives from the concern that unowned property will be wasted because there will be little incentive to care for it and make it beneficially available for others. But monopoly ownership and overvaluing assets so that they are locked away or unavailable except at an unreasonable price can also lead to waste and a reduction in social welfare. In strongly valuing reputation for the making and sustaining of creative and innovative work, these interviews suggest that property is the wrong legal construct to protect it. Current US IP law purports to build legal fences around nonrivalrous goods to incentivize their production and dissemination, but this does not align with the reputational interests and concerns of those who seek to make a living through creative and innovative work. Investment in reputation is something the law should encourage in theory, as it benefits the worker and the work they produce. But the nature of reputational values appears to make possession of and exclusion from reputational interests a near impossibility. Attempting exclusivity poses substantial problems for free speech, informational accuracy, diverse and growing community affiliations, and even market competition. Indeed, many of the interviewees describe the absence of exclusivity over reputational interests as fomenting rather than preventing these societal goods.

Whether speaking for themselves or for their company, the interviewees find that reputation serves their basic interests—that is, professional growth, autonomy, and building relationships. Reputation identifies and communicates certain qualities and sustains their character; it is a means of expression, and it grows and binds communities around common ideas and principles. Reputation is a shared resource, despite the fact that it is profoundly personal and, as the interviewees describe, "priceless." Where audience interests conflict with individual or corporate interests—in cases of negative consumer reviews, for example, or tarnishment—aggressive reputational claims are common, though not necessarily well supported in the law except in the case of trademark dilution and then only for famous brands.[49] Dilution law is unavailable for the everyday creator or business person. And although privacy torts (e.g., right of publicity) might be available, they are rare. Because no amount of money can remedy harm to dignity, overreach tends to be futile and can lead to a refusal to share or affiliate for fear of reputational harm.

Alternatively, however, protecting and building reputational interests through trusted market mechanisms and loosely affiliated consumers or fans can lead to fulsome partnerships with an audience who protect and sustain the person or company's status and good name. The protection of trademarks against likelihood of confusion between market competitors is the best-aligned IP right found in the data. It was taken for granted as a background business mechanism but largely left to self-enforcement and audience enforcement. Indeed, the diverse ways interviewees nurture and police their reputation speaks to the complexity and circumstantial nature of reputational interests and reputational protection. In the face of perceived reputational injury, IP law's meager response is inadequate to the task and, despite being the most germane area of law for creative and innovative work, largely irrelevant. Beyond the basic protection of trademark as one's business identity, interviewees successfully build, protect, and distinguish their valuable reputation in many other ways.

CHAPTER 5

Instruction

How Lawyers Harvest Intellectual Property

IT SHOULD BE CLEAR from my interviews that intellectual property is a legal construct: it exists only after creative and innovative work has begun. Why, then, is IP compared to nature and natural processes so often? For example, in-house IP lawyers frequently describe their role to me as "harvesting IP," "planting ideas," and "creating and fitting into an IP landscape." But IP is not naturally occurring. If anything arises "naturally," it is the creative flow or the innovative instinct. IP is what happens when an originator lays claim to creative or innovative work through law or when a lawyer fits creative or innovative work into a legal form.

This chapter centers on the role of lawyers and business agents in the making and claiming of IP. How does IP get made and "harvested," by whom, and under what circumstances? Of course, creative and innovative work happens without lawyers and business agents creating opportunities or incentives through legal means. As the previous chapters detail, creativity and innovation is practiced and is often profitable without IP or with less exclusivity that IP rights provide. But these interviews also contain illustrations of legal intervention via lawyers or business agents to develop IP at a decisive stage of the creative and innovative work.

It becomes clear from analyzing the behavior of lawyers and business agents (and the descriptions of their behavior) that the external force of law—its formal, classical practice of rules and exceptions—shapes creative and innovative work into something recognizable to the business world. Lawyers and business agents, working within the conventional framework of property rights to maximize investments of time and money, appear on the scene and (1) disrupt work, (2) instruct on the law, and (3) thereafter justify their intervention by appealing to economic interests, among others. These types of behavior are not mutually exclusive but a "repertoire of responses to different situations."[1] Indeed, the lawyer or business agent might execute all these functions at different times depending on the circumstances, which reflects the flexibility of law (and lawyers) to adapt to the task at hand.

How does the lawyer or business agent become involved in creative and innovative work? After Chapters 3 and 4, in which the interviewees demonstrate how they often make a living or build a business without strong IP rights (and care a tremendous amount about things like professional reputation that are only weakly protected by IP law), it is easy to forget how important and necessary IP can be. Legal categories or claims (e.g., IP rights) are, of course, more likely to arise when lawyers are involved in creative and innovative activity than when they are not. But the lawyers I spoke with also remind us of the positive role IP can have. Creating IP always happens *after* the creative and innovative work is in progress or has been completed. In lawyers' terms, IP demarcates the boundaries of the work that facilitates a foreseeable and hopefully profitable transactions. But that is not all.

Lawyers and business agents also try to use IP to maximize interests that are primary to the client—freedom to work, choice of lifestyle, and certain moral or ethical concerns of their clients—but these interests are usually secondary to IP's economic benefits. When IP takes shape with the help of a lawyer or agent who anticipates specific marketplace transactions (e.g., reproduction and distribution of client's work), its formal structure and the legal and business advice that preceded its creation reverberate onto how the creative and innovative work is made. That is, although the legal form of IP may come after much of the creative and innovative work is complete, IP's subsequent formulation (through legal disruptions, teachings, and justifications) inevitably affects the making and sharing of the individual's work in the future.

This chapter ends by comparing variations in the lawyer's role with the diverse descriptions of IP as a legal construct. Although it may appear that lawyers and business agents are an external force in the work of their clients, or that they put pressure on the creative or innovative process to fit a particular understanding of the law's role, the interviewees' descriptions of the IP's form and function that is eventually created are diverse and sometimes contradictory. According to the data, the various roles of IP as described by the lawyers or business agents do not correlate to a particular kind of lawyer or manager (in-house or firm, IP or generalist). The form IP takes and its purpose are not predetermined by legal rules or economic principles; these are the product of a particular creative context or innovative relationship. Therefore, the variations of IP's forms and purposes are likely to be as diverse as the situations in which creative and innovative work occurs. The subsequent influence that legal and business structures have on creative and innovative output—the overt channeling of the work into a legal framework—is where much of the familiar and overdetermined language of economic incentives and investment arises. This chapter sheds light on how, insofar as legal and business structures can change (and we know they can and do), legal and business structures can be tailored to more closely reflect the diverse needs and desires of artists and scientists. The first step toward doing this is to pay attention to how those needs and desires arise and are described in the lawyer-client relationship, desires regarding, for example, employment relations, corporate accountability, and property ownership.

THREE FORMS OF LEGAL INTERVENTION

Disruption

The stereotypical complaint about lawyers is that they see all the problems and none of the solutions. Lawyers see risk everywhere. Indeed, they are trained to find and assess risk in order to minimize it so that the client can work without interruption. Laura Beth Nielson and Robert Nelson describe three primary roles for in-house counsel: cop, counsel, and entrepreneur.[2] I found that this typology accurately maps onto my interview data and that its application extends beyond the in-house counsel positions in Nielson and Nelson's study. In particular, the role of "cop"—policing the conduct of business clients and serving a gatekeeping function (approving contracts, implementing compliance programs)—is a central focus in the interviews with IP attorneys.[3]

In a study of music copyright by Peter DiCola and Kembrew McLeod, the British sound artist Scanner (Robin Rimbaud) questions his lawyers' intent in providing advice; he describes them as aggressively negative and litigious, more often explaining what is unlawful and forbidden than what is possible.[4] Many of the people I interviewed likewise portray the lawyer as an arresting officer who puts up barriers to certain paths or raises the threat of sanctions. As Michael, a pharmacologist and consultant says, "Lawyers slow things down. Lawyers are not businesspeople. . . . They actually look for ways for why things won't work." Michael, who is also in law school studying to become a lawyer to enhance his pharmaceutical consulting practice, mentions one patent attorney in particular who "drove people insane because she literally told everybody who was working on this project 'None of you can talk to each other.' But you can't just say that to a client. . . . C'mon. It's not going to work from a business perspective." Lawyers are often caricatured with a stop sign, constantly halting productive movement. In describing his role in the e-book business, an in-house counsel at a very large publishing company put up his hands as if literally to halt the conversation, saying: "We built all these books, and no one had really thought about getting electronic rights. And all of a sudden, then, everyone was running to shove them on a CD. And the lawyers all go, 'Whoa, wait a minute.'" The lawyer's impulse is to slow things down (or "arrest" things) to assess the risks and payoffs, but the interviewees often find this deeply frustrating and do not contextualize it in terms of an upside.

Many attorneys know they are perceived as barriers to continued work. Even in the patent-rich medical device industry, an in-house counsel finds her colleagues "very hostile" to the lawyer's presence in the development stage. "Don't bother me" is what she hears them say. "It's a constant struggle," another attorney says, complaining about the difficulty of aligning client's expectations of workflow with the legal requirements of compliance and risk management. Susan, a director of technology licensing at a university, says, "They [the scientists] are going to start with the assumption that I'm going to get in the way of their publishing; that patenting and publishing are contradictory." And in some sense, the scientists are right. When scientists are enthusiastic about a new project and want to share their work at a conference, the lawyer or business agent in the room will remind them that sharing (in the way their academic profession encourages) might hurt the patentability of the invention. If the patent application is not filed in time, the publication may be a bar to patentability. Gary, a copyright lawyer at a large law firm, describes a similar problem:

A lot of the time, clients . . . want the "Can I do it, or can I not do it?" And we get it at the eleventh hour. [They say], "We are going tomorrow with this marketing presentation in which we are using film clips from a currently running film. But that's fine because we are just marketing our product." And I [ask], "Who is going to be there?" I try to also be practical about it. . . . I always start off by saying, "Look: under the law? No. . . . But let's look at risk factors."

But this attempt at compromise rarely satisfies the client who just wants the law and the legal representative to give a clear answer or get out of the way.

Carol, a law partner and patent attorney who was once an academic scientist herself, describes her clients' resistance to what they perceive as legal interference:

I have inventors who are academic scientists, and trying to get information out of them, it can be like a tooth extraction. . . . They're annoyed; you're an annoyance, generally. You take up their time that they could be doing other things. They're generally not interested. . . . There's an inventor . . . that I've dealt with . . . [who] founded a small company. . . . [H]e'll talk about baseball, but he didn't want to talk about his patent applications.

Clients feel that legal interference takes too much time away from their work and interrupts their flow while being unnecessarily negative and risk averse. Jacqueline, an in-house counsel and a longtime lawyer in the high-technology and computer industries, compares herself to a "surgeon," because her colleagues and clients don't want to see her, spend time with her, or pay her, unless they are "in trouble." On the other side, many clients who seek patenting advice from in-house or firm lawyers complain that the "process is difficult" and that it "takes a long time to get patents issued." To entrepreneurs, a "dream lawyer" works efficiently, is minimally invasive, and "gets" their clients' needs. But for many, this type of lawyer is the exception. A marketing professional in the content industry explains that he doesn't seek advice of their attorney often because "famously it would have taken weeks" to get her advice.

Given the disruption of time and flow that legal processes appears to cause, lawyers try to "steal moments when efficacious," as Jacqueline puts it, to ensure the overall health of their client's business. Donald, an in-house attorney, who has worked in both the high-tech and merchandising fields, recognizes the drain on time and energy for innovators to help lawyers with patent applications. He tells me about a chief technology officer who is reluctant to participate in the IP "harvesting" process because, ironically enough, he takes the science behind the work so seriously and thus patent prosecution is hugely time consuming:

Because it's work. So for [him] to work with an outside lawyer on the inevitable office actions that you get, and delays, and to help write the application, I mean, it really is [time-consuming work]. Like, [he] jokes to me that it takes me an hour to read a patent application, but it takes him a whole day. Because they are fifty pages long, and he goes, "You're just skimming it. You're not paying attention to the claims." . . . And he has to read those claims with a ruler, sentence by sentence. It's a lot of work for him. . . . The precision of it all. . . . It's an undertaking for him. . . . I think he enjoys it. But he's a very busy guy, and he wants to know that there really is value there.

The lawyers I spoke with frequently say that their clients are "very busy" and do not see the value in bringing a lawyer into the business development early on. To the attorneys, this is a mistake. Like with doctors (or "surgeons"), avoiding advice and consultation on regular business matters is like forgoing annual physicals and routine screens, which can reduce the overall cost of medical care (or doing business). Instead, people unwisely rely on emergency rooms and acute medical care, waiting for the illness to progress without the benefit of early assessment and treatment. The reasons clients and patients make this trade-off have to do with their perception of time and money. Lawyers require both, and sometimes a lot of both, without providing obvious or immediate benefits to innovators, creators, or their companies in the early stages.

The interviews contain abundant examples of frustration over the disconnect between time required for and the value of legal counsel. This is often related to the sense that the legal advice is confused or not directly on point. With a hint of frustration and resignation, Sadie, a sculptor, says, "I also think that sometimes when you ask about copyrighting art, you don't really get a clear answer about it. . . . I used to always feel like I walked away more confused." Further, the lawyers "always tell me more than I wanna know, and I have to kind of roll back a little bit." The experience of creative and innovative professionals is that lawyers overwork their question or problem, making it more complex and failing to rely on common sense or industry norms. Melanie, a documentary filmmaker with her own production company, complains that "lawyers are always going to tell you that you have to get everything signed and everything done [but I think] there's a certain amount of risk that you have take." She says:

Calling a lawyer about a release . . . was a real lesson about lawyers. Of course, they wanted everything. . . . You are not going to be safe if you don't have this . . . but we do this all the time. It was a big deal to even talk to the lawyer because the lawyer charged so much money.

Lawyers themselves are not immune to concerns over the value of time. A solo practitioner wonders, "When I do one of these [cases] and I send a client a bill, [I wonder] whether it's really a good use of the client's money." The feeling that the amount of time required to consult and the cost of legal advice may outweigh the value lawyers add is discussed in almost every interview. In describing a nasty contract dispute and how it wastes resources, Barbara, the author, says:

It bothers me enormously, but what do I do? The thing is that the amount of money on the table is going to be nowhere near what a lawyer would take out of it, so everybody is trying to do this without getting lawyers involved. But of course everyone is talking to lawyers on the side.

Unfortunately, the situation can backfire when lawyers try to reduce the cost by sharing the work of drafting the contract or patent with the client, or requesting that the client perform due diligence rather than the lawyer. "We do a lot of clean up," says one lawyer about contracts or licenses drafted by nonlawyers.

Instruction

How do lawyers and business agents combat or deflect the "arresting officer" identity? How do they build and retain client trust to facilitate the creative and innovative work to which they are committed? Primarily, as one general counsel says, they act as teachers or translators. But the sense is one of urgency. They say it is "incumbent [on lawyers] to try[] to teach" clients. Lawyers need to be "better explainers" to persuade clients that legal advice is useful and to corral effective and compliant behavior that will benefit the individual or organization. The people I spoke with had three principal ways of being instructive and guiding clients toward effective uses of IP law: by being admired or regarded as the go-to person on matters of IP; by being a gatekeeper on certain basic operations or output in a company or organization; and by explicitly teaching or coaching through training and lessons to self-consciously shape the culture to be more IP centered.

These overt instructional modes are necessary, as Jacqueline, a general counsel, reports, because you "need to remind people about the [IP] rights." For example, software engineers at her company "only realize I'm part of the equation when they see me . . . [but hardware engineers are more compliant.] . . . So getting a hardware engineer on board with legal, you just have to put a little legal button somewhere within eyesight, and they will call." Putting a "little legal button . . . within eyesight" is a way to keep the law and its requirements in view, because otherwise the engineers would not think about it. John, a university licensing and business developer, substantiates this concern: "I don't think there's any thought on the part of our researchers when they accept or seek money for research as to what, if any, IP is going to arise from it." The impression most legal actors I spoke with have is that IP simply does not cross the minds of their creative or innovative clients. It is their job, therefore, as lawyers or business agents, to incite and incent the creative or innovative professional to funnel their work into the IP framework. This section describes how that happens and the next section describes why.

IP doesn't simply happen or arise, the way a flower does after planting a seed (despite the plethora of natural metaphors for IP development). Instead, IP needs to be shaped and coaxed—sometimes even compelled. IP is not inevitable—it does not follow easily from creative and innovative activity. This is because work that may be protectable as IP (e.g., making a painting, discovering a new way to make a compound) is regularly made without thinking about IP, and the entitlements that flow from the work as IP (e.g., revenue, exclusive use) arise only after legal intervention. As earlier chapters demonstrate, comparing IP to natural processes or relationships is common throughout the interviews. Here, we see that such comparison may be a way of placing a more attractive framework on legal intervention that is otherwise disruptive or displeasing.

Status

To the artist or scientist, lawyers and businesspeople think about strange things. Lawyers and business agents seem distanced from creative and innovative professionals as they tend to focus on different priorities. The quotes so far in this chapter exhibit a disconnect between the language many lawyers use to explain IP law and the needs and interests of artists and scientists. And yet artists and scientists still consult with lawyers, and their legal blessing still matters. Seth, in-house lawyer with diverse experience in government, universities, and publishing, recalls:

There are some things I do that I think you pretty much have to be a lawyer to do, but the greater part of what I do, . . . it's not really practicing law: it's really helping to run a business. But . . . I'm the only lawyer in the building. . . . I think people tend to take my advice on a lot of issues that probably they don't have to.

Seth says later in the interview that he perceives that his colleagues believe that "because legal signed off on this . . . it's got to be OK." Even Barbara, an author who used to be an acquisitions editor and who for years worked with contracts and copyright, said that she consults a lawyer about her contracts, even if she expects that few (if any) changes will be made. She borrows from a form contract, "amending it to my tastes, and then [has] it looked at by a lawyer [who] made almost no changes." Although clients may experience lawyers as time consuming or disruptive, their status as specialists and risk managers is important to even the most astute client, even if the result of the legal counsel is simply to validate the client's work.

Gatekeeping

As clients grow their businesses, gatekeeping becomes more important and the lawyer wields a stronger influence on an individual or an organization. The lawyer then not only provides expert advice but also creates or facilitates structures through which individuals or organizations using the creative work pass. When work must be "approved" by an attorney before it is done or distributed, creative and innovative research and production slows and may be stymied. This is evident in the complaints above that describe the lawyer as an arresting officer. The legal gatekeeper is criticized by scholars, such as Patricia Aufderheide and Peter Jaszi, who fear, for example, that teachers and educators do not reproduce material in course preparation because of excessively cautious advice from supervisors and school district attorneys regarding copyright fair use.[5] On the upside, when lawyers become gatekeepers, instead of haphazardly auditing the work of a client, the lawyer and her legal advice are typically better integrated into the everyday processes of a person's or company's activities, regularly reviewing and filtering production and output.

In the interviews, gatekeeping takes place along a spectrum of informal to formal business practices. Some lawyers communicate regularly with clients and colleagues both electronically and in person to "facilitate" IP production. Peter, an in-house patent attorney at a pharmaceutical company, describes his role as providing "guidance" about how to maximize patentability and ownership, even sometimes directing attention to a "good scientific idea [that] . . . may be patentable." He "spend[s] time with scientists" working through research plans. For example:

[A] lot of it is client education . . . we really want a pretty focused research plan. Because we want it to be clear what the [collaborative research] agreement allows you to do, and what it doesn't allow you to do. So a lot of times, I'll get, you know, "I want Professor X to look at a very general field," and that's the whole research plan. So I'll spend some time with them; be like "How would we ever enforce this?" If he takes this and does X, Y, or Z, there's a good argument that that's covered by the scope of the research agreement. So let's really focus it down. What is he or she planning to really do in the clinic, or in the experimental models? Let's design it out in that way.

Here, Peter describes his role as conversational and gentle; he responds to the scientist's goals and shapes the research plan according to anticipated risks and company aims. Carol, a partner at her law firm, describes a different tactic with the same objective: to advise the client about the potential of IP and the appropriate steps for pursuing it. Carol often deals with individual inventors as well as corporate clients, but in both cases she finds she must "cross-examine" clients to determine scope of subject matter and to direct them, cautiously, toward more fruitful avenues of study:

It's like a polite cross-examination with an inventor. So when you get an invention disclosure and you call them, you make nice, and then you have them tell their story, and then you ask them questions. It's like—it really *is*—a cross-examination. And then you take notes, and then you ask them the questions. You know, when you've got a sense that you've got a novel invention and you ask, "What have others done?" and you probe it, and then, . . . "What's unexpected? . . . [I]s this exactly what you would expect to get?" And they'd say, "Well, yeah, of course. Everyone would have expected it."

Focusing the scope of research collaborations and questioning scientists about the novelty and nonobviousness of their discoveries (standards for patenting) are different kinds of gatekeeping, a sort of substantive filtering. They shape work—the object of work, with whom the work is done, and how. Attorneys create "gates" systematically and for specific reasons: to capture creative or inventive work, to define its contours, and to determine its originators in order to effectively shape it into strong IP. Indeed, without the lawyer's intervention, there may be no IP at all. Attorneys often circulate invention disclosure forms or research collaboration agreements to interject guidance and encourage a conversation to facilitate compliance with legal principles. What their compliance is for—how it is relevant and how that relevance is made clear—is the subject of the next section on justifying IP.

Other forms of gatekeeping are more systematized and hardwired into organizations or lawyer-client relationships. Sometimes the in-house lawyer is simply present at all important project meetings. When the lawyer is accepted as part of a professional's or institution's development and growth, his or her sanction and supervision becomes an indivisible element of the creative or innovative process. What the lawyer understands as "the law"—often originating with a doctrinal perspective on legal rules and a litigation focus on risks—shapes the work. As Gary, a former acquisitions editor and now a firm lawyer, describes:

[W]e would have these launch meetings for lists. And . . . the whole department would show up, and I would present. That was . . . one of my jobs, too. . . . I would present the titles that we were going to be publishing in the fall or the spring. . . . And there was my other friend who was in the legal department would always be sitting there. And he would just write it down, . . . "When you have a manuscript, I would like to see it," right? He was the only one who was sort of thinking in terms of the legal vetting side of things: what's going to get us sued?

Sometimes the gatekeeping or filtration is explicit and self-conscious, permeating the company's and individual's daily behavior. Ted, an in-house lawyer at a biotech company, says so explicitly, saying his team of attorneys at his company "indoctrinates" employees and "molds them" to "think about IP":

Because this is such a young industry . . . the vast majority of our scientists are very young. Right out of grad school, or just finished their PhD, or finished a postdoc, or something like that. So they're like blank slates. So we get them in, and we've sort of indoctrinated them . . . "OK, you need to be thinking about innovation." And we have all sorts of ways of doing that. . . . So for us . . . we've got all these people that it's just like clay we're trying to mold into "Think about IP, think about IP."

What "think about IP" means is ambiguous. Does it mean to think outside the box? Or does it mean to remember to consult an IP lawyer? Ted suggests that keeping IP law in mind may help the company innovate further (e.g., by designing around certain existing technologies). The conflation of IP and innovation in the previous quote explains a basis for the confusion that many clients experience when they believe that innovative work *inevitability* leads to IP-protected goods or services. But to "think about IP" could also mean to think about ways to commercialize the product being developed, which explains why the subsequent creation of IP is often misdescribed as "incentivizing" the early stages of innovative or creative activity. IP may arise subsequently, but its form, strength, or purpose is not necessarily predetermined by preexisting creative or innovative work.

Substantive gatekeeping through organizational routines and structured interactions may develop a company culture of innovation. Attorneys describe trying hard to evolve the company culture and encourage a positive predisposition toward IP. Recall the competition that Ted invented to cultivate a culture of innovation and disclosure of new ideas among the scientists and engineers at his company:

Every month, what we do is we just encourage the scientists to submit cool ideas. This is separate and apart from like, your standard invention disclosure form. . . . So this way, it just really tries to capture stuff . . . this little idea, this brainstorm where they see some interesting result or something like that. . . . We get people to submit them every month. . . . We collect all the cool ideas, and then . . . [w]e pick a handful of people to be judges. It's sort of an *American Idol* kind of thing where there's a panel of judges, and they get thirty seconds to stand up and extol the virtues of their cool idea. And we then rank the cool ideas in terms of coolness . . . whatever that may be. And we've actually adopted a separate ranking now where me and some of the research leaders actually rank them for IP value. Because some of the ideas, while they may be kind of cool ideas, they aren't necessarily fully baked enough to consider for IP purposes. And then people basically just get bragging rights. We then rank them, and we announce the winners. We incent people; it's like a $10 gift certificate or something that we give people. Anyone who submits a cool idea gets the $10 gift certificate.

This competition, whose purpose is to encourage innovative work and develop the associated reputational interests, has been part of the company since its founding. According to this lawyer, it has driven patent filings far and above what he had seen in previous companies. "It's been great," Ted says:

It does a couple of things. It gets people thinking about innovations and different ways to think about the same ideas or the same approaches to things. It also lets us flag things sort of early on, or as early on as possible, that, "Oh hey, this is a good idea; we have to track this and see how it plays out." Or I see once they generate some data, does this really pan out? Because if this works, this is worth filing on. So I think my numbers are outdated; we try to track this stuff: at one point near the end of last year, I think we were seeing about a 10 percent return . . . in terms of graduating on to actual patent filings . . . [w]hich was frankly amazing.

If the company measures value on the basis of number of patents filed (which many early-stage companies do for purposes of attracting potential investors and purchasers), this kind of gatekeeping has high appeal. It can also help form meaningful relationships between lawyers and creative and innovative professionals in the company by making explicit how each relies on the other.[6]

The myriad gatekeeping mechanisms—soft interviews, guided conversations, a routine presence, organizational structure, and self-conscious changes in culture—all facilitate the making and harvesting of IP. And yet facilitation is not always smooth. The gatekeeping function is frequently interpreted as another way the lawyer can be "disruptive" because they slow or stop creative and innovative production to "vet" the product for compliance. But on the whole, the gatekeeping strategies are less disruptive than other interventions; they are attempts at low-key, cordial, and even fun professional interactions, justifying the role of the lawyer and her expertise (and thus the intervention of IP generally) in the creative or innovative field.[7]

Most of these examples are drawn from corporate actors. It appears from my data that gatekeeping is more common among corporations than the instruction role I describe next. Very few of the individual artists or scientists I spoke with have relationships with lawyers or business agents that approximate those described already here, in which the lawyer-client relationship functions as a filter to select and mold the creative or innovative output in an effort to strengthen IP. Insofar as gatekeeping does in fact maximize IP rights, and those IP rights grow wealth and professional opportunity, the lack of a lawyer to play gatekeeper (either because the individuals cannot afford one or do not think to consult one) may be one explanation for the disparate wealth profiles of individuals as compared to corporations who develop IP. However, my data do not compare the wealth profiles of individuals and/or sole proprietors with employees. Nor do the data correlate wealth to IP ownership. (Most of those interviewed make a satisfactory living from their work.[8]) The sheer variation in circumstances among the interviewees—the different ways lawyers are consulted (or aren't), the variety of ways in which IP features (or doesn't)—and the relatively modest but comfortable livings made by most interviewees undermines the claim of direct causality among IP ownership, wealth, and artistic or scientific progress. However, strong assertions of IP and the use of IP for directing or recuperating investment might be robustly correlated to a close working relationship with legal counsel.

Instructional

The lawyer-as-teacher is by far the most common way in which lawyers promote creation of IP, according to the interviews. Indeed, many lawyers use the term *educate* to characterize their most important interactions with clients about IP issues. One licensing professional talks about how she "educate[s] them that . . . [invention disclosures are] real simple stuff [and] . . . we're not going to take a lot of their time." Another in-house lawyer talks about running "educational seminars" for scientists at his company. A solo practitioner explains that counseling clients is "an education process" about how IP works. The mode of instruction ranges from explicit top-down teaching—running workshops, giving talks, providing handouts—to relationship building and mentoring, ground-up engagement, and cultivation of work habits. The goal of each of these modes is to persuade individuals (and employees and managers) to "think IP," as more than one in-house counsel describes it. As with any kind of teaching, different forms of engagement work for different students; it is the teacher's job to calibrate methods of teaching to maximize learning.

It is most common for the lawyers to use classroom-like teaching as a way to persuade clients and employees to "think about IP." The lawyers conduct "seminars" at their company on patent and copyright law with "teaching materials" saved from being an adjunct professor at a local law school. Dennis, a longtime patent attorney, tells me about the in-house and industrywide "talks" he gives about patents and the development of patent law based on his experience in the pharmaceutical industry since the 1980s. He does this as a way to shape the industry to produce beneficial and profitable medicines. In-house IP attorney, Ted, tells the following story:

I . . . conduct training here for all our staff. I give an annual talk on Patents 101, and how our procedures and policies work here at [the company], and people are afforded the opportunity to ask me questions, and whenever I give that talk, I'm usually buried with invention disclosures for the next few weeks. . . . So out of sight, out of mind, if I am out in front of everybody, and preaching how important these things are, I help cheerlead and generate new inventions.

Ted is explicit about the relationship he sees between IP training and the potential for innovation and a growing patent portfolio. He believes that without his presence "out in front of everybody" "preaching" the importance of patents, patentable innovation would occur less often in his company. As he says, "out of sight, out of mind"—innovation might occur within the labs, but without the reminder of IP, those innovations might not be harvested by the company as IP to generate what he believes could be rich and potentially unexpected revenue and competitive advantage.

This kind of teaching resembles compliance training in other settings. For example, to prevent discrimination in the workplace, routine reminders and updates are often used to keep the office a dignified place to work. It may be unlike compliance training, however, in that routine anti-discrimination training does not produce a periodic uptick in the amount of complaints filed.[9] By contrast, the effect of IP training on invention disclosures in the short term versus long term—that is, the rise and fall of IP filings and assertions depending on temporal relation to the training—indicates that people need to be reminded about IP. This suggests that IP creation (as opposed to creativity and innovation) is not as firmly embedded as an expectation or behavioral norm as anti-discrimination rules are in the relevant communities.

Lawyers and business managers also talk about relationship building and mentoring, which resemble less formal processes for directing work into an IP framework. Carol, a firm lawyer, variously engages in classroom-like teaching and a more relational model of slow and steady instruction. Many of her clients, she says, "are neophytes in the process, and so you just kind of have to teach them: walk them through what you need, what a patent is, what the process of getting a patent is, . . . how you have to apply for it. . . . It's a long process." She says of her role:

[It] is to . . . write a patent application and get claims allowed. And to do that, I need to, in many ways, educate the client and the scientists. . . . [Y]ou have to teach them what this process is about. It doesn't happen overnight [even though] some do . . . think it happens overnight.

Carol shared with me many different examples of clients in which she "walk[s] them through what" they need. Despite having been through the process before, some of them would still "get all pissy" because of the time required to put a patent application together and because of her pushback on novelty and nonobviousness. Her relationships with clients are ongoing, Carol says, and many of the scientists and engineers have strong personalities. For her, it seems, regular one-on-one teaching with clients is optimal from a lifestyle and business management perspective, but it might not achieve the rate of compliance and acceptance she would like to see.

One explanation for Carol's dissatisfaction with the rate of compliance may be her position as lawyer in a firm, as opposed to being in-house counsel. While three in-house lawyers give analogous instances of relationship building and mentoring on a similarly intimate scale (one-on-one rather than classroom-style teaching and lectures), they experience less resistance to pro-IP attitudes and firm culture. One, who works in the publishing world, says confidently, "We have a fairly clear understanding. We have a process that assures that we don't have to remind everyone that we need to get the rights" to make and sell the product. His company is organized so that legal is part of nearly every transaction and conversation as either staff (contract managers) or forms (checklists and authorization forms), and not only present at trigger points or as a gatekeeper. Donald, an in-house attorney for a software and Internet company (who had previously been at a large retail manufacturer), also exudes confidence about the IP-centric nature of his firm, but only after he worked to change its culture:

When I came . . . here, we had to kind of work on the culture of getting the engineers to be interested in patents again. Because . . . as [the president and chief technology officer said] said, . . . "You know, our culture has shifted over the last three to four years, and people now just don't even think about patents." And so what we did was I started talking—first, I had to just emphasize to them that it was a priority again, and that I had a budget, and that my goal was to double our portfolio of patents every year or two.

Two points bear emphasis here. First, the "interest" in patents ebbs and flows depending on whether there is money in the budget for patent prosecution, whether counsel is interested, and whether firm culture will support it. Second, the company must choose to pursue a patent strategy. IP is not necessarily on people's minds, but IP is something that must be self-consciously pursued and woven into the business strategy.

Discouraged with the time it takes to file patents and their uncertain payoff for the company and their work in it, many engineers withdrew from initiating disclosures and coordinating with counsel. Donald developed several ways to persuade employees to shift attitudes and think more positively about patents: one is to incentivize disclosures by "giv[ing] bonuses to the engineers that have assisted in the patent applications, and in the patents being issued"; another is to set up more explicit relationships and reporting structures within the company:

You need an in-house point of contact; probably a general counsel, with the money and the desire to do it. And then you need a technology person: a person that's in charge of technology that's interested in doing it, and sees the value. And then . . . you really need an outside patent lawyer that understands your products.

With these kinds of relationships in place, Donald increased his company's patent portfolio: "in my two and a half years here, we have probably done twenty patent applications."

Not all in-house counsel find the process of education and submission to be smooth or stable. Jacqueline, a lawyer who began her legal career at the early stages of software development and commercialization in the early 1980s, describes the "heated discussions" about IP she started in her company in an effort to change its culture and grow its profitability. Jacqueline's story was mentioned in Chapter 4 in the context of reputational interests in the lives and work of creators and innovators, but I quote it at length here to illustrate how prolonged the process of encouraging innovative employees to comply with IP law and business strategies can be:

There was a very long and difficult process of changing the mind-set at [the company]—and I think at other companies, too—from hoarding the true essence of your technology to wanting to share it with the world, because you realized the tremendous impact of what you were doing. So almost as soon as we got the developers to the point where they would understand the need for protection, the open-source movement started, and I had a lot of resistance to the concept that we wouldn't make our stuff open and available. So there was this libertarian, subterranean movement afoot that created a lot of difficulty for us because of the need to protect the business. I mean, basically, you cannot give away the source code, but the sort of the artistic libertarian instincts in a software developer are to share. . . . Plus, [other organizations] suddenly started pumping out stuff. And so there was a community of people that want to share all of this, and getting them comfortable with the idea that they could do it under very, very prescribed and circumscribed environments was hard to do. . . . Internally, I spent a lot of time with the developers. I attended their meetings; I did training sessions; I just . . . had to reinforce the message. And there were— I won't say "bitter"—but there were very, very heated discussions that went on between the legal function and the development function. And there was also a lot of tension in terms of time frames. They didn't want to wait until the patent application was necessarily on file in Japan before they launched, because there was a huge push to launch. And you know, the alpha and the beta process would jeopardize the patent should the beta be viewed as an open beta. So there was an awful lot of tension between protecting the IP and getting it out to wherever it needed to go, whether it was the user community or the so-called developer community.

In contrast to the publishing executive who is confident about the ability of legal compliance to protect and enhance his company's opportunities, Jacqueline, a vice president and in-house counsel at her high-tech company, describes a much longer—and even combative—mentoring process in which she had to convince engineers and programmers that her view of the role of IP was the right one. She used a combination of personal relationships, training and retraining ("reinforc[ing] the message"), and reshaping of the community through ongoing discussions around shared notions of progress and social welfare. As she describes in this context:

So the shift over, say, ten or fifteen years was that the developers began to understand they really wanted the software protected. They embraced the idea once patents became an established form of protection . . . [It] became actually something that developers really understood. They personally benefited from it, but there was a long, long history of invention in this country. . . . [They] become part of a storied legacy of the great inventors. So patents was, in a way, a much easier sell. And you have to get the developer involved. I mean, they write the invention statement, and they work all the way through, and their name is on that in the Patent Office. So there's a real . . . ownership and pride and coolness factor to being an inventor, and being part of the company, like . . . [an] IBM or an HP.

Jacqueline considers her company's engineers to be her partners. She works directly with them, one-on-one and in groups, to change the culture at her firm. She uses historical stories of American inventiveness to teach why patents matter for their company and why her engineering colleagues should understand IP as a tool for progress (rather than a tool for control). In so doing, she appeals to ego and community rather than to profit. There is likely some skepticism among the engineers as to whether patents are really necessary to keep the company in good standing and growing. But the partnerships and communities built through "heated discussions" and working groups bind the company around common projects, such that filing for patents and protecting the companies software becomes the means for achieving a shared goal of continuing the company's projects and maintaining obligations to one another.

Jacqueline's account connects *disruption* with *instruction* insofar as instruction is an effective way to reshape norms.[10] Lawyers use a combination of gatekeeping, instructive behavior, and their status as experts to model and guide optimal behavior. Ironically, however, the lawyer is technically a fiduciary of the client, hired to pursue the client's needs and goals. The lawyer has few, if any, goals independent of the client, other than practicing law in a reputable and ethical manner (and being paid for it). "Thinking IP" and "selling" the idea of patents are, therefore, strategies that the lawyer develops in his or her *interpretation* of her client's needs and goals. The lawyers I spoke with appear to drive the normalization of IP as a business strategy (or a strategy for achieving other client goals), which then becomes routinized into an everyday practice. This in turn feeds into the client's growing awareness and use of IP in creative and innovative fields.

Persuasive and instructional tactics intended to protect and commercialize output occur in the copyright industries as well. But instead of having an attorney that acts like a "teacher," many musicians, writers, and artists have agents who fill that role. Meredith, a music agent, explains how she "coaches" her clients to create marketing strategies and sign licensing contracts (sometimes for commercials, which are unpopular among her musician-clients, and sometimes for albums, which are desirable). Sometimes, she says, she "coaxes" them into uncomfortable business arrangements to help sustain their lifestyle and achieve their professional goals—to continue to write and play music. She says:

Maybe I'm slimy in a good way? . . . I think it takes a little bit of slime . . . or "spin," for lack of a positive word for it—just to be able to coach or coax . . . an artist into doing something that they don't want to do. . . . Knowing the difference between when it's actually unhealthy for that person to do something, or when it's just outside of their comfort zone, and so it's a good thing. . . . Knowing which bits of information they need to know in order to do their best work.

Meredith's explanation illustrates how, without her intervention—be it as a coach or teacher—clients may fail to consider how brand management and copyright (as opposed to simply performing and having a website) can help achieve their goals. The "spin" (or "slime") Meredith mentions recalls the persuasive narratives of "storied inventors" that Jacqueline mentioned earlier to entice her computer programmer-colleagues to participate in IP transactions. There are no ulterior motives here. The lawyers and agents understand that clients need to be taught or coached to create IP and comply with its rules, even when doing so is in their best interest.

Optimally, working with artists and scientists to generate IP is a two-way collaboration. In my best moments as a teacher, while I help students unpack complex legal history and doctrine for use in their future as lawyers, they reveal to me new ways of understanding the history and doctrine that enrich my future teaching of it. Robert, a university professor and chemist, who is also an entrepreneur, describes one such collaboration among himself, a student, and a lawyer, as they work together to draft a patent. This professor does not need the money the patent will generate. Rather, he is attached to—and proud of—the discoveries over the course of his career, in collaboration with both university colleagues and businesspeople. Filing for a patent is one way to share the work with a larger audience, to claim it and name himself as the originator of his idea, and perhaps also to reap financial rewards from it. Robert's experience patenting his work—the reason for it and its process—is explicitly collaborative and puzzlelike. He does not complain, as do others, about the time it took to draft the patent (or to benefit from it). His focus is on learning about the innovative or creative work that occurs in the process of making or sharing IP, a dimension the previously quoted attorneys are trying to impart to their company colleagues as well. I interviewed Robert in his office at the university. He told me:

The rule [at the university] is that if you develop something that's really new that you think is patentable, you are supposed to write an invention report. . . . I mean, you can't make something done at the university into a trade secret because that's unethical. . . . [N]ot only are you taking money and doing something you shouldn't do, but it's bad for the student, because if you are concealing something that would help the student get a job, that's really totally unacceptable. So anything we did at the university, you know, we would write papers and describe what we did. . . . [O]ccasionally, we'd come across something I thought was worth patenting, and so we would in some cases we filed patents. . . . I talked with [university] patent lawyers, but I actually wrote the drafts of the patents. . . . I had one very good student, and he wrote one of them. But I helped him a lot. . . . I had to learn the stuff, and it was like playing some weird computer game. . . . It's very arcane. But normally, what would happen is that I would write a draft, and the patent lawyer would work on it, and then

I'd get it back, and I'd say, "OK, I see"—and every time I did it, it'd get a little better at it. And . . . then at [my outside, for-profit company] . . . there were a few things we patented there too, and we used a patent firm in [nearby city] who was pretty good, I think. . . . [I]t's not that he sat down and told me what to do. . . . [W]e talked about it, I got a general idea, I wrote a draft, he fixed it up, I looked at it; I said, "OK, now the next time I can do it better."

The kind of instruction this university professor receives differs in kind from the lawyer-client relationships described in the other quoted interviews. Unlike the in-house counsel, firm counsel, and for-profit employees discussed already, this university professor does not believe he *needs* the IP to continue his scientific research. That he resorts to patenting late in the process of research and discovery, and writes his own patent with a lawyer-mentor's help, could indicate that he is an outlier case. But in fact, much of the interview data confirm at least one part of Robert's experience as common among other patent holders and entrepreneurs: lawyers come late in the innovation cycle. Here, the lawyer is the last person to enter the process of perfecting or harvesting IP, which derives from the invention itself and from the ongoing and everyday work of artists and scientists. As one lawyer says, "Legal is . . . separate." Lawyers disrupt and instruct on the role of IP in creative and innovative work, thereafter (they hope) normalizing IP's presence and usefulness for future endeavors.

An exception to this theme are the cases in which lawyers instruct innovators early in research and development how to work around patented technology and, in so doing, instigate the creation of new inventions, be they objects or processes. "Design-arounds," as they are called in the patent industries, where innovators review patents for the purpose of avoiding infringement and invent something new while doing so, may be necessary to avoid licensing fees and costs of infringement. But they are also a challenge—a source of play and new innovation.[11] An in-house lawyer describes some of the value he adds to the innovative side of the business:

I have had those situations where people come to me with this great idea, and then I show them the patent that is blocking everybody from practicing their idea. . . . So that is frustrating. But see, then we get into that academic exercise of designing around a patent. And that's a pretty fun patent attorney exercise, because patents are meant to promote the useful arts, they're published out there for the world to see, the claims are published so that you know where the meets and bounds of their IP are, and working with a development team designing around patents is perfectly legal and it's a very intellectually stimulating . . . challenge.

Here, the lawyer directly provides necessary counsel to avoid liability and to guide the research within the overall business strategy. Learning how to read and interpret patent claims, in combination with the research expertise of colleagues, can lead to new discoveries.[12] This kind of innovation is often born of necessity, given the roadblocks caused by existing patents. This speaks to subject of Chapter 1—the origins innovative and creative work—and to whether or how IP plays a role in work's initial stages. Further, the design-around is a way for the lawyer to justify the value his legal expertise brings to the innovative business, as well as the value of IP more generally.

Justifications

IP lawyers justify their work for clients in a variety of ways. Scholarship about the legal profession shows that lawyers, like doctors and other professionals who render services rather than make and sell goods, must "construct[] a professional commodity" to justify their status and pay.[13] Justifications for legal services relating to IP fall into three, sometimes overlapping categories in the interviews: IP is a signal, its fuels a company, and it provides freedom for clients. These categories largely mirror the mechanisms described by literature on the legal profession more generally, suggesting that IP lawyers are not all that different from other specialized lawyers.[14] Clients purchase IP lawyers' services because IP lawyers explain how IP itself is valuable and how only lawyers can secure IP properly, and because lawyers connect IP to other things or values about which the client cares.[15]

Material Signals

The lawyers and business agents I spoke to note that IP often functions as an effective signal or a tangible "thing" that those uninvolved in the underlying creative or innovative work can recognize and understand as valuable. In other words, the legal construct literally "makes visible" the value of creative or innovative work. For example, a sculpture might inherently have value to the artist or noncommercial purchaser, but claiming IP, for the lawyer or business agent, reduces the intangible value of the sculpture into an identifiable denomination. How that denomination is measured (in money or personal rights of control) depends on how the work was made and on its maker. IP is created as a way to stabilize both the cost and control, which are relative and can be volatile. Lawyers and business agents discuss the strategies they develop to make the value of IP and their role in harvesting it obvious.

For example, Seth, in-house IP counsel in a publishing company, says that his work "isn't boilerplate. . . . [W]e do custom cabinetry here." Seth suggests the value he adds in drafting licensing agreements is like the detail, craft, and expense of making custom cabinets. The skill of lawyering requires refined, objective, and experienced judgment. The cabinet metaphor suggests another similarity between legal advice and refined carpentry—both products are everyday but invaluable—revealing how integral and useful legal guidance is perceived to be. Finally, the metaphor helps to understand and rationalize the expense of lawyers. The worth of custom cabinetry is visually and experientially obvious in its everyday use; it is considered superior in durability and beauty, and it reminds the user daily why it was worth the significant financial investment. Where at first clients may consider legal advice arbitrary or obscure, the lawyer's comparison to custom cabinetry translates his value (and the law's value) into artistry and craft—values with which the client can more easily identify.

Andrew, a software engineer and entrepreneur, uses a related metaphor to describe the role patents have in his business. He tells me that he brings together his engineering team and a lawyer and asks the group: "What do you have you think we can patent?" Then, he says:

We would go and patent those things. But . . . there is typically one or two ideas that are really valuable. . . . And then the company ends up getting a dozen or two dozen patents. The rest of them are just the blocking stuff—or not even that: they're just something you build to look very attractive to a potential buyer. But they're not real—they're like detail and documentations.

The notion that IP is made to provide "detail and documentation"—in other words, *substance*—for the company's portfolio to bulk up or demonstrate worth is similar to Seth's metaphor. The patent may or may not correspond to what the scientist or engineer believes is truly important for scientific and technological progress.[16] To Andrew, the thing created is "real" when it is "truly inventive" or "a substantial improvement" over previous inventions or processes. But for the lawyers whose goals are to build IP portfolios to bring cash into a business to invest in more research, development, and commercialization, the number of issued patents is as "real" as it gets. "It's about business edge," says another high-tech entrepreneur:

I mean, [venture capitalists] are nuts about that. I don't understand why. Because they understand so little about the [patented] space, you know, they just need some assurance. [Patents] gives you this piece of paper. . . . [The venture capitalists] go back to their investors and say, "We should invest in the company which has proprietary technology."

Donald, an in-house lawyer, shares a story about how, at a previous job, he watched a patent lawyer "create value":

[The company] did this trick. They had an in-house patent lawyer, and he really created value. . . . [W]e bought that company for $10 million . . . and we sold it for $100 million eighteen months later . . . [T]hat in-house patent lawyer, who is today at IBM—God bless him. I mean, he created value. People looked at that company, the potential buyers, and said, "Wow! This company has one hundred issued US patents. This company has sued its two main competitors and won one . . . and already has an offer to settle the other one."

By describing the growth of the company as a "trick"—like conjuring or an illusion—Donald suggests that the tenfold growth of the company may lack substantive merit or otherwise be overvalued. The relationship of patents to the "real" value of the company is left ambiguous in both of these examples. But the function of IP is clear: to signal worth in a way that appears transparent, quantifiable, and durable. (Whether the signal is "true" is a different question.) The irony, or course, is that patents are often criticized (in the interviews and elsewhere) for being ambiguous and unquantifiable in risk and reward.[17] The concrete metaphors used by lawyers and business allies to justify IP and their role in creating it only underscores the diverse (and confused) ways in which IP functions in creative and innovative fields.

As already discussed in Chapters 1 and 2, the origins of IP are often described as a natural process and creative and innovative work as a form of nature itself. It can grow from a seed or arrive like flowing water. IP is also compared to tangible things, "chits to trade," "something that [you] can put [your] hands on." This further supports the justification of IP as a stabilizing and durable form and of the lawyer's role as assembling or maintaining it. Lawyers also regularly describe law (both generally and IP law) as a kind of physical obstacle for which they are the skilled drivers who navigate it.[18] Another in-house counsel explains that "a lot of what I do [is] organize teams to work on problems":

Just today, before you came in, we were looking at having some of our US-based employees sent to Ireland to ramp up [the business]. . . . [T]here's all sorts of issues around employment law, . . . tax law, and IP. . . . At one level, it's a business . . . issue, but it has a legal nexus. . . . And the legal side tends to be a driver, because if you run into a legal obstacle, it's not so—business obstacles you can work around independently. There's no external constraint. If you have a legal obstacle . . . that tends to be a show stopper. So you've got to identify those. . . . And lawyers are pretty good at driving solutions.

Although this quote does resonate with a more malleable form of law (in which rules can be manipulated and ambiguities harnessed to suit client needs), for this lawyer, legal obstacles are less flexible than other kinds of hurdles encountered in the business world. The law is a durable edifice against which more fluid business transactions take place and with which business practices must reckon.

IP sometimes plays a crucial role in other types of business transactions. Another in-house lawyer describes specifically why he goes through the trouble of filing for copyright on software his company makes and sells, even though his company's revenue comes primarily through contracts not copyrights: "We had no copyright applications until about a year ago. And then I sued one of our customers, and . . . it was just a requisite to get my suit into the federal court." To be clear, this lawyer did not enforce the right to receive copyright royalties in federal court; he eschewed even the possibility of high statutory damages in copyright (from $750 to $150,000 per act of infringement): "You can actually get statutory damages in certain cases. And I don't care about that. I just want to have a registration on file . . . for enforcement purposes." He is simply seeking to enforce licensing terms for the software and service contracts, he says, and enforcing those agreements in federal court as part of a copyright suit under federal law is more effective than state court (as a simple contract action). As in other examples, here, IP law is a formal structure that channels a lawyer's and a businessperson's choices and activities on behalf of clients. Law is a material feature of the work and of its successful pursuit. It is something to which artists and scientists must react and against which their behavior reverberates. The lawyer in each of these cases justifies the work he or she performs for others and the time and expense spent (lawyers are a cost center, not a profit maker, as many reminded me) because they are the most ably trained to navigate the law's course.

IP as Fuel

Lawyers also justify pursuing IP as a tool for achieving clients' goals of financial viability. IP becomes a kind of fuel or currency with which future investments are made and against which credit can be extended, much in the same way service contracts, equipment, and employees are tools or mechanisms for carrying on the financial side of business. When IP signals value or growth potential, it becomes a device that sustains the capacity and assists the growth of a business.

In the initial stages of a business, IP facilitates relationships between the creators or innovators and the investors. Several licensing officers treat IP as the "proof of concept" that hooks investors into a business relationship and encourages funding to continue research through to commercialization. These licensing officers make clear that the IP doesn't ensure success as a business matter; only the existence of IP minimizes the risk that the invention or creation is not worthwhile. As one venture capitalist said, the IP works as a check on "inflated view[s] of what [the invention is] worth" and, given the expense of patenting, can prevent the "noncommercial reasons [for seeking patent protection] which make no sense." He continues: "Had we . . . no IP going in, we would never have been able to start the company."[19]

The initial business relationships facilitated by IP can be adversarial as well as productive. One investor in the high-tech industry, Kevin, describes how the potential for a patent infringement lawsuit can bring competitors together in a joint venture:

We got this huge clash, and it looked like it was going to go nowhere. . . . And we sent them a "Hey, you are probably infringing on our core patents [letter]." . . . And it certainly, you know, changes the tenor of the business conversation. . . . We sent them a nasty letter, and they came back to the table.

Kevin says later that although the patent threat may have brought folks back to the table, the substantive success of the collaboration was because "if you want this stuff to actually work, go do it with a . . . company that's solving the whole problem," meaning the collaboration succeeded because of the skill and talent of the engineers. He goes on:

Very, very, very infrequently do[] [patents] matter. I mean, all the companies that I work for, we all file patents. And we are pretty cynical about it. . . . We don't think these patents are really necessarily going to ever be worth anything to us, except in this whole morass that is people wagging sticks at each other and saying, "I am going to sue you over your patents," and "No, you are not! Ha, ha! Look at my patents here!"

In these examples, patents are business formalities that, optimally, encourage competitors to collaborate to avoid costly and time-consuming lawsuits.

Lawyers often have to teach clients why IP exclusivity is necessary or to coax them into making the investment in time that it takes to make IP. Many lawyers say simply, "Our exclusivity in certain technologies has really enabled our company to even exist." Others are more concrete about the nature of the company's existence and the benefits derived from the IP. They explain that without the patented technology—especially in drug and medical device companies—there is no revenue stream, either for the company's day-to-day needs or for further investment in research. In businesses with both copyright and patents, lawyers add that the IP provides a competitive edge through the perception of exclusivity that forces competitors to trade (take a license) or work harder at distinguishing themselves (create new and different work). Irene, a copyright lawyer, says:

IP law just sets the baseline, which is that there is this thing, and somebody has some amount of exclusivity in it, and that comes out of copyright law, the fact that one creator can say, "OK, I have this thing. Now I've got to figure out what to do with it, but I have this thing, and it's my thing, and I can keep other people from doing things with it unless they ask me." That's sort of the copyright law piece of it. And then the rest of it moves into other field—parts of law, and just basic business negotiation.

Irene is confident that she is skilled at figuring out what to do with the copyright and how to make it work for the creator as a business matter. It is a resource, and the lawyer's expertise lies in turning that raw material into something more evolved and useful. Another IP lawyer recounts hearing this question from a client: "How do you commercialize it? . . . We think this thing has value. How do we go about realizing the value of this thing we've created?" To this, the lawyer responds with a panoply of possible contractual and business arrangements, including IP. Whether IP is essential to the success of a business or one of many options is less clear to me in both of these examples. Regardless, lawyers justify the creation of IP as a basic resource—a form of currency, security, or power source—from which the ongoing business derives momentum and strength.

IP as Freedom

Lawyers also justify pursuing or protecting IP as the means through which a person or company can satisfy nonfinancial interests, such as freedom to engage in work on their own terms and the protection of other particular personal interests. This category resonates with "rights" language and is described as more vital than when IP is a fungible commodity, a flexible tool, or a resource for creating value.

IP lawyers appeal to their clients' desire to continue working at what they love for its own sake. An in-house patent lawyer says he "convince[s] [his scientist colleagues] that it's the value of protecting what we're doing from third parties doing the same thing." Another in-house lawyer at an energy-development company puts it in even starker terms: "Our exclusivity in certain technologies has really enabled our company to even exist. . . . We license some cool technology from [another entity], and we're the only ones that have these features. That's a wonderful story for me to convey to our research staff." Chapter 3 covers "freedom to operate" and rent seeking as two of the ways that IP works to help a business grow. But these examples are also relevant for how lawyers encourage clients to engage with IP on the clients' own terms.

Meredith, a music agent, recounts a similar situation in a very different market. She encouraged her client, a well-regarded folk singer, to make an advertisement by selling her voice for a national retailer. The advertisement offers generous compensation under a particular kind of performance royalty, although doing the advertisement is inconsistent with this singer's reputational interests and politics. Why does her agent encourage the singer to nonetheless perform on the commercial? For two reasons:

By doing a thirty-second spot like that, she'll get more money in the next year than she'd get from her record label in six years. . . . This was going to be money that she could make without leaving her house. And that's usually the only reason people give. [For her] . . . it was also a really big confidence builder. Like here is a woman who is known for her lyrics . . . and who people have complimented her on her voice, but never has she only used her voice as a tool. . . . And so this kind of led to this sense of her voice as a thing, . . . as another signature thing other than her words. And so in some respects, doing this was [for] very commercial reasons, and in some respects, it was a real confidence booster to see an agency and a huge company . . . choose her voice.

In these examples, the lawyer or business manager talks to the client about IP as a method of maximizing other professional goals (finishing a project or honing a skill) and subjective desires (feeling good about the work and continuing to work in a physically and fiscally comfortable manner). At first, to clients, IP creation seems to be trade-off, but with more context and explanation, they come to understand IP as related more directly to autonomy and self-direction than wealth.

The lawyers I spoke with typically understand their role in maximizing client's nonfinancial interests as one of vigilance concerning risk assessment and accounting. One lawyer describes himself "as the in-house patent guy [who] lives with a calculator right next to my keyboard." His job is to assess the costs of IP against the benefits and to monitor outside counsel fees. A businessman who works in the entertainment industry tells me his "attorney sits there and [counts] how many jellybeans we are going to have in that contract. . . . He's a bulldog and behaves like a bulldog," while he himself avoids jellybean counting in his interactions with clients because "it leaves a bad taste in the mouth of the client if we are going back and forth about petty stuff on a contract." Within companies, lawyers are perceived as being most able and best positioned to argue about money, allowing the personal, substantive relationships to be free from the corrupting influence of dollars. In each of these cases, the lawyer may play a particular role for the client vis-à-vis his or her IP, which does not necessarily achieve maximal revenue but instead preserves other client interests, such as productive relationships and a viable workplace.

A common complaint about lawyers is that they see risk everywhere. But seeing and evaluating risk is also often why we hire lawyers; assessing risk and advising on a particular course of action in compliance with the law (or addressing problems concerning noncompliance) is prototypical legal work. Clients seem to be particularly frustrated when the evaluation of risk is communicated, or understood, as a command to "stop" or even "proceed with caution." Lawyers, however, see themselves as mediating between business and scientists, as a form of "damage control" and making sure to "dot all . . . *i*'s, cross all . . . *t*'s . . . because otherwise, it's going to be a lot more unpleasant . . . when we're suing on the product." The rights IP provides, however they are explained to the client, are optimally effectuated with a lawyer's detailed-oriented expertise. As Cary, an in-house lawyer, says, "Most people think it's creating assets, these patents we write, but keeping your company out of trouble is the most important thing." I heard this sentiment from clients as well. Sadie, a public artist, painter, and sculptor,

characterizes her relationship with an attorney as comforting—she knows
that she is avoiding unwanted and particularly nightmarish outcomes:

I've since gone back to this [lawyer] periodically to get clarification on something. . . . There was a book I was asked to be part of, and I wasn't really sure
what they were asking me. They wanted to use images. . . . And I just wanted to
make sure that I hadn't signed over my life somehow.

In this situation, IP creation under a lawyer's supervision provides the
client with a sense of insurance, assurance, and sovereignty. An entrepreneur in the medical device industry finds that "initial consulting phases
[with] the [IP] lawyers . . . very helpful. They can just provide some comfort
as, 'OK, here's what I'm worried about." And although insurance is not
normally conceived of as enabling freedom and choice, of course it does
when misfortune arises. IP law may be relevant only around the edges of
a creator or innovator's daily life, but when it does become relevant, it is
important that it work for, not against, him or her. The interviews with
lawyers contain many examples of this insurance mode of IP as the lawyers' reason for encouraging its creation and protection.

The quote below is from Cary, an in-house counsel at a growing energy
company. Cary combines all the categories for justifying IP listed earlier:
the durable "landscape" or "architecture" of IP law that lawyers "navigate," IP's fungibility and flexible mechanisms, and the rights-based view
of IP law as an insurer of freedom and personal interests. The most strik-
ing metaphor is of holding the client's hand through "patent land mines":

From an IP standpoint, *architecture* . . . [and] *landscapes* are words we use a
lot, and in a previous job . . . we were looking at expanding our product line
into a whole new category, full of all kinds of patent land mines. And at the
end of the day I was able to hold their hand, and navigate the course, and we
knew there was risk of a lawsuit, but we knew we were in the right, and we had
a good argument. We launched the product, we got sued, they settled within a
few months, and we sold $100 million worth of product in first year.

The images in this quote from the interview suggest that the creation of IP
may cause disasters for some (as much as it may create riches for others)

and that a lawyer may be able to prevent those disasters from occurring. The lawyer, like a parent or caretaker, enables passage and development (a kind of protection and fulfillment) for a creator or innovator to accomplish his or her goals.

These themes of freedom and enablement resonate with literature on development as freedom, the central tenet of which is that economic development is insufficient if it doesn't also improve each person's capacity to make choices and participate meaningfully in political, economic, and cultural life.[20] To the lawyers and business folks in my study, IP protection is justified as a mechanism that increases the freedom to work (it sustains a company and/or it facilitates research and creative agendas by providing protective space) and the freedom to be acknowledged and reckoned with (to claim a seat at the table and assert preferences). Individuals and companies recognize that they need lawyers to help foment these freedoms (to reduce the risk of unfreedom from economic loss or legal barriers). As Madhavi Sunder writes, paraphrasing Amartya Sen's seminal work on this topic, "A central insight of Sen's theory of development as freedom is the recognition of 'the mutually reinforcing connection between freedoms of different kinds.'"[21] The freedom to work in conditions that are industrious and fair (for both individual employees and business owners) and to pursue inventive and creative practices relates to both economic welfare and political justice (two other kinds of freedoms). According to the lawyers and business agents in my study, the production, distribution, and enforcement of IP rights is justified as a means toward each of these kinds of freedom.

IP'S INCARNATIONS AND THE LAW

The three justifications of the time and money lawyers spend on IP correlate to three different conceptions of law more generally. Literature on both the jurisprudential categories of law and popular legal consciousness describes various ways law may be thought to order society.[22] The solidity and permanence of law's structures symbolize (and justify) its enduring strength as a system of rules under which we agree to live—it is a durable, stable form, for better or for worse. Thus, the law acts as a foundational or structural backdrop against which much else is measured. Law, here, is an edifice, dominating and strong, like the stone courthouses.[23]

Generally, law can also be a tool to wield or a game to play. "Sometimes you have to sue," several lawyers note, even if the litigation is regrettable. But many emphasize that "playing by the rules" is important for building business fairly. As much as lawyers highlight legal rules, they also highlight their ambiguous or flexible nature as a benefit. They see themselves as putting "IP to work." This implies that there are multiple ways to engage law and do business well, and that lawyers can effectively navigate these avenues. As one vice president and general counsel observes:

Some of the ambiguities are helpful to companies. . . . Maybe your competitor can patent this, or maybe they can go back and file that continuation, and get these claims. The current system . . . puts a lot of value . . . in pending applications. Even though they're not enforceable, they're still out there as a question mark.

To this businessman and lawyer, taking advantage of these ambiguities is both fair and productive. In addition to formal legal routes (some of which lead to creating IP), there are informal and nonlegal routes (e.g., interpersonal dynamics). In this context, the fluid nature of law (and IP law specifically) can be both beneficial and risky.

Law generally (and IP specifically) can also reflect and preserve fundamental values of artists and innovators, such as productive work relationships and self-determination. When IP law delineates rights like control and exclusivity, lawyers see how it may enable innovators and creators, in conjunction with their business partners, to structure and drive a working life on desirable terms. To be sure, as Chapters 3 and 4 discuss, IP law does not always satisfactorily provide all rights that artists, scientists, or business organizations seek (e.g., reputational control, business predictability, control over critical uses). But by serving as an authoritative mechanism for claiming *some* of those intrinsic rights through forms of ownership and control, IP law at least partially and symbolically designates as valuable the creative and innovative work (and emboldens those who do it). The value is both intrinsic and extrinsic: it promotes personal well-being for those who desire recognition and tribute for their talent and for those who seek to maintain productive and emotionally satisfying relationships with collaborators and audiences; and it promotes professional well-being in the form of economic welfare and work and lifestyle flexibility.

These fundamental values seem most applicable to individuals, but as the interview data demonstrate and company lawyers explain, company welfare is the real purview of lawyers. The umbrella of company welfare includes nurturing organizational characteristics that matter to employees and clients, such as enabling both collaboration and independence at work, protecting or honoring reputation, receiving fair pay, and producing excellent service or goods that are valued by peers and a paying public. It also includes characteristics more commonly viewed as shareholder concerns, such as the company's ability to be nimble, to optimize its operations, and to stay competitive. IP lawyers invoke all these values to justify the creation and assertion of IP rights—though usually not to the full extent of those rights, and rarely in isolation. The values are what clients seek, not the IP itself. This is easy to forget when lawyers and judges, in the interpretation and application of IP law, abbreviate the importance of IP to the prevention of copying and facilitating the recuperation of financial investments. This leaves too much out of the whole story to be accurate.

These incarnations of law or legality—as durable, as a game, and as reflective of intrinsic or fundamental values—are well established in the literature on legal consciousness. That each is present in my discussions with creators and innovators about the forms and functions of IP law (and the creative and innovative work that originates the IP) simply confirms that IP law has diverse functions and manifestations consistent with other fields of law. Even the lawyers and businesspeople, who may be tasked with the most narrow of economic charges (keep the company productive and keep clients away from risk), cite an array of reasons, identifying assorted times and places for IP to intervene. Far from a singular incentive to produce science and art, IP is both capacious and contradictory, even to the lawyers and businesspeople. Decades ago, Charles Fried argued that for lawyers to be moral professionals, their role as "friends"—committed to their clients interests in view of but not necessarily always aligned with a larger community's interest—was "so far mandated by moral right that any advanced legal system that did not sanction this conception would be unjust."[24] The lawyers I interviewed conceive of themselves as "friends" in this way, but the broader community, inhabited by the dominant story of incentives and property rights, has lost sight of how IP law is created as part of that friendship.

In the process of legal reform, lawyers and advocates may choose to identify the needs and desires of those doing the science and the art initially—be they individuals or companies—and to tailor legal and business structures to fulfill those needs and desires. This is not a call for "employee rights" or even, in IP parlance, strong moral rights. But it does seek recognition for the diversity of creativity and innovation that goes on within IP-rich fields and the variety of forms IP takes (without full enforcement) to promote both. Given these variations, and IP's underutilization more broadly, IP reform should proceed with an eye on flexibility. The legal community should not be restricted by theories that focus narrowly on financial incentives. These incentives account for only small slices of industry behavior. And when they are accurate, they accomplish the singular goal of aggregating firm wealth without realizing (or even articulating) the primary and precious interests of individual creators and innovators and their communities.

CHAPTER 6

Distribution

CREATIVE AND INNOVATIVE WORK is meant to circulate. It not only establishes relationships between people and organizations but also enables the creation of more objects, structures, and associations. Absent dissemination of creative and innovative work, private interests and the public good are unlikely to progress. This last chapter looks at how and why work circulates and how its protection through IP may promote or thwart its dissemination.

Before delving into the interview data on dissemination, it bears noting that Chapters 4, 5, and 6 embody contrasting philosophies of law. Chapter 5 represents a positivist legal tradition in which law is a social fact to be applied. Lawyers use external rules (IP laws) to identify and affect certain outcomes. In Chapter 4, law is a natural tradition, arising from (or should be consonant with) moral principles. The reputational interests that influence individuals and corporate agents stem from deeply felt moral beliefs but often suffer from conflict with formal legal rules. This last chapter looks at how disseminating work is inextricably entwined with IP's public function, which explicitly speaks to the constitutional goal of "progress" for copyright and patent law ("to promote the progress of science and the useful arts," art. 1, sec. 8, cl. 8). The data in this chapter also appear to resonate with theories of distributive justice. When IP works well, IP law should optimally distribute creative and innovative work, which means fairly allocating the works' public benefits and private rewards.

Too often, discussions about IP law neglect its focus on the dissemination and subsequent use of creative and innovative works. But dissemination is the *ultimate* goal of IP law—incentivizing creation is actually the secondary goal.[1] Decade after decade, Supreme Court decisions have confirmed this understanding of the purpose of IP law, whether by broadly defining fair use to facilitate access and distribution (as in *Sony Corp. v.*

Universal City Studios, a.k.a. the "Betamax" case) or by limiting the use of injunctions (as in the more recent *eBay v. MercExchange*).[2] In the 2012 case *Golan v. Holder*, the Supreme Court again affirmed its view of the original intent behind the progress clause of the US Constitution, in article 1, section 8, clause 8. *Golan* concerned section 104 of the Copyright Act, which "restores" a foreign work's US copyright under certain conditions. In that case, the Court agreed that section of the Copyright Act did not incentivize the foreign work (which was already made years earlier) but promoted its further dissemination: "Evidence from the founding . . . suggests that inducing dissemination—as opposed to creation—was viewed as an appropriate means to promote science."[3]

The statutory basis of IP confirms the important role of distribution and access to serve the public. Until 1976, copyright did not attach until the work was *published*, which was interpreted to mean publically available on a reasonably nonrestrictive basis. Patent rights are typically considered quid pro quo for the public disclosure of an invention and are claimed by filing invention specifications and written descriptions with the Patent and Trademark Office. And trademark rights do not attach until they are used in commerce and acquire trademark significance, which means they must be available and known by the consuming public to signify the source of the product or service to which they are attached (trade secret protection is an exception to this principle). Year after year, the courts confirm this understanding of IP, reminding us that "private motivation must ultimately serve the cause of promoting broad public availability of literature, music, and the other arts,"[4] and that the "sole interest of the United States" lies not in rewards to authors or inventors but in "the general benefits derived by the public from the[ir] labor."[5]

While the other chapters describe ways in which the experience of artists and scientists clashes with the formal legal rules or policy that structures IP law, here, the mechanisms of and motives for distribution appear to coincide with the original principles underlying IP. The interviewees provide accounts of distributive impulses and systems to affect and constitute a public or community interest. Moreover, the private interest of wealth aggregation (although not necessarily other private interests) is overshadowed by the dissemination and public function of creative and innovative work. Given the breadth of literature since the advent of the Internet on the generativity of networks and the benefits of sharing, on the tragedy of the anticommons, and on the ubiquity of user-generated content and inventions, it may be unsurprising that the interviewees recognize this important public or community function of dissemination. The public feature of dissemination is often overlooked—or worse, demonized as a pet cause for liberal politics. It is this chapter's focus. The chapter parses the various reasons for and forms of dissemination from the interviews as they substantiate and delineate "progress" to be a public good and as it relates creative or innovative work with IP law.

The economic rationale behind IP law contends that exclusive rights to copy and distribute are critical to fulfilling the constitutional progress mandate. Without the right to enjoin unlawful distribution, and by implication, the right to be paid for lawful distribution, widespread dissemination to the public would not occur. Publishers and other downstream distributors or intermediaries, whose function (and business method) is to market and distribute the original work, would not invest in culling, editing, storing, advertising, and selling the work without the right to control the form and breadth of its distribution. Concerns about and attacks on such intermediaries since the evolution of the digital age go the heart of distribution's function, promise, and risks. This economic rationale postulates that, without IP to protect and save distributional rights, there would be no intermediaries to fulfill the distributional mandate and the public would not benefit from access to creative and innovative work.

Neither the firm agents nor the individuals I spoke with substantiate this theory. They represent a broad range of industries—textbook publishers, media production companies, cloud-based storage companies, technology-transfer officers, pharmaceutical and medical device manufacturers and their distributors and licensees, high-technology venture capitalists. And every individual interviewee either engaged a distributor or himself or herself performed the distribution. While some also describe tightly controlling distribution through IP for pecuniary gain, these accounts must be considered in light of the many other ways these same entities generate revenue and continue operating and the other reasons they provide for distributing their work. Making money by tightly controlling dissemination is only one form and purpose of dissemination and not the most common within this data set. Thus, the focus of this chapter is not whether IP is necessary for distribution to be financially viable, but the many *forms* dissemination takes and the many *reasons* for engaging in it. This requires unpacking the relationship between exclusive rights to distribution and dissemination as a form of "progress," progress being the reason for which IP is statutorily created. The data analysis therefore requires disaggregating the maximization of economic return (one form of progress) from the dissemination impulse to locate the meanings of "progress," and identify mechanisms for achieving the latter.

Distributive forms are diversifying and business models are evolving. Older examples of intermediaries were more exclusive in their distribution mechanisms: text and music publishing companies such as Harper-Collins and EMI Music Publishers; film producers and distributors, such as Twentieth Century Fox and Paramount Pictures. Their twenty-first-century equivalents look very different: Amazon, Netflix, iTunes, Blogger, CD Baby, YouTube. Given the flourishing of online distribution, which requires a more open platform than those from the previous century, many people ask whether as controlled distribution is necessary for ongoing production of creative and innovative work. Online platforms—blogs, social media networks, search engines, cloud storage, exchange servers—now provide both the condition of production and the means of distribution. Whereas in the past, money was made by controlling distribution (fashioning scarcity) and distributors added value by functioning as gatekeepers (selecting and culling for quality), today money is made, for example, through advertising alongside the display of free content or by accumulating nominal fees for accessing the platform. This shift, which many experts consider a crisis in creative and innovative industries, is rooted in the issues surrounding the openness (or threatened closure) of distribution channels, and not necessarily in the fight against unauthorized personal use.[6] This chapter contributes to this conversation by exploring what the interview data says about the forms, risks, and benefits of distribution in our digital age.

Why do interviewees distribute their work? For the same reasons they explain making and claiming the work in the first place. The pragmatic conceptions of IP illustrated in Chapter 3 appear again in conjunction with distribution, with one crucial addition. They are making money, building relationships, fostering autonomy or self-definition, and *critically engaging and developing core competence*s. These four interests determine the form, manner, and conditions of exchange. Overall, across the interviews, there is less a focus on optimizing controlled and fee-based distribution than on elaborating the variety of valued and fruitful outcomes effected by the many forms that dissemination can take. This suggests a broader scope of application for IP law (given its distributional focus) to facilitate the various goals that dissemination and access seek to achieve. Moreover, insofar as particular forms of distribution reflect and reinforce recognizable, productive relationships—between employee and employer, creator and intermediary, manufacturer and consumer, artist-inventor and audience[7]—aligning reasons for dissemination with IP's distributive rules may assist the just formation and maintenance of those relationships and their personal and public benefits. In light of the misalignment of IP's controlled distribution with the looser distributional variations described in the interviews, distribution and its goal of progress are largely left to private choices. This may pose problems that better alignment (through less exclusive IP rights) could fix. If the data are an accurate measure of preferences, looser IP rights do not interfere with the private choices that creators and innovators make and would lead to broader dissemination in the forms selected, thus maximizing progress as defined by the interviewees.

* * *

Across the interviews, there appear to be five distinct modes of distribution:

1. *Many and more:* The interviewees manufacture or reproduce as many copies of their work as possible to distribute it as widely as possible in a market ("many and more"). Many, though not all, of the interviewees who use this method prefer distribution to occur through lawful copying, although, importantly, enforcement of unlawful copying is weak or otherwise half-hearted.
2. *Managed performance:* The interviewees also use a more selective form of distribution akin to an in-person performance. This allows

them to exercise more control over reception and receive immediate feedback from the audience ("managed performances"). While this method prevents unlawful copying to secure some revenue, it is largely preferred for its relational and reputational benefits.

3. *Sharing:* Making the work available at low or no cost for personal use is a kind of widespread dissemination among presumptive friends (those who may be strangers but are presumed to be well intentioned). The advantage of this distributional form lies in its ability to generate revenue by the sheer volume of its distribution while building an attentive audience who consumes both for pleasure and to reuse and create. Like the "managed performance," this kind of "sharing" expects an engaged audience, but unlike "many and more" is purposefully less controlled. Given the nature of this distributive impulse and form, unlawful copying is rarely mentioned. The purposes of distribution (relationship building, self-determination, and developing competence) feature prominently in this category.[8]

4. *Gifting:* The fourth method of distribution looks like donative distribution ("gifting"). The interviewees offer their work in various ways with no strings attached of exchange or engagement (e.g., outright transfer of the work or copies of the work), abiding or even encouraging unlawful copies. In these instances, interviewees seem to have no expectations except that the work be enjoyed and circulate.

5. *Holdout:* The antithesis of gifting is the "nondistribution," or "holdout," category, which some interviewees prefer when the benefit of creating or inventing is entirely internal and which benefit may be squandered by the imagined harm or anxiety of dissemination to the public.

Table 6.1 is a visual representation of the five categories and how they relate to the various goals that, for the interviewees, constitute progress (i.e., the benefits resulting from the work they do). The darker shades represent the more frequently occurring combinations and the lighter shades indicate the less frequently occurring combinations. Unshaded cells indicate that no data exists in the interviews.[9] As Table 6.1 indicates, all five forms of and reasons for dissemination exist across the interviews with varying regularity. Several forms of dissemination may also exist within a single interview, be it of an artist, scientist or engineer, business agent or lawyer. Variation within a single field, profession, or individual suggests that there are targeted reasons for choosing one form of dissemination over another. This chapter populates Table 6.1 with details of the individuals and businesses and their preferences and purposes for dissemination, in an attempt to provide a modulated or nuanced understanding of distributional control, which nuance IP laws lack.[10] The chapter also points to patterns manifest between the purpose and manner of distribution, highlighting various intermediary roles and how they partner with creators and innovators.

Some might say that dissemination of work is largely inevitable, emphasizing how the "holdout" category is the least common in the data and the most disruptive of the enumerated progress rationales. Indeed, the fact that digital rights management (DRM) and international border control have not stopped widespread dissemination attests to the momentum of distribution despite legal prohibitions. This inertia is all the more reason to understand the distinctions between the various distributional modes and the ends each facilitate—it may point to ways our current broadbrush approach to distribution (i.e., strong control with few exceptions) can be efficiently modulated to match professional norms. This chapter also discusses how the distinct reasons for ways of disseminating correlate with the particular motives for individual and group-based creativity and innovation described by behavioral science literature.[11] The categories

TABLE 6.1   Progress goals and distributional methods

Pragmatic uses for IP (progress rationales)	FORMS OF DISTRIBUTION				
	Many and more	Managed performance	Sharing	Gifting	Holdout
Making money					
Establishing relations					
Enhancing freedom					
Exercising and developing competence					

NOTE: Darkly shaded areas indicate a dense amount of interview data; the lighter the shaded area, the less interview data exists. White areas indicate the absence of interview data.

I identify in the interviews qualitatively substantiate this earlier social science research, lending validity to the data.

By connecting the modes of distribution to the kinds of "progress" each interviewee believes he or she is facilitating, we learn something about which form of dissemination promotes which kinds of goal (be it public oriented or personal) according to those doing the work. How each form of dissemination correlates to IP rules, and how each distribution form is thought to promote (or not) any of the progress rationales, teaches us how the actors in IP-rich fields minimize (or ignore), prioritize, and exploit IP law principles to achieve ends they have subjectively defined as desirable and good. If there was ever a picture of what "progress" looks like in terms of the public function of IP law (or more broadly speaking, how IP law fulfills principles of distributive justice), this chapter aims to illustrate it.

MANY AND MORE

I expected that the interviewees would, ideally, want their work to be spread as widely as possible to a diverse and growing audience at a price. To be sure, most of the interviewees seek a robust and growing market for their work so they can continue doing it. However, building an undifferentiated market—a market that is as big as possible and growing—is a fairly unusual goal across the individuals and companies interviewed. Andrew, a software engineer and successful entrepreneur with several unsuccessful endeavors behind him, says his ultimate goal all along was to build a product that grew larger and became more effective as it grew—like an online auction service. He consulted for several years to earn money to start his own company because he says, "I still wanted to build my marketplace," which he eventually did. But Andrew is unusual; few of the folks I spoke to talk explicitly, even when prodded, about the benefits of market saturation above other professional and personal goals.

One reason market saturation is not pervasive across the interviews is its close nexus with copying. Widespread distribution usually requires equally prolific reproduction of work and things (unless the distribution is in broadcast or performance form). Most interviewees did not want to or could not sustain the kind of abundant reproduction that market saturation would require. In other words, many individuals, although they want their work to be part of a robust marketplace, are satisfied with less than "many and more" as the goal of market-based distribution.

The individuals and companies that do fit into the category of "many and more" are not single minded; their goals are fairly divided between making money, building satisfying and productive relationships, and exercising their competencies. They represent various industries, from web-based commerce and its software components to patented engineering technology (both mechanical and electrical), from biological technology to writers and publishers. To be clear, these individuals and industries are also present in other distributional categories, but these particular industries largely populated this "many and more" category. So, for example, sculptors and painters did not appear to care as much about "many and more" in the data set. I had anticipated musicians and their distributors to aim for market saturation, but their described methods and goals more comfortably fit in the other three distributional categories for reasons that I discuss later. Likewise, individual inventors, academic scientists, and more traditional manufacturing industries (e.g., home goods, personal accessories) were less focused on the "many and more" distributional goal overall. This last category surprised me in particular. Wouldn't a shoe company or a cosmetic company want to saturate the market with its products? As it turns out, the interviewees in these industries (lawyers and executives) described both a more targeted and a loose distributional scheme in the "managed performance" and "sharing" categories.

The specific industries populating the "many and more" category may evidence the fact that their output is clearly and ably protected by IP, such as pharmaceuticals, medical devices, and books. Individuals involved in these industries are comfortable and able to pursue a "many and more" strategy, and they do, for all sorts of reasons. Of course, they pursue *other* distribution strategies as well when it suits them. However, those in other industries (e.g., musicians, sculptors, manufacturers of home goods) appear to distribute in slightly different ways, not only because it fits their business models but also because it more directly optimizes other goals. These other industries may be less closely tied to IP protection or care less about unauthorized copying and distribution, or they may benefit from copying and distribution unconnected to exclusive rights typically tied to IP regimes. Recall that some industries or works that populate this "many and more" category are not always seeking perfect control over the copying of the good. As Chapter 3 discusses, many industries traditionally associated with strong IP rights (including pharmaceutical companies and publishing companies) confidently build businesses around an ill-fitting IP system.

Software

The software industry and its actors are the most populous in this "many and more" category, and they do not control the copying or distribution of their work but rather seek the widest possible dissemination and use. As a high-tech consultant and former software engineer says, "If you can bring me a business that has tons of eyeballs, tons of users, with some kind of network effect . . . go for it. Let the thing get bigger and bigger and bigger and bigger, and somewhere along the way, we'll figure out how to make money." Another entrepreneur, also a former programmer, believes the key to the success of a software product is its "capacity to build an audience" of sustained users, whether the audience is paying or not. "Search is everything," another software developer says. Being found is a precursor to being used, and in the software industries, being used and appreciated usually precedes a purchase. For software companies and engineers, widespread distribution (whether lawful or unlawful) precedes the achievement of all other goals.

There are two subsidiary goals that arise among software industry actors: establishing audiences who use and appreciate the work and exercising one's own competencies. Establishing relationships with an audience is a common ambition among these individuals; they derive pleasure from having the work used and experienced and from receiving feedback from that audience. A computer scientist, who is also an entrepreneur, recalls buying back one of his patents from a company in bankruptcy because he couldn't stand seeing it sit around doing nothing. He wanted it used by people. He consciously strives to put his programs into wider use, not only because they are a way to supplement his middle-class lifestyle as an academic but also because he intends the programs to be fun and useful.

Another software entrepreneur says that one of his "biggest motivation[s] is people. Because once you get real consumers, you can actually talk to them on the phone, and if they like what you do . . . that's what really kept me going." In the same breath, he emphasizes that he also enjoys the work because it plays to his strengths: "There are people doing it for different reasons, but . . . when you see those people, when they drop their jaw, . . . like 'You can really do that?'—that's what gets you going."

Pharmaceuticals and Medical Devices

The interviewees working in the pharmaceutical and medical device industries express a similar desire to achieve these same goals (making money, establishing relationships, and challenging core competencies) through the "many and more" distributive form. In contrast to the software engineers and Internet entrepreneurs, however, these interviewees generally care about unlawful copying and closely control their distribution networks. In other words, they rarely use distribution mechanisms to drive revenue through "sharing" or "gifting." However, scientists and engineers in these fields (as opposed to lawyers and executives) often employ other forms of distribution to accomplish nonmonetary goals, such as challenging competencies and building relationships. But in general, the "many and more" category is the most common among pharmaceutical and medical device industry professionals, and it is typically invoked to the exclusion of the other distributional forms.

Predictably, folks in the business of developing patented medical devices or pharmaceuticals focus on commercializing: "We want to have an impact on health care, but we also have to make a return on investment." This global health-fund director, Richard, develops products from start to finish, with the goal of saturating the particular market his company has identified:

We looked at the market, and we said, "You know, we think the market size here is about half a billon dollars." That's just this unserved, untapped market for [particular kind of] testing in Africa. . . . [T]here's actual funding now. . . . [People are] paying for [research and development.] . . . There's a real, actual commercial market. So if there's a commercial market for it, we can actually go raise money.

Richard says later, however, that there is "not much we can do . . . unless there's some IP." He is not talking about a patent on the whole medical device, but rather about how demonstrating some patentable aspects of the device propels initial investment, which gets the project off the ground. Later, he explains, being the first to market and building complex manufacturing systems drive revenue and competitive market advantages.

Dennis, a pharmaceutical industry executive and attorney, describes a similar situation with a patented antibody that is not utilized to its full commercial potential. Dennis is frustrated with certain executive decisions to license the patent for free as part of a larger package because, as he says, "they didn't appreciate its value." Dennis says he would have done things differently:

Establish a very robust licensing program and make it cheap. . . . License it to every university for $500 a year . . . and then license it to every company for . . . $5,000 a year. And then attach a 0.1 percent royalty. I wish . . . they had given it to me. You and I wouldn't be talking now, because I'd be retired. Or I'd be running a business, but I'd be watching the checks roll in.

This in-house IP lawyer has great respect for the amount of time it takes to make a useful and novel discovery, and he understands how rarely it happens. For him, each discovery is an opportunity to create as many licensing streams as possible, using tiered pricing to maximize the amount of licensees. He measures the success of a drug by the amount of money it makes, taking for granted that widespread use is evidence of utility and public good. A technology licensing manager at a major research university echoes this statement, assessing her office's success over two decades in terms of the amount of investment it brought to early stage inventions and the eventual "exploitation of their IP." Another technology licensing manager says his company pursues patents on in-house inventions only if it thinks "there's a big enough market [to] . . . find somebody willing to license it and reimburse our patent costs."

None of this is very surprising. Especially for medical devices and biotechnology, the size of the market drives the amount of investment, and a patent appears necessary to initiate the investment process. The bigger the market—or the more it is possible to charge in a smaller market—the more likely the investment will be made with expectation of earning a return. Rarely do these same industry actors talk about the "many and more" strategy as a means to establish or cultivate particular relationships with people (although as described later, they do describe the subsequent sharing of patents in terms of building relationships).

Nonetheless, as mentioned already, the "many and more" strategy is also a way to exercise and develop competencies. This is another pragmatic dimension of IP. The interviewees explain that the more the product circulates and makes money, the more its use-value (and iterations of its scientific advances and the business model that sustains it) also circulates and develops, simultaneously benefiting and challenging the originator, competitors, and collaborators. Richard, the health-fund executive, hopes for this kind of development:

[The CEO's] trying to solve problems. . . . Merck is not going to solve these problems. There are pieces that Merck may have a role in, but they're not going to be out there saying, "Let's fix [global] health issues." And that's really what [the CEO] wants to do. . . . That's what motivates him. And . . . money's a good thing, people like money, but that's not his primary driver. And when we were having a philosophical debate on how to do this, one of the things I said, which I think he believes, is that if [our company] is successful . . . and makes a . . . ridiculous amount of money for their investors, then what's gonna happen is, people are gonna look at that and say, "Wow, they made a lot of money." And all these venture funds who are saying, "Global health, huh?" They're gonna be saying, "What's our global health strategy? Where are the other opportunities in global health? Where should we be investing?" And it creates this whole, other avenue for solving these problems that doesn't exist today. So [our company], for itself, we're gonna solve one problem. But if we create this new model, [it] can solve a whole lot more problems that we don't even have to work on. Other people are gonna work on them.

For this widespread distribution model to earn significant profits, but also to extend and improve the field through proof of concept and competition, patented inventions are key, particularly in the initial stages when controlled distribution goes hand-in-hand with its desired breadth. Interviewees in both the pharmaceutical and the medical device industries confirm that patents are key to their businesses because investment in the original research would not have been made without the IP to facilitate a large and growing market. This is very different from the software and Internet entrepreneurs who use the "many and more" form of distribution but for whom IP did not matter as much, if at all.

Publishing

The other two industries common in the "many and more" category are two content industries: writers and publishers, and filmmakers and distributors. For the publishers I spoke with, occupying a particular market—that is, selling as much as possible of the book in an identifiable market—is a main goal. This requires identifying particular markets to dominate and avoiding the problem of used-book sales in those markets. All three book publishers (a large educational and trade press, a large trade press, and a smaller trade press) talk about developing partnering strategies with other vendors and distributors of goods or services to maximize market share among the target audience. This adds another dimension of value beyond the books' particular content; the book becomes a consumer good and "fulsome resource," to use the words of one publishing executive. A publisher I spoke to at a national publishing house with both educational and trade divisions tells me the company partners with web services and social media platforms to drive the adoption and maintenance of customers. Providing changing Internet content, chat rooms, and merchandise—a "360-degree experience" of a book—attracts customers with a versatile and broad product experience. The smaller publisher, in contrast, describes more discrete partnerships, in high-end stores such as Crate and Barrel, Williams-Sonoma, and Anthropologie, to reach as wide an audience as possible and to outfit the book as a desirable houseware worth the $60 price tag.

Like publishers, writers base their financial and reputational successes on reaching a broad audience. Barbara, a well-known writer of books for children and teenagers, attributes her ongoing professional success to some of her early books, which were novelizations of popular movies:

[Doing novelizations] opened every other door that ever opened for me. Not long after that, somebody at [a national publishing company] said, "You wrote

that? You can do a girls novel. Would you like to write a book in my girls series?" So I did three books in that series, for which I got an advance and royalties, thank you very much. I did the other three [title] movies . . . for which I
got very handsomely paid. . . . But it succeeded not because of my . . . brilliant
prose. It didn't have anything to do with that. It had to do with the fact that the
movie was so successful. So that's what pulled it through.

Barbara acknowledges that her success in reaching and maintaining such
a large audience is less driven by her writing than by the nature of the
market, primed by the popularity of certain films. She considers it a lucky
coincidence that she learned to cultivate this particular market and was
able to earn a comfortable living as a writer. Lisa, another writer but with
a different audience (adult nonfiction), underscores how important having a steady audience for her books is for making a living. Of one of her
early books, she tells me:

[It] sold out immediately. They had a pretty small print run . . . but then had to
keep reprinting it. Somebody made a movie based on it, and it won a prize. . . .
I've written for a living since then. And I've done a lot of feature journalism,
reviewing, and just various writing gigs. And I'm very happy that I can make a
living out of it.

Like publishers, writers also emphasize how distributing their work facilitates productive and meaningful relationships. For the writers, these relationships are with readers and fans. During the interview, Barbara often
mentions how her readers and fans motivate her, mentioning letters from
fans she keeps by her writing desk. Lisa describes how grateful she is to
her readers who earnestly and eagerly engage her books, which deal with
troubling and serious subjects.

Some writers (and fewer publishers) also feel that widespread distribution challenges them to be better at what they do. Appealing to broad audiences is itself a complex balancing act. Two journalists-turned-novelists
(who still work in journalism when opportunities arise) spoke about being happy about reaching a wide audience when the works at issue were
particularly controversial or personal. Lisa, who authored a nonfiction

account of a famous lawsuit, was urged not to write about it because of its controversy, but it ended up being a best seller:

Everyone was furious that it was being written . . . [but] by the time it came out, people were kind of [desperate] to get hold of a copy, so it sold a bomb. It just went berserk. . . . I became very unpopular among feminists for quite some years, but . . . the sweetness of it was that it was a best seller and they just kept on reprinting it, and I know the more people [criticized me] in the newspaper, the more copies were printed. So that was more gratifying than I could tell.

Lisa explicitly chooses topics that are hard but that she feels should be discussed. She does not shy away from writing about end-of-life conflicts, sexual controversy, and murder. And when she succeeds at being widely read despite those topics, she is particularly pleased. Jennifer, another writer, contrasts writing novels with writing memoirs, both of which are "challeng[ing]" to write in contrast to news articles:

[With novels] there is no excuse for anything less than wonderful prose . . . whereas in journalism, it's just fish wrap. I mean, it's like some stories are better or worse, but really, people just want to know the facts mostly. I mean, they want to be good to read, but it's not aspiring to the same level.

Both Lisa and Jennifer aspire to cultivate a wide readership, taking as many opportunities as possible to publicize and offer their book to audiences, recognizing that their work product when widely distributed can challenge audiences as much as it challenged them in their making. Despite both, they are popular writers.

In contrast to the pharmaceutical and medical device industries, the publishers vary their modes of distribution across three fields ("many and more," "managed performance," and "sharing"), and the writers across all four (with even a few examples in the "holdout" category). This indicates a looser claim of exclusivity to their work than other industries in this category and a more flexible business model. I describe this variation in the next section, in combination with the other industry and interviewee experiences that also populate more porous distributional systems.

Filmmakers

Film industry actors, surprisingly, focus less on the "many and more" strategy as a way to make money (although they do mention it) and more as a way to build relationships with particular audiences and cultivate certain critical and engaging experiences around the film content. Many interviewees are involved in the film industry. Once I started sorting the interviewees for their engagement with film, there were few for whom the film or video medium was not in one way or another part of their professional concern: writers whose books were made into films, artists whose work is the subject of films, musicians and photographers whose work is embedded in films, or Internet entrepreneurs whose sites host films. Even scientists and engineers consider film (and television and video) important to their businesses because film and television are excellent for spreading information and shaping expectations around particular products and services.

But specifically, I focus here on four people—three filmmakers and a marketing executive whose business revolves around enhancing the film experience through alternative distribution and merchandising opportunities—because of their detailed discussion about the experience of film production and their goals for distributing film content. All four interviewees endeavor to reach as broad an audience as possible to accomplish their professional goals. The filmmakers who make documentaries primarily aim to engage an audience critically and tell a story that shapes understanding of the past and present. For the marketing executive selling Hollywood hits and advertising broadcast television shows, the goal is to enhance the film experience by providing more of it across different media (web engagement with questionnaires and quizzes, merchandise, and social media platforms). Interestingly, as part of widening distribution, they all embrace the cyclical and enduring nature of evolving technology. So whereas a common complaint in copyright industries is that new technologies threaten old media by usurping their (old) markets, all four interviewees celebrate the new technologies as opportunities to revive the original film content (and the message and experiences it conveys) for new audiences, even if the later distributions are unauthorized by the original filmmakers or their companies.

Two of the filmmakers say essentially the same thing about this underprotection of film content to maximize one's audience for that content. Ann, a documentary filmmaker, says:

I'm not trying to be known for me. I'm trying for my next film to get out there and be seen by very specific people. Like I actually want this film, I love the idea of the PBS broadcast, which it'll have, but to me that's just a blip in the world. . . . I [want] an evergreen that [will] . . . enter the schools, and I want it to have an impact on how we learn about the Civil War.

When I asked about the term *evergreen*, Ann says it's "something that's not time-specific in terms of interest." The documentary filmmakers with whom I spoke try to distribute their films as widely as possible—even by tolerating some unauthorized distribution—to create the kind of relationships they want with specific audiences, to challenge their audiences to see history in a new way, and to exercise and develop their own skill at telling a good story that will hold people's attention. Melanie, another documentary filmmaker, says:

[W]hen you make broadcast programs . . . there is a cycle to it. You work so hard and then it airs, and then it's just kind of, like, *done.* And you know, now with the Web and with DVRs and stuff, there is more life to it. . . . You meet history professors [who have unauthorized copies of the film], and they say, "Oh, I love using your film in my class." And it makes you feel better. I mean, it makes you feel like, "OK. Well, then people are still watching it. . . . [T]here is a life after the [televised] program."

It is not the case that these documentary filmmakers tolerate many forms of infringement, unauthorized distribution, or unattributed copying. But they accept the risks attendant to widespread dissemination through digital intermediaries, authorized or not, because of the benefits it affords.

The marketing executive Steve, whose clients are mainstream film, television, and toy companies, explains the widespread distribution in similar terms. Steve describes a high tolerance for leaky IP, what he calls "Swiss cheese." He says it is futile to "fight it" (infringement), because "you are always going to have an enemy. If you embrace it, and guide them," the business works smoothly. One solution is to "guide [consumers]. . . . We are going to give the audience a Swiss cheese, it's going to have all these holes in it; we know what goes in those holes. We are going to let *them* create the stuff that goes in the holes." His broad distribution strategy embraces less exclusive IP to build a paying customer base. Here, Steve describes the strategic opportunities and the social benefits of widespread distribution:

We come in and . . . direct [that] the packaging copy [of a toy, based on a film character] affects the entire franchise. So you are learning something new [from] that [packaging] copy: what is actually [the toy's] backstory? So then when you open up that toy, it's more than just opening up the toy—you are experiencing that character's life in a different way than you saw in the film. Still connected.

Steve's goal is to connect the consumer to the product on an emotional level that encourages further engagement in all sorts of ways. He admits his strategy is not new, but it takes advantage of new technology and new systems of distribution and engagement (e.g., online platforms, user-generated content sites) to augment the experience:

It used to be the way records were sold. . . . [I]n the old days, when it was vinyl, and you bought a record, you opened up that record, and you smelled the paper, and then you read the liner notes before you put the record on. . . . Now you download everything, and when you download it, after three weeks, throw it away. Or it sits on your iPod until it shuffles to when you hear it again. Because there is not an experience when you buy records anymore. . . . [We] tell [clients] . . . how [to] . . . enhance [their media product] through narrative, through story, through continuity. . . . [T]he term [now] is *transmedia*. And in a few years, it'll change to something else. But *cross-platform* used to be [the term for] repurposing material. The big one, the big announcement, years ago was watching *Shawshank Redemption* on your telephone. So you can watch it on your iPhone, or you could watch it on your BlackBerry. And, you know, we sit here and go, "Why would I want to watch *Shawshank Redemption* on my phone?" And it failed, because nobody wants to watch that. What are you going to learn—if you learn something *new* about *Shawshank Redemption* on your phone, that's a different story. If . . . Tim Robbins's character, if you learn something about [his] case, where he was accused of killing his wife, the back[story,] now we are talking about something different. . . . We are hired to do a bunch of that [new] stuff. . . . A lot of times, we are brought in, we create the mythology, and then [the client] create[s] those ancillary tidbits from our mythology. . . . The mythology is the spine of the franchise. And everything that comes out of it are the nerves that come from that spine. So the film is one, books are another, comic books are another.

In contrast to the filmmakers, who cite explicit educational goals for their films, Steve's goal as a marketing executive is to grow his client's audience by enhancing the pleasure of the consuming experience. He does so by multiplying its platforms and attracting audience members to engage the creative content in diverse ways. Audiences, he says, can "learn" new things about the characters and evolve the story themselves through video games, comic books, and other entertainment media. He is not talking about critical engagement that changes how people think about history or contemporary welfare, as some of the documentary filmmakers are. As much as Steve's approach builds relationships for their own sake, this focus is also relevant to making money on behalf of his company (and his clients)—what he describes as "monetizing the experience." His goal with "many and more" distribution is to establish and sustain consumer relationships rather than to develop the competence of the storyteller or the audience. His business began with the idea of being a story generator, a new kind of "skin that you could tell stories through," the goal of which was to energize communities. He tells me of his first job in the business (which was unpaid):

[It was in the] New York school system to start talking to kids about heroism and life experiences, because the school said the kids were suffering [after the events of September 11, 2001]. . . . [T]hese kids were screaming for help. And the schools called us and said, "Can you come in and talk to them about heroes, and about . . . certain aspects of heroism and everything?" So we went in and we launched this program.

* * *

Industry professionals in this distribution category are evenly dispersed among the rationales for progress they identify. Notably, however, none of the interviewees who discusses the "many and more" distributive strategy describes it as a way to develop identity or establish autonomy. Autonomy and identity are more prevalent reasons in the interviewees' engagement with the other forms of distribution.

MANAGED PERFORMANCE

Three industries dominate the distributive category of "managed performance," especially regarding three of the four progress goals. Interviewees in the fields of publishing and writing, music, and sculpture tend to cultivate opportunities to "perform" their work—either through controlled in-person spaces or closed-digital environments—for three primary purposes: revenue generation, establishing desired relationships with collaborators or customers, and nourishing professional identity and autonomy. Among these industries, revenue generation is the most frequent explanation for managed performances, but the other two goals are also common. However, many more creative and innovative industry actors (including those already identified) employ this kind of selective and in-person dissemination to facilitate the fourth type of progress—exercising and challenging their own (and others') competencies—which leads to improved and evolved goods and services.

The managed performance takes various forms. Musicians and sculptors, as well as their managers and lawyers, may control the method of delivery (e.g., by selling tickets), control the performance space, or restrict recordings or photographs. They also selectively reproduce and disseminate their work by carefully choosing collaborators, marketing methods, and media formats. For writers and publishers, managed performances complement the large-scale distribution characteristic of the "many and more" category. Writers, and especially their publishers, may also exert more control over distribution by managing permissions for reprinting and distribution; controlling and marketing digital content; and carefully identifying audiences who will sustain the business and cultivate intellectual, emotional, and financial support for their content creators. As for the engineering and science professionals, be they licensing officers, in-house attorneys, or engineers and scientists, managed performances monitor the exchange of information, goods, and services in two ways:

they control unauthorized copying and distribution to ensure a competitive edge in the market, and they selectively identify partners in the industry with whom improvements to the utility and experience of the good or service can be made.

Managed performances openly concern IP protection. The people I spoke with control the distribution of their work by asserting exclusive rights to the work (whether or not they understand those rights as IP rights). While IP rights do not necessarily sustain the work or business (as Chapter 3 describes), assertions of exclusivity and control are typical, convenient, and perceived as effective. This "managed performance" category is not as populous as the "sharing" category, which is described in the following section. So, despite the alignment between this category and IP entitlements, that coincidence remains less typical among the interview data overall. The category is noteworthy, however, given the presence of all four progress goals within it and the wide variety of creative and innovative fields represented.

Music

Musicians and music agents target audiences to maximize performance opportunities, both radio and live. Meredith, a music agent, explains how she identifies musicians she can help become well-respected and professional performers:

I don't have the "I think that person is so amazing . . . I want to make them famous" drive. And I don't think any artist who has that hope would come to me to manage them. I have the "that person has some really important things to tell the world that no one else is telling the world, and so I think we can market that. We can get that word out there."

Meredith has been working with budding folk musicians for approximately six years to develop their careers as musicians and songwriters. But she has been in the music business for much longer, and she worked in advertising before music. In managing her musicians, she prefers to select audiences and venues carefully, and to maximize potential within those audiences. She encourages the sharing of music, but she also heavily markets the music, seeking focused recording opportunities outside the musician's comfort range to enable other desirable circumstances, such as prolonged studio time or preferable travel arrangements. One of her clients, Mary, talks about the choice of label to distribute and market her albums in a similarly targeted way:

They have a really solid mailing list, and they have a really solid relationship with a lot of radio and . . . people everywhere. . . . The label thing just sets you apart, enough that people are going, "OK . . . they like her enough to put her on the label." And it just allows you a little bit more attention . . . [because] everyone can do [their] own CD. . . . [P]eople are getting barraged with CDs.

Both agent and musician understand that managing the audience—shaping content and calibrating reputation to target certain groups or individuals—is a way to maximize play time, which in turn develops reputation and earns revenue. Neither seeks to disseminate music as widely as possible; both aim to optimize reputational and performance goals through targeted distribution.

In addition to performance opportunities, selling merchandise (CD and other goods) also builds reputation and revenue. As Kim, a New York musician tells me:

You have to understand that as a working musician, you cannot go to a show and not have product. And I am not talking about download cards—I am talking CDs. . . . It would not behoove me ever to go do some major show and not have product. It just doesn't make sense.

Mary also supports this strategy, explaining how the "most steady stream of income is merchandise sold at shows. . . . iTunes is [also] one of the major streams. Also, performance right royalties."[12] Merchandise and music recordings (including CDs that are copyright protected and branded goods that are trademarked) will sometimes be unlawfully copied and distributed. But the musicians generally feel that both lawful and unlawful distribution increase their renown among the particular communities who will support them, which translates into professional success.

Targeted and specialized distribution in the music industry achieves two other goals related to professional progress in the arts. First, it helps develop productive, meaningful relationships with recording labels and audiences. Second, working with certain producers and performing in front of choice audiences challenges musicians to improve their skill and deepen their art. Kim explains, "Bringing in a producer, and . . . having to step back and have someone else say, 'This doesn't make sense to me when I hear it for the first time,' or 'What are you trying to do here?' . . . just [to] have someone break it apart [is a good thing]." Professional interactions like this one can allow musicians to learn new things about their own songs and to explore the potential for music to bring pleasure and enlighten. This can also happen when audiences connect with the music in unexpected ways. Mary learned how a song she wrote about her personal experience nonetheless resonated with others when she performed it:

Like that little moment right before you lose your innocence in your childhood, I think that strikes a nerve somehow. But I've been surprised because that was such a personal song. I thought that that was just for me, you know? . . . [But] you're never quite sure what people are going to respond to. No idea. . . . With this new record, I haven't really started playing a lot of stuff live. I have no idea yet what people are going to pick out of it.

The musicians I spoke with explained that performing for live audiences is critical to their happiness as musicians. "Delivering the song is still, for me, very important," Mary says. She continues:

Like the electricity that happens when someone is lighting up—like a stranger is relating somehow to what you are saying . . . when the room is quiet and people are just right there, there is a circuit of energy where you wind up with more energy at the end of the show because you feel like in some tiny way, you have been of service.

In these ways, live and structured music performances accomplish all four of the goals that define progress: developing professional identity, building relationships, generating revenue, and challenging the artist (and his or her audience) to grow and learn through the experience.

Sculpture

Sculptors appear to have a somewhat different relationship to controlled distribution. Controlling copies and distribution of their work is more often a matter of professional identity and ego than revenue. This makes sense, since sculpture is not as readily reproducible as music, nor is it made for reproduction. But despite this, the sculptors I interviewed describe acute attention to distributional choices: where to show, how to show, and with whom to collaborate in order to make and display their work. I interviewed both public artists with large installation projects and more traditional sculptors who produce smaller museum pieces. Choosing sites for displaying (or installing) work is critical to both kinds of sculptors, for many reasons.

First, controlling the nature of the work's distribution may determine how, and how successfully, it earns money. As Sadie says:

When I joined [an artist collaborative], it was part of my long-range plan to develop bodies of work that I could then package and travel. . . . Because I think that's a very effective way of getting the work out, you can make money off of yourself that way, without having to sell the work, and if you do sell it, it goes into a collection.

Second, targeted distribution of work also anchors supportive relationships for their further development. According to Sadie, "[Early in my career] I had a kind of belief that people . . . believed in me being an artist. I mean, why else were they commissioning [my work]? These were not collectors. . . . I think they felt good. You know, like they were helping to make [my art] possible."

Third, the location of the work is central to its challenge as a unique piece. Sculptors describe how reconceptualizing the nature of a place in terms of the work is part of their creative endeavor, as it is inextricably entwined with personal expression and professional development. That is, for sculptors more than musicians, the *geography* of their art is central to the personal and public significance of the work. Here are two examples. First, Karen's sculptures are often indistinguishable from the context in which they sit. She says:

I was having a lot of problems as a student, because . . . I like being outside, meeting people, and just being out in the world rather than being in a studio and making something that seems very disconnected from real life. But nobody in the painting department . . . was really able to help me. They didn't know what I was doing, so . . . when I saw that [work of another artist], I realized, "Oh, you don't have to be in a studio, and you don't have to make an object."

Karen has become well known as someone who extracts the essences of certain natural objects or processes, reproducing them in sculpture; she isolates objects in nature and rebuilds them in ways that make us look anew upon them. Not being confined to a studio or traditional gallery space, and learning how to control the space (by broadening it), was key to Karen's personal and professional success. Indeed, the place and manner in which her art is displayed (e.g., the particular form of distribution) is the focus of Karen's art. As such, Karen ruminates deeply on the places she chooses to make and display her art.

Joan, also a sculptor, though better known and more financially stable than both Karen and Sadie, confirms that managing the place and manner of display is crucial to the success and significance of her art. She says that the pieces of which she is most proud "changed the whole city. . . . It's meant a lot to people who live there." The design of most of her work is also influenced by place, centering on the nature of geological and man-made landscapes:

I do a lot of research [when I design a piece]. And I like talking to all different kinds of experts. . . . [For a recent piece] I was looking at the interconnectedness of the countries of the Americas, and I picked [an] . . . earthquake that shifted the earth's mass and changed the orbit of the Earth . . . [which] became the subject of the sculpture.

When her art is successful, Joan explains, it shapes relationships with its audience, fulfills her personal desires to explore natural surroundings and its complex history, and challenges her to reconceive places in terms of nonrepresentational art. The distribution of her sculptures is highly controlled—perhaps the most strictly controlled—because they cannot travel and they are uniquely built for their place.

By the same token, the sculptors understand that their work will inevitably be distributed by others through photography, with or without permission, because their most successful pieces are displayed in or as part of public spaces. Indeed, the sculptors I spoke with strive for such circulation because it increases public recognition and appreciation. But while most sculptors encourage photographs for personal use, they worry about photographic use for profit by others without permission (e.g., as an aesthetic background to an advertisement for a car). In the interviews, distributing a photograph of a sculpture is more common and more often tolerated than circulating a photograph of a painting or an unauthorized excerpt of writing or an unlawful copy of a song. Most of sculptors I spoke to give up control—"What am I going to do?" they say—but underneath this complacence I believe they recognize that a photograph of the sculpture in no way competes with the experience of the original. The original is tied to its place, its unique and actual distributional form, and copies (via photographs or miniatures) are just not the same. Therefore, for sculptors, the managed performance involves picking the site and controlling how it is viewed. Doing so is integral to the sculpture's nature, value and uniqueness. This is not the same for writing or music, because in those media, the difference between the "original" and the "copy" may be minimal.

Curiously, however, sculptors regularly contract around the protections built into the fixed placement of their work. To win commissions, on which they depend for livelihood and professional growth, sculptors waive the protections of the Visual Artists Rights Act (VARA). The VARA is part of the Copyright Act and protects certain "moral" rights of visual artists (especially sculptors), such as the right to attribution and rights against destruction or integrity of the work. Despite having a strong interest in preserving the work as conceived and made in the specific place, most sculptors with whom I spoke indicate they have no choice but to waive these legal provisions that protect their work from being altered or moved. Joan's experience is typical of those I interviewed:

The city . . . required me to give up VARA, and they said that's what they require . . . of all their artists. It was awful. And actually, it has been to my detriment because I have lost control over the lighting, which is very important to me. . . . In the contract, I waive VARA and then they give me other rights, but much less. And that is not completely uncommon. And one of the main reasons cities that have big programs ask you to waive it is because they want to be able to remove it.

Despite the fixed nature of the sculpture and its ostensibly unique distribution, sculptors (like musicians) seek control of their work in ways that preserve its integrity and the audience's experience of it, even if that control is not airtight.

Notably, both musicians and sculptors populate this distributive category even though they are protected differently from the dangers of unauthorized dissemination of their work, and despite having different relationships to the distributive possibilities of the digital era. Sculptors formally have the benefit of VARA but waive it in practice to see their work installed. Unlike musicians, they don't face the risk of widespread unauthorized reproduction that would reduce their revenue. Music files, by contrast, are easily copied and distributed so musicians anticipate and tolerate sharing (and hope it will build their reputation) and manage their distribution less through IP than by controlling performance opportunities and being choosy about collaborating with labels. In both artistic fields, the kind of managed or controlled display or performance is not well facilitated by IP law.

Publishing

Recall that the writers and publishers among my interviews describe a *very broad* approach to distributional forms, populating all the forms of distribution I identify. In addition to using a "many and more" approach, the writers and publishers also target audiences or control the dissemination of their copyrighted content. (This is in contrast to musicians and sculptors, who, according to my data, do not aim for market saturation as much as they seek a targeted dissemination with more control over forms and audiences. Musicians and sculptors will populate other categories, however, such as "sharing" and "gifting.") Writers and publishers manage permissions for reprints and distribution through subscriptions and paywalls (as in journal subscriptions and licenses), and they "curate" collections of work on the basis of particular audiences' intellectual or emotional interests. For example, Samuel, a lawyer and business executive for a publisher of a consortium of academic journals, says:

[A] journal is not a bucket of content. A journal has a personality, it has an editor in chief; it has aims and scope; it has a mission; it has placement within a discipline. . . . So publication in journal X is significantly different from publication in journal Y.

According to industry actors, including this publishing executive, curated content represents the value of the work as a whole, and it is the reason people pay for access to it. Joseph, who works for a different publishing company, contrasts his company's approach with other publishers who fit better in the "many and more" category: "They'll print a hardcover book . . . maybe there is a lot of buzz around this book. They print 100,000 of them, and they put it in every store across [the nation]. And it just doesn't sell. They will remainder it four months after it's been pressed." Joseph, in contrast to Samuel, works at a small but elite trade press whose strategy is to find a "limited audience" and, "take titles that appeal to that [audience]," to market them in a variety of targeted ways, including product placement outside of bookstores.

Writers confirm that targeting audiences for distribution is appealing, although in each individual case targeting has less to do with generating revenue as it does with fulfilling other aspirations. Reaching specific kinds of readers can help establish an appreciative audience, for instance, or challenge themselves and others. Writers still want to be widely read, but when controlling the dissemination of their work—by not letting their novels freely circulate on the Internet, for example, or monitoring their use for derivative works (e.g., films, plays)—writers can maintain control over their expressive message and also cultivate relationships with certain readers. Lisa, a book author, feels wary about putting her work (or portions) up on the Internet:

I have great anxiety about it. But that's because of the age I am. . . . I am thinking, "What the fuck is this Internet, and where is it going to go?" And if I let my little book go out there, will it get lost, and . . . it'll be out of my control. . . . [W]hen a book is published and it's an actual, physical object . . . I know what that is, and I have sold the rights and I know there's a contract and the money has to come in twice a year. . . . It's not just about making heaps of money, but it's some old-fashioned "gentlemen's agreement," as it were. Whereas the Internet to me is this phenomenon that I don't understand.

While worried about letting her book "out of [her] control" on the Internet, Lisa nevertheless derives pleasure from being very generous with her work's dissemination and reuse in other ways, but only with a specific and defined audience:

I was invited to speak at a conference [for people who are experts on grief]. And I went along, and I thought, "Well, I'll throw myself on their mercy." And so I did, and I looked out at the crowd, and there are a couple hundred people there . . . who had faces of extreme . . . wisdom. . . . And I could see that there wasn't a single person in the room who was shocked by [the book]. And a woman came up to me at the end and she said, ". . . Don't ever be ashamed of the anger. We *all* feel it. We all feel it. So never be ashamed of it." And, phew! What a relief. And so then I felt that . . . [I] was justified [publishing the controversial story], because these people really knew about . . . this stuff on a much deeper and longer level than I did.

The book Lisa refers to is controversial because of the ethical dilemma at its core (about end-of-life decisions) and its autobiographical basis. Lisa may be shy about distributing this book online in excerpts or for publicity purposes, but she is eager and happy to distribute it to this audience from whom she sought comments because of their particular expertise and interest in the subject of the book.

Lisa lives off her royalties and continues to write books, but her books do not aim to be crowd-pleasers. Instead, they explore difficult and sometimes uncomfortable questions about love, power, and violence. Like other writers I interviewed, she moderates her desire to be read across diverse audiences with the goal of being understood and appreciated by specific groups of readers. This challenges her to be a better writer and enriches her relationships with fans and other writers. Similarly, Jennifer, who is a more recent novelist but a longtime news reporter, says that being a writer "feels like you are responding" to outside influences, questions, and audiences. She is not making up stories to tell or being a "gatekeeper" for content. Jennifer, like some other writers I interviewed, describes selecting and targeting her work, reaching out to specific kinds of readers with specific stories, to fulfill goals related not only to earning a living but also to developing expertise, self-determination, identity, and professional relationships. Intellectual property protection (particularly copyright and sometimes trademark) can help exercise this selective distribution.

* * *

A wide variety of professionals, not only musicians, sculptors, and writers, strive to exercise and develop expertise by disseminating their work in a controlled or managed way. Filmmakers and distributors, biotechnology and engineering professionals, manufacturers and inventors of home goods (e.g., batteries, lightbulbs, other home products), all find that controlled dissemination (as an exchange or targeted transfer) facilitates the improvement of their own work as well as others' while also enhancing the experience of their targeted audiences. In these circumstances, the managed performance controls the exchange of content, innovation, ideas, and information. Interviewees in a wide variety of fields control access to their work through restrictive licenses, price, and the enforcement of ancillary rights to facilitate these ends. For example, Cary, an in-house lawyer in a publicly traded energy company, says the company benefits from the restrictive agreements he drafts and enforces:

The flow of information is important. It's also a tough thing to control. You're used to collaborating. You're used to having those coffee shop conversations . . . so that kind of flow of information is perfectly healthy and fun within the confines of our little world, but you need to know that you have to turn that off if you're collaborating or talking with a vendor or potential [joint venture] participant until we have the proper agreements and things in place.

Speaking about another company he worked for in the home goods business, Cary says:

[It] was very buttoned-up on confidential things, to the nth degree. It was the poster child on how to protect confidential information. . . . They didn't use third-party vendors for manufacturing equipment. They did all the development in-house. In fact, they didn't have a single inventor that was responsible for an entire product line, because you wanted to make sure you [had downstream] control.

Sometimes "buttoning up" confidential business information—managing the distribution of data and goods—is a precursor to a fruitful collaboration, driving both revenue and business relationships. But more often, the controlled transfer creates market advantage by limiting supply. In the next section, I discuss the category of "sharing," which includes sharing confidential business information and data as a way of more directly facilitating collaboration and product improvement.

Cary confirms that "models [of controlled access] are kind of dictated by the management team," suggesting that whether an individual or company prefers a targeted and controlled approach or a more diverse and widespread dissemination of data and material depends on the individuals involved and on the industry. The interview data bears out this diversity in distributive choices and their use to achieve the four progress goals. Although some patterns exist among the varied forms of dissemination, given the limited data set, the most robust conclusion concerns the *existence* of the variations rather than their particular distribution across the industries represented. Quantitative studies are necessary to test these emerging patterns and examine the frequency of the variations in larger populations.

Throughout the interviews, in this category of "managed performance," more direct use of IP rights (whether or not identified as such) are a means to control and target dissemination for an array of goals relating not only to revenue but to other personal and professional aims. As Chapter 3 describes, claiming and asserting control through IP rights is sometimes done to grow revenue and build a business, but doing so is not necessarily critical to sustaining it. As this discussion about targeted dissemination illustrates, IP law can also be a means of managing and targeting distribution to achieve other professional ambitions.

SHARING

Sharing is the most popular form of distribution among the interviews. As I identify it, sharing has several key aspects: it aims to make work widespread, at low or no cost, and typically the shared work is for personal use although interviewees tolerate noncompetitive commercial use as well. The sharing often occurs involuntarily (e.g., without permission), but the interviewees accept this access by others because of its potential benefits and tend to assume that the subsequent use is well intentioned.

That is, they believe the work will ultimately foment creativity or innovation by others; oftentimes, the use is not consumptive but a purposive reuse. As mentioned earlier, this kind of sharing may generate revenue by the sheer volume of its dissemination, directly or through its reputational boost, nominal payments, productive exchanges, or sales of complementary products and services. But the interviewees focus less on the financial exploitation of the work than on the effect the work has on others. This category, like managed performances, anticipates an attentive audience. But unlike managed performances, because of the general anonymity that sharing entails, the interviewees exercise little or no control over the shared work, and there is little immediate or direct feedback from recipients. Predictably, then, the motives of relationship building (however amorphous or anonymous), self-determination, and developing competence feature prominently in this category. But as already emphasized, the interviewees frequently cite "making money" as a benefit of sharing the work, even though with sharing, it occurs without exploiting or maximizing rights of exclusion (IP rights). This category is also the most diverse in terms of the fields and professionals who populate it. There is less clumping of specific industries, and although individuals and companies are present, individuals are more heavily represented.

A variety of industries and individuals describe sharing as an optimal way to connect with audiences so that the work can permeate culture and remain there. For instance, we already heard from Mary how she tolerates fans ripping CDs so that her music can be enjoyed and other musicians can build on it, especially when purchasing the music is an unlikely option:

[Ripping CDs] It's just free marketing. . . . [T]he people that actually buy CDs [are] still there. . . . But I feel like if you're not going to buy it, but you're going to give it to your friend, great. If you're going to give it to five friends, that's fine. Because I'd rather you have it if you're not going to buy it. I mean, I'm not saying I want everyone to do that, obviously, because like I said, I'm still depending on the sales. But . . . I discover a lot of good stuff by someone just bring me a CD.

As described earlier, the filmmakers I spoke to similarly express an ambition to make "evergreen" films—films that have staying power, that continue circulating and growing in culture but without necessarily strong exclusive rights of distribution.[13] In fact, as described previously, the documentary filmmakers appreciate that the sharing of their work can occur beyond their control. As Melanie says:

You meet history professors [who have unauthorized copies of the film], and they say, "Oh, I love using your film in my class." And it makes you feel better. . . . people are still watching it."

Melanie tolerates unauthorized use of her film because she wants it to have a life beyond the singular (or rerun) episode on television or in theaters. To be sure, she expects to generate renown and revenue from its diffuse distribution, but what she really seeks in reuse is the film's continued life with others. By allowing the sharing of their work, these filmmakers successfully find diverse audiences for their films (other filmmakers, teachers, interested viewers) that challenge and propel their content toward evergreen status.

Many writers, artists, and scientists also feel flattered when their work is shared widely in new venues or for new audiences, expressing a range of emotions from true pleasure to anticipation and acquiescence. Lisa talks about how pleasing it is to see her written work quoted by others:

I would be flattered to be quoted. I mean, it's very flattering and pleasing to think that something that you have written has kind of entered the public domain. . . . I think that probably what enrages people: the failure to ask permission. I bet if people asked permission, a lot of writers would either charge a small amount of money, or they would say, "Sure." You know, it could be free. "Take it, and I'm glad."

Like flower pots or used books stationed on a residential curbside for giving away, Lisa conceives of sharing as donating her words for others to use, discuss, or build on. Indeed, she suggests that this kind of sharing and adoption is precisely what successful writing accomplishes—it gives a voluntary gift without any expectation of exchange. Sharing, in fact, resembles a gift because it attaches very few, lenient conditions, but it is unlike a gift because the author does not explicitly initiate voluntary giving (outside publication). Even beyond quoting or making "mash-ups," which is a reuse that changes the message of the original, artists clarify their tolerance for unauthorized reproduction and distribution as an assumed sharing that is part of participating in an artistic community. Melanie, a filmmaker, says: "Everything's kind of derivative. Like art in general. You know, people are always emulating. . . . [if people were to quote or copy my work] I think that I would be flattered." Not only is sharing flattering; it is simply the way art gets made.

Like filmmakers, visual artists seem generous with their work, with a few caveats. Recall Leo, the painter who is particularly concerned with reputational interests and control:

Ultimately . . . I paint because I want to share . . . my sense of how I see the world, how I see color, with other people. I think I've got to . . . not be totally possessive about that. . . . As long as someone was [using my work] in a way that I felt was up to the quality [that would be one thing] . . . but if you think they are degrading your work, that's [another] thing. Right?

For Leo, the sharing alone is motivation to paint, and exclusivity can be frustrating for his personal production goals. He shares to build his relationships, his sense of self-worth as a painter, and his reputation. His sharing is largely free of caveats, except when the derivative works that result from his paintings are in his opinion "degrading." His exception further reveals the assumption that the audience with whom one "shares" is presumed to be well-intentioned and producing acceptable work. Sharing is, after all, a norm in the artistic industry. Most artists (writers, musicians, sculptors, and visual artists) assume that sharing work—and borrowing from others—is a crucial part of how creativity occurs and flourishes.

Scientists and engineers, in both academic institutions and firms, describe their desire to share in comparable terms: as "talking" and "a conversation." That is, the essence of research is discussion with others. As one biologist says, "what scientists do is they disclose: they share, they talk." University technology licensing professionals, corporate counsel, and firm executives confirm this proclivity among scientists and engineers to "share," to "talk," even at the expense of IP rights which may require secrecy.

At times, business managers and lawyers find this tendency appealing, but at other times it is frustrating, because sharing and talking can lead to a loss of exclusivity in IP rights. Michael, a pharmaceutical consultant, describes the tensions that arise when he tries to convince scientists to refrain from disclosures: "They are researchers. . . . So they are proud of [the work], and they love to talk about it. So they go to conventions and industry forums . . . 'I want to present a paper on this.' 'No, you can't. I know you want to. You can't.'" Another pharmaceutical executive critiques the assumption that scientists are always altruistic in their impulse to share: "They may not be directly doing it to create a drug that's going to sell a billion dollars, but they want . . . the Nobel Prize. They want to publish in *Science*." In these instances, sharing accomplishes at least two goals. It is reputational—it cultivates an identity in a community and contributes to self-definition and autonomy in one's field. Second, it is relational—it facilitates collaboration and networks that advance one's research. Despite the frustration that corporate agents, licensing professionals, and lawyers experience, these sharing impulses and desires are strong among the scientists and engineers doing the work, and they likely can be operationalized within the workplace to maximize job satisfaction and performance.[14]

Some individual inventors enjoy observing their work circulate because it means others appreciate the work as a productive tool. Lauding the invention's circulation is not disguised enthusiasm for the financial benefits of its marketability, but an expression of pride in the invention's utility to others. This is both an intrinsic and extrinsic good. Leora, an inventor of home goods, describes how she felt joy at seeing her invention on store shelves: "It was out in stores. . . . [Y]ou could buy them at the grocery store. It was thrilling. It was more thrilling than getting the patent. I mean, I have [the items] at home, I bought some, and I have them still." Another inventor, Dan, a chemical engineer, recalls an instance when he felt proud that the tool he developed was produced and circulated in a midsize company where it could make a difference to its operations: "[It was] a design tool for a certain type of remediation process, which people still use today . . . almost twenty years later. It was great fun just working there. . . . I could make a difference companywide." When I followed up with Dan, asking how the tool was owned and whether it was still proprietary, he didn't know anything except that the company for whom he worked owned it upon its creation, was later bought, and its acquirer went bankrupt. He says, shrugging, "Probably the program is floating around in a variety of places now." He has no further information about the tool's status, except that it is likely still in use, and this pleases him.

Sharing widely so that others will experience the work is so important to some of the people I spoke with that they describe taking costly steps to ensure that their work remains in circulation. Jack, the computer scientist who talked about his motives for inventing and disseminating in reputational, problem-solving, and financial terms, laments that one of his inventions was sold to a small company and became entangled in a bankruptcy proceeding. So he bought his own invention out of bankruptcy to put it back into circulation: "I made a deal with the guy who had the small company, and the shysters who stole it from him in bankruptcy, to get [the invention] back, if I gave 'em each 25 percent stake." When I ask if he wanted it back because he knew it was valuable, Jack says:

No, I was just really frustrated that the patent was stuck in bankruptcy, and nothing was being done with it. . . . I just didn't like it being stagnant. You know, and iPhone's coming, and . . . something's gonna happen. . . . [I]t took about ten years to get the patent. So the original patent issued in '95. The patent was paid for by the small company, and then by 2000 or so they had gone bankrupt, and it was all locked up.

Visibly upset at the "stagnan[cy]" of his invention and the patent, Jack bought back his own patent so that it would be free to be used and licensed in the future. Primarily, he did so not in the hopes of financially benefiting from the patent (he otherwise has a well-paying job), but, it seems, to experience the intrinsic pleasure of witnessing the invention's use by a large and appreciative audience.

*　　*　　*

Despite the variety of progress rationales that sharing accomplishes, the aims and hopes that interviewees have for sharing can be summarized in two core convictions: first, if the work is meant to be used and appreciated, it must be in the hands of many people to exploit and develop its value; and second, sharing produces revenue. The people I interviewed, on the whole, do not talk about achieving these goals through exclusivity.

This is true even for the firms and institutions the data set covers. For example, Susan, one of the university licensing officers I interviewed, defines the value of sharing as nonexclusive, low-cost dissemination with an eye toward derivative uses that generate more innovation:

> There's two purposes [for] the patent. The primary one is to get somebody else to invest in [commercializing the invention], and they become [the exclusive licensee]. . . . We will sometimes get a patent that we think ought to be nonexclusively licensed that has great commercial potential, but because we don't think it's appropriate to allow a single company to tie it up, we would then go into a fairly generous nonexclusive licensing strategy. The close model for that . . . was the Stanford [University California San Francisco] patent. You would not have wanted that exclusively licensed to one company, because then you would have funneled the entire genetic engineering industry through one portal.

Charged with facilitating the dissemination and commercialization of the institution's inventions, Susan's job is explicitly to build competencies and generate revenue. And her strategy is not unique to nonprofit or small inventors.

Even in brand-name pharmaceutical companies, business agents seem to pursue similar strategies and goals. Dennis, the in-house lawyer who worked in large pharmaceutical companies his entire career, and is quoted earlier in the "many and more" category, says he was frustrated with a prior employer's licensing strategy because he believed it thwarted subsequent innovation. By pricing the invention too high, the company prevented widespread use, leading to sunk and unrecovered costs.[15] Dennis's preferred distributive technique of widespread affordable distribution fits better with "many or more" than "sharing," but the strategy is notable here given that, despite working for pharmaceutical companies his entire career, he aligns his motives and mechanisms with research universities and individual inventors. Both pursue a strategy of sharing widely to affect others' creative and innovative work. And each assumes a reuse for play and modest pay and pursues a respectable revenue stream to further one's own work and industry. The language of obligatory exclusivity, typical of dominant IP discourse, is missing from this distributive strategy, despite the emphasis on licensing potential and revenue. Individuals speak in terms of duties rather than rights, of relationships with their work and with others rather than of personal entitlements. This makes sense given that the act of dissemination inherently contemplates an audience with whom one will share a consequential relationship; it confirms that artists and scientists work to have an effect on others.

The impulse to share, then, is not an individual characteristic but also is present as an attitude or quality in firms or institutions. Both industry actors and firm managers, some of whom have already been quoted here, laud the benefits of sharing for both the company culture and its productivity when it takes the form of a "flow of information" and relationship building through "coffee-shop conversations" that are "perfectly healthy and fun." As I previously described, one technology company harnesses employees' interest in sharing and disclosing their work by creating monthly competitions among researchers for the "coolest idea." The winner receives a meager $10 gift certificate and priceless collegial accolades. This idea incorporates the employees' natural behavior into the company's culture:

> The whole Cool Ideas program got started because one of our researchers saw some kind of crazy result when they did something, and that's what started me and the president of the company talking about how . . . we need to hear about this. We need to have people talking about it and hearing about it.

Ted, a company executive, recognizes that individual motivation to share originates in a desire for self-expression and for building and challenging expertise. He harnesses these intrinsic motives, which normally manifest as open and playful sharing, in a structured work-time activity, thereby funneling inventive behavior into developing more useful and desirable products. To be sure, his company doesn't share its products externally in the same way employees and scientists seek to share their ideas internally. But establishing a culture of dissemination encourages employees to challenge one another, grows reputations both individually and as a company, and develops "cool ideas" for the company to commercialize—and this has become hardwired into the firm. As such, the firm's business strategies and public persona are shaped in large part by its principle innovators, who lead by the example they set internally.

Dispersed but active engagement is a major reason for disseminating works. So it is not surprising that among the interviewees, sharing widely, at low cost with few strings attached, appears to be the most common way to engage audiences and promote further circulation. With this comes an organizational tolerance for secondary uses that may technically be unlawful under IP law. The musician, filmmakers, writers, and painter mentioned here demonstrate this acceptance. Sculptors, photographers, web designers, and software engineers express similar attitudes. More surprising are the business agents and lawyers who exhibit forbearance and lenience for conditions under which audience engagement likely leads to infringement and marketplace competition. Even in these circumstances, commercial entities and individuals encourage the broad sharing of business models and products to promote the development of capabilities. As quoted earlier in the "many and more" section, Richard, an entrepreneur in the medical device industry, says that his new company's business strategy, the goal of which is to be viral and replicate, is meant to encourage follow-on and second comers in the field. Richard says of the company, "We're gonna solve one problem. But if we create this new model, [it] can solve a whole lot more problems that we don't even have to work on. Other people are gonna work on them." This entrepreneur and his business partner welcome competitive and complementary global health companies. His goal in distribution is to saturate a market with his product and services, but he encourages other companies to emulate his business model and join forces in the global health market to fight human diseases. In this way, I consider him to be "sharing" his business model, openly inviting collaborators, competitors, and even copiers. While his company needs to make money to exist, he makes clear that its primary goals are to solve health problems and enlist more people to do the same. Pursuing these goals shapes his engagement in the field (and the company CEO's engagement) and encourages him to be more open with his business strategies.

These last examples demonstrate how the "many and more" and the "sharing" categories overlap in terms of a mutual interest in widespread dissemination and a public-oriented outlook. They differ in their emphasis on payment exchanges ("many and more" assumes payment, whereas sharing may not) and on their reliance on IP ("many and more" often presumes a baseline exclusive right, however loosely enforced, whereas sharing appears to sideline IP). In addition, "sharing" includes more individuals than institutional actors, whereas "many and more" includes many of both. Moreover, "sharing" by institutions or firms is clearly driven by individual motivations or behaviors, suggesting that where it is embraced as a corporate or institution-based distribution strategy, it comes from the ground up. Sharing differs from "many and more" in another important way. As a diffuse and optimistic distributional form, it achieves all four of the progress goals the interviewees exhibit, whereas "many and more" does not. Like "many and more," sharing establishes and builds relationships in that it is emotionally fulfilling, collaborative, and productive. It stimulates reuse and creative or innovative production—and it generates revenue. But sharing also develops identity and professional reputation by enhancing autonomy and self-definition, whereas "many and more" distribution is not described in this way. This suggests that firms, by embracing a "many and more" strategy, may fail to fulfill (or even address) this employee or user interest.

The right to exclude dominates property and IP claims, inevitably evoking metaphors of trespass and dominion. Sharing emphasizes a very different focus, highlighting the desire for widespread dissemination at low or no cost between people and within or between firms. The impulse to share is remarkably distinct from traditional IP discourse when interviewees describe tolerance toward and even acceptance of secondary users. In fact, secondary uses—including borrowing, reusing, and complementing—appear sought by the interviewees as a reason for dissemination in the first place. Furthermore, disagreeable uses are not the market harms we might expect but the uses that threaten professional reputation. And as already established, those uses are rarely, if ever, covered by IP law.

That so many interviewees embrace sharing recommends it as a normative choice, although further research is necessary to draw more refined conclusions about the preferences among industries and the actors within them. Importantly, many of these same industries and actors also describe engaging in other forms of distribution (which may be more or less controlled). These interviews nonetheless paint an initial picture of creative and innovative communities that seek to elaborate their competencies, collaborations, financial well-being, and professional autonomy by broadly and loosely disseminating their work. Their emphasis on sharing also collapses the distinction frequently reified in discussions about corporate welfare and institutional prerogatives between making money and doing good.[16] The choice to share innovative or creative work achieves all four progress goals, thereby avoiding the zero-sum binary of self-interested versus public-oriented behavior. Indeed, this binary either emerges as false or is heavily contested throughout the interviews.

GIFTING

Examples of gifting come from only a few industries and individuals in the data. With some exceptions, musicians, sculptors, and writers populate this category, although a few scientists and software engineers, and their business agents (e.g., licensing officers, lawyers), are also present. Because of the nature of qualitative sampling and analysis, I cannot say more about the distribution of these examples over a larger population (or confirm the absence of other professionals in this category); I can only suggest that more research should be done to discern whether other professionals (how many and which kinds) in creative and innovative fields also exhibit gifting behavior. As Table 6.1 at the beginning of this chapter shows, the incidence of gifting in the data is less frequent than that of sharing or managed performances. Again, that is not a claim I can make beyond this data set. But the variation in the data set and its dimensions, as described in this section, is notable for how gifting accomplishes goals related to IP, despite the lack of any exclusivity or excludability associated with the gift itself.

As for gifting's role in making artistic or innovative progress, I expected that gifts, which are purely donative without strings attached, were not intended for financial gain. The data bear this out; no one uses gifts to make money directly. I also expected that gifts would be used to facilitate relationships. The data also support this intuition. More surprising, however, is that gifting facilitates autonomy and self-determination, and it promotes community expertise and competence. Actually, the latter goals are the most common explanation among the interviews for giving gifts of creative or innovative work.

A rich anthropological literature explains that a hallmark of a gift is that its value derives from its circulation.[17] A gift is not something you keep; it is something you give away: "The gift that is not used will be lost, while the one that is passed along remains abundant."[18] In other words, dissemination is necessary for the gift to have value. Moreover, by giving it away, the gift's value grows—and that value cannot be used up. This is a different view of value from what is usual for rules governing ownership and control. Instead of exercising dominion and control or excluding others to protect or retain the value of exclusivity for oneself—a premise of IP law—gifting embodies the opposite impulse: it relinquishes control and includes others without restrictions to extend or amplify value.

For example, years ago, a professional chemical engineer and amateur composer, Dan, started writing music for himself and his son. Family circumstances propelled him to retire early (in his fifties), and his music soon became the focus of a small opera company he founded and for which he now works nearly full-time. He speaks about his early music composing this way:

[There was] no pressure because none of it was going to be judged. It was just for us to sing together. So I started writing these songs, and [my son] would sing them . . . and his friends would come over and sing them. And our friends would come over and sing them. And fifteen months after I started, I had generated about . . . two and a quarter hours of music.

When his wife suggested a community concert, Dan protested: "Why? . . . We can sing it anytime we want." Dan says his wife responded, "'Well, because we have to share it, because it's cool.'" Soon thereafter, the group put on a local performance, the first of many, propelled by further demand from the community audience. Dan explains how he realized that, to experience fully the music's benefits, which began as a way to enrich a child's life and build relationships among family members, the music seeks a larger community. Its value grew upon giving it to more people:

I thought we were just making music, that I was giving [my son] an opportunity to sing that he wouldn't otherwise have. But in fact I was doing something much more important without even realizing it. And we had our show, and it was great fun. . . . We did act one at . . . the [local elementary] school. . . . And act two we did at the parking lot of the [local] . . . school of dance. We were going to do it inside, but it was such a beautiful day we just set up outside. We just sang it as an oratorio basically. We just put these mics up, and people put costumes on and stood in front of the mics and sang into the microphones.

Dan is describing the transformation from keeping his music to himself to giving it to the community. Mary—a working musician all her life, from a different generation and working in a different genre—makes a similar statement but explicitly evokes the idea of giving away music:

For me, [making music has] always been like, "What am I working on [emotionally]?" And then, of course, I was saying, you *want* [the music] to be useful. You want it to somehow get from you to being someone else's story. Like I want them to belong to other people.

Music is a likely candidate for gifting because, once heard, it becomes part of its audience, living in our heads as we hum tunes long after hearing them on the radio. In many ways, music is the quintessential example of a creative act that is always and necessarily given away and, as such, grows in significance. It can never be used up.

What about other forms of creativity? Sculpture appears the least likely of the creative arts to be "constantly circulating" the way music does, especially in light of sculpture's static and often cumbersome form. And yet I spoke with several sculptors who overcome this potential limitation in their art by mimicking a gift economy with their work. For instance, Karen is an artist whose sculptures tend toward unique installations that are built into the environment or made of transient material. She tells me that she sometimes crafts small books to give away at her shows:

Because there was no system for selling things, so I wasn't part of that exchange where you make something and somebody wants to buy it. I was making things and I would give them away. Like that's why I made a lot of books, because you could just give away books. . . . I made a lot of installations that would be completed by a bookshelf with books, then photocopied ones, and people could just help themselves and take it away. . . . So instead of just reading a press release or whatever, they would have more of a . . . little work in its own right, this little book.

These small books, like party favors, are valuable "in [their] own right," each being unique and created by a well-known artist. But they are not sold or traded. They are gifts for visitors to the gallery who come to see the show. Several other gallery artists, like photographers and other sculptors, describe making and distributing similar tokens of thanks or small memorials for visitors.

There are more traditional gifting exchanges as well. For example, one interviewee describes his experience with a good friend who is a sculptor and is always giving away his art:

He is actually quite a good sculptor, and we have several bronzes that he's done . . . and they're stunning. . . . [But] he is very modest about it . . . he'll never give you a bill. I have to say to him, "Don't we owe—can I give you some money for what you did?" . . . [H]e's uncomfortable with money or something. I don't know. . . . He also earns a living making corporate logos, [but] he's poor. . . . I was introduced to him by [my other artist friend], and [he] always says to me, "You have got to remember to pay [him]. He won't ask you."

The sculptor earns a living by developing corporate brands, even though he could earn money selling his art. Apparently, he chooses not to sell his art, only to give it away. For him, paying for logos is acceptable and functional, but paying for the sculpture is "uncomfortable" and undercuts his artistic experience.

Yet a third sculptor, Sadie, talks about how gifting is reciprocal: sometimes audiences give to artists. One of her major works consists of hundreds of pieces piled together, inscribed with words and phrases. The sculpture as a whole is meant to be touched, handled, and read. By design, it demanded interaction with its audience. Sadie says:

People talk to each other, and so . . . everybody's in their own little world. But people start to talk to each other and you get whole groups of people that are like, "Hey, look at this one," and you know it just gets really fun. And I never know any of these people, and they all have stories and people started sending me boxes of [similar objects] because it was really nice because I was having trouble finding a thousand of [them]. . . . People have been great. I have people that have been emailing me or writing letters and sending stuff for ten years.

She describes her primary goal and pleasure in doing her work is the feeling of reciprocity created by the art. For her, such reciprocity is generative of new ideas, more creativity, and more enjoyable interactions and relationships.

These examples demonstrate how gifts seek and perpetuate momentum between the gifter and the recipient. With the circulation of the gift, there are more experiences, more interactions, more communication, and sometimes even more art. Whereas the market is a zero-sum game for many interviewees—balancing debts of sunk investment with value transferred for costs recuperated—gifting is generative, without the need for a balance sheet. It also appears to break down the binary relationship between artist and audience (or grantor and grantee, buyer and seller). With gift circles, over time it becomes difficult to figure out who originated the gift. When everyone is a beneficiary, the vector of giving loses importance.

Just as gifts are things one gives away, they are also things over which one relinquishes control. Indeed, if the giver retains any rights in the thing given, it is less a gift and more an obligation (a duty or contract). The interviewees express this lack of control in several ways. Some talk about how their work becomes part of the public domain, over which no one does or should have exclusive control. For example, Lisa tells me about learning of a play that mirrored one of her well-known novels. For many reasons, she is certain the playwright copied from her book. But she shrugged it off because her book is based on a true story. She says, "I didn't chase it up, but I just thought . . . 'That's interesting.' . . . [T]he story was in the public domain, so . . . I had no ownership of the story." This is not entirely accurate under copyright law. A novel based on a true story has copyright protection in the original expression of the public domain facts, which would include character embellishment, organization, and imagined plot details—all of which Lisa says the playwright copied. But, and this is consistent with the rest of her interview, Lisa renounced control over the work when it became a circulating story in her community at large. As quoted earlier, Lisa says, "I would be flattered to be quoted. I mean, it's very flattering and pleasing to think that something that you have written has kind of entered the public domain." To her, publishing her work can be an opportunity for relinquishing control to the public domain.

Similarly, Robert, a scientist, who is an entrepreneur and a university professor, believes that in his profession, withholding work from the public is unethical. Whether or not this implies that he is actually "gifting," his gesture nonetheless has the characteristics of a gift. Robert believes his research *must* circulate; its goal is to be generative, and for that to occur, he must relinquish control over its critique:

I feel a legal obligation *and* a moral obligation that anything that's done at the university we are supposed to publish. . . . [W]e would write papers and describe what we did, presumably to the point where people could reproduce it. . . . Occasionally, we'd come across something that I thought was worth patenting, and . . . in some cases, we filed patents.

Although patents are exclusive rights, intended to prevent others from making, using, or selling the invention as claimed, Robert understands that the value of the patent lies in its public disclosure (i.e., the grant of exclusivity is exchanged for disclosing and not keeping confidential the useful, nonobvious, and novel invention). He makes clear, however, that patents are the exception to the rule—for him, liberating research for others to replicate and develop is paramount.

Alex, a software developer and entrepreneur on his third or fourth business, talks about building a customer base the way musicians and writers talk about building fan communities. His strategy is like a Kickstarter campaign in reverse. He gives away product in hope that eventually a "fan base" (a paying audience) will come his way:

If you have a user who can't afford your software, give [it] away for free. Because you're gonna lose them anyway, right? You'll never see money from those guys. Give it to them, let them use it. Maybe in six months they'll get money and they buy and upgrade.

This "free pays" strategy for business development is also an example of gifting. There are no strings attached to downloading this software program, no obligations of repayment. Alex simply hopes to establish relationships based on appreciation and admiration, which may or may not come back in the form of devoted users. His success since he began as an entrepreneur has cemented his commitment to this method.

The anti-remuneration impulse in the quotes here may reflect a perception among interviewees that the talent and desire to be creative or innovative is a gift in and of itself. Lewis Hyde posits that artists experience their talent in terms of a gift, and the same is true of scientists and engineers with whom I spoke. Hyde writes:

An essential portion of any artist's labor is not creation so much as invocation. Part of the work cannot be made, it must be received; and we cannot have this gift except, perhaps, by supplication, by courting, by creating within ourselves that "begging bowl" to which the gift is drawn. . . . In an autobiographical essay the Polish poet Czeslaw Milosz speaks of his "inner certainty" as a young writer "that nothing depended on my will, that everything I might accomplish in life would not be won by my own efforts but given as a gift." Not all artists use these very words, but there are few artists who have not had this sense that some element of their work comes to them from a source they do not control.[19]

Some interviewees agree with this philosophical explanation of creative processes. Mary, describing how she became a musician, says, "I don't think I decided. It decided me." And Karen, the artist, says, "I always felt that's . . . who I was . . . ever since I was little." Folks in the sciences also talk about special talents or interests that seem to be with them from an early age. Jack, a computer scientist, says, "[In my youth] there was just an ability to translate any idea into working computer program, and there were other people around who could do it, but I was better and faster. It was just sort of like chess or math, there was just this sort of order." A biologist unenthusiastically reports that she didn't feel she had much reasonable choice:

Why I went into science is very simple: I did very well in it in school. So it was easy. And so it seemed like the logical thing to do. . . . I actually really liked math, because I like to problem solve, and I like to read and I like mystery. [As a kid] my father took me to the library every Saturday . . . and I would go through and read . . . scientific mysteries, and . . . do math problems.

Whether these are "gifts" or "natural instincts" or "special talents," many of the interviewees describe their origins in art and science in this manner.

That interviewees sometimes disseminate the work produced with their "gifts" without regard to market forces—without exerting exclusivity in order to charge monopoly rents—consequently seems appropriate and unsurprising. They experience their talents in some significant measure as beyond their control, and using their talents to benefit an audience or their community is a form of reciprocity and a fulfillment of their identities as artists or scientists. While Lewis Hyde calls this "closing the circle,"[20] for many of those I interviewed, closure is not descriptive of their work. Rather, they open themselves and their work to the world. Their talents or gifts propel them to work diligently to refine their craft in service of three progress goals: to express themselves as creators or innovators, to form community (establish relationships), and to enrich it (build and challenge capabilities).

HOLDOUT

The ubiquity of market capitalism, especially in IP law, sometimes makes the category of gifting hard to discern. This contrasts with the holdout behavior I sometimes heard about in interviews, behavior that is infrequent but nonetheless conspicuous. Interviewees describe refusing to disseminate work by appealing to rights that resemble but are not necessarily coincident with those protected by IP law (e.g., rights of exclusion to control identity and reputation). This is troubling when thinking about the IP prerogative of progress as a public-natured good.

Interviewees who did engage in holdout behavior account for their refusal to disseminate in terms of ego and identity interests or to maintain quality and/or challenge their own capabilities. Mary recalls resisting a lucrative commercial deal because it would have associated her music with a big-box store; Kim, another musician who struggles to make ends meet, refused a gig because it would have supported a fast-food restaurant. Sadie, a sculptor, does not show her work when she doesn't think the space dignifies it: "I'm not sure [the work will] be cared for. I don't think that they know what they're doing . . . they're just trying to get stuff up." Elizabeth, a writer who has yet to publish her novel, refuses to work with an agent because she finds the marketing of her work "boring." She says she won't mind if others read her work, but only after she is dead:

When I first started out, I had this idea because I had read a lot of literature and a lot of people's letters . . . that I wanted to be this part of the cultural conversation and write letters to the editors. . . . I wanted to feel like I was part of *that*. And now, . . . sure, I would love to get published. But . . . when I look at the best-seller list, most of those books don't interest me. And even the books that are pressed on me by people, I try them, but for me, I need the sediment of history. . . . I need one hundred years to go by and all the bad stuff to fall to the bottom to be able to find the books that I like to read. So I wouldn't want to go on a book tour. . . . [A]ll those sort of trappings—I wouldn't want to teach. Like all of the trappings today of the modern writer's life don't interest me. If I could be Salinger, OK. That would be fine. . . . I would be very happy with that. But I'm happier just working. I mean, maybe it sounds disingenuous. But it's been arrived at after many years.

To be sure, Elizabeth doesn't eschew publication of her work entirely, but she chooses to write everyday and not to promote it. She believes great literature, which she wants to write and believes she can write, takes time and, for her, solitude. Distributing that work in her lifetime is not a priority as compared to just doing it. Her resistance to publication rests on both an annoyance at how trade publications are market-driven and a sense that it is not worth publishing something that is not truly excellent. Elizabeth is worried about putting something out there that isn't good enough (that will not stand the test of time), and that putting out work prematurely fails to enrich culture. So, she exempts herself from the process. She hopes that an audience will read her writing someday, but only if it is excellent. She appears insecure about the quality of her writing, even in midlife after twenty-five years of doing it, but she is also content to work on her writing everyday, trying to produce something worthwhile and saving its circulation for a time far into the future.

There are other clear examples of holdout behavior based on ego claims, which closely resemble moral rights in the European IP tradition. A painter, for instance, is described by his attorney and friend as being very particular about his reputation: "He has been very careful about it. [H]e . . . keeps track of every painting he has sold, he knows who has it because he wants to control reproduction. He gives almost no reproduction rights because he doesn't want his paintings becoming mass produced in any way." According to the attorney, refusing to disseminate, for the artist, boosts reputation and the appearance of quality because it protects the value of the original, which is uniquely tied to the hand of the artist. Similarly, Ann, a filmmaker, recounts how an archivist restricted access to his archive of public domain photographs because he did not approve of the way she was going to use one of them for her film. Because the archivist owns the only tangible copy of the photograph in question, Ann cannot use the photograph in her film, despite its public domain status, except by copying a copy, which degrades the quality of the visual image. Ann explains the situation:

I am held captive by people who claim ownership of particular photos that are rare and important to telling my story . . . and the person has decided he doesn't want me to use it. Now he's said, "Doesn't matter how much money I have," he decided he doesn't want to.

As it turns out, this kind of story is not uncommon among archivists with regard to historical photos.[21] Archivists appear to believe they have a moral right, akin to authorship of their archival collection, that justifies denying access to other artists and researchers even when the underlying material is not protected by IP. This is similar to the overclaiming described in Chapter 4.

If we accept that developing one's professional identity and enhancing one's freedom to work within a chosen field are forms of "progress," then these examples of holdout behavior certainly promote progress. But they do so in a very limited way; this kind of progress is narrowly conceived, individualistic, and without meaningful regard for external or public welfare. That is, this form of progress does not appear to be sustainable on a large scale because it fails to account for the public interest—it serves only as an aggregate of private preferences. If progress is to have any public dimension, which I believe the constitutional prerogative demands, holdout behavior fails to serve constitutional progress. And yet IP law not only enables this kind of restrictive and private control; it is often used to fortify it. Aside from the archivist example, publication of any of the works mentioned here deliberately withheld by the authors, musicians, or artists would be a violation of copyright law.[22]

* * *

The diversity of distributive impulses among the interviewees that rely on some IP implies that IP may be working fine as a mechanism for dissemination. It doesn't appear to restrict the circulation of creative and innovative work. Individuals and firms are able to tighten control when they desire and to relinquish available rights when doing so serves their underlying goals. One problem with this formulation, however, is that ownership and preferred control do not often coincide, especially when creators and innovators are employees or independent contractors. Even though sharing and gifting behaviors could achieve their goals, because firms are less likely to engage in these behaviors, ownership over creative and innovative work may not correspond with the ambitions and aspirations of the actors doing the creating and innovating. Unless the individuals doing the work have the opportunity to shape or reconstitute the firm culture around the variety of personal and professional goals described, a disconnect between employee and organization will develop and likely make the organizations devoted to creative and innovative work inefficient and unsatisfactory. In these circumstances, IP—too often described narrowly and inaccurately as necessary to financial health—serves only as corporate capital. As long as we ignore the diverse incarnations and functions of IP, its presence and absence for creative and innovative industries, and its frequent irrelevance for the people who must be supported to get the work done and make it available to the public, IP's service to firms will continue to be a self-fulfilling prophecy. To reverse this trend, we may need to replace the role of gatekeepers with those who originate (rather than sustain) the work. I discuss these issues more in the conclusion.

Another implication of IP's ill-fitting role in the diversity of distributive impulses is that IP's public function is left to private choices. Individuals and companies are left to decide on their own when to enforce or not enforce their broadly protective IP rights, relinquishing the maintenance and monitoring of public benefits of broad dissemination of creative and innovative work to preference, chance, or mood. Given that most interviewees acknowledge, praise, and enjoy the widespread dissemination of others' creative and innovative work and were provoked to produce more of it themselves, it is ironic (or perhaps emblematic of a collective action problem) that the United States has developed stronger not looser IP rights over the past fifty years.

The progress goal that emerges in this discussion of dissemination—that spreading work can enhance and challenge competencies for oneself and others—is a quintessential good. To "progress science and the useful arts," IP should provoke and support a creative and innovative community. Instead, its role appears to be hit or miss. Law cannot function well within a community based in durable principles with a breach so profound.[23] As a game to be played or a tool to wield, as a set of functional, sometimes malleable (albeit formidable) rules, skilled lawyers can manage and manipulate IP law to their client's advantage. This is what Chapter 5 illustrates. But IP should matter to the people and the entities for whom it was constitutionally fashioned: "authors," "inventors," formal or informal organizations of each, and the public. By working around IP's excessively broad exclusivity rules to promote various kinds of progress, the beneficiaries of IP are signaling their preference for how to reshape these laws to reflect shared values.

Conclusion

WHEN I TAKE A STEP BACK from the interviews and accounts they contain, and I consider both their breadth and detail, I find them simultaneously inspiring and unremarkable.

Artists and scientists seek quality and stability in their work, not abundance. (To me, this is unremarkable.) When interviewees focus on finances, they do so to enable more art or science or to form relationships, not to collect money for its own sake. (For me, this is inspiring.) Lawyers or business managers confirm that their clients and creative or innovative partners define themselves by their work. (This is unremarkable.) The objects they produce or the services they render are not everyday work goals, despite their likely monetization or distribution to develop fans and consumers. Work itself is the goal. They enjoy doing the work, meeting the challenges, thinking about and achieving the next step with cultivated skills and interests. (This is inspiring.) These people work to be free, and free to pursue what interests them. (Unremarkable.) If they are lucky, as the many artists, scientists, and business folks I interviewed feel they are, their work is what interests them. If they can work under favorable conditions, their work is a form of freedom. (Inspiring.)

Scott, a thirty-eight-year-old Internet entrepreneur on his second successfully company, sums up his work ethic and philosophy:

One of the sort of speeches I give everybody we interview [for a job in the company], is people have this perception that the CEO makes the most money, sits in the corner office, does whatever he wants, you know, gets all the choicest cuts of meat kinda thing. And the greatest irony is that in a company like mine at least, I'm the one guy who can't quit. So you want a place to work that's a good culture, that's gonna make my career grow, where I'm gonna learn? I [as the CEO and owner] want that more than anything else, because at the end of the day, you can walk out the door, and I can't go anywhere. You want a good place to work? I have to have a good place to work! 'Cause I'm stuck here.

What are favorable work conditions in the creative and innovative fields? This is a critical question, and it likely involves the contours of intellectual property among other forms of legal regulation. Work conditions concern the distribution of ownership and control over the financial rewards associated with intangible work product. Distribution of ownership and control may benefit those doing the work as well as those organizing it (e.g., employers, managers, advisers). The interviewees consider fruitful collaboration and creative autonomy to be crucial for favorable work conditions. They also cite as important fair distribution of resources and accurate attribution and credit, as well as the opportunity to pursue intellectual interests and refrain from demoralizing or degrading behavior that devalues the person and work product associated with them. They value the opportunity to share and distribute work output and to continue working without unreasonable hurdles to sharing, distributing, and carrying on. And they want these interests to align across owners, investors, employers, and employees.

Legal distinctions between the making of art and science and its ownership and control disrupt the alignment of relevant interests. And the assumptions made about the differences between corporate concerns and individual motivations also distort our views on the appropriate legal regulation of ownership and control over creative and innovative work. In the United States intellectual property law has been designed and delineated in statutes and cases with a model of self-interested, wealth-maximizing, and risk-averse individuals and corporations in mind. But this is the wrong model.[1]

Scott continues, illustrating this point:

So this is why I say people are the hardest piece of a company, right? . . . How are we gonna derive [economic] value from our activities? . . . Well, the only way we're gonna do it is if we can convince people to buy the product and if we can build a good product, and make it work, and that's all people driven. Technology, you know, it's all people-built technology, but at the end of the day people like to do business with other people, and people are social by nature, and . . . I think one of the greatest secrets about being a good entrepreneur and keeping your payroll down is understanding that people don't actually work for money. People need money, and you have to pay them, and if you didn't pay 'em they wouldn't work, but people don't work for money. You can pay people dramatically less money if you give them a chance to grow and learn and be part of something bigger than themselves.

Carol Rose explains in *Property and Persuasion* that a "property regime presupposes a kind of character [a cooperative and empathetic person] who is not predicted in the standard story about property." "That is why," she says, "classic theories of property turned to narrative at crucial moments" to explain away the inconsistencies in the central characters' motivations and behaviors.[2] "In short, there is a gap between the kind of self-interested individual who needs exclusive property to induce him to labor and the kind of individual who has to be there to create, maintain and protect a property regime."[3] The interviews, including the one quoted earlier with Scott, are replete with the kind of characters upon whom Rose claims property regimes tacitly depend but nowhere acknowledge. Instead of suppressing or ignoring such people, Rose argues that the law should recognize and support them, in both their personal and their collective resistance to the crude market-driven model of property rights that protects investment-backed guarantees instead of human interests more broadly.

Incentives to create and innovate exist independently of the market-protecting mechanisms of intellectual property.[4] In fact, IP rights function as strategic business tools, attribution mechanisms, signs, sticks, and land mines—uses that are far afield from the risk-reducing device it was intended to be in the United States. As William Patry says about copyright's misunderstood relationship between right and value:

Copyright is not fairy dust, vesting everything it touches with magical economic value. Copyrights do not create value at all. Rather, economic value is derived from buyers' willingness to pay for a product or service. Who cares if you have a copyright on a movie that no one wants to see or a musical composition no one wants to hear?[5]

Patry further clarifies: "Copyright laws are a form of legal insurance protecting value otherwise created."[6] And that is all they were intended to do. The notion that stronger and broader IP laws will facilitate more creativity and more innovation rests on false assumptions. Creative and innovative work is not necessarily valuable because it can be owned. And as the interviews in this book demonstrate, creators and innovators do not necessarily do or make their work so that they can exclusively own or control it. Value, to them, comes from diverse sources. Therefore, IP with its exclusive rights does not necessarily incentivize creativity or innovation for those who are producing or commercializing output. Otherwise put, artists, scientists, and their business partners do not describe knowing of or relying on intellectual property in a robust way that suggests they substantially depend on its contours to "progress" their science or art. Instead, as Scott, the businessman quoted earlier, explains, "The only way we're gonna [derive value from our activities] . . . is if we can convince people to buy the product and if we can build a good product, and make it work, and that's all people driven." At the very least, the qualitative data from this study should undermine the frequent assertions that producing intellectual goods requires the set of robust external incentives that our IP regimes provide.

People continue with their work against long odds, sometimes working for a lifetime getting by with just enough money, and often with less than they'd originally hoped. They work as sculptors, writers, chemists, technologists. The choices they make to share, collaborate, or otherwise enable the distribution of their work are not risk-free, but the risk of others *copying* their work is not foremost in their minds. The people I spoke with consider diverse distributional choices as central and inevitable to their success, to how their work is made, admired, nurtured, advanced, and expanded. Absent a concern over copying (or the more pointed accusation of free riding), IP's rationale withers—it is no longer a justifiable insurance mechanism against threats to the value of created work. Although some interviewees (especially the lawyers) do describe IP as a risk-reducing mechanism for business investments in intangible work, most others evoke IP in a manner adverse or extraneous to US IP law. They seek instead to protect moral rights or to foster productive and emotionally fulfilling relationships or to earn enough to continue working every day.

"We're artists. We make our own moral universe," Sean, a photographer, said to me. He was speaking earnestly about how he understood the ownership and control over his photographs to be different from those asserted by his former employer (an international news agency). Sean contested his former employers' assertion of rights over his pictures even while recognizing that he probably had a weak legal claim to the photographs' copyright. But he nonetheless perceives himself to have the moral high ground. He imbued the photographs with value. They contain his vision, and he is the person who won awards. He continues to believe the news agency he worked for should have little control over how he chooses to reproduce and circulate "his" photographs beyond their initial newsgathering and distribution function, but not because he expects to earn money from his photographs. He was paid by the news agency after all.

The layers of corporate or business interests that dictate control and ownership over creative or innovative work exhaust artists and scientists. The layers feel wasteful and inefficient. They stall and misdirect work efforts. Because of this, many seek independence. As one very successful sculptor explains, "When you're an artist, no one can fire you and it's as challenging as you make it." This is, of course, not always true. Artists are often commissioned to make art, directed by clients, and they can be fired from the commission. As much as lawyers experience frustration from their clients (and vice versa), artists become frustrated with their audiences, paying or otherwise. Nonetheless, these relationships are vital to understanding the trade-offs artists and scientists face when building a satisfying life around their work. They seek autonomy *and* challenge, where the challenge often comes from developing appreciative work relationships. If employment fails to provide either autonomy or challenge, people are likely to move on despite the steady income employment situations may supply. The interviews are full of accounts of abandoning or forgoing lucrative work opportunities because focal nonpecuniary interests were left unfulfilled.

When discussing IP law and legal reform, we have long resorted to a particular discursive script explaining how exclusive rights incentivize creation and innovation: "IP law is based on the idea that the problem with openness is we won't get enough creation."[7] But this is simply not the case. Not only is openness a priority for developing and facilitating relationships with collaborators and audiences; openness appears to "breed creativity" in myriad contexts.[8]

If IP primarily functions as a restriction on openness, it is suboptimal for those who seek to create and innovate, even for those who want to make money from their creations and innovations. Although this is not always true, it is strongly represented by the data here, which indicate that we should worry about the trend in IP law reform to shrink openness rather than to maintain or expand it. In fact, reforms should reverse their course; loosen the reins of exclusivity and seek better alignment with the needs and interests of those initiating, producing, and distributing creative and inventive goods.

There is much at stake in the current IP misalignment. For one, work production and quality may suffer when too much exclusivity is in the hands of employers or organizations whose interests fail to coincide with creators and innovators. As the businessman, the photographer, and the sculptor here illustrate, autonomy and creative self-direction matter a great deal. Lawyers and agents try to explain and justify to their clients why shaping work into IP will help. But the variability of their justifications and the malleability of the rules strongly suggest that client interests should shape whatever exclusivity results, not the other way around. Rather than fitting the creative and innovative work into an IP framework, the IP rules should reflect the interests of those making and distributing the work. At the very least, doing so will not hurt the production and dissemination of intellectual output, given that it is how many people behave (or strive to behave) anyway.

Second, the material boundaries between public and private spheres and the interests those boundaries protect hang in the balance. Exclusivity assumes a private sphere controlled with sanctions to prevent access. But many interviewees draw a line between the private and the public spheres that is not determined by maximizing revenue with access charges. Instead, that line depends on which relationships individuals seek to foster, the nature of the space, the range of harms from intrusion, remedies available for those harms, and long- and short-term needs and desires. Indeed, the conceptual boundaries between the public and private spheres are being challenged everywhere in the twenty-first century.[9] IP law and its raison d'être, science and art, are in no way immune to these shifting boundaries. For IP, the private and public spaces may have different import than they do in family law, criminal law, or health law where the public-private divide is also highly contested. With IP, given the volatility of the private sphere in light of the omnipresence of digital access as the starting place for creative and innovative platforms, we would be smart to reevaluate whether in IP the line that divides exclusivity from open access for the purposes of fomenting creative and innovative work is drawn in the right place.

Third, the ubiquitous practice of contracting around IP defaults may be reckless. Instead of relying on IP rights, both individuals and companies report frequently using contracts to effectuate optimal business relationships in creative and innovative fields. Although IP may be a subject of the contract, the contract usually concerns much more than statutorily granted IP and often recasts the product, service, or idea in terms that IP may not recognize or allow. This has several consequences. It can dilute the IP regime's statutory default that arguably benefits the individual creator's interest (as when visual artists regularly waive their rights under the Visual Artists Rights Act to win a public art commission). It can also hide or force contractual terms via contracts of adhesion, such as mandatory arbitration clauses or waivers of liability commonly seen in clickwrap agreements.[10] Indeed, these contracting patterns raise the specter of whether meaningful consent exists to enforce the agreements. Other consequences follow from this promiscuous contracting, such as the restriction of exhaustion doctrines that otherwise would help grow a secondary market in used (and often cheaper) goods and transactional tangles that create uncertainty,[11] all of which should alert us to the possibility that IP rules are not meaningfully or productively aligned to advance individual or industry needs and preferences. Although the interview data may support the factual assertions made in IP scholarship concerning the widespread practice of contracting around IP rules, in the aggregate it may not help us determine how this widespread practice will affect the progress of art and science in the long run. Normative assertions remain tentative. The interviews do, however, provide some indication as to why some people and organizations rely on contracts:

IP rights are perceived as deficient in critical ways and people pursue values other than growing wealth through exclusivity.

The "Goldilocks" complaint that IP rights are "too strong" in some cases and "too weak" in others is not new to the IP literature.[12] The overenforcement of IP rights often protects interests underserved by IP regimes (e.g., attribution, preventing lawful competition). Underenforcement of IP rights likewise seems to further interests related to creative and innovative production that are undercut by exclusivity (e.g., building an audience, collaborating, developing complementary goods). And so the ongoing practices of harvesting and asserting IP perpetuate ill-fitting regulatory regimes. Compared to the law on the books, these IP practices are full of gaps and overhangs, both intentional and accidental.

Therefore, a fourth issue is whether IP reform should patch some holes and embrace or formalize others, or rebuild the system from the ground up. Some might say that we should leave the system alone because leakiness is an essential feature and not a bug. Indeed, several of the interviewees claim that imperfect control is an advantage (rather than a detriment) to the IP system. Moreover, leakiness might be a tool for transforming the IP mismatch into an acceptance of IP's less dominant role in the business strategies and health of IP-rich fields. The freedom to choose when to enforce and when not to enforce leaves the decision in the owner's hands and maintains an informal breathing space.[13]

It is easy to see the good in exercising or promoting "choice." But "choice," as with "freedom," is always exercised against a backdrop of foundational constraints set by someone or something. If those constraints reproduce inequalities of resources or opportunities, if they perpetrate patterns of harm via restraint of expression, community, or welfare, these foundations should be questioned. It is not enough to say, "People make do within the IP system we have." People make choices based on resources and risk, and our system of exclusive rights (pursued through litigation and access to lawyers) rewards the repeat player, the highly resourced one, or the one who is unruffled by financial or personal risk. This is not a system for everyday people. As such, the celebration bells of "choice" ring hollow.

And so we face this choice: do we leave enforcement in the rights holders' hands, even when ownership and origin may be divided and motivations misaligned, or do we formalize the breathing space to provide clearer and suitable rules for all of us? Together, the costliness and relative uncertainty of copyright and trademark fair-use claims, the complexity of threading patent thickets, licensing trails, and the legitimacy of patent and copyright trolling in light of IP policy suggest that leaving enforcement entirely with the rights holder may risk substantial and harmful imbalances. This debate resembles analyses of rules versus standards in legal philosophy:[14]

If we try to promote clarity by adhering to rigid rules, and people fail to follow those rules because of social custom, excusable mistake or unacceptable cost, we will wind up undermining the stability of property rights by upsetting legitimate expectations. And when rules allow the bad man to walk the line, they undermine property rights rather than promote them.[15]

Better alignment between desires for protection and legal parameters of protection might ameliorate these problems.

Some may also say that the fact that IP laws are both overenforced and underenforced is a feature of law generally. Its misalignment, in other words, may simply be the way law works as a regulatory mechanism, imperfect for the varieties of situations in which it is implicated.[16] But, for instance, when overenforcement claims lead to disappointing results in court or a private settlement, they diminish the rule of law in the eyes of those involved in the dispute. What good is the law when precisely that which the artist and scientist care most about (e.g., attribution, reputation, stability) is left unprotected or underprotected by the IP system that claims to incentivize the progress of art and science? A similar frustration exists when overclaiming succeeds, but should not have succeeded in light of normative principles and legitimate expectations. It is often the case that "when enforcement is perceived as unfair not by a small marginal group, but by a larger group . . . the resulting rift between the legal norm and the social norm not only makes the benefit of compliance non-existent, it also tends to reduce greatly the degree of internalization of the legal norm."[17] Rule-of-law principles depend on a more accurate alignment between practice norms and legal rules.[18] For IP to serve the goals it claims are vital, "to promote the progress of science and useful arts" and to facilitate a fair marketplace in goods and services, a better fit, at least of a certain kind, may be in order.

What kind of steps might we take to move forward in reforming IP law for the benefit of creative and innovative communities? If informal routes are preferred, we might encourage erring on the side of underenforcement. Best-practice communities can help informally shape entitlements, limitations, and exceptions industry by industry, and through subsequent development and assertion, they can inform business practices and risk assessments. Best practices may clarify the parameters of the lawful breathing space mentioned earlier without formal rule making. I am not the first to suggest such measures.[19] This book adds fodder to these projects and hopefully strengthens trust in community practices on which lawyers and judges rely. At the very least, it further adds to the growing quantity of facts and analyses that undermine both legislative and judicial assessments of intellectual property's "necessity" for progress. We should be beyond the point at which courts can comfortably assume that intellectual property "provides the economic incentive to create and disseminate ideas."[20]

Formally, we might propose legal reform that shifts the burden during litigation and disincentivizes overenforcement of IP with penalty provisions. This kind of reform has recently been proposed in the patent context.[21] Patent law is also currently the only statutory regime that has a formal misuse provision.[22] Copyright and trademark misuse claims are rare and rarely succeed. Developing shorter, more successful paths for copyright and trademark infringement claims—potentially through more opportunities for motions to dismiss, counterclaims, or declaratory judgment actions—would be welcome from the perspective of cost and time. Refining the application of fair-use factors statutorily or with strategic litigation may also be useful.[23] Reducing or refining damage awards has been a rallying cry for some time, especially in the copyright context, where statutory damages tend to far outweigh any realizable monetary harm from infringement. Given that the interviewees tend not to be focused on the economic value of creative work alone, reforming statutory damages seems an easy target. By the same token, a strong desire for credit suggests that providing proper attribution should mitigate damage awards and might even help avoid litigation in the first place. Others have already proposed reviving a copyright notice requirement for those serious about preventing others from copying their work,[24] and some have proposed abolishing software patents.[25] The data in this book further support such proposals.

I could go on proposing more statutory tweaks or even wholesale reforms based on the data. But this is less a book about legal reform than it is about legal stories—stories that tell how law structures relationships and serves the personal and professional goals of creators and innovators, and their partners. Despite suggestions for informal or formal legal change, I do not want this conclusion to imply that better alignment will always solve the problems faced in the production and distribution of creative and innovative work from which we may diversely benefit. We must be careful to avoid the tendency to regulate with rigid protocols, be they technological measures or otherwise (e.g., the Digital Millennium Copyright Act). If better alignment means losing the productive leakiness of the IP regimes, and the dissipation of the freedoms and flexibility individuals and their businesses need to pursue diverse professional goals, then we do not want it. But because the interview data overwhelmingly indicate that those in IP-rich industries can make do with less IP and that IP does not always incentivize production or facilitate dissemination of creative or innovative work, we should rethink its structure and its purposes.

IP law primarily serves to facilitate the retention or alienation of work to which people are deeply attached. Its purpose may be partly economic, but the attachment itself is based on human attributes or *properties* (to revive a pun developed by Margaret Radin[26]). People crave work and relationships that are remote from wealth. When it comes to IP, therefore, we need to rethink the opposition of the individual and the business organization and thus also the unique focus on economic growth as "progress." Companies producing creative and inventive work are made of and run by people. The firm's interests are not, nor should they be legally formalized as, so different from the individuals that constitute them or are affected by them. Separating the people who do and make everyday IP from those that benefit from it generates unproductive schisms and irrelevant rules. The misalignment of IP with the myriad goals creators and innovators pursue helps us identify and thereafter preserve only those IP rules that remain right for these individuals and industries.

I leave the last words to Max, an architect and sculptor with his own business, whose long, successful career has sustained him and his family. He is responding to my question about professional goals and optimizing his time. His answer is matter-of-fact but also profound in its summary of his thoughts on creative work, personal and professional progress, and the communities to which he belongs:

Of course, it's very possible that three weeks from now we have about fifteen glitches that we haven't quite worked out yet, and [finishing the public art project] is gonna take a lot longer. Most likely will. But you know, I mean, that's one of the issues, is that [the art] it's like raising children. You're never quite finished.

Research Methods and Data Analysis

THE RESEARCH FOR THIS BOOK started in the summer of 2008, when I began conducting the interviews. I was interested in learning from those engaged in making and facilitating creative or innovative work about the role, if any, intellectual property law played in their professional lives and work. The interviews explored various mechanisms and motives for generating creative and innovative work by talking at length with those in relevant fields. I had no specific hypothesis to test. I was interested only in hearing whether and how the incentive theory that dominates US legal doctrine in intellectual property manifests in the accounts of making and distributing creative work.

I chose a qualitative empirical method for two primary reasons. First, there is a growing body of quantitative empirical work in intellectual property scholarship providing data on the collection and assertion of intellectual property but very few qualitative studies of the experiences of creators and innovators, be they individuals or organizations. Second, qualitative research complements and enriches (and can be especially useful when combined with) quantitative research. When the purpose of an empirical study is exploratory and hypothesis generating, as this study is, qualitative methods are useful to

develop insights about the underlying forms and dynamics of the phenomenon under study. Unlike quantitative research in which researchers seek to generate precise estimates based on a sample that can be generalized with estimated degrees of error to a larger population, qualitative researchers seek "analytic generalizations" that attach meaning, rather than measurement, to the phenomena observed.[1]

Qualitative research tries to identify the situated knowledge (i.e., actors' experiences and interpretations) about a particular object, practice, or field by identifying variations in events and interpretations through data that is "densely textured, locally grounded, meaningful to the subjects themselves."[2] Generating categories for further exploration and developing explanations for those categories from within the narrative structures that interviewees provide is a hallmark of qualitative research.

Moreover, I am interested in the narratives and categories as explanatory and justificatory tools in the constitution of law and culture. Qualitative fieldwork (and systematic analyses of the data) collects actors' accounts of their lived experiences, displaying how interviewees build and make sense of their professional lives, offering explanations of how they work and why. If we are interested in understanding or more precisely defining the human motivations and incentives that intellectual property doctrine asserts is present in creative and innovative fields, interviews provide direct evidence from the individuals who actually do the work. Short of actually living with and shadowing the inventors and artists, accounts from a cross section of diverse actors provide the most reliable evidence concerning purposes and interpretations of intellectual property for its producers. Given the choice between abstract theories based on hypothesized models of economics or organizational behavior and the experience of individuals in those organizations who make (or fail to make) a living from their creative or innovative work, lessons from experience are preferable.

From the interviews, I hoped to generate a database of language terms and a catalog of narratives that describe (1) how interviewees generate or engage in creative and inventive processes and (2) how people make sense of intellectual property in relation to their creative and inventive work. A study of this sort is limited, as are all studies that rely on respondents' self-reports (including surveys), by the interviewees' responsiveness, self-interestedness, and possible lack of candor. Survey research attempts to control for the variations in the reliability of self-reports with large sample sizes. In-depth, face-to-face interviews like those that constitute this study rely on both the interviewer's skill (demeanor, techniques for establishing comfort and rapport, and careful question design and probes) and theoretical framing to address issues of reliability and validity.[3]

This study also sought to explore popular consciousness about the role of intellectual property law in creative and inventive processes. As a database of language and narratives about creativity, invention, and intellectual property, the interviews provide evidence of the culturally circulating schema, memes, interpretations, and understandings of law as it relates (or doesn't) to creative and innovative work. Moreover, stories people tell and the language they use to describe their work (here, involving art and science) are important in and of themselves.[4] Stories are political insofar as they are justifications for the status quo or change. Language and narratives participate in the constitution of consciousness and community.[5] The repeated use of words, phrases, and stories reify concepts, categories, and expectations that structure our identities and our relationships in society.

INTERVIEWING

I followed a method of nonrepresentative stratified sampling. Utilizing four significant variables—occupation (creator-innovator or intellectual property professional), relevant intellectual property regime for work product (copyright or patent), whether the interviewee was an independent contractor or an employee, and duration of career—sixteen possible variations were generated. (Trademarks permeated all industries and interviews, and so were not a relevant variable on which to sample.) Interviewees were as evenly divided as possible among the categories, as depicted in Table A.1.

Although this qualitative project does not aim for inferential generalizability the way an analysis of a randomized sample would, the key to analytic generalizability derives from the extent of the diversity in the sample from or about which data is collected. The sample should include all possible variations that might exist along critical dimensions relevant

TABLE A.1 Case variations

CREATOR OR INNOVATOR				BUSINESS AGENT OR LAWYER			
Independent contractor		Employee		Independent contractor		Employee	
C-rich field	P-rich field	C-rich field	P-rich field	C-rich field	P-rich field	C-rich field	P-rich field
1st 2d	1st 2d	1st 2d	1st 2d	1st 2d	1st 2d	1st 2d	1st 2d
25 y 25 y	25 y 25 y	25 y 25 y	25 y 25 y	25 y 25 y	25 y 25 y	25 y 25 y	25 y 25 y

NOTE: C = copyright; P = patent; y = years.

to the subject being studied in the sample. In this way the sample, while not random, saturates the variation and is in that sense qualitatively but not proportionately representative. Thus, this study includes a wide variety of professions: filmmakers, photographers, painters, sculptors, journalists, novelists, musicians and composers, biologists, chemists, hardware and software and chemical engineers, web designers, computer scientists, lawyers (firm, solo, and in-house), agents, and publishers, as well as business executives working with pharmaceuticals, medical devices, telecommunication, e-commerce, marketing, media, and entertainment. Appendix B contains a descriptive list of the interviewees and their professional fields. Interviewees were located through letter campaigns and recommendations (snowball sampling). For this study, each of the cells at the most specific level (fourth tier) contained at least three respondents, and at the next higher tier (third tier), at least six respondents.

Among the creators and innovators studied, all generate work that is or could be protected in some way by intellectual property law. Among the legal professionals, all have experience working in the intellectual property field on behalf of creators and innovators and their organizations (as lawyers, licensing professionals, or business managers). When possible, I collected documents from the interviewees, including, for example, invention disclosure sheets, corporate policies regarding intellectual property, sample licenses, and contracts. These additional sources of data were used to supplement and "triangulate" interviewee's accounts, sometimes providing substantiation and occasionally evidence with which to critique respondents' accounts.

In qualitative fieldwork studies, there is no easy way to determine how many interviews are needed for the set.[6] Some social scientists recommend between twenty and fifty, depending on the dimensions of the phenomena, including, for example, the logical variation in the subject of study.[7] This book is based on a set of fifty interviews. By approximately the thirtieth interview, I had reached what is called "saturation," after which I began to hear the same themes repeatedly.[8] However, I continued to conduct interviews to achieve robust stratification of creative and innovative professionals across the variables. As explained earlier, this is not a study based on random sampling logic. It is based on the aggregate of the events, examples, and cases that each interview presents, and the method is particularly "effective when asking how or why questions about processes unknown before the start of the study."[9]

Interviews lasted between one and two hours, and they were semi-structured, face-to-face, and digitally recorded for later transcription. Interviewees were guaranteed anonymity, which ensured that they could speak truthfully about, for example, personal issues, employers, or competitors, without worry of reputational injury or retaliation. I followed an interview protocol, which was developed in advance and designed to elicit both in-depth and open-ended conversation. I guided the interaction with scripted topics and questions but was responsive with follow-up queries and comments depending on the interviewee's particular answers. Improvised questions were asked when they were appropriate and made sense within the unfolding conversation. Interviews tended to begin with questions about details of the interviewee's professional workday and business, current or past projects, and particular joys of his or her work. I also asked interviewees about challenges they face in their work, optimal changes to their work, and the reasons they continue pursuing their work despite difficulties they experience or anticipate. I also asked interviewees to consider how their professional life has transformed over time and why, thinking back to aspirations and goals they had missed or attained. I asked respondents for examples of work of which they are most proud and why, and examples of work that has disappointed them and why. Almost always, interviewees described some point in their professional life when they asserted a claim over their work (or wished they had) because of some conflict. I devoted special attention to these instances of claiming and conflict because they were times when the interviewees were most clearly evoking and justifying an entitlement to their work, evoking rights and wrongs that sounded like legal or equitable interests. I sought to discern the scope of the entitlement and the basis for it within the interview. There were, however, other subtler ways in which the interviewees claimed work as "theirs" and justified it as worthy of protection from use or misuse by others. I pursued those descriptions as well, probing the reasons and explanations. If moments like these—of claims of title and ownership—did not arise or were not sufficiently clear, I posed hypotheticals to test the interviewee's tolerance for behavior that would be akin to infringement or unlawful takings in intellectual property law. Because I wanted to discover respondents' understandings and interpretations without directing them or broadcasting particular conceptions of IP, I never directly asked about intellectual property until the end of the interview. At that point, I did so to test the interviewees' understanding of IP and to compare what they understood and believed about intellectual property law and policy with the events, behaviors, and beliefs they had already described regarding their professional work (or their client's professional work) in creative or innovative fields.

DATA ANALYSIS

Analysis of the interview transcripts proceeded at the level of language (word choice, narrative structure, and content) and conceptual themes (from reading across the transcripts and from the literature on innovation and intellectual property). Drawing on my experience and training as a literary scholar, analysis of the interviews isolated and analyzed the various linguistic and narrative components that form a particular moral ordering (or "point") and that often reflect or maintain a particular institutional or social structure.[10] The analysis of conceptual themes in the interviews also developed from the socio-legal literature on innovation and legal policy. As interviews were read, reread, and coded with help of the analytic software, I revised data searches on the basis of reformulated questions and categories that emerged from the ongoing study of the interviews and the scholarly literature.

Interviews were analyzed in various steps. First, transcripts were read and summarized in a two- to three-page synopsis. These condensations include any notes made during the interview, a description of particularly interesting stories related by or quotations from the interviewee, and a list of overarching themes from the interview. During this initial process, I generated a list of code words developed deductively from preliminary findings and inductively from the emergent language, repetitions, narrative structure, and conceptual themes contained in the interviews. Then, the transcripts were read again and coded using a qualitative software system called Atlas.ti, which I used to manually attach codes (the themes, concepts, and words) to particular parts of the transcripts. (I had a research assistant do the same thing—so all transcripts were coded twice—and I managed the process for purposes of intercoder reliability.[11] This produced highly consistent and reliable coding based on a mutual understanding of the concepts and developing themes within the data.) Atlas.ti allows users to search and sort the data by code or any other category the user establishes (e.g., word, phrase, category of respondent). Atlas.ti also allows users to connect transcripts (or parts of them) to each other and to other documents within the database, thus adding depth and relations to the data set for yet further analysis. While coding, I drafted memos relating to certain subsets of transcripts within Atlas.ti that cross-referenced codes and transcripts, adding further dimensionality to the data analysis. Users can initiate queries in Atlas.ti, asking it to find all the instances in the transcripts when a code exists [PATENT] or of a particular combination of codes (e.g., [PATENT and INFRINGEMENT and SOFTWARE]) either within a subset of transcripts or across them all. The resulting output can be analyzed independently, saved in the system, further narrowed (or broadened), and compared to other query results.

As a database of language about intellectual property formation, creativity, and invention, the interviews provide empirical evidence of the culturally circulating schema, memes, interpretations, and understandings of intellectual property law. Treating each interview as a text exposes its structural features as a story of law-in-action and of creative and innovative culture. In conducting an inductive, qualitative analysis of the data, one goal was to arrive at a systematic understanding of popular legal consciousness regarding intellectual property. Another goal was to provide a "thick description" of the origins and output of creative and inventive processes and their relationships to the legal entitlements that may (or may not) flow therefrom.[12] Interview transcripts reveal understandings and interpretations of rights to the fruits of labor enacted by the interviewees through their accounts of their work and its concrete output, as well as connections and disconnects between popular consciousness and self-reported behavior. This project thus maps the relationship between the creative and innovation processes (how art and science proceed) and intellectual property law (what intellectual property is for and how it functions).

LIMITATIONS

The current project produces a typology of interpretations concerning intellectual property and creative and innovative work, whereas a larger sample size might generate quantitative information about the distribution of the identified variations, possibly uncovering additional variations. Follow-on surveys or further interviews can test for the applicability of these models across more professional fields and types of creativity or innovation. Preliminary findings from this study suggest that photography and some text publishing in the copyright space and pharmaceutical, and some medical device businesses in the patent space, rely more heavily on the traditional role of intellectual property as a mechanism to recuperate sunk costs in initial development and necessary distribution. Further research is required to draw firmer conclusions regarding this role of intellectual property in these fields.

That this sample was concentrated in a localized geographic area (New England and New York) may be considered a limitation. The geographic concentration did, however, increase the ability to conduct face-to-face interviews with minimal cost. The US Northeast is also a region of abundant scientific and artistic creativity; it may, however, be distinctive, and as such, additional research will have to test these types against data collected in other distinctive regions.

As already mentioned, an interview study (though one supplemented by document analysis) is limited to interviewees' self-reporting. This is a study of cultural scripts and beliefs. Inasmuch as it seeks to produce an account of legal consciousness (what people say as well as what they do), studying these narrative structures is critical. And because the project explores the relationships among interpretations about creative and innovative processes and their transformation (or not) into intellectual property, the validity of this study depends on how much of the interview responses reliably describe recognizable practices, whether the descriptions are sufficiently thick to be credible, and whether the theoretical interpretations are sufficiently grounded in these and comparative data.[13] I did my best to emulate the methods of well-regarded and robust qualitative interview studies to ensure optimal validity. Quality of interviewing matters a lot, and for this reason, I personally conducted all the interviews instead of relying on research assistants. Another scholar conducting qualitative research describes the importance of interviewing technique:

The more discursive, conversational style of the interview affords opportunities to prompt respondents to explain seeming oversights and inconsistencies, which serve as consistency or reliability checks of sorts. These same in-depth techniques are also well suited for getting underneath the superficial, socially desirable, or conventional responses people give when accounting for their behavior because the depth of information generated allows the researcher to detect deeper levels of meaning that the respondent herself may not be aware of, but which reveal underlying motivations that conventional or initial accounts belie.[14]

Despite my confidence that the interviews are robust and probing, my findings and conclusions are suggestive rather than exhaustive. Those attempting to generalize should proceed with caution. I hope, and encourage, further research, both qualitative and quantitative, to build on this initial framing.

In the end, I hope that the stories of those doing and facilitating creative and innovative work speak louder than my own analysis of them. Providing a platform to distribute the stories of creativity, innovation, and intellectual property was a primary goal of this project, so that when we talk about intellectual property law and the reasons for it, we might have those engaging in the underlying work foremost in our mind. My second aim was to organize the stories (and the concepts and themes embedded in them) into several coherent structures—theoretical and descriptive—so that we might test and question the categories, themes, and their connections as they inform our thinking about and reforming of intellectual property law in the future.

Interviewees

KEY

- First half of career (in their first twenty-five years of professional work).
- Second half of career (in their second twenty-five years of professional work).
- Unless otherwise noted, interviewees work full-time at their described profession.
- Where noted with an asterisk (*), interviewee is both an attorney or businessperson and a creator or innovator.

CONDITIONS

Interviewees were promised anonymity according to consent forms that each signed to participate in the study. The consent form was approved by the Institutional Research Board of Suffolk University. The biographies listed in the following sections use pseudonyms and lack detail in order to honor the promise of anonymity. I have tried to give enough information for readers to evaluate the stratification of the sample but not so much that anonymity is compromised.

ATTORNEYS, AGENTS, AND OTHER BUSINESS FACILITATORS

First Half of Career

Ted. An in-house attorney who is also vice president of a small start-up energy company that is in its second decade. He was an IP attorney at a law firm prior to working in-house.

Peter. An in-house patent attorney at a publicly traded, global pharmaceutical company. He began his career at a large law firm as a patent prosecutor.

Paul. An intellectual property attorney (partner) at a midsize law firm serving individual and corporate clients.

Richard. A business executive whose focus is building companies around core products in the medical and health fields. He currently works at an international nonprofit, building their research and development ventures. An experienced venture capital investor, he has been partner and founder of several funds focusing on bioengineering and life sciences.

Michael. A pharmacologist with his own consulting company that advises scientists, start-ups, and small and large businesses on how to manufacture their product for large-scale production and distribution. He recently graduated from law school to provide his clients with a more comprehensive consulting service.

Samuel. A copyright attorney and general counsel of a nonprofit licensing organization. In an earlier career, he was a senior in-house attorney for a national retail chain, and senior attorney at a big-city law firm, where his focus was intellectual property and antitrust.

Gary. An intellectual property lawyer in a large law firm whose focus at the firm is on copyright and trademark issues. Before law school, he worked in a national publishing company advising on the selection and cultivation of authors and markets.

Frank. A copyright attorney who is general counsel for global educational publishing company with particular focus on scientific and medical publications.

Meredith. A music agent with her own marketing firm that specializes in promoting singer-songwriters but also represents other kinds of artists and small businesses. Previously, she worked as a marketing executive at a large advertising agency. At the time of the interview, her firm was several years old and growing.

Joseph. A publishing executive working on product development and marketing at a niche press with an international reputation. He previously worked as a buyer in bookstores.

Steve. A marketing and business executive who co-owns a small but prosperous company that focuses on developing brands and merchandise lines through brand extension for entertainment companies (film, television, and toys). He previously worked as an executive in marketing and development in a Fortune 500 company.

Scott. A marketing executive with his own company that develops web-based marketing platforms and strategies. He began his career as an investment banker, but left to found his first company (also an online advertising and direct marketing company), which he sold after several years.

Second Half of Career

Cary. An in-house intellectual property counsel for an alternative-energy company start-up that was recently acquired by an international conglomerate. He previously worked as chief patent counsel in various companies with diverse focuses: consumer goods (longest tenure of over a decade), semiconductors, and electronic test equipment. He began his career as a chemical engineer.

Dennis. An in-house patent attorney at a publicly traded, global pharmaceutical company. In his earlier career, he worked in a similar positions as in-house patent counsel for similarly large pharmaceutical companies.

Leora.* An in-house counsel at an international medical device company, with a focus on intellectual property, compliance, and contracts. She began her career as an engineer and is a named inventor on several patents involving consumer goods.

Carol.* A former academic biologist, who achieved tenured status at a nationally regarded university but then changed careers, went to law school, and became partner in a boutique law firm counseling diverse clients on intellectual property issues, with a particular focus on patent-related issues, including patent prosecution.

Susan. A director of the technology-transfer office and its operations at a top-tier university known for its research in science and engineering.

John. A senior licensing officer in the technology-transfer office at a top-tier university known for its research in science and engineering.

Howard. An intellectual property lawyer since the 1980s, for a long time as a partner in a large law firm and now a partner in his own small boutique law firm that specializes in advising companies about their intellectual property strategies. He works with all sorts of intellectual property (e.g., patents, copyright, trademark, and trade secrets).

Jacqueline. An in-house general counsel of privately held Internet company that sells online content and space, and whose initial public offering (IPO) was recently stalled. In her earlier career, she was in-house counsel for leading technology companies.

Donald. An in-house attorney who is also vice president for an e-commerce company that provides e-commerce platforms to clients, is in its third decade, and was recently acquired (after the interview) for $1 billion. In his earlier career, he worked for a publicly traded, multinational toy and entertainment company.

Bob. An in-house attorney who is also a vice president of a large, privately held publishing company with educational and trade division offices around the world. He has been in publishing nearly his entire career, with early stints as a litigator.

Seth. An in-house attorney for a small and profitable print and online publishing company. In his earlier career, he was a litigator working for the government and in-house at a university.

Irene. A solo practitioner specializing in copyright and trademark issues, serving companies and individual clients, with a specialty in publishing and media issues, both for profit and nonprofit clients. In her earlier career, she worked at a large big-city law firm specializing in copyright and trademark law and worked in-house as senior and general counsel at several large publishing companies.

CREATORS AND INNOVATORS
First Half of Career

*Andrew.** A scientist and high-technology entrepreneur, with a graduate degree in physics, who currently runs his third company and is seeking a purchaser or IPO. A previous company was sold for $30 million, and another failed to get off the ground. He is a named co-inventor on several patents.

*Ilene.** A genetic biologist who recently graduated from law school and has become a patent attorney with a boutique law firm. She first spent several years as a biologist in academia and many more in the pharmaceutical industry.

*Alex.** A computer scientist and entrepreneur with a company (one of many he started, some of which he sold) that develops and sells access to a web-based product for online use. He is a named inventor on several software patents.

*Kevin.** A software and hardware engineer who no longer designs programs or products but is a consultant and entrepreneur, investing in high-technology companies with a focus on telecommunications. He worked in some of the founding computer companies as a software engineer when the companies were still small, and he helped them grow. He has since been involved in both start-ups and public companies in the industry.

*Matthew.** An information architect, with a background in software development and architecture, who previously had his own company developing websites and Internet commerce and marketing strategies for a variety of companies. Currently, he is a senior account developer at an Internet commercial and marketing company, where he works with clients to develop strategies for Internet interaction and client engagement.

Elizabeth. A writer, formerly a copy editor at various national magazines, who holds an MFA in writing. She is writing a novel and is supported by her husband.

Jennifer. A journalist, formerly bureau chief in Europe for an international news organization, and currently on staff at a nationally syndicated radio station. She is coauthor of a well-regarded first book.

Mary. A singer-songwriter with more than three solo albums and a busy professional performing schedule. She is in her midthirties, and represented by a music agent and a well-regarded music label. At the time of the interview, she had a flexible part-time job, but at the time of publication, she was working full-time on her music.

Karen. An artist with a growing international reputation. Her sculptures, paintings, drawings, and diverse installations have earned her international accolades, awards, and grants. She works on her art full-time and always has.

Joan. A sculptor with an international reputation and her own studio employing several assistants. She began as a painter but became a sculptor after several years. She works on her art full-time and always has.

Melanie. An award-winning documentary filmmaker who has her own film production company. She regularly works in public television, but she began her career as a photographer, photographic journalist, and later assistant producer to an acclaimed filmmaker.

Kim. A musician, with her own band and several albums, who is also an aspiring actress. She works in healing arts and as a freelance writer in addition to performing.

Sean. A former award-winning photographic journalist who worked with national and international newspapers. He left professional photography within the first decade to work in a family business.

*Theo.** An advertising executive with an expertise in film and video working in an internationally acclaimed advertising agency. He also makes his own films, having made several shorts, and recently finished his first feature film, which won awards at national and international film festivals.

Second Half of Career

Dan. A chemical engineer who worked at global companies on product development, earning awards for his work. He is also a co-inventor on several patents. Later, he worked as chemical engineer in several civil engineering firms that were smaller in scale. He retired early to work on music composing and performing full-time. He currently runs a nonprofit community opera company that performs his operas as well as others.

Robert. An award-winning chemist at a major research university who also started a company (with outside investment and expertise) based on a patented invention that combines his expertise in computer software, math, and chemistry.

*Thomas.** A software engineer who founded his own company before graduating from college and has worked as co-owner and partner since then, growing and diversifying his company's products and services, which revolve around data management. His company remains private.

Jack. An award-winning computer scientist at a major research university. He is the inventor on several patents, some of which were sold or were the foundation of companies in which he had a financial stake.

Barbara. An author of books for children from ages eight to the early teens. She has written more than 120 books in various series, and she began her writing career with novelizations of successful films. Her first work in publishing was as a contract manager and editor in a national publishing company. She left that work after many years to support herself with her own writing.

Lisa. An author of adult fiction and nonfiction, with several writing awards and best sellers. She began her career as a teacher and a journalist.

*Leo.** A painter (and retired lawyer) in the later stages of life who is developing a reputation as an up-and-coming artist in the contemporary art scene. He spends most of his time painting and showing his art in galleries.

Helen. A sculptor who focuses on public installations. She has worked full-time as a sculptor nearly her entire career. She employs a studio assistant.

Sadie. An artist who focuses on sculpture (but works in other media) and supports herself with a combination of her own work and salaried employment curating public art projects. She lives in subsidized housing for artists.

Camille. A sculptor with an international reputation whose focus is public art. She employs a studio assistant and has worked on her art full-time nearly her entire career. She taught for some years before working on her public installations full-time.

Max. An artist with a focus on architectural works and sculpture with an international reputation. He employs a studio assistant and has worked on his art and architecture his entire career.

David. A photographer who shows and sells his work but also works part-time in retail. Earlier in his career, he worked full-time as a fashion and advertising photographer.

Ann. An award-winning documentary filmmaker who has her own film production company and recently won several national awards for her films. She is a former staff producer for public television.

Notes

1. In referring to "antlike persistence," Dennis may consciously or unconsciously be referring to a 1924 court decision written by the famous judge Learned Hand in which he used the language of "antlike persistence" to describe patent lawyers and their own resolute pursuit of valid patent claims. *Lyon v. Boh*, 1 F.2d 48 (S.D.N.Y. 1924). If Dennis is referring to this, then he has switched the focus of Learned Hand's praise from lawyers to scientists.

2. Mihaly Csikszentmihalyi, *Creativity: Flow and the Psychology of Discovery and Invention* (New York: Harper Collins, 1996); Howard Gardner, *Creating Minds: An Anatomy of Creativity Seen Through the Lives of Freud, Einstein, Picasso, Stravinsky, Eliot, Graham, and Gandhi* (New York: Basic Books, 1993); Keith Sawyer, *Explaining Creativity: The Science of Human Innovation* (New York: Oxford University Press, 2006); but see Teresa Amabile, *Creativity in Context* (Boulder, CO: Westview Press, 1996).

3. Other books that engage a similar set of questions from different angles (only a few of which are based on systematic empirical analysis) include Jason Mazzone, *Copyfraud and Other Abuses of Intellectual Property Law* (Stanford, CA: Stanford University Press, 2011); Kal Raustiala and Chris Sprigman, *The Knockoff Economy: How Imitation Sparks Innovation* (New York: Oxford University Press, 2012); Peter DiCola and Kembrew McLeod, *Creative License: The Law and Culture of Digital Sampling* (Durham, NC: Duke University Press 2011); Joanna Demers, *Steal This Music: How Intellectual Property Affects Musical Creativity* (Athens: University of Georgia Press, 2006); John Tehranian, *Infringement Nation: Copyright 2.0 and You* (New York: Oxford University Press, 2011); James Bessen and Mike Meurer, *Patent Failure: How Judges, Bureaucrats, and Lawyers Put Innovators at Risk* (Princeton, NJ: Princeton University Press, 2008).

4. But see *Citizens United v. Federal Election Commission*, 558 U.S. 310 (2010) (treating corporations as people for the purposes of rights concerning political speech under the First Amendment).

5. As I will explain shortly, this is a contestable assertion.

6. Certainly, the law and economics literature asserts a strong relationship between IP and firm structure, suggesting that IP might influence profit strategies, organizational form, conflict management tactics, and research and development. See, e.g., Jonathan Barnett, "Intellectual Property as a Law of Organization," *Southern California Law Review* 84 (2011): 785–858; Dan Burk and Brent McDonnell, "The Goldilocks Hypothesis: Balancing Intellectual Property Rights at the Boundary of the Firm," *University of Illinois Law Review* (2007): 575–636; William Landes and Richard Posner, *The Economic Structure of Intellectual Property Law* (Cambridge, MA: Harvard University Press, 2003).

7. But see Mark Rose, *Authors and Owners: The Invention of Copyright* (Cambridge, MA: Harvard University Press, 1993), in which he traces the copyright regime as founded on corporate and organizational interests of book sellers and publishers, not individual interests of authors.

8. See Julie E. Cohen, "Copyright as Property in the Post-Industrial Economy: A Research Agenda," *Wisconsin Law Review* (2011): 141–165.

9. Mary Douglas, *How Institutions Think* (Syracuse, NY: Syracuse University Press, 1986), 9.

10. "Marxist theory assumes that a social class can perceive, choose and act upon its own group interests. Democratic theory is based on the idea of the collective will." Ibid.

11. This is the central claim of Émile Durkheim in his *Elementary Forms of Religious Life* (first published in 1912) and later Robert Merton, in both *Social Theory and Social Structure* (New York: Free Press, 1968) and "Social Structure and Anomie," *American Sociological Review* 3, no. 5 (1938): 672–682.

12. Douglas, *How Institutions Think*, 8.

13. See Appendix A for in-depth discussion of the benefits and limitations of qualitative empirical studies such as this one.

14. See, e.g., Peter DiCola, "Money from Music: Survey Evidence on Musicians Revenue and Lessons from Copyright Incentives," *Arizona Law Review* 55 (2013): 301–372; Stuart J. H. Graham et al., "High Technology Entrepreneurs and the Patent System: Results of the 2008 Berkeley Patent Survey," *Berkeley Technology Law Review* 24 (2009): 1255–1328, 1258.

15. James Boyd White, *From Expectation to Experience* (Ann Arbor: University of Michigan Press, 2000), 114.

16. See ibid. (making a similar claim interpreting a statute that defines a business organization).

17. Ibid. at 119.

18. For an explanation of storytelling and story forms being self-fulfilling in the adjudication of particular disputes, see Carol Rose, *Property and Persuasion: Essays on the History, Theory and Rhetoric of Property* (Boulder, CO: Westview Press, 1994). See also Anthony Amsterdam and Jerome Bruner, *Minding the Law: How Courts Rely on Storytelling and How Their Stories Change the Ways We Understand the Law and Ourselves* (Cambridge, MA: Harvard University Press, 2000).

19. Hayden White, "The Value of Narrativity in the Representation of Reality in *On Narrative*," *Critical Inquiry* 7, no. 1 (1980): 5–27.

20. Ross Chambers, *Story as Situation: Narrative Seduction and the Power of Fiction* (Minneapolis: University of Minnesota Press, 1984).

21. Ann Southworth, *Lawyers of the Right: Professionalizing the Conservative Coalition* (Chicago: University of Chicago Press, 2008); Pamela Stone, *Opting Out: Why Women Really Quit Careers and Head Home* (Berkeley: University of California Press, 2007); Patricia Ewick and Susan Silbey, *The Common Place of Law: Stories from Everyday Life* (Chicago: University of Chicago Press, 1998).

22. See, e.g., Charles Ragin and Lisa Amoroso, *Constructing Social Research* (Thousand Oaks, CA: Sage Publications, 2011), 173 (describing how quantitative research is constrained by its frames).

23. Brett Frischmann and Mark Lemley, "Spillovers," *Columbia Law Review* 107 (2007): 257–301.

24. Diamond v. Chakrabarty, 447 U.S. 303 (1980).

25. 447 U.S. 303 (1980).

26. 15 U.S.C. §1127.

27. Laura Heymann, "Overlapping Intellectual Property Doctrines: Election of Rights Versus Selection of Remedies," *Stanford Technology Law Review* 17 (2013): 239–277; Andrew Beckerman-Rodau, "The Problem with Intellectual Property Rights: Subject Matter Expansion," *Yale Journal of Law and Technology* 13 (2011): 35–89; Laura Heymann, "The Trademark/Copyright Divide," *Southern Methodist Law Review* 60 (2007): 55–102.

28. Beckerman-Rodau, "Problem with Intellectual Property Rights."

CHAPTER ONE

1. Jessica Silbey, "The Mythical Beginnings of Intellectual Property," *George Mason Law Review* 15 (2008): 319–379 (describing "origin stories" as myths to justify a social or legal status). The story of Isaac Newton and the apple tree is one such story. The origin of the lyrics of the "Star-Spangled Banner" (written by Francis Scott Key after watching a battle during the War of 1812) is another. See also Mihaly Csikszentmihalyi, *Creativity: Flow and the Psychology of Discovery and Invention* (New York: Harper Collins, 1996) (describing the aha moment as arriving after a period of incubation).

2. David M. Engel, "Origin Myths: Narratives of Authority, Resistance, Disability, and Law," *Law and Society Review* 27 (1993): 791.

3. To preserve anonymity, I have generated pseudonyms for the interviewees. Appendix B contains a full list of all the interviewees.

4. Silbey, "Mythical Beginnings of Intellectual Property."

5. For relevant academic literature distinguishing incentives and motives, see Henry Sauerman and Wesley M. Cohen, "What Makes Them Tick?" (Working Paper No. 14443, National Bureau of Economic Research, Cambridge, MA, 2008), 2, http://www.nber.org/papers/w14443 (and citations therein). Sauerman and Cohen describe benefits that are contingent on effort or performance as incentives, whereas they describe individual's *preferences* for the contingent work benefits as motives. For clarity purposes, I prefer extrinsic versus intrinsic motives, and consider both of them "incentives" of a kind.

6. Campbell v. Acuff-Rose Music, Inc., 510 U.S. 569, 584 (1994) (quoting Samuel Johnson in his letters found in James Boswell, *The Life of Samuel Johnson, LL.D.* [1791; republished as George Birkbeck Hill, ed., *Boswell's Life of Johnson*, revised and enlarged by Lawrence F. Powell, 6 vols. (Oxford, UK: Clarendon Press, 1934–1950)]).

7. Henry Sauerman, Wesley Cohen, and Paula Stephan, "Doing Well or Doing Good? The Motives, Incentives, and Commercial Activities of Academic Scientists and Engineers" (paper presented at the 2010 summer conference at Imperial College London Business School, June 16–18, 2010), http://www2.druid.dk/conferences/viewpaper.php?id=501180&cf=43; Katherine J. Strandburg, "Curiosity-Driven Research and University Technology Transfer," in *Advances in the Study of Entrepreneurship, Innovation & Economic Growth*, ed. Sherry Hoskinson and Donald Kuratko (Oxford, UK: Elsevier Science and JAL Press, 2005), 16:93–122.

8. See Rebecca Tushnet, "Economies of Desire: Fair Use and Marketplace Assumptions," *William & Mary Law Review* 51 (2009): 513–546 (describing the importance of

attribution and pleasure in producing creative work); Ben DePoorter, Adam Holland, and Elizabeth Somerstein, "Copyright Abolition and Attribution," *Review of Law and Economics* 5 (2009): 1063–1080 (citing work regarding varieties of social recognition and other nonpecuniary rewards); Catherine L. Fisk, "Credit Where It's Due: The Law and Norms of Attribution," *Georgetown Law Journal* 95 (2006): 53–67 (describing why attribution matters). See also Peter S. Menell and Suzanne Scotchmer, "Intellectual Property," in *Handbook of Law and Economics*, ed. A. Mitchell Polinsky and Steven Shavell (Amsterdam: Elsevier, 2007), 2:1479–1524 (describing how relationship between patent protection and innovation is complex and often diverges from an overly simplistic incentive story).

9. Silbey, "The Mythical Beginnings of Intellectual Property," 323.

10. Csikszentmihalyi, *Creativity*, 47.

11. Ibid.

12. Ibid., 83, 95. See also Jeanne C. Fromer, "A Psychology of Intellectual Property," *Northwestern University Law Review* 104 (2010): 1441–1510 (citing literature on "problem finding" and "problem solving" perspectives among scientists and artists).

13. Csikszentmihalyi, *Creativity: Flow and the Psychology of Discovery and Invention*, 83.

14. Ibid. at 95.

15. Ibid. at 94–95. The reason for this, in part, is because of the selection of his subjects, famous individuals in their field. My selection was not of "geniuses," but I tried for a fair cross section of industry actors.

16. This kind of problem solving comports more directly with the psychology literature. Csikszentmihalyi, *Creativity*, 83–98.

17. Csikszentmihalyi's interviews described the same sentiment. Ibid at 107.

18. Rebecca Tushnet, "Economies of Desire: Fair Use and Marketplace Assumptions," *William & Mary Law Review* 51 (2009): 513–546 (describing creativity as a form of addiction-satisfying activity).

19. This is consistent with studies conducted by Mihaly Csikszentmihalyi, among others; see Csikszentmihalyi, *Flow: The Psychology of Optimal Experience* (New York: Harper & Row, 1990); Daniel Pink, *Drive: The Surprising Truth About What Motivates Us* (London: Penguin, 2009).

20. Pink, *Drive*, 89.

21. For arguments about the importance of autonomy in business organizations, see ibid. at 72, 163.

22. See ibid. at 61 (describing internal competitions to disclose all new ideas).

23. See ibid. at 86–95 (citing studies in behavioral economics and psychology, among them Paul P. Baard, Edward Deci, and Richard Ryan, "Intrinsic Need Satisfaction: A Motivational Basis of Performance and Well-Being in Two Work Settings," *Journal of Applied Social Psychology* 34 [2004]: 2045–2068, which in turn cites a study of 320 small businesses in which those that granted workers greater autonomy grew at four times the rate of control-oriented firms. These are just a few of the many such studies bearing out similar conclusions).

24. See, e.g., Fiona Murray and Scott Stern, "Do Formal Intellectual Property Rights Hinder the Free Flow of Scientific Knowledge? An Empirical Test of the Anti-Commons Hypothesis," *Journal of Economic Behavior and Organization* 63 (2007): 648–687; Julie E. Cohen, "The Place of the User in Copyright Law," *Fordham Law Review* 74 (2005): 347–374; Michael A. Heller and Rebecca S. Eisenberg, "Can Patents

Deter Innovation? The Anticommons in Biomedical Research," *Science* 280 (1998): 698–701.

25. Invention disclosures are questionnaires scientists fill out when they believe they've invented something new, nonobvious, and useful, and therefore have discovered something that may be patentable.

26. Tim Wu, "Tolerated Use," *Columbia Journal of Law and the Arts* 31 (2008): 617–635; John Tehranian, "Infringement Nation: Copyright Reform and the Law/Norm Gap," *Utah Law Review* (2007): 537–550; Shyamkrishna Balganesh, "The Uneasy Case Against Copyright Trolls," *Southern California Law Review* 86 (2013): 723–779.

27. Csikszentmihalyi, *Creativity*, 107.

28. Mark Lemley, "The Myth of the Sole Inventor," *Michigan Law Review* 110 (2012): 709–760; Robert K. Merton, "Resistance to the Systematic Study of Multiple Discoveries in Science," *European Journal of Sociology* 4 (1963): 237–249.

29. Robert Merges writes about how in the digital age "collectivities are the more essential unit of analysis" and that we should therefore stop "talking in terms of individuality and instead about the reasons for autonomy in the first place." Robert P. Merges, "The Concept of Property in the Digital Era," *Houston Law Review* 45 (2008): 1247–1274.

30. Margaret J. Radin, "Property and Personhood," *Stanford Law Review* 34 (1982): 957–1015; Roberta J. Kwall, *The Soul of Creativity: Forging a Moral Rights Law for the United States* (Stanford, CA: Stanford University Press, 2009).

31. Julie Cohen posits something similar: that the author-centered model of incentives for copyright is simply wrong as a descriptive matter and that we should be talking instead about how copyright sustains and generates corporate welfare in specific industries. In other words, "the incentives-for-authors story impedes clear-eyed assessment of copyright's true economic and cultural functions. In the contemporary information society, the purpose of copyright is to enable the provision of capital and organization so that creative work may be exploited." Julie Cohen, "Copyright as Property in the Post-Industrial Economy: A Research Agenda," *Wisconsin Law Review* (2011): 143. My interview data bear out this theory empirically.

CHAPTER TWO

1. Mihaly Czikszentmihalyi, *Creativity: Flow and the Psychology of Discovery and Invention* (New York: HarperCollins, 1996), 107–126; Teresa M. Amabile, *Creativity in Context: Update to the Social Psychology of Creativity* (Boulder, CO: Westview Press, 1996), 133–138.

2. See, e.g., Michael J. Madison, "Creativity and Craft," in *Creativity, Law and Entrepreneurship*, ed. Shubha Ghosh and Robin Paul Malloy (Cheltenham, UK: Edward Edgar, 2011) (discussing the role of crafted-goods in copyright law and defining craft for his purposes in the broader sense of "human-produced artifacts even if their tangible manifestations are digital or virtual . . . to physical things, or at least to material [including digital] things, rather than to the cognitive or imaginative processes that produce them").

3. Anthony Giddens, *The Constitution of Society: Outline of the Theory of Saturation* (Cambridge, UK: Polity, 1984), xxiv–xxvi, 110–162.

4. See Czikszentmihalyi, *Creativity*, 107–126.

5. See ibid. at 105; see also Jeanne C. Fromer, "A Psychology of Intellectual Property," *Northwestern University Law Review* 104 (2010): 1441–1510.

6. Lyon v. Boh, 1 F.2d 48 (S.D.N.Y. 1924).
7. Robert K. Merton, *The Sociology of Science: Theoretical and Empirical Investigations* (Chicago: University of Chicago Press, 1973).
8. Feist Publications, Inc., v. Rural Telephone Service Co., Inc., 499 U.S. 340 (1991) (holding that sweat of the brow—one's labor—does not determine whether a work is copyrightable).
9. Jessica Silbey, "The Mythical Beginnings of Intellectual Property," 15 *George Mason Law Review* 319 (2008): 327–337 (describing the myths of scientific inventorship embodied in patent law) and 342–351 (describing the myths of romantic authorship embodied in copyright law).
10. Alasdair MacIntyre, in his influential 1981 book *After Virtue*, discusses the ethics of practice and everyday work as a defense to the corrosive effects of capitalism and that routine work binds communities around shared values. Alasdair MacIntyre, *After Virtue: A Study in Moral Theory* (London: Duckworth, 1981).
11. Howard Risatti, *A Theory of Craft: Function and Aesthetic Expression* (Chapel Hill: University of North Carolina Press, 2007), 219–231.
12. See Laurel Thatcher Ulrich, *The Age of Homespun Objects and Stories in the Creation of an American Myth* (New York: Knopf, 2001) (studying everyday craft objects as a form of material culture to understand the people who used them).
13. See *Feist*, 499 U.S. 340 (1991). But see Adam D. Moore, "Toward a Lockean Theory of Intellectual Property," in *Intellectual Property: Moral, Legal, and International Dilemmas*, ed. Adam D. Moore (Lanham, MD: Rowman & Littlefield, 1997), 81–103; Wendy J. Gordon, "A Property in Self-Expression: Equality and Individualism in the Natural Law of Intellectual Property," *Yale Law Journal* 102 (1993): 1533–1609; Lawrence C. Becker, "Deserving to Own Intellectual Property," *Chicago-Kent Law Review* 68 (1993): 609–629.
14. See *Feist*, 499 U.S. 340 (1991).
15. Ibid.
16. 35 U.S.C. §101 (The Patent Act): Silbey, "The Mythical Beginnings of Intellectual Property," 329–337.
17. Margaret J. Radin, "Property and Personhood," *Stanford Law Review* 34 (1982): 957–1015. Radin's contributions are indebted to both Lockean and Hegelian philosophies, but her theories go well beyond both to innovate their applications to the modern property and intellectual property regimes. See Margaret J. Radin, *Reinterpreting Property* (Chicago: University of Chicago Press, 1993).
18. David Fagundes, "Property Rhetoric and the Public Domain," *Minnesota Law Review* 94 (2010): 652–705; Molly S. Van Houweling, "The New Servitudes," *Georgetown Law Journal* 96 (2008): 885–950.
19. This makes sense given that lawsuits are extremely costly and that full-blown litigation is worthwhile only when the assets being protected are worth the hundreds of thousands (or millions) of dollars a lawsuit will cost. Kevin M. Lemley, "I'll Make Him an Offer He Can't Refuse: A Proposed Model for Alternative Dispute Resolution in Intellectual Property Disputes," *Akron Law Review* 37 (2004): 299–327; William M. Landes, "An Empirical Analysis of Intellectual Property Litigation: Some Preliminary Results," *Houston Law Review* 41 (2004): 749–779, 753; Michael J. Meurer, "Controlling Opportunistic and Anti-Competitive Intellectual Property Litigation," *Boston College Law Review* 44 (2008): 509–544, 515–516. Alternatively, lawsuits may be

filed to send a message about the lengths to which a business or organization will go to protect its IP assets, even if the asset is not worth as much. See Stephanie F. Ward, "Plaintiff to RIAA: Download This!" *ABA Journal*, November 2007, 15 ("'Our companies have every right to protect their product, just as those who have been robbed have every right to claim damages for what was stolen from them,' [Jonathan Lamy, (the Recording Industry Association of America's) senior vice president of communications] says. '[Filing these suits] is simply a means to an end—that is, communicating the message that illegal downloading has consequences and encouraging fans to turn to any one of the great legal ways to enjoy music.'").

20. See Dastar Corp. v. Twentieth Century Fox Film Corp., 539 U.S. 23 (2003).

21. Christopher Buccafusco and Christopher Sprigman, "Valuing Intellectual Property: An Experiment," *Cornell Law Review* 96 (2010): 1–45 (describing results of an experiment that demonstrates overvaluation by creators of expressive works as compared to the price at which buyers are willing to license the works, thus leading to suboptimal transactions).

22. I am grateful to Bill Patry for conversations with him discussing this point. See also William Patry, *Moral Panics and the Copyright Wars* (Oxford: Oxford University Press, 2009), 131.

23. See Jonathan M. Barnett, "Is Intellectual Property Trivial?" *University of Pennsylvania Law Review* 157 (2009): 1691–1737; Dan Burk and Brent McDonnell, "Balancing Intellectual Property Rights at the Boundary of the Firm," *University of Illinois Law Review* 275 (2006): 575–636; Dan Burk, "Intellectual Property and the Firm," *University of Chicago Law Review* 71 (2004): 3–14; Joanne E. Oxley, "Institutional Environment and the Mechanisms of Governance: The Impact of Intellectual Property Protection on the Structure of Inter-Firm Alliances," *Journal of Economic Behavior and Organization* 38 (1999): 283–309.

24. See Julie E. Cohen, "Copyright as Property in the Post-Industrial Economy: A Research Agenda," *Wisconsin Law Review* (2011): 141–165 (making this same argument from the perspective of the development of postindustrial property, that is, corporate capital).

25. Eldred v. Ashcroft, 537 U.S. 186 (2003).

26. "Congress passed the CTEA in light of demographic, economic, and technological changes, and rationally credited projections that longer terms would encourage copyright holders to invest in the restoration and public distribution of their works" (ibid. at 188), and later the Court confirms that copyright secures a bargain, "this for that," such that authors receive the benefit of the copyright term, including any extension. Ibid. at 214.

27. Ibid. at 207 (note 15).

28. Ibid. at 242 (Breyer, J., dissenting).

29. In the trademark context, for example, the argument that trademarks protect consumers diverts attention from (and obfuscates the fact of) the expansion of trademark rights that benefit mark owners. See Mark P. McKenna, "The Normative Foundations of Trademark Law," *Notre Dame Law Review* 82 (2007): 1840–1915. Thanks to Mark McKenna for bringing this comparison to my attention.

30. Barton Beebe, "An Empirical Study of U.S. Copyright Fair Use Opinions, 1978–2005," *University of Pennsylvania Law Review* 156 (2008): 551–623, 617 (describing how commerciality—and market harm—competes for dominance in the fair-use analyses with transformativeness).

31. 35 U.S.C. §§116, 261 (the Patent Act allocating ownership).
32. Similarly, if we really want to protect and benefit the originator of IP (the author or inventor), we would regulate the creator-intermediary relationship much more than we do, through either employment doctrine or IP-related rules. See, e.g., Catherine L. Fisk, "The Role of Private Intellectual Property Rights in Markets for Labor and Ideas: Screen Credit and the Writers Guild of America, 1938–2000," *Berkeley Journal of Employment and Labor Law* 32 (2011): 215–268.

CHAPTER THREE

1. I am grateful to Jennifer Rothman for the phrase "taking a backseat."
2. Leah Chan Grinvald, "Shaming Trademark Bullies," *Wisconsin Law Review* (2011): 625–691; Siva Vaidhyanathan, *Copyright and Copywrongs: The Rise of Intellectual Property and How It Threatens Creativity* (New York: New York University Press, 2003); Shyamkrishna Balganesh, "The Uneasy Case Against Copyright Trolls," *Southern California Law Review* 86 (2013): 723–779.
3. Wendy Gordon, "Fair Use Markets: On Weighing Potential Licensing Fees," *George Washington Law Review* 79 (2011): 1814–1856, 1823 and note 52; Brett Frischmann and Mark Lemley, "Spillovers," *Columbia Law Review* 107 (2007): 257–301.
4. Mario Luis Small, "How Many Cases Do I Need? On Science and the Logic of Case Selection in Field Based Research," *Ethnography* 10, no. 5 (2009): 5–38, and especially 21, 25 (speaking to the value of qualitative work to produce "emergent knowledge").
5. Consider President Obama's statement in a speech at the Export-Import Bank's annual conference in March 2010, where he remarked: "We're going to aggressively protect our intellectual property. Our single greatest asset is the innovation and the ingenuity and creativity of the American people. It is essential to our prosperity and it will only become more so in this century. But it's only a competitive advantage if our companies know that someone else can't just steal that idea and duplicate it with cheaper inputs and labor. There's nothing wrong with other people using our technologies, we welcome it—we just want to make sure that it's licensed, and that American businesses are getting paid appropriately." See "Remarks by the President at the Export-Import Bank's Annual Conference" (press release), March 11, 2010, White House Office of the Press Secretary, http://www.whitehouse.gov/the-press-office/remarks-president -export-import-banks-annual-conference.
6. Balganesh, "The Uneasy Case"; David Fagundes, "Efficient Copyright Infringement," *Iowa Law Review* 98 (2013): 1791–1846.
7. See, e.g., Martin Kretschmer, "Does Copyright Law Matter? An Empirical Analysis of Creator's Earnings" (working paper, University of Glasgow), 3, http://papers.ssrn .com/sol3/papers.cfm?abstract_id=2063735; David M. Gould and William C. Gruben, "The Role of Intellectual Property: IP Rights in Economic Growth," *Journal of Development Economics* 48 (1996): 323–350.
8. Claims made over work in terms of time resonate with traditional views of real and personal property that incorporate elements of labor, occupancy and notice to the world. Susan S. Silbey, "Locke, op. cit.: Invocations of Law on Snowy Streets," *Journal of Comparative Law* 5, no. 2 (2012): 66–91.
9. George Lakoff and Mark Johnson, *Metaphors We Live By* (Chicago: University of Chicago Press, 1980); see also William Patry, *Moral Panics and the Copyright Wars* (New York: Oxford University Press, 2009), 43–60.

10. Stefan Ambec, Mark Cohen, Steward Elgie and Paul Lanoie, "The Porter Hypothesis at 20: Can Environmental Regulation Enhance Innovation and Competitiveness?" *Review of Environmental Economic Policy* 7, no. 1 (Winter 2013): 2–22; Sandra Roussea and Kjetil Telle, "On the Existence of the Optimal Fine for Environmental Crime," *International Review of Law and Economics* 30, no. 4 (2010): 329–337.

11. Barton Beebe, "Intellectual Property and the Sumptuary Code," *Harvard Law Review* 123 (2010): 809–889. This has echoes of the dawn of the anxieties, both theoretical and real, at the beginning of the "mechanical age" and modernism. Walter Benjamin, *The Work of Art in the Age of Mechanical Reproduction in Illuminations: Essays and Reflections* (New York: Harcourt, Brace, Jovanovich, 1968), 217–262.

12. Julie Cohen, "Pervasively Distributed Copyright Enforcement," *Georgetown Law Journal* 95 (2006): 1–48.

13. Cohen (ibid.) defines "constitutive freedom" as the autonomy to choose within a meaningful range of constraints for the diverse communities for whom IP matters. See more generally Julie Cohen, *Configuring the Networked Self* (New Haven, CT: Yale University Press, 2012).

14. Cohen, "Pervasively Distributed," 46.

15. James Boyd White, *From Expectation to Experience: Essays on Law and Legal Education* (Ann Arbor: University of Michigan Press, 2000), 114.

16. Ibid. at 113.

17. Clarissa Long, "Patent Signals," *University of Chicago Law Review* 69 (2002): 625–681. Whether the signal is a quality one, however, of course depends on many factors and matter of empirical debate. See, e.g., David Hsu and Rosemarie Ziedonis, "Patents as Quality Signals for Entrepreneurial Ventures," *Academy of Management Proceedings*, August 1, 2008, 1–6; David Hsu and Rosemarie Ziedonis, "Strategic Factor Markets and the Financing of Technology Startups: When Do Patents Matter More as Signaling Devices?" (working paper, 2011).

18. Richard Posner, *The Little Book of Plagiarism* (New York: Pantheon Books, 2007), 12.

19. Barton Beebe, Intellectual Property and The Sumptuary Code, *Harvard L. R.* 123 (2010): 809–889 (describing IP claims as authenticity claims).

20. See, e.g., Jonathan Barnett, "Do Patents Matter? Empirical Evidence on the Incentive Thesis," in *Handbook on Law, Innovation and Growth*, ed. Robert E. Litan (New York: Edward Elgar, 2011), 178–211.

21. Harold Bloom, *The Anxiety of Influence: A Theory of Poetry* (New York: Oxford University Press, 1973).

22. "Me too" drugs are medicines that may treat a similar symptom or target a similar biological mechanism but be composed of different molecules. They may also be quite similar in molecular structure to the original drug but different enough to be non-infringing variants of the original. They may be inspired by the original drug (which is the point of the interviewee's criticism), and they may also be the product of simultaneous invention. See, e.g., Rosanna Spector, "Me Too Drugs: Sometimes They're Just the Same Old, Same Old," *Stanford Medical Magazine*, Summer 2005, http://stanmed.stanford.edu/2005summer/drugs-metoo.html. See also, "Me Too! Me Too!" *Economist*, April 17, 2007, http://www.economist.com/blogs/freeexchange/2007/04/me_too_me_too.

23. See, e.g., Daniel Pink, *Drive: The Surprising Truth About What Motivates Us* (New York: Penguin, 2009).
24. Chris Anderson, *Free: The Future of a Radical Prices* (New York: Hyperion, 2008). See also Chris Anderson, "The Economics of Giving It Away," *Wall Street Journal*, January 31, 2009; Chris Anderson, "Free! Why $0.00 Is the Future of Business," *Wired*, February 25, 2008.
25. 17 U.S.C. § 504 (providing for statutory damages ranging from $750 to $150,000 per act of infringement).
26. This was Jonathan Barnett's point in "Do Patents Matter?," where he explains how patents might level the playing field between large firms and small by providing the smaller companies a level of exclusivity with their patent that larger companies can get through early entry market dominance. Jonathan Barnett, "Do Patents Matter? Empirical Evidence on the Incentive Thesis," in *Handbook on Law, Innovation and Growth*, ed. Robert E. Litan (New York: Edward Elgar, 2011), 178–211. A problem with this assertion is that both large and small companies can use patents to protect market share, and so the theory of the equal playing field only works if the larger firm forbears from patent protection.
27. Randal Picker, "The Razors-and-Blades Myth(s)," *University of Chicago Law Review* 78 (2011): 225–255; *Lexmark International, Inc. v. Static Control Components, Inc.*, 387 F.3d 522 (6th Cir. 2004).
28. The particular role of contracts in business has long been studied and is beyond the scope of this book. Notable in this context, however, is Stewart Macaulay's seminal article from 1963 that describes tentative findings from an interview-based qualitative empirical study on the role of contracts in varied industries in Wisconsin. Stewart Macaulay, "Non-Contractual Relations in Business: A Preliminary Study," *American Sociological Review* 28, no. 1 (1963): 1–23. In the article, Macaulay explains how businesspeople rely on contracts to define the scope of the desired performance by both parties, but less frequently to address contingencies, resolve disputes regarding the relationship, or determine legal sanctions for breach. The partial nature of the contract as a reflection of the actual business relationship (its present contours and implied or assumed future obligations) is commonplace among businesspeople and a source of potential anxiety among lawyers. The present study reflects both the centrality of contracts as a dominant mechanism for business relations and the inevitability of gap filling with business methods, including less formal legal ones, such as loyalty (personal relationships) and reputation.
29. The proliferation of Creative Commons licenses also reflects the tendency of using copyright—and underenforcing it—to achieve goals that are other than economic.
30. Catherine Fisk, "Credit Where It's Due: The Law and Norms of Attribution," *Georgetown Law Journal* 45 (2006): 49–117 (describing the history of the disassociation of IP rights from individuals to companies and attribution and credit as the inalienable right that employees value).
31. Macaulay, "Non-Contractual Relations."
32. Keith Blois, "Trust in Business to Business Relationships: An Evaluation of Status," *Journal of Management Studies* 26, no. 2 (1999): 197–215; Henry Abodor, "The Role of Personal Relationships in Inter-Firm Alliances: Benefits, Dysfunctions, and Some Suggestions," *Business Horizons* 49, no. 6 (2006): 473–486. See also Fred Reichheld, *The Loyalty Effect: The Hidden Force Behind Growth, Profits and Lasting Value* (Allston, MA: Harvard Business School Press, 1996).

33. See, e.g., Traci B. Warrington, Nadia J. Abgrab, and Helen M. Caldwell, "Building Trust to Develop Competitive Advantage in E-Business Relationships," *Competitiveness Review: An International Business Journal incorporating Journal of Global Competitiveness* 10, no. 2 (2000): 160–168.

34. Blois, "Trust," 210.

35. The literature on the ill-fitting nature of reputational interests and IP law is growing. See Daniel Solove, *The Future of Reputation* (New Haven, CT: Yale University Press, 2007); Laura Heymann, "The Law of Reputation and the Interest of the Audience," *Boston College Law Review* 52 (2011): 1341–1439.

36. Robert P. Merges, *Justifying Intellectual Property* (Cambridge, MA: Harvard University Press 2011), 18.

37. Gordon, "Fair Use Markets," 1839.

38. Merges, *Justifying Intellectual Property*, 83.

39. Ibid. at 72.

40. Ibid. at 81.

41. Michael Heller, "The Boundaries of Private Property," *Yale Law Journal* 108 (1999): 1163–1223.

42. Merges, *Justifying Intellectual Property*, 75–76 and 338 notes 24–25. Here, Merges is talking about Kant's personal will, which is related to but separate from the rational will.

43. Feist Publications, Inc., v. Rural Telephone Service Co., 499 U.S. 340 (1991).

44. IP exclusivity is the purported mechanism by which creative and innovative work is made and disseminated. IP exclusivity is not an end in itself.

45. I am grateful to Abraham Drassinower for helping me think through the ideas in this paragraph, as well as to Brett Frischmann, Wendy Gordon, Mark Lemley and Mark McKenna. Remaining ambiguities or mistakes are my own.

46. Daniel Gervais, "The Price of Social Norms: Towards a Liability Regime for File-Sharing," *Journal of Intellectual Property Law* 12 (2004): 39–73, 49–50.

47. "Property systems cannot function without widespread confidence in their legitimacy, including a sense that it is immoral to infringe on property rights." Joseph Singer, "The Rule of Reason in Property Law," *University of California Davis Law Review* 46 (2013): 1369–1434, 1382.

48. Jessica Litman, *Digital Copyright* (Athens, NY: Prometheus Books, 2001).

49. Bill Herman, *The Fight over Digital Rights: The Politics of Copyright and Technology* (New York: Cambridge University Press, 2013).

50. Indeed, there is indication that the hostility has arisen and is growing. See ibid. at 1–25 (discussing the recent legislative failures of the Stop Online Piracy Act and the Protect IP Act as evidence of newly mobilized coalitions seeking to halt the growth of IP rights).

CHAPTER FOUR

1. Ray Madoff, *Immortality and the Law: The Rising Power of the American Dead* (New Haven, CT: Yale University Press, 2010), 120.

2. Robert C. Post, "The Social Foundations of Defamation Law: Reputation and the Constitution," *California Law Review* 74 (1986): 691–692 (describing the "obligatory reference to Shakespeare" when writing about reputation).

3. Laura Heymann, "The Law of Reputation and the Interest of the Audience," *Boston College Law Review* 52 (2011): 1241–1342.

4. Madoff, *Immortality and the Law*, 119.

5. Daniel J. Solove, *The Future of Reputation: Gossip, Rumor and Privacy on the Internet* (New Haven, CT: Yale University Press, 2007); Hassan Masum and Mark Tovey, eds., *The Reputation Society: How Online Opinions Are Reshaping the Offline World* (Cambridge, MA: MIT Press, 2012); Eric Goldman, "The Regulation of Reputational Information," in *The Next Digital Decade: Essays on the Future of the Internet*, ed. Berin Szoka and Adam Marcus (Washington, DC: TechFreedom, 2011), 293–304.

6. There is a growing body of research that substantiates this observation in my interviews. See, e.g., Christopher Jon Sprigman, Christopher Buccafusco, and Zachary Burns, "What's a Name Worth? Valuing Attribution in Intellectual Property," *Boston University Law Review* 93 (2013): 1389–1435 (showing through empirical experiments that creators value attribution and receiving recognition for their work more than getting paid). Certainly, the long history of moral rights in Europe and the revival of moral rights (to a limited extent) in the United States supports this proposition as well.

7. Mark McKenna, "The Normative Foundations of Trademark Law," *Notre Dame Law Review* 82 (2007): 1839–1916.

8. See the Visual Artists Rights Act (VARA), 17 U.S.C. §106A (granting limited rights of integrity and attribution, subject to fair-use determinations, to paintings, drawings, prints, sculptures, still photographic images produced for exhibition only, and existing in single copies or in limited editions of two hundred or fewer copies, signed and numbered by the artist).

9. The Patent Act requires the inventor be named on the patent application (35 U.S.C. §111) and has a provision for correcting inventorship when it is listed in error (35 U.S.C §256), but nothing in the patent law gives the inventor any right to have his or her name associated with the invention as it is made, sold, or used in the marketplace.

10. With regard to right of publicity, arguably the broadest of the rights, it provides a person with the right to protect and profit from the commercial value of his or her name or likeness and to prevent others from unfairly appropriating either for commercial purposes. This started out as a personal right (akin to privacy) and has shifted to a property interest capable of transfer, descendability, and commercialization. See Madoff, *Immortality and the Law*, 133. For the difficulty of this and other claims to protect reputational interests, see Madoff, *Immortality and the Law*, 119–151; Eric Goldman, "The Regulation of Reputational Information"; Laura Heymann, "The Scope of Trademark Law in the Age of the Brand Persona," *Virginia Law Review in Brief* 98 (2012): 61, 69 and note 25.

11. Heymann, "Law of Reputation."

12. Heymann, "Scope of Trademark Law," 69.

13. Jeremy Sheff, "Marks, Morals, and Markets," *Stanford Law Review* 65 (2013): 772.

14. Indeed, the different ways reputation can be protected splits between those rights that are inheritable as property (e.g., publicity rights, copyright, trademark) and where the right ends with the life of person to whom the reputation is attached (e.g., defamation, privacy). Madoff, *Immortality and the Law*, 127.

15. As Barton Beebe explains, the ubiquity of copies in our digital age, and intellectual property law's failure to maintain desired distinctions between goods and people regarding value and status, foretells the situation in which differentiated identity and reputation will depend on production rather than consumption. The interviewees'

focus on work and works—the interrelatedness of everyday practice with output—instead of on unauthorized copying as a bulwark against foiled reputation, in large part bears out Beebe's prediction. Barton Beebe, "Intellectual Property Law and the Sumptuary Code," *Harvard Law Review* 123 (2010): 809–889.

16. Robert G. Bone, "Hunting Goodwill: A History of the Concept of. Goodwill in Trademark Law," *Boston University Law Review* 86 (2006): 547–622.

17. "When brands are commonly described as having personalities, and marketers have long talked about brands in anthropological terms, it is not a huge leap for brand owners to claim reputational injury and disruption to self-definition as salient harms." Heymann, "Scope of Trademark," 69.

18. Ibid. at 68.

19. A notable exception is the case of Louis Vuitton Malletier, S.A. v. Hyundai Motor America, 2012 WL 1022247 (S.D.N.Y., March 22, 2012), in which the company Louis Vuitton successfully sued Hyundai for dilution by blurring as a result of Hyundai's use of the Louis Vuitton trademark on a basketball in an advertisement.

20. Mark Lemley and Mark McKenna, "Irrelevant Confusion," *Stanford Law Review* 62 (2010): 413–457; McKenna, "Normative Foundations," 1839; Sandra Rierson, "The Myth and Reality of Dilution," *Duke Law and Technology Review* 11 (2012): 212–312; Leah Chan Grinvald, "Shaming Trademark Bullies," *Wisconsin Law Review* 2011 (2011): 625–685; William McGeveran, "Rethinking Trademark Fair Use," *Iowa Law Review* 94 (2008): 49–124.

21. Rierson, "Myth and Reality of Dilution," 213–214.

22. Heymann, "Scope of Trademark Law."

23. Martha Ertman and Joan Williams, eds., *Rethinking Commodification* (New York: New York University Press, 2005).

24. Walter Isaacson, *Steve Jobs* (New York: Simon and Schuster, 2011), 290–291. Of course, it must be pointed out that Jobs went on to commission the building of a very expensive yacht later on in his life.

25. Ibid.

26. As Laura Heymann has written, "[W]e should not be too surprised when consumers base purchasing decisions on the reputation of the brand—after all, they are responding to the encouragement they are given to view their connection to the brand as a relationship rather than simply as a transaction. Nor should we be too surprised when trademark owners claim to have experienced harms from unauthorized uses of their mark that sound more in defamation or right of publicity rather than diversion of sales. When brands are commonly described as having personalities, and marketers have long talked about brands in anthropological terms, it is not a huge leap for brand owners to claim reputational injury and disruption to self-definition as salient harms." Heymann, "Scope of Trademark Law," 69.

27. Grinvald, "Shaming Trademark Bullies." Metaphors comparing brand value or trademarked goods to children may even contribute to the weakening raison d'être of trademark law, which is fair and robust marketplace competition, and may explain the expansion of trademark law to robust likelihood of dilution claims in which actual harm need not be shown.

28. McKenna, "Normative Foundations," 1860–1861.

29. Mark McKenna and Mark Lemley, "Owning Mark(et)s," *Michigan Law Review* 109 (2010): 137–190; Mark A. Lemley, "Property, Intellectual Property, and Free Riding,"

Texas Law Review 83 (2005): 1031–1089. But see McKenna and Lemley, "Irrelevant Confusion," 413–421 (providing examples of overly broad sponsorship claims that courts have upheld as infringing despite empirical evidence to the contrary).

30. For examples of the high tolerance consumers have for different entities, services, and goods being labeled with similar names without being confused or brands being diluted, see Mark McKenna, "A Consumer Decision-Making Theory of Trademark Law," *Virginia Law Review* 98 (2012): 67–145; Laura Heymann, "The Grammar of Trademarks," *Lewis and Clark Law Review* 14 (2010): 1313–1350.

31. Dan Burk and Brett McDonnell, "Trademarks and the Boundaries of the Firm," *William & Mary Law Review* 51 (2009): 346 ("A recognized trademark is frequently the most valuable asset held by the modern firm").

32. Laura Heymann, "A Name I Call Myself: Creativity and Naming," *UC Irvine Law Review* 2 (2012): 585–626; Laura Heymann, "Naming, Identity, and Trademark Law," *Indiana Law Journal* 86 (2011): 381–445. Similarly, misnaming (misattribution or failure to attribute) can be equally offensive for the same reason. The "value of attribution" has been shown experimentally to be high, such that those seeking attribution (a reputational boost) will transact at lower costs as long as proper and prominent attribution is provided. By the same token, people may refuse to transact altogether or to transact at much higher costs if publication or distribution occurs without attribution. See Sprigman, Buccafusco, and Burns, "Valuing Attribution."

33. Heymann, "A Name I Call Myself," 585; Heymann, "Naming, Identity, and Trademark Law," 381.

34. Yale Electric Corp. v. Robertson, 26 F.2d 972, 974 (2nd Cir. 1928).

35. Sprigman, Buccafusco, and Burns, "Valuing Attribution"; Eric Goldman, "Regulating Reputation," in *The Reputation Society: How Online Opinions Are Reshaping the Offline World*, ed. Hassan Masum and Mark Tovey (Cambridge, MA: MIT Press 2011), 51–62; Catherine Fisk, "Credit Where It's Due: The Law and Norms of Attribution," *Georgetown Law Review* 95 (2006): 49–117.

36. For an overview of moral rights in the United States and Europe in the context of US film history, see Peter Decherney, "Auteurism on Trial: Moral Rights and Films on Television," *Wisconsin Law Review* (2011): 277–280.

37. Ibid. at 304–305.

38. Dastar Corp. v. Twentieth Century Fox Film Corp., 539 U.S. 23 (2003).

39. Dastar, at 539 U.S. 31 (2003).

40. Decherney, in "Auteurism on Trial," 316, describes a situation in which, in order to protect their work's integrity, the group Monty Python would rather (and did) upload its content for free in the form it approves of rather than sell its work and have it be altered without their permission or approval.

41. Douglas Holt, "Why Do Brands Cause Trouble? A Dialectical Theory of Consumer Culture and Branding," *Journal of Consumer Research* 29, no. 1 (2002): 70–90.

42. McKenna, "Normative Foundations of Trademark Law," 1839.

43. McKenna and Lemley, "Irrelevant Confusion," 413.

44. A recent case decided by the US Court of Appeals for the Ninth Circuit, *Cindy Lee Garcia v. Google, Inc.* (No. 12-57302) (Kozinski, J., writing for majority), exemplifies the mischief that can be caused by broad intellectual property claims brought to defend

or vindicate reputation and identity interests. In that case, an actor, Cindy Garcia, sued Google (and YouTube) under the Digital Millennium Copyright Act (DMCA) to "take down" a video in which she appeared. She claimed copyright ownership over her performance in the film (despite *disclaiming* copyright ownership in the film itself) and thus that she had standing to assert her rights under the DMCA to remove the unauthorized copies and enjoin the unauthorized distribution of her "work" from YouTube's sites. The court ruled in her favor, sympathetic to the death threats Garcia received because of her role in the film (*Innocence of Muslims*, which instigated a fatwa because of its offensive content). That a single actor with a marginal role in a film can, acting alone, enjoin the distribution of the film profoundly undermines the transactional efficiency and doctrinal cohesiveness of the joint-authorship rules in copyright law. This mischief of a disaggregated copyright claim in the name of protecting identity and reputation is caused largely by the competing interests of reputation (identity protection) and copyright interests (creation and dissemination). Trademark or right of publicity claims could be extended in similar contexts in support of related ends. The First Amendment stands as a bulwark against such overreaching, and yet when passionate personal or private interests arise, they can overpower disciplined application of IP laws.

45. Trademark law is especially agile and threatening given its expansive growth over the years and since the federal anti-dilution legislation passed in 1995, which doesn't require confusion or competition as a measure of trademark injury.

46. There is significant debate about the utility of dilution as a cause of action for trademark owners in light its potential for mischief and overextension. See Rierson, "Myth and Reality of Dilution," 213–214. Regarding the likelihood of confusion action in trademark cases, there is a growing body of research asserting the efficiency of clearer defenses and formal or informal expedited dispute resolution procedures. See, e.g., McGeveran, "Rethinking Trademark Fair Use," 49; William McGeveran, "The Trademark Fair Use Reform Act," *Boston University Law Review* 90 (2010): 2267–2321; Chan Grinvald, "Shaming Trademark Bullies," 625; Mark McKenna and William McGeveran, "Confusion Isn't Everything," *Notre Dame Law Review* 89 (2013): 253–318.

47. Patricia Ewick and Susan Silbey, "The Common Place of Law: Stories from Everyday Life" (Chicago: University of Chicago Press 1998), 50–52.

48. There are many intellectual property scholars and lawyers who recognize and strongly argue that intellectual property cannot simply be understood as founded on utilitarian principles. Excellent examples include Margaret Radin, *Reinterpreting Property* (Chicago: University of Chicago Press, 1993); Robert Merges, *Justifying Intellectual Property* (Cambridge, MA: Harvard University Press, 2011); and Madhavi Sunder, *From Goods to a Good Life* (New Haven, CT: Yale University Press, 2012). When I claim an overemphasis on utilitarian and economic principles for intellectual property protection, I am referring to the long-standing explanation for intellectual property (that as a property right it incentivizes early and significant investment) with its basis in the law and economics movement and also in the legislative history and case law asserting that unauthorized copying usurps the market for original creators and inventors and disincentives their further production.

49. Heymann, "Law of Reputation," 1344.

CHAPTER FIVE

1. Robert L. Nelson and Laura Beth Nielsen, "Cops, Counsel, and Entrepreneurs: Constructing the Role of Inside Counsel in Large Corporations," *Law and Society Review* 34, no. 2 (2000): 463.
2. Ibid.
3. Ibid. at 463.
4. Kembrew McLeod and Peter DiCola, *Creative License: The Law and Culture of Digital Sampling* (Durham, NC: Duke University Press, 2011), 123.
5. Patricia Aufderheide and Peter Jaszi, *Reclaiming Fair Use* (Chicago: University of Chicago Press, 2011), 110 (describing teachers as being afraid to learn more about copyright fair use for fear of being in trouble from their vice principal or librarian [intermediary gatekeepers], who are themselves instructed by lawyers [primary gatekeepers] about risks of reproducing and distributing copyrighted material for educational purposes).
6. Richard L. Abel, "American Lawyers," in *Lawyers: A Critical Reader* (New York: New Press, 1997), 117–131 (describing how the legal profession constructs a marketable commodity in their legal advice).
7. Ibid.
8. Those who can't survive economically on their creative output alone find ways to make ends meet with part-time jobs in order to continue their creative work.
9. David Sherwyn, Zev Eigen, and Michael Heise, "Don't Train Your Employees and Cancel Your 1-800 Harassment Hotline: An Empirical Examination and Correction of the Flaws in the Affirmative Defense to Sexual Harassment Charges," *Fordham Law Review* 69 (2001): 1265–1304.
10. I am grateful to Julie Cohen for helping me make this connection explicit and for spurring ideas in this paragraph.
11. Katherine J. Strandburg, "What Does the Public Get? Experimental Use and the Patent Bargain," *Wisconsin Law Review* (2004): 81, 101–102.
12. See ibid. See also Ron D. Katznelson and John Howells, "Inventing around Edison's Incandescent Lamp Patent: Evidence of Patents' Role in Stimulating Downstream Development" (working paper, 2012), http://bit.ly/Inventing-around-Edison (discussing how disclosure of Edison's invention in the patent claims leads to subsequent inventor activity that adjusts to and designs around Edison's invention leading to downstream innovation).
13. Abel, "American Lawyers," 117.
14. William Gallagher, "IP Legal Ethics in the Everyday Practice of Law: An Empirical Perspective on Patent Litigators," *John Marshall Law Review of IP* 10 (2011): 309–364 (explaining how his empirical study shows that "patent litigators, among the contemporary legal profession's most elite . . . practitioners, are not immune to many of the pressures and cultural and structural influences that shape and potentially undermine ethical decision-making in legal practice").
15. Abel, "American Lawyers," 117.
16. The disconnect between the invention and the IP can be surprising to some scientists and artists. As another interviewee said describing one of her first experiences patenting an invention when she was an engineer (she later became a lawyer): we "took a feature that was there, that really wasn't the sexy part of the invention . . . but maybe . . . has potential to be interesting. . . . It was a complete revelation to me. . . . [W]hen we got that patent . . . we claimed [something different from what I invented]. . . . We spun

it, you know. So getting a patent is different, or can be different from the actual thing that you have."

17. See Chapter 3 in this volume; see also Dan Burk and Mark Lemley, *The Patent Crisis and How the Courts Can Solve It* (Chicago: University of Chicago Press, 2009); James Bessen and Michael Meurer, *Patent Failure: How Judges, Bureaucrats, and Lawyers Put Innovators at Risk* (Princeton, NJ: Princeton University Press, 2008).

18. Abel, "American Lawyers," 117 (describing the construction of the professional commodity in terms of convincing a client "they cannot produce the [legal] services themselves").

19. This interviewee is right that the patent prosecution process may weed out unpatentable inventions and, given its cost, may deter people from filing unless they can recoup their money. But many people spend money (whether to file patents or to paint houses) not to recoup costs or make more money, but because they like the result for what it is: a patent, or a beautiful house. His assumption is that people seek to patent for reasons related to reputation and status rather than to protect an invention to monopolize its commercial exploitation. While, of course, people seek patents for all sorts of reasons, whether seeking a patent for reasons of ego "makes no sense" and other "noncommercial reasons" are not worth pursuing depends on particular situations and interests.

20. Amartya Sen, *Development as Freedom* (New York: Knopf, 1999); Amartya Sen, Commodities and Capabilities (Oxford: Oxford University Press, 1985); Martha Nussbaum, *Women and Human Development: The Capabilities Approach* (New York: Cambridge University Press, 2000); Madhavi Sunder, *From Goods to the Good Life* (New Haven, CT: Yale University Press, 2012), 88–89.

21. Madhavi Sunder, *From Goods*, 90 (quoting Sen, *Development as Freedom*, 4).

22. Patricia Ewick and Susan Silbey, *The Common Place of Law* (Chicago: University of Chicago Press, 1998).

23. Judith Resnik and Dennis Curtis, *Representing Justice: Invention, Controversy, and Rights in City-States and Democratic Courtrooms* (New Haven, CT: Yale University Press, 2011).

24. Charles Fried, "Lawyers as Friends," *Yale Law Journal* 85 (1976): 573–586.

CHAPTER SIX

1. Paul Goldstein, *Copyright's Highway: From Gutenberg to the Celestial Jukebox* (Stanford, CA: Stanford University Press 2003), 216 (describing IP "law's early aim of connecting author to their audiences" and to promote "cultural diversity").

2. Sony Corp. v. Universal City Studios, Inc. 464 U.S. 417, 431–432 (1984); eBay v. MercExchange LLC, 547 U.S. 388 (2006).

3. Golan v. Holder, 132 S. Ct. 873 (2012).

4. Sony Corp v. Universal City Studios, Inc. 464 U.S. 417, 431–432 (1984).

5. Ibid. at 429 (quoting Fox Film Corp. v. Doyal, 286 U.S. 123, 127 [1932]).

6. William Patry, *How to Fix Copyright* (New York: Oxford University Press, 2012), 183.

7. I do not mean to imply with this list of artificially binary relationships that the relationships created by distribution channels are necessarily or optimally binary. These are just some of the overdetermined relationships customarily associated with IP-protected work and that some of the large IP-invested industries, such as Hollywood,

continue to instantiate through closed systems of innovation and circulation. See Andrew Currah, "Hollywood, the Internet and the World: A Geography of Disruptive Innovation," *Industry and Innovation* 14, no. 4 (2007): 359–384, 380.

8. This kind of distribution reflects Clay Shirky's comment that "the sharing, in fact, is what makes the making fun. Clay Shirky, *Cognitive Surplus: Creativity and Generosity in a Connected Age* (New York: Penguin, 2010), 19.

9. Given the nature of qualitative empirical work, the research demonstrates the existence of categories rather than the significance of any absence of data. Further quantitative work is needed to draw conclusions about the distribution of data across categories.

10. Music copyright may be the exception to the lack of variation in distributional modalities. There are many different ways to distribute music under the music copyright system, including various forms of and bases for compulsory licenses that resist a binary analysis of the distribution right.

11. Bruno Frey, *Happiness: A Revolution in Economics* (Cambridge, MA: MIT Press, 2010). See also Teresa Amabile and Steven Kramer, *The Progress Principle: Using Small Wins to Ignite Joy, Engagement and Creativity at Work* (Cambridge, MA: Harvard Business Review Press, 2011).

12. Peter DiCola confirms the various sources of revenue from a survey of more than five thousand musicians, and the small amount of revenue from traditional copyright sources. Peter DiCola, "Money from Music: Survey Evidence on Musicians' Revenue and Lessons About Copyright Incentives," *Arizona Law Review* 55 (2013): 301–342.

13. The term *evergreen* in the film context is not the same as in the patented invention context, where "evergreening" a patent elongates the life of the patent exclusivity through continuation filings. Where evergreening in the film context does not presume exclusivity, evergreening in the patent context does. For a discussion of the economic effectiveness of evergreening in patented pharmaceuticals, see C. Scott Hemphill and Bhaven N. Sampat, "Evergreening, Patent Challenges, and Effective Market Life in Pharmaceuticals," *Journal of Health Economics* 31 (2012): 327–339.

14. See Daniel Pink, *Drive: The Surprising Truth About What Motivates Us* (New York: Penguin Press, 2009), 72–73. See also Daniel Goleman, with Howard Gardner, *Good Work: Aligning Skills with Values* (Wired to Connect: Dialogues on Social Intelligences) (Florence, MA: More Than Sound Productions, 2008), audio CD.

15. As previously quoted, Dennis says, "What should've been done with that IP, that patent, is [the company] should've established a very robust licensing program, and made it cheap[,] . . . publicized they were licensing it . . . to every university for $500 a year . . . so that . . . there's consideration, but make it so cheap that every university's going to do it. And then license it to every company, but for like, $5,000 a year and then attach a 0.1 percent royalty."

16. James Boyd White, *From Expectation to Experience* (Ann Arbor: University of Michigan Press, 2000), 113–114 (interpreting laws regulating corporations as challenging the questionable opposition between economic goals of a corporation and public-spirited or philanthropic goals).

17. See Lewis Hyde, *The Gift: How the Creative Spirit Transforms the World* (New York: Random House, 1983); see also Arjun Appadurai, introduction to *The Social Life of Things: Commodities in Cultural Perspective*, ed. Arjun Appadurai (Cambridge: Cambridge University Press, 1986), 3–62. Much literature on gift economies refers to and reinterprets Marcel Mauss, "Essai sur le don: Forme et raison de l'échange dans

les sociétés archaiques," *L'année sociologique* 1 (1923–1924): 30–186, available in English as *The Gift: Forms and Functions of Exchange in Archaic Societies* (New York: Norton, 1967).

18. Hyde, *The Gift*, 21.
19. Ibid. at 146.
20. Ibid. at 149.
21. Deborah Gerhart, "Freeing Art and History from Copyright's Bondage" (unpublished manuscript, University of North Carolina School of Law), http://papers.ssrn.com/sol3/papers.cfm?abstract_id=2213515.
22. The archivist, however, likely has no copyright basis to enjoin the copying or display of the public domain images in his archive, although he likely has physical control (and rights against trespass) over the space of and physical objects in his archive.
23. Joseph Singer, "The Rule of Reason in Property Law," *University of California Davis Law Review* 46 (2013): 1369–1434.

CONCLUSION

1. See, e.g., Yochai Benkler, *The Penguin and the Leviathan: How Cooperation Triumphs over Self-Interest* (New York: Crown Books, 2011), 14; Julie E. Cohen, "Copyright as Property in the Post-Industrial Economy: A Research Agenda," *Wisconsin Law Review* (2011): 141–165.
2. Carol Rose, *Property and Persuasion: Essays on the History, Theory and Rhetoric of Ownership* (Boulder, CO: Westview Press, 1994), 37.
3. Ibid. at 38.
4. Brett Frischmann, *Infrastructure: The Social Value of Shared Resources* (New York: Oxford University Press, 2011), 267–268 (explaining how intellectual property is often misunderstood as creating incentives rather than markets).
5. Email from Bill Patry, June 17, 2013 (on file with author).
6. Ibid.
7. Mark Lemley, "The Dubious Autonomy of Virtual Worlds," *UC Irvine Law Review* 2 (2012): 575–583, 581.
8. Ibid.
9. See, e.g., Jeannie Suk, *At Home in the Law: How the Domestic Violence Revolution Is Transforming Privacy* (New Haven, CT: Yale University Press, 2009).
10. Margaret Radin, *Boilerplate: The Fine Print, Vanishing Rights, and the Rule of Law* (Princeton, NJ: Princeton University Press, 2012).
11. Aaron Perzanowski and Jason Schultz, "Digital Exhaustion," *UCLA Law Review* 58 (2011): 889; Ariel Katz, "The First Sale Doctrine and the Economics of Post-Sale Restraints," *BYU Law Review* (2014): 55–142; Niva Elkin-Koren, "What Contracts Can't Do: The Limits of Private Ordering in Facilitating a Creative Commons," *Fordham Law Review* 74 (2005): 375–422; Paul A. David, "Mitigating 'Anticommons' Harms in Science and Technology Research" (Stanford Institute for Economic Policy Research Discussion Paper No. 10-030, 2011); Fiona Murray and Scott Stern, "Do Formal Intellectual Property Rights Hinder the Free Flow of Scientific Knowledge? An Empirical Test of the Anti-Commons Hypothesis," *Journal of Economic Behavior and Organization* 63 (2007): 648–687; Rosemarie Ham Ziedonis, "Don't Fence Me In: Fragmented Markets for Technology and the Patent Acquisition Strategies of Firms," *Management Science* 50 (2004): 804–820.

12. Dan L. Burk and Brett H. McDonnell, "The Goldilocks Hypothesis: Balancing Intellectual Property Rights at the Boundary of the Firm," *University of Illinois Law Review* (2007): 575. See also Shyamkrishna Balganesh, "The Uneasy Case Against Copyright Trolls," *Southern California Law Review* 86 (2013): 723–781.

13. Balganesh, "Uneasy Case"; Julie Cohen, "Pervasively Distributed Copyright Enforcement," *Georgetown Law Review* 95 (2005): 1–48.

14. Louis Kaplow, "Rules Versus Standards: An Economic Analysis," *Duke Law Journal* 42 (1992): 557–629.

15. Joseph Singer, "The Rule of Reason in Property Law," *UC Davis Law Review* 46 (2013): 1369–1434.

16. "[I]t is a mistake to conclude . . . that the best way to achieve these ends is to reduce property law to mechanical rules that can be applied without the need to think or exercise judgment. Property law is a practical art that requires practical reason to work. Property rules never operated without such judgment; nor could they. The rule of law is not a Procrustean bed. Rules of reason shape the infrastructure of property law and we are lucky that they do." Ibid.

17. Daniel Gervais, "The Price of Social Norms: Towards a Liability Regime for File-Sharing," *Journal of Intellectual Property Law* 12 (2004): 39–73, 49–50.

18. Singer, "Rule of Reason in Property Law," 1382.

19. Patricia Aufderheide and Peter Jaszi, *Reclaiming Fair Use: How to Put the Balance Back in Copyright* (Chicago: University of Chicago Press, 2011); Leah Chan Grinvald, "Shaming Trademark Bullies," *Wisconsin Law Review* (2011): 625–691.

20. Golan v Holder, 132 S.Ct. 873, 895 (2012), citing Harper & Row, Publishers, Inc. v. Nation Enterprises, 471 U.S. 539, 558 (1985) and Eldred v. Ashcroft, 537 U.S. 186, 206 (2003).

21. The Obama administration recently proposed rebalancing the patent litigation system to disincentivize lawsuits by patent-assertion entities (otherwise known as patent trolls) because of their cost to innovative industries. See "Factsheet: White House Task Force on High-Tech Patent Issues," June 4, 2013, http://www.whitehouse .gov/the-press-office/2013/06/04/fact-sheet-white-house-task-force-high-tech-patent -issues.

22. See the Patent Act, 35 U.S.C. §271(d)(4).

23. William McGeveran, "The Trademark Fair Use Reform Act," *Boston University Law Review* 90 (2010): 2267–2321; Michael Carroll, "Fixing Fair Use," *North Carolina Law Review* 85 (2007): 1087–1154; see also Brad Greenberg, "Copyright Trolls and Presumptively Fair Uses," *Colorado Law Review* 85 (2013): 53–128.

24. Christopher Sprigman, "Reform(aliz)ing Copyright," *Stanford Law Review* 57 (2004): 485–568.

25. Colleen Chien, "Reforming Software Patents," *Houston Law Review* 50 (2012): 325–388, 350 (discussing various proposals, including limitations and abolition).

26. Margaret Radin, *Reinterpreting Property* (Chicago: University of Chicago Press, 1993), 191.

APPENDIX A

1. Pamela Stone, *Opting Out: Why Women Really Quit Careers and Head Home* (Berkeley: University of California Press, 2007) 243, 248.

2. Jack Katz, "Ethnography's Warrants," *Sociological Methods and Research* 25, no. 4 (1997): 391–423, 392.

3. Joseph Maxwell, "Understanding Validity in Qualitative Research," *Harvard Educational Review* 62, no. 3 (Fall 1992): 279–300; Uwe Flick, *An Introduction to Qualitative Research* (Thousand Oaks, CA: Sage Publications 1998).

4. Francesca Polletta, *It Was Like a Fever: Storytelling in Protest and Politics* (Chicago: University of Chicago Press, 2006); Patricia Ewick and Susan Silbey, *The Common Place of Law: Stories from Everyday Life* (Chicago: University of Chicago Press, 1998).

5. George Lakoff and Mark Johnson, *Metaphors We Live By* (Chicago: University of Chicago Press, 1980).

6. Mario Small, "How Many Cases Do I Need? On Science and the Logic of Case Selection in Field-Based Research," *Ethnology* 10, no. 5 (2009): 5–38.

7. Anthony Onwuegbuzie and Nancy Leech, "The Role of Sampling in Qualitative Research," *Academic Exchange Quarterly* 9, no. 2 (2005): 280–288.

8. Small, "How Many Cases," 25–27.

9. Ibid. at 25.

10. Paul Ricoeur, *Time and Narrative*, 3 vols. (Chicago: University of Chicago Press, 1984–1988); Hayden White, *The Content of the Form: Narrative Discourse and Historical Representation* (Baltimore: Johns Hopkins University Press, 1987), 1–25.

11. To ensure that my research assistant understood the codes in the same way, we met regularly to review the coding of transcripts we each coded and compared the coding. Where there were differences, we discussed and resolved them. We reviewed already-coded transcripts to ensure that agreements forged on the common transcript were transferred to independently coded interviews. Memos were shared on a regular basis again to produce a common framework for preparing the transcripts and ongoing analysis. By its very nature, working with qualitative data is an interpretive process. Nonetheless, strong consensus can be achieved by regularly sharing coding on a common text and thus collectively developing common parameters for interpretation.

12. Clifford Geertz, *The Interpretation of Cultures* (New York: Basic Books, 1973).

13. Matthew Miles and A. Michael Huberman, *Qualitative Data Analysis* (Thousand Oaks, CA: Sage Publications, 1994), 245–285.

14. Stone, *Opting Out*, 254.

Bibliography

Abel, Richard. "American Lawyers." *Lawyers: A Critical Reader*. New York: New Press, 1997.

Abodor, Henry. "The Role of Personal Relationships in Inter-Firm Alliances: Benefits, Dysfunctions, and Some Suggestions." *Business Horizons* 49, no. 6 (November–December 2006): 473–486.

Amabile, Teresa M. *Creativity in Context: Update to the Social Psychology of Creativity*. Boulder, CO: Westview Press, 1996.

Amabile, Teresa M., and Steven Kramer. *The Progress Principle: Using Small Wins to Ignite Joy, Engagement and Creativity at Work*. Boston: Harvard Business Review Press, 2011.

Amsterdam, Anthony, and Jerome Bruner. *Minding the Law: How Courts Rely on Storytelling and How Their Stories Change the Ways We Understand the Law and Ourselves*. Cambridge, MA: Harvard University Press, 2000.

Anderson, Chris. "Free: Why $0.00 Is the Future of Business." *Wired*, February 25, 2008. http://archive.wired.com/techbiz/it/magazine/16-03/ff_free?currentPage=all.

———. *Free: The Future of a Radical Price*. New York: Hyperion, 2008.

Anderson, J. Jonas. Review of *Gene Patents and Collaborative Licensing Models: Patent Pools, Clearinghouses, Open Source Models and Liability Regimes*, ed. Geertrui van Overwalle. *IP Law Book Review* 1, no. 54 (2011): 54–60.

Appadurai, Arjun. Introduction to *The Social Life of Things: Commodities in Cultural Perspective*, edited by Arjun Appadurai, 3–62. Cambridge: Cambridge University Press, 1986.

Arthur, John. "Resource Acquisition and Harm." *Canadian Journal of Philosophy* 17, no. 2 (1987): 337–347.

Aufderdeide, Patricia, and Peter Jaszi. *Reclaiming Fair Use*. Chicago: University of Chicago Press, 2011.

Baard, Paul P., Edward L. Deci, and Richard M. Ryan. "Intrinsic Need Satisfaction: A Motivational Basis of Performance and Well-Being in Two Work Settings." *Journal of Applied Social Psychology* 34 (2004): 2045–2068.

Balganesh, Shyamkrishna. "Debunking Blackstonian Copyright." *Yale Law Journal* 118 (2009): 1126–1181.

———. "The Uneasy Case Against Copyright Trolls." *Southern California Law Review* 86 (2013): 723–729.

Barnett, Jonathan. "Intellectual Property as a Law of Organization." *Southern California Law Review* 84 (2011): 785–858.

Becker, Lawrence C. "Deserving to Own Intellectual Property." *Chicago-Kent Law Review* 68 (1993): 609–629.

Beebe, Barton. "An Empirical Study of U.S. Copyright Fair Use Opinions, 1978–2005." *University of Pennsylvania Law Review* 156 (2008): 549–625.

———. "Intellectual Property and the Sumptuary Code." *Harvard Law Review* 123 (2010): 809–889.

Benjamin, Walter. *The Work of Art in the Age of Mechanical Reproduction in Illuminations: Essays and Reflections.* New York: Harcourt, Brace, Jovanovich, 1968.

Benkler, Yochai. *The Penguin and the Leviathan: How Cooperation Triumphs over Self Interest.* New York: Crown Books, 2011.

———. *The Wealth of Networks: How Social Production Transforms Markets and Freedom.* New Haven, CT: Yale University Press, 2006.

Bernstein, Gaia. "In the Shadow of Innovation." *Cardozo Law Review* 31 (2010): 2257–2312.

Bessen, James, and Michael J. Meurer. "Direct Costs from NPE Disputes." Working Paper No. 12-34 (June 25, 2012), Boston University School of Law, Boston.

———. *Patent Failure: How Judges, Bureaucrats, and Lawyers Put Innovators at Risk.* Princeton, NJ: Princeton University Press, 2008.

Bigelow, Gordon. "Let There Be Markets: The Evangelical Roots of Economics." *Harper's Magazine,* May 2005, 33–38.

Blois, Keith. "Trust in Business to Business Relationships: An Evaluation of Status." *Journal of Management Studies* 36, no. 2 (1999): 197–215.

Bloom, Harold. *The Anxiety of Influence: A Theory of Poetry.* New York: Oxford University Press, 1973.

Boldrin, Michelle, and David Levine. *Against Intellectual Property.* New York: Cambridge University Press, 2008.

Bone, Robert G. "Hunting Goodwill: A History of the Concept of Goodwill in Trademark Law." *Boston University Law Review* 86 (2006): 547, 604–606.

Breyer, Stephen. "The Uneasy Case for Copyright: A Study of Copyright in Books, Photocopies, and Computer Programs." *Harvard Law Review* 84 (1970): 281–351.

Buccafusco, Christopher, and Christopher Sprigman. "Valuing Intellectual Property: An Experiment." *Cornell Law Review* 96 (2010): 1–45.

Burk, Dan, and Mark Lemley. *The Patent Crisis and How the Courts Can Solve It.* Chicago: University of Chicago Press, 2009.

Burk, Dan, and Brett McDonnell. "The Goldilocks Hypothesis: Balancing Intellectual Property Rights at the Boundary of the Firm." *University of Illinois Law Review* (2007): 575–636.

———. "Trademarks and the Boundaries of the Firm." *William & Mary Law Review* 51 (2009): 345–394.

Carens, Joseph H., ed. *Democracy and Possessive Individualism: The Intellectual Legacy of C. B. Macpherson.* Albany: State University of New York Press, 1993.

Carroll, Michael. "Fixing Fair Use." *North Carolina Law Review* 85 (2007): 1087–1154.

———. "One Size Does Not Fit All: A Framework for Tailoring Intellectual Property Rights." *Ohio State Law Journal* 70 (2009): 1361–1434.

Chambers, Ross. *Story as Situation: Narrative Seduction and the Power of Fiction.* Minneapolis: University of Minnesota Press, 1984.

Chan Grinvald, Leah. "Shaming Trademark Bullies." *Wisconsin Law Review* (2011): 625–685.

Chander, Anupam. "Everyone's a Superhero: A Cultural Theory of Mary Sue Fan Fiction as Fair Use." *California Law Review* 95 (2007): 597–625.

———. "The New, New Property." *Texas Law Review* 81 (2003): 715–798.

Chander, Anupam, and Madhavi Sunder. "The Romance of the Public Domain." *California Law Review* 92 (2004): 1331–1374.

Chien, Colleen. "Reforming Software Patents." *Houston Law Review* 50 (2012): 325–388.

Cohen, Julie E. *Configuring the Networked Self.* New Haven, CT: Yale University Press, 2012.

———. "Copyright as Property in the Post-Industrial Economy: A Research Agenda." *Wisconsin Law Review* (2011): 141–165.

———. "Pervasively Distributed Copyright Enforcement." *Georgetown Law Journal* 95 (2006): 1–48.

———. "The Place of the User in Copyright Law." *Fordham Law Review* 74 (2005): 347–373.

Cross, Gary S. *An All-Consuming Century: Why Commercialism Won in Modern America.* New York: Columbia University Press, 2000.

Currah, Andrew. "Hollywood, the Internet, and the World: A Geography of Disruptive Innovation." *Industry and Innovation* 14, no. 4 (2007): 359–384.

Czikszentmihalyi, Mihaly. *Creativity: Flow and the Psychology of Discovery and Invention.* New York: HarperCollins, 1996.

———. *Flow: The Psychology of Optimal Experience.* New York: Harper & Row, 1990.

Decherney, Peter. "Auteurism on Trial: Moral Rights and Films on Television." *Wisconsin Law Review* (2011): 273–316.

———. *Hollywood's Copyright Wars: From Edison to the Internet.* New York: Columbia University Press, 2012.

Demers, Joanna. *Steal This Music: How Intellectual Property Affects Musical Creativity.* Athens: University of Georgia Press, 2006.

DePoorter, Ben, Adam Holland, and Elizabeth Somerstein. "Copyright Abolition and Attribution." *Review of Law and Economics* 5 (2009): 1063–1080.

DiCola, Peter. "Money from Music: Survey Evidence on Musicians Revenue and Lessons from Copyright Incentives." *Arizona Law Review* 55 (2013): 301–342.

DiCola, Peter, and Kembrew McLeod. *Creative License: The Law and Culture of Digital Sampling.* Durham, NC: Duke University Press, 2011.

Dinwoodie, Graeme B., and Rochelle C. Dreyfuss. "Intellectual Property Law and the Public Domain of Science." *Journal of International Economic Law* 7, no. 2 (2004): 431–448.

Dogan, Stacey. "Beyond Trademark Use." *Journal on Telecommunications and High Technology Law* 8 (2010): 135–156.

———. "Trademark Remedies and Online Intermediaries." *Lewis and Clark Law Review* 14 (2010): 467–489.

Dogan, Stacey, with Mark Lemley. "The Merchandising Right: Fragile Theory or Fait Accompli?" *Emory Law Journal* 54 (2005): 461–506.

———. "Trademarks and Consumer Search Costs on the Internet." *Houston Law Review* 41 (2004): 777–838.

Dogan, Stacey, and Mark Lemley. "What The Right of Publicity Can Learn from Trademark Law." *Stanford Law Review* 58 (2006): 1161–1220.

Douglas, Mary. *How Institutions Think.* Syracuse, NY: Syracuse University Press, 1986.

Drassinower, Abraham. "Authorship as Public Address: On the Specificity of Copyright Vis-à-Vis Patent and Trade-Mark." *Michigan State Law Review* 1 (2008): 199–233.

———. "Copyright Is Not About Copying." *Harvard Law Review Forum* 125 (2012): 108–119.

———. "A Rights-Based View of the Idea/Expression Dichotomy in Copyright Law." *Canadian Journal of Law and Jurisprudence* 14 (2003): 3–21.

Dreyfuss, Rochelle C. "Designing Intellectual Property Institutions for the Twenty-First Century." *Journal of World Intellectual Property* 12, no. 5 (2009): 341–347.

———. "Does IP Need IP? Accommodating Intellectual Production Outside the Intellectual Property Paradigm." *Cardozo Law Review* 31 (2010): 1437–1473.

———. "Evaluating the Public Impact of Open Innovation." *Australian Economic Review* 44, no. 1 (2011): 66–72.

———. "Pathological Patenting: The PTO as Cause or Cure." *Michigan Law Review* 104 (2005–2006): 1559–1578.

Dreyfuss, Rochelle C., Harry First, and Diane Zimmerman, eds. *Working Within the Boundaries of Intellectual Property: Innovation for the Knowledge Age.* Oxford: Oxford University Press, 2009.

Dreyfuss, Rochelle C., Diane Zimmerman, and Harry First, eds. *Expanding the Boundaries of Intellectual Property: Innovation Policy for the Knowledge Society.* Oxford: Oxford University Press, 2001.

Durkheim, Émile. *The Elementary Forms of Religious Life.* London: Allen and Unwin, 1912.

Elliot, Richard. "Existential Consumption and Irrational Desire." *European Journal of Marketing* 31 (1997): 285–296.

Engel, David M. "Origin Myths: Narratives of Authority, Resistance, Disability, and Law." *Law and Society Review* 27 (1993): 785–826.

Ertman, Martha, and Joan Williams, eds. *Rethinking Commodification.* New York: New York University Press, 2005.

Ewick, Patricia, and Susan Silbey. *The Common Place of Law: Stories from Everyday Life.* Chicago: University of Chicago Press, 1998.

Fagundes, David. "Efficient Infringement." *Iowa Law Review* 98 (2013): 1791–1846.

———. "Property Rhetoric and the Public Domain." *Minnesota Law Review* 94 (2010): 652–705.

Fisher, William W. "The Implications for Law of User Innovation." *Minnesota Law Review* 94 (2010): 1417–1477.

———. "Intellectual Property and Innovation: Theoretical, Empirical, and Historical Perspectives." *Industrial Property, Innovation, and the Knowledge-Based Economy, Beleidsstudies Technologie Economie,* edited by Gerrit Ybema, 47–72. Den Haag: Directoraat-Generaal Innovatie, Ministerie van Economische Zaken, 2001.

———. *Promises to Keep: Technology, Law and the Future of Entertainment.* Palo Alto, CA: Stanford University Press, 2004.

Fisk, Catherine L. "Credit Where It's Due: The Law and Norms of Attribution." *Georgetown Law Journal* 95 (2006): 49–117.

———. "The Role of Private Intellectual Property Rights in Markets for Labor and Ideas: Screen Credit and the Writers Guild of America, 1938–2000." *Berkeley Journal of Employment and Labor Law* 32 (2011): 215–278.

———. *Working Knowledge: Employee Innovation and the Rise of Corporate Intellectual Property 1800–1930.* Chapel Hill: University of North Carolina Press, 2009.

Frey, Bruno. *Happiness: A Revolution in Economics.* Cambridge, MA: MIT Press, 2010.

Fried, Charles. "Lawyers as Friends." *Yale Law Journal* 86 (1976): 573–587.

Frischmann, Brett. *Infrastructure: The Social Value of Shared Resources.* New York: Oxford University Press, 2011.

Frischmann, Brett, and Mark Lemley. "Spillovers." *Columbia Law Review* 107 (2007): 257–301.

Fromer, Jeanne C. "A Psychology of Intellectual Property." *Northwestern University Law Review* 104 (2010): 1441–1508.

Fueller, Johann, and Eric von Hippel. "Costless Creation of Strong Brands by User Communities: Implications for Producer-Owned Brands." Sloan School Working Paper 4718-08 (August 1, 2008), Massachusetts Institute of Technology, Cambridge, MA.

Gallagher, William T. "IP Legal Ethics in the Everyday Practice of Law: An Empirical Perspective on Patent Litigators." *John Marshall Law Review of Intellectual Property* 10 (2011): 309–364.

————. "Trademark and Copyright Enforcement in the Shadow of IP Law." 28 *Santa Clara Computer and High Technology Law Journal* 3 (2012): 453–497.

Gardner, Howard. *Creating Minds: An Anatomy of Creativity Seen Through the Lives of Freud, Einstein, Picasso, Stravinsky, Eliot, Graham, and Gandhi.* New York: Basic Books, 1993.

Gerhart, Deborah. "Freeing Art and History from Copyright's Bondage." Unpublished manuscript, http://papers.ssrn.com/sol3/papers.cfm?abstract_id=2213515.

Gervais, Daniel. "The Price of Social Norms: Towards a Liability Regime for File-Sharing." *Journal of Intellectual Property Law* 12 (2004): 39–73.

Ghosh, Shubha. "The Fable of the Commons: Exclusivity and the Construction of Intellectual Property Markets." *University of California Davis Law Review* 40 (2007): 855–890.

————. *Identity, Invention, and the Culture of Personalized Medicine Patenting.* New York: Cambridge University Press, 2012.

Ghosh, Shubha, and Robin Paul Malloy, eds. *Creativity, Law and Entrepreneurship.* Cheltenham, UK: Edward Elgar, 2011.

Giddens, Anthony. *The Constitution of Society: Outline of the Theory of Saturation.* Cambridge, UK: Polity, 1984.

Goldman, Eric. "Regulating Reputation." In *The Reputation Society: How Online Opinions Are Reshaping the Offline World*, edited by Hassan Masum and Mark Tovey, 51–62. Cambridge, MA: MIT Press, 2011.

————. "The Regulation of Reputational Information." In *The Next Digital Decade: Essays on the Future of the Internet*, edited by Berin Szoka and Adam Marcus, 293–304. Washington, DC: TechFreedom, 2011.

Goldstein, Paul. *Copyright's Highway: From Gutenberg to the Celestial Jukebox.* Stanford, CA: Stanford University Press, 2003.

Goleman, Daniel, with Howard Gardner. "Good Work: Aligning Skills with Values." *Wired to Connect: Dialogues on Social Intelligences.* Audio CD. Florence, MA: More Than Sound Productions, 2008.

Gordon, Wendy J. "Fair Use Markets: On Weighing Potential Licensing Fees." *George Washington Law Review* 79 (2011): 1814–1856.

————. "Of Harms and Benefits: Torts, Restitution, and Intellectual Property." *Journal of Legal Studies* 21 (1992): 449–482.

————. "A Property in Self-Expression: Equality and Individualism in the Natural Law of Intellectual Property." *Yale Law Journal* 102 (1993): 1533–1609.

————. "Render Copyright unto Caesar: On Taking Incentives Seriously," *University of Chicago Law Review* 71 (2004): 75–92.

————. "Trespass-Copyright Parallels and the Harm-Benefit Distinction." *Harvard Law Review Forum* 122 (2009): 62–80.

Gould, David M., and William C. Gruben. "The Role of Intellectual Property Rights in Economic Growth." *Journal of Development Economics* 48 (1996): 323–350.

Graham, Stuart J. H., Robert Merges, Pam Samuelson, and Ted Sichelman, "High Technology Entrepreneurs and the Patent System: Results of the 2008 Berkeley Patent Survey." *Berkeley Technology Law Review* 24 (2009): 1255–1328.

Greenburg, Brad. "Copyright Trolls and Presumptively Fair Uses." *Colorado Law Review* 85 (2013): 53–128.

Greenfield, Kent. *The Myth of Choice: Personal Responsibility in a World of Limits.* New Haven, CT: Yale University Press, 2012.

Heller, Michael. "The Boundaries of Private Property." *Yale Law Journal* 108 (1999): 1163–1223.

Heller, Michael A., and Rebecca S. Eisenberg. "Can Patents Deter Innovation? The Anticommons in Biomedical Research." *Science* 280 (1998): 698–701.

Hemel, Daniel J., and Lisa L. Ouellette. "Beyond the Patents-Prizes Debate." *Texas Law Review* 92 (2014): 303–382.

Hemphill, C. Scott, and Bhaven N. Sampat. "Evergreening, Patent Challenges, and Effective Market Life in Pharmaceuticals." *Journal of Health Economics* 31 (March 2012): 327–339.

Hemphill, C. Scott, and Jeannie Suk. "The Law, Culture, and Economics of Fashion." *Stanford Law Review* 61 (2009): 1147–1200.

Heymann, Laura. "The Grammar of Trademarks." *Lewis and Clark Law Review* 14 (2010): 1313–1350.

———. "The Law of Reputation and the Interest of the Audience." *Boston College Law Review* 52 (2011): 1241–1342.

———. "A Name I Call Myself: Creativity and Naming." *University of California Irvine Law Review* 2 (2012): 585–625.

———. "Naming, Identity, and Trademark Law." *Indiana Law Journal* 86 (2011): 381–445.

———. "The Scope of Trademark Law in the Age of the Brand Persona." *Virginia Law Review in Brief* 98 (2012): 61–70.

Holt, Douglas. "Why Do Brands Cause Trouble? A Dialectical Theory of Consumer Culture and Branding." *Journal of Consumer Research* 29, no. 1 (June 2002): 70–90.

Hsu, David, and Rosemarie Ziedonis. "Patents as Quality Signals for Entrepreneurial Ventures." *Academy of Management Best Paper Proceedings* (2008): 1–6.

———. "Strategic Factor Markets and the Financing of Technology Startups: When Do Patents Matter More as Signaling Devices?" Unpublished manuscript, 2011.

Hughes, Justin. "American Moral Rights and Fixing the *Dastar* Gap." *Utah Law Review* (2007): 659–714.

———. "Champagne, Feta and Bourbon: The Spirited Debate About Geographical Indications." *Hastings Law Journal* 58 (2006): 299–386.

———. "Copyright and Its Rewards, Foreseen and Unforeseen." *Harvard Law Review Forum* 122 (2009): 81–96.

———. "Fair Use Across Time." *University of California Law Review* 43 (2003): 775–804.

———. "Size Matters (or Should) in Copyright Law." *Fordham Law Review* 75 (2005): 575–637.

Hyde, Lewis. *Common as Air: Revolution, Art and Ownership.* New York: Farrar, Straus & Giroux, 2010.

———. *The Gift: How the Creative Spirit Transforms the World.* New York: Random House, 1983.

Irr, Caren. *Pink Pirates: Contemporary American Women Writers and Copyright.* Iowa City: University of Iowa Press, 2010.

Isaacson, Walter. *Steve Jobs.* New York: Simon and Schuster, 2011.

Kaplow, Louis. "Rules Versus Standards: An Economic Analysis." *Duke Law Journal* 42 (1992): 557–629.

Katyal, Sonia, and Eduardo Penalver. *Property Outlaws: How Squatters, Pirates and Protesters Improve the Law of Ownership.* New Haven, CT: Yale University Press, 2010.

Katznelson, Ron D., and John Howells. "Inventing Around Edison's Incandescent Lamp Patent: Evidence of Patents' Role in Stimulating Downstream Development." Northwestern University School of Law Working Paper (2012), http://bit.ly/Inventing-around-Edison.

Kelty, Christopher M. *Two Bits: The Cultural Significance of Free Software.* Durham, NC: Duke University Press, 2008.

Kretschmer, Martin. "Does Copyright Law Matter? An Empirical Analysis of Creator's Earnings." Unpublished manuscript, http://papers.ssrn.com/sol3/papers.cfm?abstract_id=2063735.

Lakoff, George, and Mark Johnson. *Metaphors We Live By.* Chicago: University of Chicago Press, 1980.

LaMonica, Paul R. "NBC Sued over *Heroes* Scene by Garbage Disposal Maker." CNN, October 17, 2006. http://money.cnn.com/2006/10/17commentary/mediabiz/index.html.

Landes, William M. "An Empirical Analysis of Intellectual Property Litigation: Some Preliminary Results." *Houston Law Review* 41 (2004): 749–776.

Landes, William, and Richard Posner. *The Economic Structure of Intellectual Property Law.* Cambridge, MA: Harvard University Press, 2003.

Lemley, Kevin M. "I'll Make Him an Offer He Can't Refuse: A Proposed Model for Alternative Dispute Resolution in Intellectual Property Disputes." *Akron Law Review* 37 (2004): 287–327.

Lemley, Mark. "The Dubious Autonomy of Virtual Worlds." *University of California Irvine Law Review* 2 (2012): 575–583.

———. "Ignoring Patents." *Michigan State Law Review* (2008): 19–34.

———. "The Myth of the Sole Inventor." *Michigan Law Review* 110 (2012): 709–760.

———. "Property, Intellectual Property, and Free Riding." *Texas Law Review* 83 (2005): 1031–1075.

Lemley, Mark, and Mark McKenna. "Irrelevant Confusion." *Stanford Law Review* 62 (2010): 413–457.

Lessig, Lawrence. *Code and Other Laws of Cyberspace.* New York: Basic Books, 1999.

———. *Code Version 2.0.* New York: Basic Books, 2006.

———. *Free Culture: How Big Media Uses Technology and the Law to Lock Down Culture and Control Creativity.* London: Penguin Press, 2004.

———. *The Future of Ideas: The Fate of the Commons in a Connected World.* New York: Vintage Press, 2001.

———. *Remix: Making Art and Commerce Thrive in a Hybrid Economy.* London: Penguin, 2008.

Liu, Joe. "Copyright and Breathing Space." *Columbia Journal of Law and the Arts* 30 (2007): 429–451.

———. "Copyright and Time: A Proposal." *Michigan Law Review* 101 (2002): 409–481.

———. "Copyright Law's Theory of the Consumer." *Boston College Law Review* 44 (2003): 397–438.

———. "The New Public Domain." *University of Illinois Law Review* (2013): 1395–1456.

Long, Clarissa. "Patent Signals." *University of Chicago Law Review* 69 (2002): 625–679.

Macaulay, Stewart. "Non-Contractual Relations in Business: A Preliminary Study." *American Sociological Review* 28, no. 1 (1963): 1–23.

MacIntyre, Alasdair. *After Virtue: A Study in Moral Theory*. London: Duckworth, 1981.

Madison, Michael. "Beyond Creativity: Copyright as Knowledge Law." *Vanderbilt Journal of Entertainment and Technology Law* 12 (2010): 817–851.

———. "Creativity and Craft." In *Creativity, Law and Entrepreneurship*, edited by Shubha Ghosh and Robin Paul Malloy, 22–48. Cheltenham, UK: Edward Elgar, 2011.

———. "Some Optimism About Fair Use and Copyright Law." *Journal of the Copyright Society USA* 57 (2010): 351–360.

Madison, Michael, Brett M. Frischmann, and Katherine J. Strandburg. "The Complexity of Commons." *Cornell Law Review* 95 (2010): 839–850.

———. "Constructing Commons in the Cultural Environment." *Cornell Law Review* 95 (2010): 657–710.

Madoff, Ray. *Immortality and the Law: The Rising Power of the American Dead*. New Haven, CT: Yale University Press, 2010.

Masum, Hassan, and Mark Tovey, eds. *The Reputation Society: How Online Opinions Are Reshaping the Offline World*. Cambridge, MA: MIT Press, 2012.

Mauss, Marcel. "Essai sur le don: Forme et raison de l'échange dans les sociétés archaïques." *L'année sociologique* 1 (1923–1924): 30–186. Available in English as *The Gift: Forms and Functions of Exchange in Archaic Societies*. New York: W. W. Norton, 1967.

Maxwell, Joseph A. "Causal Explanation, Qualitative Research, and Scientific Inquiry in Education." *Educational Researcher* 33, no. 2 (2004): 3–11.

Mazzone, Jason. *Copy Fraud and Other Abuses of Intellectual Property Law*. Stanford, CA: Stanford University Press, 2011.

McGeveran, William. "Rethinking Trademark Fair Use." *Iowa Law Review* 94 (2008): 49–124.

———. "The Trademark Fair Use Reform Act." *Boston University Law Review* 90 (2010): 2267–2321.

McKenna, Mark. "A Consumer Decision-Making Theory of Trademark Law." *Virginia Law Review* 98 (2012): 67–145.

———. "The Normative Foundations of Trademark Law." *Notre Dame Law Review* 82 (2007): 1839–1916.

McKenna, Mark, and Mark Lemley. "Owning Mark(et)s." *Michigan Law Review* 109 (2010): 137–190.

Menell, Peter. "Intellectual Property and the Property Rights Movement." *Regulation* 30, no. 3 (2007): 36–42.

———. "Knowledge Access and Preservation Policy in the Digital Age." *Houston Law Review* 44 (2007): 1013–1071.

———. "The Property Rights Movement's Embrace of Intellectual Property: True Love or Doomed Relationship?" *Ecology Law Quarterly* 34 (2007): 713–754.

Menell, Peter S., and Suzanne Scotchmer. "Intellectual Property." In *Handbook of Law and Economics*, edited by A. Mitchell Polinsky and Steven Shavell, 2:1473–1570. Amsterdam: Elsevier, 2007.

Merges, Robert P. "The Concept of Property in the Digital Era." *Houston Law Review* 45 (2008): 1239–1275.

———. *Justifying Intellectual Property*. Cambridge, MA: Harvard University Press, 2011.

Merton, Robert K. "Resistance to the Systematic Study of Multiple Discoveries in Science." *European Journal of Sociology* 4 (1963): 237–282.

———. "Social Structure and Anomie." *American Sociological Review* 3, no. 5 (1938): 672–682.

———. *Social Theory and Social Structure*. New York: Free Press, 1968.

———. *The Sociology of Science: Theoretical and Empirical Investigations*. Chicago: University of Chicago Press, 1973.

Meurer, Michael J. "Controlling Opportunistic and Anti-Competitive Intellectual Property Litigation." *Boston College Law Review* 44 (2008): 509–544.

Moore, Adam D. "Toward a Lockean Theory of Intellectual Property." In *Intellectual Property: Moral, Legal, and International Dilemmas*, edited by Adam D. Moore, 81–106. Lanham, MD: Rowman & Littlefield, 1997.

Murray, Fiona, and Scott Stern. "Do Formal Intellectual Property Rights Hinder the Free Flow of Scientific Knowledge? An Empirical Test of the Anti-Commons Hypothesis." *Journal of Economic Behavior and Organization* 63 (2007): 648–687.

Nelson, Robert L., and Laura Beth Nielsen. "Cops, Counsel, and Entrepreneurs: Constructing the Role of Inside Counsel in Large Corporations." *Law and Society Review* 34, no. 2, (2000): 457–490.

Nussbaum, Martha. *Women and Human Development: The Capabilities Approach*. New York: Cambridge University Press, 2000.

Patry, William. *How to Fix Copyright*. New York: Oxford University Press, 2012.

———. *Moral Panics and the Copyright Wars*. Oxford: Oxford University Press, 2009.

Picker, Randal. "The Razors-and-Blades Myths(s)." *University of Chicago Law Review* 78 (2011): 225–255.

Pink, Daniel. *Drive: The Surprising Truth About What Motivates Us*. London: Penguin, 2009.

Posner, Richard A. *The Little Book of Plagiarism*. New York: Pantheon Books, 2007.

———. "Misappropriation: A Dirge." *Houston Law Review* 40 (2003): 621–641.

Post, Robert C. "The Social Foundations of Defamation Law: Reputation and the Constitution." *California Law Review* 74 (1986): 691–742.

Radin, Margaret J. *Boilerplate: The Fine Print, Vanishing Rights, and the Rule of Law*. Princeton, NJ: Princeton University Press, 2012.

———. "Property and Personhood." *Stanford Law Review* 34 (1982): 957–1015.

———. *Reinterpreting Property*. Chicago: University of Chicago Press, 1993.

Ragin, Charles, and Linda Amoroso. *Constructing Social Research*. Thousand Oaks, CA: Sage Publications, 2011.

Raustiala, Kal, and Chris Sprigman. *The Knockoff Economy: How Imitation Sparks Innovation*. New York: Oxford University Press, 2012.

Reichheld, Fred. *The Loyalty Effect: The Hidden Force Behind Growth, Profits and Lasting Value*. Boston: Harvard Business School Press, 1996.

Resnik, Judith, and Dennis Curtis. *Representing Justice: Invention, Controversy, and Rights in City-States and Democratic Courtrooms*. New Haven, CT: Yale University Press, 2011.

Rierson, Sandra. "The Myth and Reality of Dilution." *Duke Law and Technology Review* 11 (2012): 212–312.

Risatti, Howard. *A Theory of Craft: Function and Aesthetic Expression*. Chapel Hill: University of North Carolina Press, 2007.

Rose, Carol M. "Introduction: Property and Language, or, the Ghost of the Fifth Panel." *Yale Journal of Law and the Humanities* 1 (2006, supp.): 1–28.

——. *Property & Persuasion: Essays on the History, Theory and Rhetoric of Property*. Boulder, CO: Westview Press, 1994.

Rose, Mark. *Authors and Owners: The Invention of Copyright*. Cambridge, MA: Harvard University Press, 1993.

Rothman, Jennifer. "Initial Interest Confusion: Standing at the Crossroads of Trademark Law." *Cardozo Law Review* 27 (2005): 105–191.

——. "The Questionable Use of Custom in Intellectual Property." *Virginia Law Review* 93 (2007): 1899–1982.

Rustichini, Aldo. "Emotion and Reason in Making Decisions." *Science* 310 (2005): 1624–1625.

Samuelson, Pamela. "Are Patents on Interfaces Impeding Interoperability?" *Minnesota Law Review* 93 (2009): 1943–2019.

——. "The Copyright Principles Project: Directions for Reform, Symposium: Copyright @ 300." *Berkeley Technology Law Journal* 25 (2010): 1175–1246.

——. "Mapping the Digital Public Domain: Threats and Opportunities." *Law and Contemporary Problems* 66 (2003): 147–171.

——. "The Quest for a Sound Conception of Copyright's Derivative Work Right." *Georgetown Law Journal* 101 (2013): 1505–1564.

——. "Should Economics Play a Role in Copyright Law and Policy?" *University of Ottawa Law and Technology Journal* 1 (2004): 3–20.

——. "The Uneasy Case for Software Copyrights Revisited." *George Washington Law Review* 79 (2011): 1746–1782.

——. "What Effects Do Legal Rules Have on Service Innovation?" In *Handbook of Service Science*, edited by P. P. Maglio, C. A. Kieliszewski, and J. Spohrer, 603–622. New York: Springer, 2010.

Sauerman, Henry, and Wesley M. Cohen. "What Makes Them Tick?" Working Paper No. 14443 (2008), National Bureau of Economic Research, Cambridge, MA, http://www.nber.org/papers/w14443.

Sauerman, Henry, Wesley Cohen, and Paula Stephan. "Doing Well or Doing Good? The Motives, Incentives, and Commercial Activities of Academic Scientists and Engineers." Paper presented at the 2010 summer conference "Opening Up Innovation," Imperial College London Business School, June 16–18, 2010. http://www2.druid.dk/conferences/viewpaper.php?id=501180&cf=43.

Sawyer, Keith. *Explaining Creativity: The Science of Human Innovation*. New York: Oxford University Press, 2006.

Scafidi, Susan. *Who Owns Culture? Appropriation and Authenticity in American Law*. New Brunswick, NJ: Rutgers University Press, 2005.

Scotchmer, Suzanne. "Incentives to Innovate." In *New Palgrave Dictionary of Economics and the Law*, edited Peter Newman, 273–277. New York: Macmillan Press, 1998.

——. *Innovation and Incentives*. Cambridge, MA: MIT Press, 2004.

——. "Openness, Open Source and the Veil of Ignorance." *American Economic Review* 100, no. 2 (2010): 165–171.

——. "Protecting Early Innovators: Should Second-Generation Products Be Patentable?" *Rand Journal of Economics* 27 (Summer 1996): 322–331.

———. "Standing on the Shoulders of Giants: Cumulative Research and the Patent Law." *Journal of Economic Perspectives* 5 (1991): 29–41.

Scotchmer, Suzanna, Ted O'Donoghue, and Jacques Thisse, "Patent Breadth, Patent Life, and the Pace of Technological Improvement," *Journal of Economics and Management Strategy* 7 (1998): 1–32.

Scotchmer, Suzanne, and Jerry Green. "On the Division of Profit Between Sequential Innovators." *Rand Journal of Economics* 26 (Spring 1995): 20–33.

Sen, Amartya. *Commodities and Capabilities.* Oxford: Oxford University Press, 1985.

———. *Development as Freedom.* New York: Knopf, 1999.

Sheff, Jeremy. "Marks, Morals, and Markets." *Stanford Law Review* 65 (2013): 761–816.

Sherwyn, David, Zev Eigen, and Michael Heise. "Don't Train Your Employees and Cancel Your 1-800 Harassment Hotline: An Empirical Examination and Correction of the Flaws in the Affirmative Defense to Sexual Harassment Charges." *Fordham Law Review* 69 (2001): 1265–1304.

Shirky, Clay. *Cognitive Surplus: Creativity and Generosity in a Connected Age.* New York: Penguin, 2010.

Silbey, Jessica. "The Mythical Beginnings of Intellectual Property." *George Mason Law Review* 15 (2008): 319–379.

Silbey, Susan. "Locke, op. cit.: Invocations of Law on Snowy Streets." *Journal of Comparative Law* 5, no. 2 (2012): 66–91.

Singer, Joseph. "The Rule of Reason in Property Law." *University of California Davis Law Review* 46 (2013): 1369–1434.

Small, Mario Luis. "How Many Cases Do I Need? On Science and the Logic of Case Selection in Field Based Research." *Ethnography* 10, no. 5 (2009): 5–38.

Solove, Daniel J. *The Future of Reputation: Gossip, Rumor and Privacy on the Internet.* New Haven, CT: Yale University Press, 2007.

Southworth, Ann. *Lawyers of the Right: Professionalizing the Conservative Coalition.* Chicago: University of Chicago Press, 2008.

Sprigman, Christopher. "Reform(aliz)ing Copyright." *Stanford Law Review* 57 (2004): 485–568.

Sprigman, Christopher Jon, Christopher Buccafusco, and Zachary Burns. "What's a Name Worth? Experimental Tests of the Value of Attribution in Intellectual Property." *Boston University Law Review* 93 (2013): 1389–1435.

Stone, Pamela. *Opting Out: Why Women Really Quit Careers and Head Home.* Berkeley: University of California Press, 2007.

Strandburg, Katherine J. "Curiosity-Driven Research and University Technology Transfer." In *Advances in the Study of Entrepreneurship, Innovation & Economic Growth,* edited by Sherry Hoskinson and Donald Kuratko, 16:93–122. Oxford, UK: Elsevier Science and JAL Press, 2005.

———. "What Does the Public Get? Experimental Use and the Patent Bargain." *Wisconsin Law Review* (2004): 81–152.

Subotnik, Eva. "Originality Proxies: Toward a Theory of Copyright and Creativity." *Brooklyn Law Review* 76 (2011): 1487–1552.

Subotnik, Eva, and Jane Ginsburg. "Speaking of Moral Rights, A Conversation." *Cardozo Arts and Entertainment Law Journal* 30 (2012): 91–104.

Suk, Jeannie. *At Home in the Law: How the Domestic Violence Revolution Is Transforming Privacy.* New Haven, CT: Yale University Press, 2009.

Sunder, Madhavi. *From Goods to a Good Life: Intellectual Property and Global Justice.* New Haven, CT: Yale University Press, 2012.

Swanson, Kara. "Biotech in Court: A Legal Lesson on the Unity of Science." *Social Studies of Science* 37 (2007): 357–384.

Tehranian, John. *Infringement Nation: Copyright 2.0 and You.* New York: Oxford University Press, 2011.

———. "Infringement Nation: Copyright Reform and the Law/Norm Gap." *Utah Law Review* (2007): 537–550.

Tushnet, Rebecca. "Economies of Desire: Fair Use and Marketplace Assumptions." *William & Mary Law Review* 51 (2009): 513–546.

———. "Gone in 60 Milliseconds: Trademark Law and Cognitive Science." *Texas Law Review* 86 (2008): 507–568.

———. "Naming Rights: Attribution and Law." *Utah Law Review* (2007): 781–820.

———. "Payment in Credit: Copyright Law and Subcultural Creativity." *Law and Contemporary Problems* 70 (2007): 135–174.

Ulrich, Laurel Thatcher. *The Age of Homespun: Objects and Stories in the Creation of an American Myth.* New York: Vintage Books, 2001.

Vaidhyanathan, Siva. *Copyrights and Copywrongs: The Rise of Intellectual Property and How It Threatens Creativity.* New York: New York University Press, 2003.

———. *The Googlization of Everything (and Why We Should Worry).* Berkeley: University of California Press, 2011.

Van Houweling, Molly S. "The New Servitudes." *Georgetown Law Journal* 96 (2008): 885–950.

Von Lohmann, Fred. "Fair Use as Innovation Policy." *Berkeley Technology Law Journal* 23 (2008): 1–36.

Wagner, Polk. "The Perfect Storm: Intellectual Property and Public Values." *Fordham Law Review* 74 (2005): 423–434.

Wagner, Polk, and Gideon Parchomovsky. "Patent Portfolios." *University of Pennsylvania Law Review* 154 (2005): 1–77.

Warrington, Tracy B., Nadia J. Abgrab, and Helen M. Caldwell. "Building Trust to Develop Competitive Advantage in e-Business Relationships." *Competitiveness Review: An International Business Journal incorporating Journal of Global Competitiveness* 10, no. 2 (2000): 160–168.

White, Hayden. "The Value of Narrativity in the Representation of Reality." *On Narrative, Critical Inquiry* 7, no. 1 (1980): 5–27.

White, James Boyd. *From Expectations to Experience.* Ann Arbor: University of Michigan Press, 2000.

Woodmansee, Martha, Maria Biagioli, and Peter Jaszi, eds. *Making and Unmaking Intellectual Property: Creative Production in Legal and Cultural Perspective.* Chicago: University of Chicago Press, 2011.

Wu, Tim. *The Master Switch: The Rise and Fall of Information Empires.* New York: Knopf, 2010.

———. "Tolerated Use." *Columbia Journal of Law and the Arts* 31 (2008): 617–634.

Yen, Alfred C. "Copyright Opinions and Aesthetic Theory." *Southern California Law Review* 71 (1997–1998): 247–302.

———. "The Danger of Bootstrap Formalism in Copyright." *Journal of Intellectual Property Law* 5 (1997–1998): 453–466.

———. "*Eldred*, the First Amendment, and Aggressive Copyright Claims." *Houston Law Review* 40 (2003–2004): 673–696.

———. "A First Amendment Perspective on the Construction of Third-Party Copyright Liability." *Boston College Law Review* 50 (2009): 1481–1502.

Zimmerman, Diane L. "Modern Technology, Leaky Copyrights and Claims of Harm: Insights from the Curious History of Photocopying." *Journal of the Copyright Society* 61 (2014): 1–58.

Zittrain, Jonathan. *The Future of the Internet and How to Stop It*. New Haven, CT: Yale University Press, 2008.

Ziedonis, Rosemarie Ham. "Don't Fence Me In: Fragmented Markets for Technology and the Patent Acquisition Strategies of Firms," *Management Science* 50 (2004): 804–820.

Index

Page numbers followed by "t" indicate material in tables.